An Erking Good Life

by
Ken J. Rutterford

Published 2013 by arima publishing

www.arimapublishing.com

ISBN 978 1 84549 592 3

© Ken J Rutterford 2013

All rights reserved

This book is copyright. Subject to statutory exception and to provisions of relevant collective licensing agreements, no part of this publication may be reproduced, stored in a retrieval system, or transmitted in any form or by any means, without the prior written permission of the author.

Printed and bound in the United Kingdom

Typeset in Garamond

This book is sold subject to the conditions that it shall not, by way of trade or otherwise, be lent, re-sold, hired out, or otherwise circulated without the publisher's prior consent in any form of binding or cover other than that which it is published and without a similar condition including this condition being imposed on the subsequent purchaser.

arima publishing
ASK House, Northgate Avenue
Bury St Edmunds, Suffolk IP32 6BB
t: (+44) 01284 700321
www.arimapublishing.com

DEDICATION

I here dedicate this book to all of the pilots and aircraft owners who have given me so much pleasure throughout my lifetime by letting me be with their aeroplanes. Either in the air or on the ground. Without these kind people, I could never have written this book. To all of them, I here extend my thanks.

ABOUT THIS BOOK

This book is all about myself and my devotion to old aeroplanes. I was born the son of a gamekeeper and I have always been an aircraft enthusiast. My interest in this subject has grown keener and stronger as I grew older. As I have never been a wealthy person, I never became a pilot. I now regret on not having tried to do so. Money, or the lack of it, is the reason that I have stayed grounded. My interest and the liking for old aeroplanes, especially the civil aeroplanes has gradually dominated my life. I have always treasured my memories of the many old aeroplanes that I have seen throughout the years of my lifetime. Within the pages of this book, I am hoping that I may be able to share just a few of my treasured memories with you.

Tiger Moth GADGV

WHAT CONSTITUTED AN ERK

An Erk is a bloke that can be found clambering all over an aircraft. The aircraft he calls a Kite. Without the work that is performed by Erks, then the aircrews could never had flown. If he was an engine bod, then he would take on an oily greasey appearance. He is known to come in all shapes and sizes and was known to be very fond of WAAF company. Whenever work was needed on a kite he would be there and hard at it. Once that he had satisfied himself that his work was well done, he would then skive away until he was needed again. He could detect a NAAFI van long before it came into site. He would never fail to visit it. It was a wad and a mug of char that kept him active. When not found on an aeroplane, and if he was to be seen at all, then he would probably be riding a bike.

CONTENTS

1. MY INFANT YEARS 12
2. THOSE SPARTAN THREE SEATERS 15
3. A DEHAVILLAND INFLUENCE 17
4. TO SCHOOL AT LAST 28
5. WORKING IN WARTIME 37
6. WARTIME ACTIVITY 43
7. A TASTE OF SERVICE LIFE 55
8. I BECAME A ROOKIE 70
9. I GOT SOME IN 73
10. TRAINING TO BECOME AN ERK 77
11. A FULLY FLEDGED ERK 85
12. I GOT PLUCKED 102
13. BACK ON MY BIKE 104
14. MOTORCYCLES & PHOTOGRAPHY 108
15. THE VINTAGE AEROPLANE CLUB 115
16. FOR THE HISTORIANS 121
17. MY CHANCE TO OBSERVE 125
18. THE RETURN OF UNCLE SAM 135
19. UP IN YOURS 141
20. ROMAN TIGERS 161
21. YE'LL TAK' THE HIGH ROAD 179
22. WAY DOWN UNDER 188
23. DRAGE AIRWORLD AND DISTANT DOCUMENTS 206
24. RETURN TO UP OVER 212
25. MAINLY ON THE LIGHTER SIDE 217
26. SEEING IS BELIEVING 227
27. WITH THE AIRCRAFT RESTORERS 236
28. TWO PAGES FROM MY LOG BOOK 243
29. A PICTURE GALLERY 244

GENERAL ARRANGEMENT DRAWINGS

1. Taylor Watkinson Dingbat G-AFJA 147
2. Piper PA-17 Vagabond 148

ILLUSTRATED DRAWINGS

1. Shooting at Sarson Wood 16
2. The Iron House 20
3. The aircraft pen as I remember it 20
4. Those two Hawker biplanes 36
5. This Leyland was often our school bus 36
6. The deHavilland D.H.93 Don 44
7. The downed Waco CG-4A 44
8. The Queen Mary and the Junkers Ju.188 wreckage 49
9. We watched the searchlights 50
10. Imperial Airways liners flew low over our home 51
11. Steaming into Stockcross 59
12. U.S.A.A.F. Welford's D-Day over Wickham Heath 59
13. The remaining bombing watch tower 64
14. Harwell's Wellington DV871 and Harrow K7000 64
15. My first flight, BM826 with u/c problems 72
16. The Royal Oak and a Jupiter Class 83
17. The only time that I became airborne in the RAF 91
18. The hanger nosedive 95
19. The Kamikaze attack 119
20. Aeronca G-AEVS and "Constance" at Denham 118
21. Avro 638 Club Cadet G-ACHP in the Chiltern Hills Air Race 120
22. Handley Page Hastings WD485 taking-off over the hump 134
23. A B-47E Stratojet lands on Greenham Common 140
24. Short S.25 Sandringham "Southern Cross" VP-LVE in Poole Harbour 160
25. "Dee Jay" over Uffington White Horse 165
26. Circling over my home in HU 166
27. We were forever overtaking Tiger Moths 183
28. Whittaker's Westland Widgeon 199
29. Catalina flying boat sections in a garage yard 199
30. Flying between the Swiss mountains 222
31. Bobbing between the trees in the Thunder Balloon "Twiley's Golf Finger" 222
32. Southern Sailplanes, Membury 240
33. Removing the 90 h.p. Pobjoy Cataract from a B.A. Swallow Mk.II 240

THE PHOTOGRAPHS
(Not including, The Picture Gallery)

1. The little Aeronca 100, G-AEVS at a V.A.C.'s event 4
2. Grandfather attending to his young pheasants 26
3. My treasured signed photograph of the D.H.88 Comet G-ACSS 27
4. My Mother and my Wife in the snow, Chapel Road, Wickham Heath 83
5. Boscobel House 84
6. R.A.F. Cosford's huts 84
7. Produce my camera and the erks would clamber for a snap shot 91
8. Spitfire Mk.IX MK.188 away for a compass swing 95
9. Spitfire Mk.IX, MA592 for South Africa 99
10. Spitfire Mk.IX, NH539 having an engine run 99
11. Avro Lancaster TW923 100
12. The 'Highways Hostel', Euxton, Lancashire 101
13. Walk-about in the Farnborough bush 107
14. Myself standing by the Turkish Spitfire Mk.IX, RR182 113
15. The Newbury EoN, G-AKBC 114
16. My photograph of that flying bomb 114
17. Flying at Cranwell 176
18. Peter and Ian Trask and HU on Seven Barrows field 176
19. Calleva's Tiger Moth G-AJHU by the D.H. memorial stone 176
20. Flying with Captain Fred. Tiger Moth G-ACDJ 177
21. Tigers were designed to be inverted, but only in the air 177
22. Brother William and Mark Peters working on DJ 177
23. Self standing by Hotel Uniform on 8th March 1986 178
24. The pranged HU. Photographed on 5th of June, 1986 178
25. Rendall's Dragon Rapide G-AIYR at Hatfield 186
26. Peter's new Tiger Moth at Hatfield 186
27. A view of the many Moths at Hatfield 187
28. The Flying Doctor's Nomad, VH-MSF 202
29. Commonwealth CA-28 Ceres VH-SSY at WAngaratta 202
30. Drage Airworld, Wangaratta, Victoria, Australia 203
31. The badge on the Nomad VH-MSF 208
32. Walking out to board the DC-10 at Melbourne 215

33. Boarding the Junkers Ju 52/3m, HB-HOS/A-107 224
34. The Junkers Ju 52/3m, HB-HOS/A-107 225
35. I might have made a Zeppelin raid over London 225
36. The Bloody Tower 226
37. Snow circles on my driveway 233
38. Our son's home is in the centre of the photograph 234
39. My home is in between the struts 234
40. About to board the Skyship at Radlett 235
41. The ball of wool crop circle photographed from the Cessna 235
42. Klemm L.25 "Clementine" G-AAUP 241
43. Aeronca C.3. G-ADYS. "Gladys" 242

ITEMS OF INTEREST

1. Newton Ferrers Sailing School letter 15
2. Our Mother's 1930 flight ticket 16
3. My Spotters Club membership card for 1942/43 52
4. My Spotters Club, No 51 certificate...52
5. My 1965 gun licence 54
6. An unsuccessful chit for an Oxford flight..60
7. My registration card 67
8. My call-up papers 68
9. My pay book..69
10. My medical card 69
11. Three Spitfire engine data cards...89
12. My very proud deHavilland Propellers certificate 98
13. The charter ticket for G-AWCH 124
14. The 1982 Henlow Gala keepsake 175
15. The 'Famous Grouse' cloth badge..183

MY INFANT YEARS

I was born the eldest of two sons to a gamekeeper. My parents had set up their first home deep down in a keeper's bungalow in beautiful lush green woodland and a long way away from the nearest cottage. This woodland consisted of mainly hazel with a few other larger trees dotted in here and there. These were of beech, oak and a few firs. To the front of our home there was along stretch of grass in which during the winter months the guns would stand. On the far side of this grass running on an embankment was the Southern Railways Grateley Incline. This rail line ran between Andover and Salisbury. Beyond this there were more woodlands. It was a very lonely life for my mother and an under keepers life was much harder in those days than what it is today. There were no such luxuries as Land Rovers and incubators and they did have to rear far more pheasants. This place was then called Sarson Wood and it was part of the Amport Estate then owned by Colonel Whitburn. My parents were to live here for seven years and for me, it was the first six years of my life. I had no playmates, and what you never had you never missed. I found it to be a very happy life and I grew up to love the beauty of nature and these woodlands. My only brother Richard was also born in this same dwelling, but four years later on. My mother had insisted that he should be christened 'Dick'. She was then told by some person that I now have forgotten that come later in life he might just be knighted. How could one ever call him 'Sir Dick'. Richard he was christened, but as Dick he has always been known,

In order to get to our home we first walked down a long gravel road and then once entering the woodlands it was down a very muddy track. Motors trying to reach our home had often got stuck in deep sticky mud under some mature beech trees. Tradesmen just refused to come to our home. A large wooden boxed cupboard was provided that was mounted upon for wooden posts just inside the wood. Here all groceries were left. Each week, mother had to drag the pram and me to this box to collect what the tradesmen had left in it. I do not remember if we ever bought coal, or how that would have been delivered. Well as I write this I am now in my mid eighties and I was only six years old when we left there. Although the working class were not fond of reaching our home, the gentry would make their way down to our home and in the worst winters weather conditions. There were times when they also had royalty among them. They would line up at their pegs along that grass strip and blast away with their most expensive guns at all of those pheasants that dad had reared. After the shoot had moved away, they had left the ground around the stands littered with fresh brightly coloured empty cartridge cases. I was then allowed to go out and collect some of them. These colourful paper tube empty cartridge cases with their fresh smelling burnt powders then became my building bricks. I was given those wooden cubed toy building bricks, but these did not hold for me that same fascination as what did those empty cartridge cases with their shining brass metal ends.

During the spring and the summer months this place was a haven. Much of the ground cover was that rich green dog mercury. In the spring there were bunches of primroses. These were my father's favourite flower. Mixed in with the primroses were those dainty little white anemones and yellow celandines. Later on would then come the bluebells. Every evening come eight o'clock a long goods train would come puffing its way up the incline in the direction of Salisbury. This I was to know as 'Old I Think I Can' by the sounds that it made by its labouring exhausting steam. It was constantly repeating to its self those words ' I think I can'. I was always allowed to stay up to watch this goods puff its way out of sight and then it was strictly to bed. Come the morning and there were the sounds of the many small songbirds singing with the calls of the woodpigeon.

These I would put the words to, 'My Toes Bleeding betty'.

My interest in aviation started here at Sarson. To start with, my father was always interested in aircraft and this was to rub off on to my brother and myself. Being born whilst the letters G-E were still being allocated, I was far too young as to be able to read these registrations, but I well recall seeing civil aircraft flying over having these large registration letters applied across the bottoms of their lower wings. Most of these aircrafts were biplanes. I still have one or two vivid memories from these early days. One of them was my father pointing out to me a tail-less aeroplane. It was obviously one of those Westland Pterodactyls, though I shall now never know which mark of them was the one that I saw. Most likely it was the Mark IV.

My most vivid toddler memory was the sound and then the sight of a very large multi-empire biplane. This noisy flying monster was at tree top height and heading straight for our home.

To the other side of the bungalow and in the direction that this monster was heading there stood a very tall mature Douglas fir tree. I can remember Dad passing a remark like 'By Jove, it's a big one, he will never get over that tree'. His remark was as much as what I could stand and so I rushed indoors to Mother crying my eyes out. Well it must have got over that tree.

I now realise that it could have been navigating by 'Bradshaw'. In other words, it was following the railway line. On the other hand it could have been a Vickers Virginia or a Boulton & Paul Sidestrand that had taken-off from RAF Andover. I shall never know.

It was while I was living at Sarson that I saw my one and only giant airship. I was being walked across Amport Park with my parents when this large vessel of the air was seen heading in a northwesterly direction. Once a week, Mother would take me in to Andover to do her shopping on Mr Raisey's bus. This then took us past Andover Aerodrome and I would try to count the number of silver biplane fighters that were always parked on the grass and to be seen between the buildings. An aunt and uncle would often pay us a visit from the Newbury area on their 500cc AJS motorcycle that was registered MO 9287. I have a memory of this motorbike when it was fitted with a sidecar and had broken down. We were being taken to a seaside when the ball bearings broke up in the rear wheel. Perhaps it was having me in the chair as it was then known by, might have been just that too much extra weight for it to contend with. It would have been on one of these visits that Mother was taken to an air display that was held on Andover Aerodrome. This was in 19330 and I would have been two years old. It was then that she took her one and only aeroplane ride. This cost 5/- (25p) in today's money. I know this as I still have her flight ticket. It was with the Brooklands School of Flying Ltd. Dad would have liked to have gone, but his work would not let him.

Living down Sarson Wood was a very lonely life for our mother. In those days keepers were expected to put in very many hours and often stay away from home on some nights. This if poachers were known to have been active in the area. Also many long hours had to be put in during the spring on the rearing fields. Due to this, mother had got herself into a situation where she might have had a nervous breakdown. Because of her condition, Dad decided to look for new employment and so he took a keepers post on the Benham Settled Estates near Newbury, which was near our mothers parents home. It was to be on this estate that Dad was to spend the rest of his life. Now here at the age of six, I was about to start my schooling.

Now while living at my second home, this same aunt and uncle, Aunt Nance and Uncle Rudolph took me for a week's holiday with them on Hayling Island. Uncle never liked the name Rudolph and always went by his second name Fred, to us, we knew him as 'Uncle Doo-dah', and please do not ask me why as I cannot tell you. Keepers could only take one weeks holiday a year and this had to be taken between the end of shooting season and the starting of rearing the birds for the coming years shoot. It was not the time of year for wanting to spend the holiday at a seaside resort. I remember being chauffeur driven in a large car from Newbury to Hayling. Each time that the driver throttled back there was a loud backfire. Needless to say, that by the time that we arrived at the holiday bungalow on the island the silencer on the car resembled a colander. I very much enjoyed being given this holiday, but sure enough there was one thing that I very much wanted and that they made sure that I could not have. I very much wanted it to have been my very first flight in an aeroplane.

Throughout each day, a solitary low flying biplane with large letters painted across its lower wings would keep flying past us and close to the waters edge. As it flew close to the beach it always did so and in the same direction. Well I had to ask uncle 'why did it keep on flying past us and why did it always do so in the same direction'? The answer was then given to me. It was flying joy rides around the island and it was operating from a field, which was close to the main, land bridges. That did it. This aeroplane continually flying past us all week made me that determined that the time had come for my very first venture up into the air. The trouble was that aunt and uncle thought otherwise. This would have been far too expensive for me to have a go at and they also did not have my parents consent. But try telling that to a young lad like me who did not understand these situations. Due to my continual persistence they would not even take me there to see it take off and land. I now think that this old biplane would have been a Spartan Three-Seater. It could have been just one of several. Either G-ABTR or G-ACAF. I am including here a copy of a letter, which is headed, Newton Ferrers Sailing School which mentions these old Spartan Three-Seaters. Also while on this holiday I remember seeing several all silver biplane flying boats that flew past us and heading in a westerly direction. At that time I did not know what they were. It was in later years while we had the unpleasant task of turning out aunt and uncles old home that we came across a snap shot. I now know that they were Supermarine Walrus and that they would have been brand new.

THOSE SPARTAN THREE SEATERS

This letter was sent to me very many years ago and I am now sorry, but I have forgotten who the person was that sent it to me. I have a feeling that it was when I was searching for the colours of these Spartans. The ink on this letter had faded to the extent that it would not reproduce. As I considered that it was worth including in this book, I have had to run a pen over the original writing.

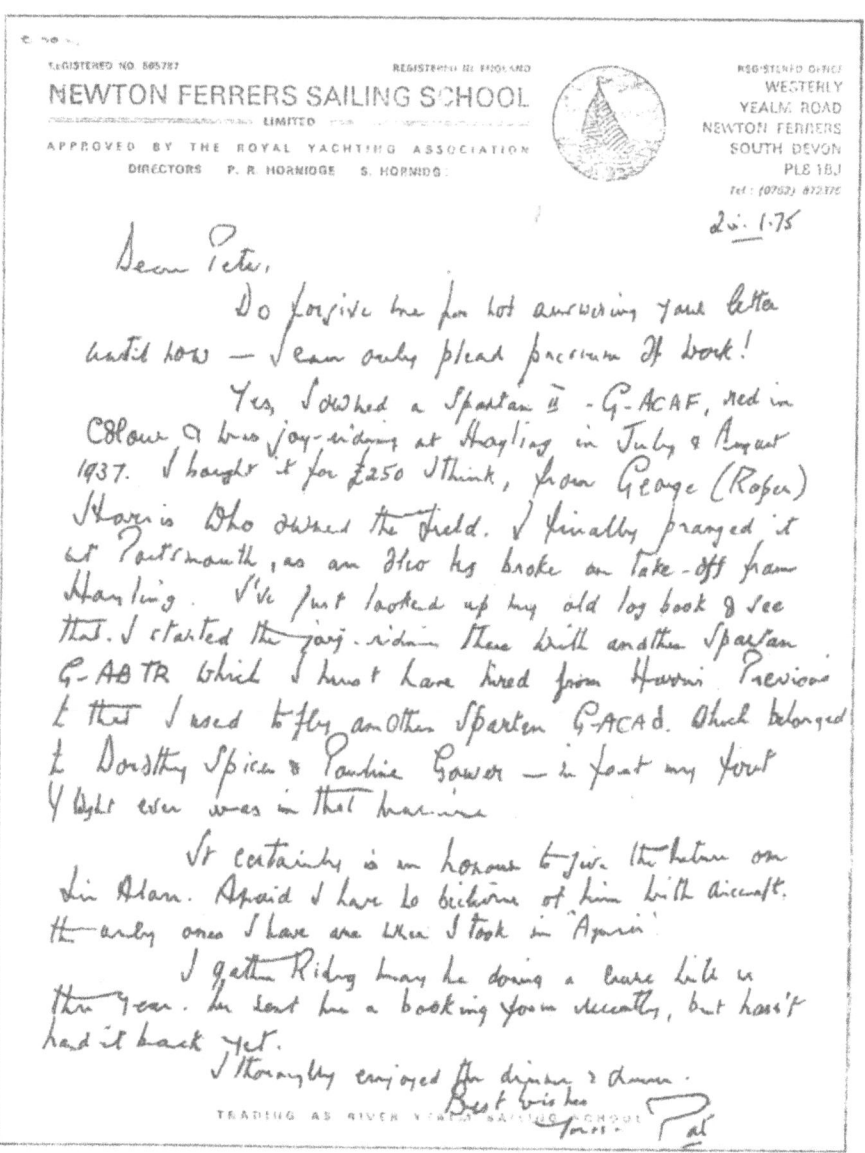

Mother's 1930 flight ticket

Shooting at Sarson Wood

A DE HAVILLAND INFLUENCE

As I have previously said, our father was very interested in aircraft and this was to rub off on to my brother Dick and myself. The majority of our interests could be traced back to Captain Geoffrey de Havilland who in later years became Sir Geoffrey. Our father was born in 1898 on the Highclere Estate in what this estate named, the Iron House. We got to know of it as the Tin Bungalow. This large country estate had it especially built for our grandparents to move into. They had got married and having lived for a year on the Elveden Estate near Thetford, grandfather had taken a gamekeepers position on the North Hampshire Downs. Their new home was clad on its outside with corrugated iron sheets painted in red oxide. On its inside it was lined with varnished wood boarding. This boarding on all of its interior walls and also the interior linings to the roof. It had no ceilings as in a normal bungalow. For very many years the stove pipes ran up through the roof and several times I have heard it said on how it was a wonder that the place never got burnt down. Those wooden boards had charred where the stove pipes had entered the roofing. This Iron House was built at a place named Easton Park. It was situated nestling under Beechhanger Copse in a location between two churches. These churches were Woodcott and Crux Easton. The vicar for these two churches was the Reverend Charles de Havilland who was the father to Geoffrey.

Dad had two elder brothers who emigrated to Australia only to return back to Europe where they lost their lives in France fighting in the First World War. He also had two younger brothers who were both to work for the de Havilland Aeroplane Company, and he also had five sisters. There was a story that circulated. A gun whilst standing at his peg along the strip of grass that was to the front of their home and to the side of Easton Park Great Wood, had said to his loader, 'What is that place up there', as he pointed towards the bungalow. 'It looks like a small factory', his loader said, 'You are quite right Sir, that is exactly what it is'. They were a large and very happy family and many are the stories that have been told to me about their lives while living at Easton Park. The one that I liked best about Dad was when he was given a bicycle. It had no brakes and its wheels were shod with solid rubber tyres. He was riding it down the track which led up to their home from the roadway when the rear tyre which had a join in it came partly away from the rim. The result was that this rubber strip thrashed him on his back all of the way down the hill. I do not know if he had deserved a thrashing, but he got one.

It was the Reverend Charles de Havilland that christened our father. Dad once described him to me as being a thick set man with a clumped foot. He said that he could be easily upset, and when he was, he would stumble away muttering in a foreign tongue. Perhaps he was praising his maker, who knows. Myself I would think that he most likely started speaking in french. Charles lived with his wife Nettie along with their family in the rectory at Crux Easton which was close to the small church and the village school in which our father and his brothers and sisters did all of their schooling. The de Havilland boys were much older than Dad and his brothers, but they were always known to have been up to something. They would shoot airgun pellets at the church bell and make it ping. They also flew model aircraft. This influenced our father and his brothers to also construct model flying machines. The so called fuselage would have been a straight hazel stick. Beneath this for its full length would have been the rubber motor which when wound would have driven a hand carved propeller. The wing and tail being a shaped one piece wire frame with no spars. The ribs were also of wire and twisted at their ends to hold them in place. I am now not sure as to what the covering was, but I expect that it was glued on brown or white paper. Some of their models were of the tractor design while others were what Dad called, tail first being a canard.

Our Aunt Annie who was a younger sister to father has told me on how our father and his brothers had carved a large wooden propeller and had fitted it to a rig which they had made. They then revolved it at high speeds via a hand crank and a bicycle chain. This she said had frightened her as she had expected it to have spun off.

Geoffrey was to be the boy that made the de Havilland name famous when in later years he founded the de Havilland Aeroplane Company. I will not here dive into the history of that great firm as it has been well documented in other books. But I will mention a little on Geoffrey de Havilland's first attempts into aviation. He built his first flying machine that was powered by his own designed engine in a workshop at Fulham in London. This aircraft was to become known as de Havilland Aeroplane Number One. It was in 1909 when our father would have been about eleven years old that Geoffrey assisted by his friend, Frank Hearle transported this aircraft on a solid tyred chain driven lorry from Fulham to a place called Thorndown on the Earle of Carnarvon's Highclere Estate. Here there were two sheds that had been erected by Moore-Brbazon by the kind permission of the Earle of Carnarvon. This being only a few miles as the crow flies from the small hamlet of Crux Eason. Mr Moore-Brabazon then decided not to use these sheds and so it was that Geoffrey de Havilland was able to purchase one of them and to be given the use of the other. Here in one of these sheds the aeroplane was assembled. This place is located just to the southern side of Beacon Hill. It was on the eastern side of Thorndown on the field known as Seven Barrows that Geoffrey and Frank attempted to fly the aircraft. This field being so named because there are seven barrows to the Litchfield side corner to this field. Dad, and I presume along with his two elder brothers, Billy and Richard walked across the downs to have a look at his aeroplane. They were to be too late as Geoffrey's first attempt at taking to the air had failed. The aircraft had started to take to the air but Geoffrey had over controlled and pranged it. This would have been his first stall. One has to remember that in these early years of powered aviation, Geoffrey had yet to teach himself to fly. What our family did find was many small pieces from the wreckage and some of these they took home with them. How I would liked to have owned a piece of that wreckage today.

Geoffrey was not to be beaten. His engine was still sound and he recovered what he could from the wreck and along with Frank they returned it all back to Fulham. Geoffrey then set about designing his second aircraft and this one became known as de Havilland Aeroplane Number Two. By the summer of 1910 they returned back to those sheds on Thorndown. Here on the Seven Barrows field they had success at last. Dad was one of several of the older school children that were given a half-day off from their schooling to walk across the downs and to watch Geoffrey fly. This must have been one of his early flights that they witnessed as it was only a straight hop up and down again. Later on he was able to fly circuits around the area. What they then saw was aviation history in its making. The landing must have been on the heavy side as some of the flying wires were in need of attention. We lost our father in 1981 and so I can no longer ask him, but I do not now know if any wires were broken or just in need of tensioning. This was the only flight that they saw him make, but they had seen it.

We were to lose our grandmother on our father's side while I was still but a small boy, my brother never knew her. Aunt Annie who was a little younger than Dad then stepped into the breach and kept the homestead going for grandfather and the rest of the family. She was never to marry. Dick and I lost our own Mother in 1964. Our Aunt Annie was at that time living in a cottage on her own. She then gave up her cottage home and came and lived in with Dad.

It was during the 1930's that Dick and I would be taken on visits to Easton Park when our parents would visit grandfather and Aunt Annie. Geoffrey de Havilland now having the title of Captain was very fond of Crux Easton with its downlands and woodlands and who could blame him for that. To start with, he had a caravan that was designed on aircraft lines built for himself in the Stag Lane factory. For one year he had this caravan parked under the edge of the Easton Park Great Wood (now long gone) that was to the front of the Tin Bungalow. On many weekends the Captain would fly one of his many moth aeroplanes to Crux Easton and spend time in his caravan. He would always fly if the weather allowed him to do so. Our Uncle George who was the next son to be born after our father was nearly always given the job to take him water. 'He did not have that caravan made large enough', said George as he continued. 'On one occasion when I was taking him the water I tripped over a guest of his that had spent the night sleeping outside'. DH was friendly with Grandpa and often walked in the woods with him. Several of our family photos were most likely taken by DH as in those days not so many people had cameras. I have one photograph that our Aunt Annie always treasured and this I am showing in this book. She told me that it was taken by the Captain of Grandpa attending to his pheasant coops while Mrs de Havilland is seen looking on. Captain Geoffrey was a very keen entomologist. During each night that he stayed in his caravan he would keep an outside light burning. I imagine that he must have had some kind of a generator as he made his own electricity. By the use of this lamp he would attract through the night many kinds of moths (insects). Our family would often watch him gathering up his nightly catch from their windows. Note the shapes of the de Havilland tail empennages and compare them with the shapes of moth and butterfly wings. Later on he was to have his own bungalow built in the village of Crux Easton and close to what is known as the John Wallis Titt self-regulating geared wind engine. This wind engine and its well house stand to the front of this de Havilland built bungalow. Several times a year the Crux Easton wind engine is open to the public. In the well house there is a collection of 1/72 scale de Havilland aircraft. For details of openings, visit the website http:/www.freewebs.com/windengine/. This wind engine was here before Dad was born.

On most weekends when the weather was flyable, Mr DH would travel by air to spend the weekend in his bungalow. This building has since been added on to. His moth type aircraft he would park in a fenced off enclosure in the corner of the field which was the nearest to his residence. This field was to become known as the de Havilland field but I do not think that he ever owned it. Whenever Dick and I were taken there in the 1930's it was most likely at a weekend. We would give Auntie Annie little piece until she had walked us up through the woodland and across that field so that we could go and inspect the captain's aeroplane. We were never to meet the great man or to see him fly. His aircraft was always parked in that wired enclosure pen. The first registration that I thought that I had remembered of being parked in that pen was G-ACPK and this belonged to a D.H.85 Leopard Moth. I have since learnt that Mr DH did privately own the Leopard Moth G-ACKP. As both of these registrations belonged to Leopards, I cannot now be certain as to which one of them that it was that I saw. DH could easily have borrowed one straight off of the production line. On another visit it was the D.H.87B Hornet Moth G-ADMT which filled the enclosure pen. In much later post-war years, Cliff Lovell was to restore this old Hornet after it had languished for quite a while in the Strathallan Air Museum. It was on the 17th of August 1997 at a de Havilland Moth Club's annual event on Woburn Park that its then owner, Pat Swoffer kindly gave me seven minutes in the air in this grand old side-by-side seat cabin biplane. That quick ride in 'MT' made my weekend for me. When I had first set my eyes on G-ADMT, I most likely would have been wearing short trousers.

The Iron House

The aircraft pen as I remember it

The captain was very kind to the local people who had to get use to an aviator in their midst. He was known to have given aeroplane rides as prizes at village fetes. Several local people were given joy rides. Grandfather and many others of our aunts and uncles were given flights by him. One person who did miss out on an aeroplane ride was our Uncle Fred. Dad had told me on how he had just walked up to him, and as he put it, cheeked him for a ride. He had done this just as the Captain had finished securing his pen. Having then told him who he was, the Captain then asked him where he would like to go. Dad then replied, 'Just up and around so that I can see what the place looks like from up in the air'. With this, Mr DH undid his pen and our father, like our mother, then enjoyed their one and only aeroplane ride. I do not know what he was flown in, but I would think that it was most probably a D.H.60 Moth. Aunt Annie and her sister Sue were taken up in what I think was most likely to have been a D.H.85 Leopard Moth. There is just a very small chance that it could have been a D.H.75 Hawk Moth. This is because they had sat to the rear of the Captain being side-by-side in a high wing monoplane. Afterwards, Geoffrey then said to them, 'I had wanted to take you to the south coast to see the sea, but because it had been so dull I decided to take you above the clouds instead'. Aunt Annie had done some house work for Mrs de Havilland. There became a sequel to their flight and so I will tell you about it here.

My wife Daphne and I had been taking holidays in Cornwall in a very old cottage which belonged to one of my work-mates. Its slate roof had been given a cement wash which was its last result. Having booked this cottage we were about to go on our holiday when we were told that the rusty nails that had held the slates had given way and that the roofing had slid off. Daphne was doing some house work for a gentleman farmer and she then told them on how we had lost out on our holiday. Mary, the farmer's wife then told Daphne that she had a friend who lived in London who owned a weekend holiday cottage in Helhoughton. This being a small village in the north of Norfolk. Mary then got in touch with her friend and we were told that we could have it for a week providing that we gave it a bit of a spring clean. In other words, a good going over. We could then use all of its facilities for the week and it would not cost us a penny, but if it was fine would we please mow the grass. From then on we took several holidays in that little old cottage and the owners were pleased to let us have it. On one such holiday I did a repair to the stairway and they were as pleased as punch. We only stopped going when the owners decided to sell their cottage. On one of the later years we took Dad and Aunt Annie with us. Then on the following year we lost Dad, and so we just took along Aunt Annie.

It was in 1982 while I attended the R.A.F. Gala that I mentioned to Henry Labouchere that I would be staying for a week in Helhoughton. I had got to know Henry by being a member of the de Havilland Moth Club (deHMC). Henry then kindly invited us to his home which was about the same distance from Fakenham as what it was from Helhoughton but on the other side of the town. Henry then said that if I paid him a visit then he would take me flying. Henry had an aircraft business on the old wartime airfield of Langham. Henry then owned two aeroplanes. A very nice Australian built Tiger Moth in which he loved flying it in aerobatics and also the Leopard Moth G-ACMN. Having motored to the airfield I was wondering which of his two aircraft that he would wheel out. I might just be given a nice session of aero's, but it was the Leopard which he wheeled out of the hangar. Prior to us setting off, he then asked Daphne if she would like to come. Daphne who was never that keen on flying, politely refused the offer saying that she would sit in the motor and keep Annie company. Henry then flew me along the salt-marsh while out to sea there was a thick fog that stopped at the water's edge. On our return back to Langham, I then told Henry of aunties one and only aeroplane ride and I said, 'I bet she would have loved to have come with us'. 'What a pity you did not mention it before', said Henry. Having landed back, Aunt Annie was offered a ride and by sitting by the side of me we were quickly flown to the coast and back. Henry was getting a little concerned in case that sea fog started to roll in land. Aunt Annie had sat on my left hand side. Henry then asked her how she had enjoyed the flight and he also added, 'This time you did get to see the sea'. Auntie then replied, 'It was just the same as that last flight all those years ago, except this time I was sitting on the opposite side'. At eighty-two years young, this little flight was one for the history books.

Captain Geoffrey was also kind to some of the Crux Easton lads by offering them jobs in his factories. By what I have been told, not one of these lads that accepted ever let him down. Dad's two younger brothers our uncles Fred and George, were two such lads that gave up living in the green countryside to move out of the sticks to live in the bricks and to take up a factory life. Freddie was first to go then followed by George after he had finished serving in the Grenadier Guards. Our two uncles were to marry two sisters who also had moved from the countryside to get jobs in London. Then for the rest of their lives they settled for suburbia. George once told me on how Sir Geoffrey, as he had become, suddenly entered his workshop. Having spotted George he made straight to him. This was long after that famous name of de Havilland had been removed from the factory wall to be replaced by the name, Hawker Siddeley. Work then ceased for a while as they chatted on old times. 'Do you know', said Geoffrey, 'They called me up for a short period into the R.F.C. (Royal Flying Corps) and they gave me the rank of captain and I have never done a day's drill in my life'. George who had done little else but drill decided to keep his thoughts to himself. Sir Geoffrey then left the shop as quickly as what he had entered it. George then told me on how this had upset the shop foreman so much as he had considered that it should have been him that this great man should have spoken with.

Another young lad that left Crux Easton and joined the de Havilland enterprise was Frank (Toby) Cox. When he had left school he had started out in life with living in with Grandpa as a trainee gamekeeper. Later in my life, when I had come out of the R.A.F. I was to work under Frank for a year when I secured a job in Newbury with Vickers Supermarine in their Shaw factory. This was doing horizontal milling. When Vickers in Newbury shut down, Frank was then to work for the firm that I had worked for during the war, Opperman Gears in Hambridge Road, Newbury. It was with one of the Opperman brothers that Frank left the factory life to start up a game farm in south Hampshire. After a while Mr Opperman pulled out and Frank continued running the business on his own. He had finally found the life that he loved and had first started out with. He once told me that he had been one of the lucky ones as on some weekends he had been flown back to Crux Easton with his boss in the Leopard Moth G-ACKP. I was to last see Frank when he turned up out of the blue at Stockcross village church when he attended Aunt Annie's funeral, though I have since spoken with him over the phone. One thing that I remember Frank telling me about and this was when he was working with 'Old Joe' (Grandpa). He was told that to be a good gamekeeper was to do nothing. Just to sit down in the middle of a wood and then listen to all of the sounds that were going on around you. It is a Mr Opperman who is a relative from that firm who now owns that so called de Havilland field today.

It was in the October of 1934 that the red and white D.H.88 Comet racer named "Grosvenor House" and registered G-ACSS won the England to Australia Air Race. It was entered by A.O. Edwards and flown to victory by C.W.A. Scott and T. Campbell-Black. This race was run in two sections and so it became two races in one. These sections were the speed and the handicap. This Comet won both, but it could only claim one victory and so it took the prize for the speed section.

In the early 1930's, the citizens of Melbourne prepared to celebrate their city's centenary. It was in 1932 that Sir Harold Geingoult-Smith who was then Melbourne's lord mayor conceived the idea of having an air race from London, England and finishing in Melbourne, Victoria, Australia. Their city being founded in 1834, this would then highlight their city and place their country firmly on the world map. In 1933 an approach was made to Sir MacPherson Robertson who was a millionaire philanthropist. MacRobertson as he was universally known then agreed to put up the prize money, but he only agreed to this air race by having certain conditions. His first condition was that everything that could possibly be done on safety, had to be done. He stipulated that the race had to be international and that it had to be run in two sections, the speed and the handicap. Competitors could enter in one or both sections, but a competitor could only take away one prize. Another stipulation was that the race had to be completed within sixteen calendar days. Mildehall in Suffolk was finally chosen as the departure airfield. On Friday the 19th of October, King George V along with his wife, Queen Mary and the Prince of Wales made a royal visit to the new Mildenhall airfield. Here they chatted to the contestants and the race officials and wished them all well. There had been sixty-four entrant applications and the 20th of October was set as the starting date. The prize in the speed section was £A,10,000 with second and third awards of £A,1,500 and £A,500. The first prize for the handicap section was £A,2,00. Also the winner would receive a gold cup to the value of £A,650. This was all very serious money in those days.

Meanwhile at de Havillands, Captain Geoffrey had called a board meeting as he did not visualise this race being won by a foreign aeroplane. The Americans at that time had two new twin-engine metal constructed monoplane airliners. These were the Boeing 247 and the Douglas DC-2. The later being the forerunner of the famous Douglas C-47 Dakota. Holland was also entering a new three engine monoplane, the Pander S.4. England at that time had nothing that could equal these foreign aircraft in the speed section. If no other British aircraft company could get up off of their backsides, then Captain Geoffrey suggested that they should. In other words, Geoffrey wanted to take a gamble and to wave the union flag. The board agreed and the captain gave his chief designer, Mr A.E. Hagg a rather rush job. The future of their company was then staked on him. His job was in a very short space of time to design a twin engine wooden constructed monoplane that was capable of global racing. The firm placed a lot of capital into this new venture and needless to say, Mr Hagg delivered and on time. De Havillands did not disclose too much about their new venture and they kept things very much hush-hush. What they did release was that it would fly at over 200 mph and that it would be capable of stage lengths of 2,600 miles. To all entrants that placed an order by the 28th of February, the selling price would be just £5,000 with a guaranteed delivery in the coming September.

Three of these Comets were ordered for the race straight off of the drawing board. They were all British registered. Their registrations were, G-ACSP, 'SR and 'SS. The winning Comet being the last one registered. The handicap section was won by a Douglas DC-2. On Tuesday the 23rd of October, Scott and Campbell-Black flew G-ACSS "Grosvenor House" between the two pylons on Flemington Racecourse and then landed at Laverton aerodrome. Altogether, five de Havilland aeroplanes flew in the races which included the three Comets. The other two aircraft being a Dragon Six (later to be known as a Dragon Rapide). This was a New Zealand entry registered ZK-ACO. The other was a D.H.80A Puss Moth an Australian entry registered VH-UQO and named "My Hildegarde". It was flown to England by C.J. (Jimmy) Melrose. He then flew it all the way back to Australia on his own where he came in third. Sadly just two years later he was to lose his life along with his passenger. He was flying his Heston Phoenix VH-AJM through a storm when a wing failed. It was considered possible that he may have had a lightning strike. Fifty years later on, a commemorative flight to that of "My Hildegarde" took place. I will write about this in a later chapter.

Why all of this history on the Comet racers and the MacRobertson air race you may well be asking yourself. What I have been leading up to is a specially framed photograph of that winning Comet "Grosvenor House". Before I discussed this photograph with you, I needed you to be able to judge its importance for yourself. It was on the date of this magnificent achievement that Captain de Havilland had some dated and autographed framed photographs of G-ACSS, this winning Comet. He did this so that he could give them to some of his close friends. Our grandfather 'Old Joe' as he was locally referred to was given one of these framed photographs. As a child I always admired this photograph as it hung on their living room wall. This prized picture has now been handed down to me. As I now turn my head I can see it hanging on my study wall. A few years back I obtained a very small portion of DH marked plywood skinning. This had been removed from the wing of 'SS when it was being restored back to a flying condition by its new owners, The Shuttleworth Trust. This small plywood sample now lives by the side of this photograph.

A few years back it became my turn to give a lecture at the Aviation Group of the Swindon Branch of the U3A (University of the Third Age) of which I was a member. I chose for my subject the D.H.88 Comet. Not the airliner which came years later and was their type D.H.106. A life-long friend of mine, Dennis Simmons who is now long deceased. (now most of the people who I am writing about in this book are now deceased, but I cannot keep referring to them as the late so-and-so). Well Dennis said that he would bring me along an article on this famous Comet racer, but he must have it back as it belonged to his brother-in-law. I did not give his offer much thought as I have shelves full of aviation books and many of these are on de Havilland aircraft. True to his word, Dennis brought along a small book which had a picture of G-ACSS in it. To my surprise it was signed by Captain de Havilland and dated and it was credited to the Shuttleworth Trust. Now I have only ever seen one other framed photograph that is similar to the one that is in my possession. That other one was in the ownership of a licensed engineer who had been an ex de Havilland apprentice and his parents had also lived at Crux Easton. On close inspecting my photograph and making a comparison with the one printed in the book I then found that both signatures were identical and had been signed over the same portion of the photograph exactly. No person could possibly do a thing like that, not even the great man himself. This then proved to me that this picture had been pirated. The only time until now in this book that I have let this picture be published was in the de Havilland Moth Club's 'Enterprise No 20'. Later the deHMC dropped the name 'Enterprise' in favour of 'The Moth'. It would not have been so bad if they had credited it to Sir Geoffrey. The other framed photograph that I had been shown had at one time been removed from its frame and cleaned. Mine is very much in a need of cleaning and I was considering of getting this done. Now my brother Dick who also would have very much liked to have owned it then took for himself a photograph from this photograph. This came out so well that I could hardly spot the difference between the two of them. Due to this, I have now decided to keep mine in its original sealed dirty state. I have often wondered who it was that took the original. Perhaps it was the great man himself.

Having spoken so much about the family life at Crux Easton, I think that it is only fitting to say a few words about our grandfather, 'Old Joe'. What I am about to reveal here could not have been spoken about all of those years ago. It would have carried a stigma. In today's world, these things are looked upon in a different kind of way. Grandfather was one of the most pleasant of persons that you could ever wish to meet. Over the years I have heard many people speak of him and no one has ever given him a bad name or have said anything nasty about him. When we were children, and also later on in life, my brother and I were never told anything that related to our great grandfather. All that we were ever told was that our grandfather was a step-son and it was left at that. In later years, Dick and I have made several journeys to Bury St. Edmunds and to Elveden while researching our family history. When one traces back in time it is quite a common thing to find that you have a skeleton in the cupboard. We half expected to find one and we did. On one of our researching visits to Suffolk, we called in on our Aunt Rose and Uncle Fred who lived in Stevenage. Rose then let the cat out of the bag when she said, 'You boys just as well know now that your great grandmother was seduced by the lord of the manor'. Uncle Fred did not know that his wife knew about this and having it been made a family secret for so long he then showed his surprise with anger. The manor was Elveden Hall and its lord was the Maharajah Duleep Singh who was often referred to as 'The Black Prince'. He had been removed from ruling the Punjab in India by the British and then to purchase the Elveden Estate. He called Queen Victoria 'Mrs Fagin' as he considered that she had stolen from him the Koh-i-noor diamond. This she had cut and it is now a part of the crown jewels where it is on the late Queen Mother's state crown. All the same, Queen Victoria thought very highly of him. Today the maharaja's shady doings are still with us and also with very many more other families that can trace their histories back to those servant girls of Elveden Hall. Together we made a visit to the Ancient House Museum of Thetford Life which was given to the town by Prince Frederick who was one of the maharajah's sons. His sons were also known as 'The Black Princes'. A curator in that museum told us that all of the maharajah's strain had died out, but the strain from all of those servant girls is still very much alive. We were told that at least a dozen or so families like our own had come to this museum while undertaking family research. Some people had come from as far away as Canada in order to do so.

Maharajah Duleep Singh died in Paris in 1893 while he was only in his mid forties. He is buried along with his wife Maharani Bamba and his two prince sons in Elveden church yard. Without digging the old boy up to prove the DNA you may think that our families have no proof that he was my great grandfather. Our proof is the blue blood that once flowed through his veins. Throw-backs in the family have shown that a few have had extra dark skin and some have been born with the Mongolian Asian blue spot on their backsides. What other proof should one need. Maharajah Duleep Singh and the Earle of Carnarvon at that time were great shooting buddies. I have since learnt that through this kind of thing, many families were moved one way and the other between the counties of Suffolk and Hampshire. This may have been one of the reasons that our grandparents found their way into living in Hampshire. It is no wonder that it was the reason that we were not told and it had to be kept such a secret. I do not like the word seduced. I call a spade a spade and I would sooner call it rape. Those servant girls stood no chance. Their parents were most likely living in tied houses on the estate. This seems to have been the common norm at that time. This must have been how the lords of the manors treated their servant girls and most of them being in their teens. On my book shelf I have a book called, 'The Big Shots, Edwardian Shooting Parties'. It was published in the late 1970's and was written by Jonathan Garnier Ruffer. To the front of this it has an introduction by Lord Walsingham of Merton Hall which is also near to Thetford. Here his lordship is speaking of his great uncle, Tom de Grey, the 6th Lord Walsingham. Here he acknowledges that this scandal took place as he states that he usually slept with his housemaids. That statement made in that introduction is proof that rape was often taking place. All the same, woe-betide a peasant who got caught poaching a pheasant to feed his family. He could have been transported off to Australia. Perhaps he might have been better off if he had been. Even today I have no faith in what is called British justice. If you are up against a person with lots of money you stand little chance of winning your case. I was to find this out when I was taken to court in Newbury. I was driving a telephone lorry when I was rammed by a speeding Bentley at a cross roads and it was no fault of my own. As soon as that judge was told that the Bentley was a write-off, he found me guilty even though I had an independent witness that proved that I was not.

I seem to remember once that on reading in a newspaper that India had requested the return of that famous Koh-i-noor diamond. My thoughts on the subject are this. It should be sold back to India and the monies from the sale should be placed in a fund to help any person in need that can trace their relations back to those Elveden servant girls even if it required to dig the maharajah up to obtain his DNA. I would not wish to leave him on the top, after all, he was my great grandfather. Our great grandmother did get married after she had had our grandfather. She then raised a family of her own and lived to be nearly one hundred.

Just to close this chapter, I will tell you just one of the many stories that I have been told about our grandfather, 'Old Joe'. Two boys had climbed up a tree. This being the kind of thing that I might have got up to when I was a child. The one that had climbed up way above the other then shouted down to the one below. 'Coo, you can see Old Joe's house from here'. Then a voice from under the tree said, 'But can you see Old Joe'. Grandfather was waiting for them to climb down.

My Grandfather, Joe Rutterford is seen attending to his pheasant coops to the rear of the Easton Park homestead, Crux Easton/Woodcott. Mrs deHavilland is looking on and Captain Geoffrey, her husband, most likely took this old photograph. The Captain was very friendly with 'Old Joe', my Grandfather.

DeHavilland Comet - England to Australia in 2 days 4 hours - October 1934

TO SCHOOL AT LAST

It was at the close of the 1933-34 shooting season that my parents moved their home from Sarson Wood near Andover to the small hamlet of Wickham Heath in Berkshire. Dad had changed his employment and he now became a gamekeeper on the Benham Estate which was and still is owned by the Sutton family. This large Berkshire country estate is situated between the towns of Newbury and Hungerford. Father had bought himself a very small two-stroke motorcycle. It was a Francis Barnett that was powered by a Villiers engine. Its triangular frame was constructed from many metal tubes which were all bolted together. The front forks were sprung by a large rubber block that had a hole through its centre. The drive was to a rim on the rear wheel by a leather belt which was known to slip and often to break. It was on this machine that Dad had set out to find his new employment. Maybe he found the cost of running it to high as after we had moved to Wickham Heath he never used it again. He gave away or sold the engine and the engineless bike then took up one side of the largest shed. Eventually after much pestering, Dad finally relented and us two boys then got a lot of fun by playing with it between the many tall and mature scots pine trees. It had the registration NX 8569.

Dad had taken this job on the Benham Estate for the sake of our mother's health. Through no fault of our father, the location and his job at Sarson had taken its toll on mother's nerves. Mother was now only a bus or a cycle ride away from her parents and she now had neighbours on each side of us. Our other grandfather was a head gardener for a large house called, 'Foley Lodge'. This place was roughly halfway between our new home and the town of Newbury. It was just on the other side of the estate's village of Stockcross where I was to do all of my schooling. On this estate Dad was to spend the rest of his working days and he had his cottage for life. He could have moved away and become a head keeper or a single handed keeper, but mother was not for moving. The only move that she wanted to make was into Stockcross village where she then would have electric lighting and water on tap. We could not have wished for better parents, but in my eyes, our mother was not cut out to be a gamekeeper's wife. A good keeper's wife in those days had to be something special. She had to get use to a life of solitude. Both of our parents endured a very hard life and they were a happy couple. My brother and I now realise that we should have done a lot more to have helped them with all of the chores, but at the time we did not see it that way.

Now that my home was at Wickham Heath I had become over six years old. Due to brother Dick coming along and the outlandish location of my old home, plus mother's upset nerves, I had not started my schooling at the age of five like all the other kids. My excuse has often been that on missing out on that first year of schooling was the reason why I never became a brilliant scholar. It is true that this did not help me a bit, but to be fair, they did try and help me along while I was in the infant class. Just how my parents got away with me losing that first year of schooling I do not know, but get away with it they did.

Our new home in the countryside was in a semi-detached cottage that was modelled on a Tudor styling. To the eastern side of our home were six small cottages all built in a row under one thatching. Today they have been made into only four and the estate has sold them off. To each end of our row of eight cottages was a small farm. These two farms were leased to tenants by the estate. To the rear of all of these houses it was woodland. This wood was called 'Long Plantation', but we always knew it as, 'The Firs'. It consisted of nearly all scots pine, but here and there were dotted a few other trees. These were of oak and beech and that dainty weed of the wood, silver birch which made up for the rest. Nearer to the rear of our houses the pine trees were more mature and below them there was very little ground cover. It was just a carpet of old pine needles. Beneath these older trees we spent a lot of time playing and together with our new playmates we had a lot of fun. These new playmates lived next door but one to us in that long row of thatched cottages. They were starting from the oldest down; Enid, Dennis and Maurice Simmons. Enid was about two years older than myself and she would climb to the top of any tree providing it had branches that would allow her to do so. For the rest of our lives they then became life-long friends. Sadly, as I write this, Maurice is the only one left of that family. Dick and I grew up to loves these woods and the beauty of these old scot pines. They are at their best when a late evening yellowish sunlight highlights their pinkish-purple barks. Fallen branches from these trees would help us in fuelling our stoves. Many are the hours that we have been spent wooding and collecting up pine cones to kindle our fires.

Life was very hard for our parents. Not one of these cottages had a drain to it. All of the down pipes from the guttering had a tub at the bottom of it. Our home did have a rudimentary sink in the scullery, but this had to have a bucket standing under it to catch the used dirty water. Many were the times that this bucket had overflowed. There was no water on tap. A well that was at the top of a very long vegetable garden that was to the front of the houses provided us and our next door neighbour with water. After you had drawn your bucket of water, you then had to remove all the floaters before you carried it back to the house. The laundry had to be boiled in an old cast iron copper. First you had to do your trips up the garden to part fill the copper with water. You then had to bring in fresh cut wood which you placed underneath. You then had to get the fire going to heat up the copper. The clean washing was then removed from the copper with a long wooden copper stick and then placed in a galvanized bath to drain off the water. It then had to be wound through two wooden rollers by turning a large handle at the end of the mangle. Now it was to be carried out and hung on the washing line. The dirty water had to be ladled out into buckets and carried out into the woodland where it was slung away. Having dried out the copper, you then had to remove all of the ashes from its fireplace. Taking a bath was a similar procedure. You lit up the copper to heat the water. A long galvanized bath which was kept hanging on an outside wall was brought into the house. It was then the same procedure in cleaning out the copper and throwing away the dirty water. If it was a dry season and the well was low in water, this dirty water would be saved for the garden by being emptied into one of the gutter tubs.

All of the lavatories were out of doors. They consisted of a lavatory bucket under some elm wood seating. On an average of once a week, these buckets needed emptying. This we referred to as, burying the pig. First, a hole had to be dug way out in the woodland. Not an easy job as you had to contend with tree roots. Also the ground had a thick layer of clay. In wet weather conditions, this layer of clay made for stagnant surface water. Chamber pots under the bed served for night time. In the winter you would not want to run down the stairs, unlock the door and then run across a snow covered yard in order to drain off a little water. Then to reverse your procedure to return back into your nice warm bed. The next day these bedroom slops had to carried down stairs and slung into the woods at the rear of our houses.

Heating and cooking was by a kitchen range, either open or closed. It was made of cast iron and had to be black leaded. Like the copper, it needed wood logs and a little coal. It also needed its ashes to be removed. There was an oven door to one side of the fireplace. Most of the cooking was done on this range. To assist in cooking, we had a Valor paraffin oil stove and also a paraffin Primus stove. This became useful for making toast or heating up the flat irons to iron our clothing. Lighting was by paraffin oil lamps and these had to be trimmed and filled. Yes life was primitive, but we did enjoy it. Now that I cast my mind back to those days, it was understandable on how our mother had longed to have had a chance to make a move into the Stockcross village. Now we had tradesmen call on us. The grocer, the baker, the coal man, the accumulator man and the paraffin man. This gent, a Mr Sawyer had a large paraffin tank fitted to the rear of his vehicle and he also sold other odd items. Our milk was delivered by bicycle. This by Lesley Stacey who had the small farm at the end of our row. Dad being an estate worker had a load of wood delivered to him about once a year. But in order to use it, then it had to be cut up. It became a common sight to see our father walk off with a cloth sack of pheasant feed over his shoulder. On his return he would often carry a shoulder stick which he would then add to his wood pile.

The estate owned village of Stockcross was where we did our schooling. Today, nearly all of the houses in the village have been sold off and have become private. The estate no longer has a large working force to find homes for. This village has many Tudor styled houses similar to the one in which we lived. At that time this village had the school, a church and a chapel, three pubs and two shops. One of these also held a Post Office. It also had a village policeman, but not today. There was a recreation ground complete with tennis courts and also a nice brick built hall. A portion of this hall was a working man's club. This village had what we had not got, the luxury of electric lighting and water on tap. This water was pumped up to the village on a daily basis from a large lake that was to the front of the big house, 'Benham Valence'. Our school was built in two sections. The infants class and the kitchen being one part. The other was the main class rooms. As I write this, the village has lost one of its shops and a pub. The way that things are looking, it may quite well lose another. The school buildings in which we once attended have since been pulled down, but a new school has been built on the other side of the large playing field. Where the village has changed is in its class of people. More upmarket. In my terms, yuppie-fied. They are still nice country people, but somehow, not quite the same as what we were. I have to face it, some of my children that are now grown up with families of their own have become yuppies. Nothing today stays the same anymore. It is to the church in this village that I still like to attend their services whenever I can, but I now live in Swindon which is a good twenty-five miles distant. Some of my family which includes my parents and my wife Daphne are buried in the churchyard there. It is to this churchyard that one day I hope that I will eventually end up.

I realise as I write this that I have deviated somewhat from the subject of aircraft and aviation, but I do intend to get back to it towards the end of this chapter. As a country school, I could not have wished for a better one. Although this Berkshire C of E school was far from the standard of a modern comprehensive of today, we had first class teachers and had every chance of obtaining a good education. Several of the children that I went to school with did very well for themselves much later on in life. We did not have to sit for 'A' levels and pocket calculators were yet to be invented. We used pens that had to be dipped in inkwells. We did not wear uniforms or any school colours or badges. There was also no homework. All of this work was done in the school's time and in a classroom. I for one have always been against children having to bring homework home with them. To start with they have to carry heavy packs and it is not all of them once they are home that can have the comfort of a heated quiet room in which to perform their work. Many of them having to work in a crowded room with a television set switched on. I am a strong believer that all school work should be done in a school classroom.

For those of us who sat an exam and past it, then they could leave the village school and go to a Newbury school. The girls went to the town's High School while the boys went to the Grammar School. Yes, our Stockcross School was a mixed school of both sexes. We sat two to a desk and it was not uncommon for a boy to share a desk with a girl. Although our parents would have liked Dick and myself to have taken that examination and past it, they were secretly relieved that we did not do so. To have gone to the Grammar would have meant them trying to find the money in order to kit us out with uniforms and satchels. Money was short. In order to have done so, they would have to have gone without other commodities. Those boys that made it to the Grammar School had to wear red caps. To these, us village boys gave some nick-names. We referred to them as either grammar grubs or red topped matches.

It was during the later years of my education that our school became swamped with evacuee children from London. These poor unfortunate children were placed on special trains and sent away from the bombing and into the safer countryside. Many of them had never seen a farm with animals on in their lives. It was all so new to them. For many of them it was an adventure, but not to all. Some found it very traumatic. Labels were tied on to them and on their backs they carried their gasmasks in special satchels. Well we all at that time had to carry them, especially to school. Each one of them also carried a small case with not much more than a change of clothing in them. There was not any room to cram in any toys. What they left behind them was not only the blitz, but their parents, relations, pets, toys and their ways of living. It was the love of their homes. They were not to know where they would end up or who would then be looking after them. They did not know if they would be shown any love in their new homes. Some thoughts must have always have been going through their minds such as, if it is not safe for me, then will it be safe for my parents. Would I ever see them again? Would I still have a home to go back to and how long will I have to be away? They were all very brave children and for them I think that it must have been worse than being called up into the armed services.

With our capital city and many other ports, towns and cities being blitzed night after night, who in their right mind could blame Bomber Command for hitting back at Germany. They had asked for the whirlwind which they later received. All along, our country new that the Germans had got heavy water plants and that their aim was to produce a nuclear weapon. Had they had succeeded in doing so, then little old England would have been the place that they would have tried it out on. Hitler had given up the thought of invading us, but a nuclear bomb would have served him just as well. In those days, no one knew the terrible effects that radiation would leave. Had Bomber Command not have done what it did, it would have failed our country in its time of need. I see no glory in warfare. Should there have been some, then it should not all have gone to Fighter Command, brave as what they were. All of those that took to the air to fight for our country were just as brave. Another thing that has always niggled me is that every week you can turn on the TV and you can watch programs on wartime aviation. What you get is what the air crews got up to. Nothing at all about the ground crews or come to that, any of the other trades which struggled to keep the stations active. I see no reason why the air crews should get all of the so called glory. Without the other trades, they would not have got off of the ground. Myself, I received my call-up papers in 1946 and so I just missed out on active service. Several of my pals who were just a little older than what I was did see active service. Had I had been that little bit older and knowing how much I have always loved flying, I most likely would have volunteered for aircrew. All the same, I now thank God that I was not called up to go to war and help in dropping bombs on other people.

I am now getting side tracked again and so it is back to my school days. The buildings were of hard brick and the roofs were slate covered. To start with we had four teachers which included the infant teacher and the head. With the coming of so many evacuees, two extra teachers came along with them. One of which was a conscientious objector. Back in those days we had much colder winters which often brought along deep snow that blocked many of our country lanes. In order to keep us children warm, our classrooms were heated by large coke burning tortoise type stoves. In very cold weather, parts of these stoves would glow red hot. During the warm summer months these stoves would not be lit and the sash windows would be wide open. I well remember when one of these stoves was lit up for the first time after the summer. Its chimney, or stove pipe went straight out through the wall and then took a bend and continued up the outside of the wall. It was made from asbestos and during the summer the dampness had penetrated it. The heat from the fire then turned this dampness into steam. With ear shattering bangs it then blasted asbestos shrapnel all over the school playground. That playtime we had to be kept in the buildings. A similar thing was to happen with us kids in the Methodist Chapel at Wickham Heath where on Sunday mornings we would attend a Sunday school. Several of us children were detailed to go and light a fire in a much smaller stove which was situated in the centre of the chapel. It was the first time that the fire had been lit after the summer break. It also had an asbestos stove pipe which ran straight up from the stove and through the roof. We placed in it some old newspapers and some kindling wood and set fire to it. Having got the fire started, we left the stove and started to play some tunes on the harmonium. No sooner had we started playing than there was an almighty, not taking the pun, explosion from the stove. Together we all went back to the stove to investigate as it was still there and had not blown itself to pieces. What we found was that a large portion of outer layer of the stove pipe had blasted away. It had hit the side wall with so much force that it had bounced back and landed on a pew close to the stove. Well we thought, that having done that all would now be well and so we returned back to the harmonium. No sooner had we got back and there was another loud bang followed by another. This asbestos pipe was inside a building and not on the outside like the one at the school. It had only taken a bit of kindling wood to have generated so much steam in such a short place of time. We were not able to vacate the chapel as we would have had to risk passing the stove. Together we all took cover behind the pulpit until the fire had burnt itself out and the asbestos shrapnel had stopped flying. This gave us a lesson in the power of steam. I now know that asbestos can be very dangerous in more ways than one.

I had been schooling for several years when two aeroplanes decided to look us up. I cannot now remember if it was before or after the time when we had to carry those satchels that contained our rubber gasmasks. These we were made to wear for periods of a time during lessons. This so that we got use to wearing them as in those days a gas attack was very real. Wearing these made breathing much harder and it also created lots of snorting noises and some steaming up condensation on the inside of the celluloid windows. As children we did not take the situation seriously as we would often play some distance from home without them. Each village had a lime painted coloured board mounted on top of a post. In the event of a gas attack, these boards would then change colour. But by the time that you got to see that board, it could well have been too late. I have no idea how we would have received an all clear from a gas attack out in the country. But the powers to be did take things very seriously. Army lorries had this special paint applied on a metal disc. Some aircraft in the training role had diamond shaped patches of this paint applied on an upper surface where it could easily be seen. This might be found on the top of a fuselage just forward of the tailplane. I am pleased to say that none of this paint ever had to change colour.

It was on a Friday afternoon between two and three–o-clock on a fine summer's day when two Hawker biplanes started to use us boys as a training exercise. This was a period in the school syllabus when in fine weather all of the boys would go to the school allotments to be taught gardening. All of the girls were kept in the classroom learning needlework. Us boys were busy at pronging the ground when we were spotted from the air by the pilots of two Hawker Hart variants. This event happened over seventy years ago and I knew that they were Hawker biplanes but I was not then that clued up as to identify which kinds it was that they were. They were powered by Rolls-Royce Kestrel engines which was the forerunner of the famous wartime Merlin. These pilots had decided that we were just the right kind of candidates in which to practice some low level beat-ups on. The Hart was a pre-war fighter-bomber that was later to be used as an advanced trainer. It was also used as a training glider tug. All of the remaining Hawker Kestrel engine biplanes were to end up in the training role. These two biplanes first came in on us from behind a row of oak trees at the bottom end of the school's grass playing field. All of the time, one then followed the other playing a game of follow my leader. If the first one went low, I am sure that the second one tried hard to go lower. They then circled around with one always on the others tail. Dipping down low over the main road and close to a horse chestnut tree, they then skimmed over the school roof where they upset the girls with their racket as they made their way back to us boys. Our headmaster, Mr (Inky) Penwill was shouting out to us boys to lay flat on the ground. He himself was already flat on the ground and could not get any flatter. This manoeuvre they repeated and as they did so they got lower every time. In the end they were as good as bouncing their wheels in the school's playing field before lifting back up over the hedge which separated the field from the school gardens. Thinking back on that event, very foolish as it was, it could not have been so easy for the second pilot while continually flying in the first aircraft's slipstream. Like some person who likes to position himself at an air show close to the end of an active runway, at that time I did not see any danger. If I could have been given an air show like this every time we were taken for gardening lessons, then I might have got to take more interest in gardening.

Whenever the outside weather conditions were unsuitable for gardening and during the winter months we boys were then kept in a classroom being given art and drawing lessons. It was on one of these Friday afternoons that a wartime teacher who had joined us with the evacuees was taking us lads on a drawing lesson. His name was Mr Llewllyn of Welsh origin and so we had nick-named him Loo-Loo. One of the evacuees was suffering with a genuine winter's cold. This poor lad could not help it but he developed a coughing fit. This then started another boy coughing who had a similar problem. The reaction of this was that the whole class then developed a coughing fit. We were then all coughing for all we worth and poor old Loo-Loo then lost it as the coughing grew worse. He just stood there facing us all and he did not seem to know what to do next. In fact, he was the only one not coughing. A pal of mine named Desmond Newport, sadly one of the many that is no longer with us, suddenly in his excitement, he forgot himself. He did not cough, but he shouted out the word cough at the top of his voice. This then brought old Loo-Loo to his senses and he stood poor old Desmond behind the blackboard for the rest of the afternoon. There then became a little silence before the whole class broke into a fit of laughter. Desmond had cured the coughing fit and even the boy that had started it all was no longer coughing.

Toys also featured in my young life. I once did own a very nice flying model, but only in name. It was given to me by my Uncle Doo-Dah, the uncle that had given me that holiday on Hayling Island. As I was considered too young for it, the grown-ups decided that they had better fly it for me as I might break it. It was a Frog ready to fly rubber powered job and I seem to remember that it had a geared propeller. The wings had pressed out metal ribs with a skin covering of printed paper. I also believe that it could be wound up within the box in which it came. It is now nearly over three quarters of a century ago and so perhaps my memory might be failing me. To shorten a long story by cutting, they decided to fly it for me and obviously also for themselves. It flew very well until they crashed it into the tiled roof of my grandfather's (on my mother's side) henhouse. That was the last flight that that model made. I also remember having a wire framed silk covered rubber powered job that came out of Woolworths. It could only have cost sixpence in old money as in those days that was the stores top price. There was an exception. A toy articulated lorry that I owned had cost one shilling. It was sold in two parts. The tractor portion was sixpence and the trailer portion was sixpence. Many years ago we had a wind-up gramophone. One small record that we played went, 'Sixpence in Woolworth's. I wonder what kind of price that record would fetch today.

As we grew older, we were to design and build balsa constructed rubber powered aircraft models which we covered with tissue paper. Also we made model gliders. A glider from which I obtained a lot of pleasure was made from a kit and I remember that Dad helped me in the building. It was called, a Beauglider. It flew quite well until one day it ran into the upper branches of a mature oak tree. Eventually it did reach the ground, but only in pieces. It was never to fly again. Dick designed and built two rubber powered jobs. These he named the Skylark and the Owlet. Both of these flew very well. He also designed and built a very special model that had elliptically shaped wings. This model took him very many hours to design and to build. One night he at last finished it and it was ready to be air tested. Impatience then got hold of him. In the dark of night he took it just outside the back door, he gave the rubber motor just a few turns and then launched it into the blackness. It obviously was a very good flyer as it travelled a lot farther than he had thought it would. We were unable to see where it had landed, but we did hear next doors dog growling and a lot of crunching noises. It had flown into next doors dog pen which was out in the wood. The dog had then attacked it in fury and all that Dick could salvage was the undercarriage. At the time when most of these balsa models were built I had then left school, but Brother Richard was still there.

We were also given other toys. One Christmas our parents bought us each a large tin three engine airliner. It was based on the Armstrong Whitworth Argosy. These toys were fitted with navigation lights. Three torch bulbs. A red on the port and a green on the starboard wing tip. A white was on the tail. They were painted bulbs. To power them there was a flat type torch battery under the lower centre section of the fuselage. I believe that they were bought from out of Marks & Spencer. We were also given a few die-cast Dinky Toys. These we took to be the cat's whisker. Dick was given two de-Havilland types. A Comet Racer and the Albatross G-AEVV. I was also given a Comet racer and the Armstrong Whitworth Ensign G-ADSR. I later had a Short Singapore III and a green de-Havilland Leopard Moth. These Dinky's were very popular and several of us boys would take some to school with us where we would play together with them at playtimes. I well remember on how I came by a Cierva C.30 Autogiro. That particular morning I had gone to school on the bus. Also on that bus was a red topped match who was to continue his journey on into Newbury. His name was Roy Burgess. Just before I got off of that bus I did a swap with him for that C.30. What I did not know was that he had painted it yellow the night before. I then became covered in yellow and it was all over my clothing. Mother was not that pleased with my Swap. Come to that, neither was I.

There were three different methods of going to school. Walk, cycle or go on the bus. If we went by bus, then we had to leg it home and if we walked, we also had to leg it home. One day I went to collect my cycle from the cycle shed and it was not there. I then went back into the school where I told 'Inky' that my bike had been stolen and then I legged it home. Having walked in doors I then had to tell mother that my bike had been stolen. She then reminded me that on that morning I had gone to school on the bus. Sure enough, there in the shed was my bike. Come the following morning I was then left with the unpleasant task of telling my headmaster as to how I had got my bike back. Come to think about it, I was not that brilliant at the time. I had started my schooling one year later than everybody else.

When I was not at play, I would spend quite a bit of time on Stacey's farm. This farm being called 'Peewit Farm'. Jobs that I tackled were horse raking, help in rick building and shocking up in the harvest fields. I also spent many hours just sitting on the right side mudguard of an old Fordson model N tractor whilst Bert Kempster was ploughing with it. This was quite safe, but today with all of this health and safety, it would not be legal. One thing that has stayed in my memory was the time when Bert stopped the tractor while he went into the wood to attend the call of nature. This old tractor was not the best to swing on the handle or to get started once the engine was hot. Sometimes also when cold for that matter. He had made me get down and stand well away from the tractor and had kept the engine running and the tractor stationary by placing a large spanner holding down the clutch pedal. The old girl was vibrating so much that the spanner slipped away from where it had been placed and the tractor took off on its own. It was the fastest that I had ever seen Bert move as he made after it and catching up with it just before it got to the far hedge. I was shown how to milk cows. This I never did manage. I did not want to manage it because I knew that had I had done so, they would have had me milking cows for ever more.

Dad had spent many hours in making us two boy's bicycles. This from the many bits and pieces that he had managed to get hold of. Both Dick and I became very good at bending them badly after all of his efforts in building them. There was a craze going round where you could buy a carrier that fitted over the rear mudguard and it also had a stand so that you could stand the bike up much like that on the rear of a motorbike. Brother Dick was not happy until they bought him one. For the first time out with this attachment fitted he rode his bike down Hoe Benham to the harvest field. He did no more than stand it up on its stand in the gateway into the field. No sooner had he done this and then along came Bert driving the old Fordson and pulling the binder. As Bert was looking back to see where the binder would be going he failed to notice a pushbike that was stood in the centre of the entrance. The tractor then bent that bike badly. That became the end of the bike with the stand and it failed to please father, that I can tell you.

I was one year late in starting my schooling. I also left school before I had reached the age of fourteen. This was due to one of those school illnesses. It may have been mumps, but I have now forgotten which illness that it was. Being as we had a war on at the time it could quite well have been German measles. I could not take up keepering as the war had closed this down. The time had come when it was suggested that I should start working for the war effort. At the time I was eager to leave school, but many has been the time when I had wished that I was still back there.

Those two Hawker biplanes

This Leyland was often our school bus

WORKING IN WARTIME

Having reached the age of fourteen, it was time for me to leave school and to start out in life helping to pay for my own keep. Our country now had its back to the wall and was in need of all the war effort that could be mustered. Not that my little bit would do very much. My parents were determined that the best thing for me was to go into an engineering factory and help in manufacturing those vital munitions. My father and his father had been gamekeepers. Due to Hitler's war, I was to break this chain. By now, Dad had packed up as a keeper and was then sent to mix up concrete as a labourer to the builders who were constructing a chain of pillboxes along the Kennet Valley. These pillboxes would have formed a vital line of defence had the Germans invaded. I remember Dad being very angry when some of these builders went on strike for more money. I feel sure that had they had been in Germany then they would have been shot. We looked upon them as performing an act of mutiny. As soon as all of the pillboxes had been constructed, Dad then came back to the Sutton Estate workforce where he was placed on forestry work. It was in this trade that he was to finish his working days. Full-filling my parents wishes, I started my working life in a factory that specialised in manufacturing industrial reduction gearboxes of all sizes. They also specialised in the cutting of gearwheels. This firm was Opperman Gears. They had just moved west into the Newbury area from Clerkenwell, London. Their London factory had been blitzed and the building was made unsafe. They had come to Newbury bringing with them many of their original work-force. They also brought with them all of the salvaged machinery which was then reassembled into a brand new brick building. Many of their machines were ancient and some of their lathes could be continually heard chattering away to each other.

I was to be trained as a turner. My first job was working on a very small capstan (turret) lathe. I was given a very simple job to start with. It was parting off spokes for the spectacle control wheels for the pilot's control columns that were to be fitted into Wellington bombers. The capstan being loaded with long lengths of alloy tubing. Oppermans were then making most of the control columns for the Vickers Armstrong Wellingtons. They were also manufacturing several other components for Vickers. What we called Vickers shafts were produced in two separate lengths. I have often wondered if they had anything to do with holding the wings on the Wellington bombers. Another thing that we made were what was known as, flap control boxes. During the war, many small parts were manufactured by many firms and so you never knew just how they were used. Secrecy was the key word of the day. What you did not know about, you could not talk about. Careless talk cost lives, was the general slogan. Due to the two types of components that this factory was producing, there were two sections of fitters. These were, the aircraft and the gearbox. Later on in the war this firm designed and built some potato harvesters. To me, these looked clumsy. I do not think that they would have been very popular with the farmers. These kind of things had to be tried out as our nation had to be fed with as much food as was possible being grown in our own country.

For a short period in the morning and again in the afternoon we were played over the factory speaker system the BBC program, Music While You Work. This we always enjoyed, it help in breaking the monotony of the repetition work that most of us workers were having to do. By keep on doing the same old thing over and over each day could get very tiring. We were only allowed two visits to the toilets each day for doing a number two job. For this you drew a key from the tool stores and you were timed and had to return that key within seven minutes. It was while I was working on one of these small early capstans that I came very close to having a serious accident.

These old lathes were powered from a short over-head line-shaft. There was a large electric motor that fed this shafting that was situated on the top of the gantry. To start the lathe you pushed sideways a long wooden handle that hung down from above. By doing this you moved a leather belt from an idle pulley on to a live pulley. I had turned around to talk to another person when my right hand accidentally moved that starting handle. I was very lucky, as I just managed to snatch my hand away in the split second that I felt the pulley wheel of the lathe. One split second longer and it would have pulled my whole arm in. It was a clear case of the left hand not knowing what the right hand was doing. I made sure that I would not do that again. Like the saying goes, and it is very true, all aeroplanes can bite back. I found that this could also be very true of all things that are mechanical. During the war, the Health and Safety were then not so concerned about such matters as what they are today. That is, if they existed.

Working under a factory roof was to rob me of seeing a lot of the air activity that was always taking place in our skies. Father working out in the open air was to see much more. It was while he was still a gamekeeper, and so this would have been very early on in the war, a group of keepers standing together saw a German bomber. It flew past them along a small valley. They could not identify it, but they did all see the crosses painted on it. As it flew by them, for some reason it started machine-gunning. It may have been at them, but if it was then it had missed them clearly. One of the keepers raised his shotgun and fired at it, but as would be expected, it just flew on.

It was around this time that my family had been singled out to act as the local fire service. We were to perform this task for the rest of our small community. We had to sign for a stirrup-pump and because of this we had to be shown how to use it. Our homes were situated in the parish of Boxford. We were never to know what social events might be happening in Boxford, any events that we went to was always in the village of Stockcross in the adjoining parish. The only time that Boxford parish knocked on our doors was when they needed some money for something. It was to Boxford that Dad had to go to when he joined the L.D.V. (Local Defence Volunteers). Later to be called The Home Guard. To the now younger generations they would know it as 'Dad's Army'. Had Germany invaded, and they could have done, then the Home Guard would have given Gerry quite a bit of stick. It was also from Boxford that Dick and I were given a belated sister named Betty. She was an evacuee from London's East End. The thing that I remember about her coming was that the lady that came knocking on our doors wanted every cottage to take in one evacuee. She owned a very large house with many rooms, but she was not keen on filling up her own home with these poor unfortunate children. She was of typical English gentry. The other thing that I well remember is that at that time we all caught fleas. On a close inspection of Betty's hair we then found that she was infested with them.

It was to Boxford that Mother and I had to go for the lesson on how to use that stirrup-pump. Here it was presumed that incendiary bombs would fall through a roof to a place where we could get at them. What rubbish. They had not given any thought that these bombs would have been dropped at a time in quantity. Also that if we had been bombed by them, many would have landed in the dry woodland which they would have then set on fire. If those woods had gone up, then so would our homes. Also they had not given any thought as to where we could get a constant supply of water. If acres and acres of woodland had gone up in flames then we would have stood no chance. After the war we were given the option of buying or returning that pump. We bought it and it did then come in useful as a garden spray.

For the purpose of getting to work and back which was a journey of seven miles each way, my parents helped me with the finance on a new bicycle. This was my first ever new bike. It was a

Raleigh Sports and it was made to wartime standards. I became very proud of it, and my bike and I became as one. In all weathers I would use my bike. If it was wet, I donned a yellow cycle cape and a pair of similar leggings. I could cycle over fifty miles without getting fatigued. This I could do when I was fresh, but by the end of each working day it was a different story. After standing all day on a duck board working a machine, it would sap the energy out of me. My journey home was an uphill ride and it generally took me nearly twice as long.

On my journeys to and fro' from work I would always be on the lookout for aircraft. Either seeing them in the air, or travelling along the roads on motor transport. Many of these that were being transported by road were heading north to a large repair and salvage depot at Cowley, Oxford. The majority of aircraft that I saw on road while being transported were British. The amount of forced landings that were taking place in Britain at that time was enormous. Nearly every one of them had to be recovered necessitated a road journey. At that time, many sections of aircraft were being manufactured by small firms in isolated factories. These also necessitated a road journey to take them to their final assembly locations. Often a fuselage would be seen travelling on an R.A.F Queen Mary (60 feet in length transporter). The wings with its other bits and pieces would often follow on a second transporter. Wellington fuselages took up the complete bed of these trailers. Airspeed Oxfords continually held up every other vehicle that was travelling along the road. Their outer wings were removed from either side of their A.W. cheetah engines which were left sticking out taking up near enough both sides of the road. Journeys were different then as main roads had sharper bends and steeper gradients. They were also much narrower. Heavy lorries were then regulated to 20 mph and there were often convoys of military vehicles travelling in one direction or another. These were often assisted by DR's (dispatch riders) on motorcycles. Short Stirling fuselages would not fit on to Queen Mary's. These were seen being transported on flat bed lorries with their rear portion of the fuselage over-hanging the back of the bed for nearly the length of which they were sitting on. Military convoys when encountered were often made up of all kinds of vehicles. They could include jeeps, quads, gun-tractors pulling guns or even track laying vehicles such as tanks and bren-gun carriers. These long convoys were always accompanied by DR's.

On one dark morning while on my way to work, I met up with one of these long military convoys that was slowly on the move from the north to the south. My journey took me from the west to the east. There was a DR who had parked his motorbike and was content at stopping all the traffic at this road junction until he had seen all of his convoy safely through. He had held up his hand and stopped me. Now I had to punch a factory time clock and on being late cost me money and it was also looked upon as being a black mark. My mind decided that come what may, I had to get past this guy. I chose my moment and made a dash to get by the side of him. At the same time he spotted my action and stepped out in front of me. This resulted in my front wheel going between his legs and I think that it hit him where it hurts most. He then took a dislike to me as his language was not from out of an English dictionary. I do not know if he had the power to summons a civilian, but he could not do much about it as he was stuck at his post. During the winter's nights I was never to see my home in daylight during the working week. One very dark winter's morning I crashed into a grey painted eight wheel rigid pool petrol tanker. This eight legger was sideways on and right across the road as it was backing into a filling station. Its headlamps were fitted with black-out masks and the rear light was not visible. I crashed into its rear bogie and I was lucky that I had not crashed into the centre of its chassis or I might have broken my neck. Another worker from our factory was close behind me riding his Norman autocycle. He told me that the only thing that saved him from also crashing into it was when he saw my rear lamp go out.

At that time there was an essential works order in force. Because of this, once I had turned sixteen I was not allowed to change the type of work in which I was doing. Having reached the age of sixteen, I was then expected to work more hours per day and to partake in overtime. As I have previously mentioned, I had a seven mile uphill bike ride after I had clocked out. Now that I had become sixteen, the law would allow me ride a motorcycle. I saved up £20 and bought a 1934 Triumph 147 cc Model XO. It was a pretty little four-stroke sloper and it was registered, NV 4132. I then applied for a petrol allowance and then received some coupons to buy this red wartime petrol, but not enough for me to use the motorcycle for all of the time. I had to display L-plates. There was no driving testing being done until after the war. It was also stipulated that I could only use my motorcycle on the shortest route between my home and my place of employment. Because of these stipulations and short supply of petrol, I was not able to practice riding it before I got myself mixed in with the large volume of wartime traffic. I got on it and rode it to work and I was chuffed and throughout that day I was longing for the factory hooter to sound so that I could motor back home on it.. On my way home, as I motored through Newbury I was faced with a dilemma. On a narrow section in Oxford Street to the front of me were two cyclists who were from my works that were riding side by side. On coming towards me was a wide flat-bed US Army aircraft transporter. It was then that my brain took a pause as I had forgotten how to stop the thing. I aimed it for a line between the outer cyclist and the transporter. My left arm brushed the right arm of the outer cyclist and my right leg slid along the full length of the bed of that lorry. Unfortunately for me, my motoring days were to be very short lived. Although I had made sure that the engine had plenty of oil, I was not to know that it was not being pumped around the engine and so it was back to flogging those pedals round again. I did draw all of my petrol and this I placed in a five gallon drum in the shed. Unfortunately the chap who delivered us our paraffin decided to put some of this in the same drum that held my petrol. In later years we boys used some of this and it then became known as, Ken's Blended. Strange as it may seem, it was at that very same part of Oxford Street when I was cycling home that a U.S.A.A.F. Douglas C-47 flew over extra low. I could not help myself from looking up at it. This resulted in me hitting the kerb and then crashing on to the pavement.

In those wartime days we had a police force that did what it was meant to do, it policed. In fact it over policed. Our factory was situated away and to the east of the town. Nearly all of the work force used cycles. During those dark winter months one had to have lights on those cycles. Most people used battery powered lamps as carbide lamps were not allowed. One was forced to make these journeys to and fro' from the works and these cycle batteries were in a very short supply. For those that lived in the town, their wives had a better chance of queuing up and obtaining these batteries. Even then, the supply of batteries could run out before the end of the queue was reached. Living out in the country, the chances of being able to be in the town when some batteries came into the shops was much slimmer. Our work force got very annoyed when the police waited for us at a spot just before reaching the factory gates. This was just`` to catch those of us that had got flat batteries. What a difference it is today. Many cyclists can quite often be seen riding on roads, also on walkways and often with no lights, mudguards or reflectors and the police seem to do nothing about it.

The year of 1942 brought the Americans into the war. It was on one fine summer's day when the news quickly spread around the factory that the yanks had arrived. Working under the cover of a factory roof was to rob me of a lot of aircraft spotting. The event that was happening was to me, something special. In ones and twos, those of us that were interested in aeroplane spotting left our machines and made our way to the nearest open factory door. The doors were already wide open to let the fresh air into the works. The sky was filled with a mass of DC-3's. We did not know of them as Skytrains, C-47's or Dakotas in those early days of the war. This mass formation was flying in a westerly direction and could have been following the Great Western Railway which bounded the rear of our factory. On the other side of the railway embankment was the very busy rail-strewn, what was once the Newbury Race Course. I have often wondered as to which airfields this mass of aircraft would have been flying to and where they had all come from. There must have been between fifty or a hundred of them and many had already passed, by the time that I reached the door. Each one displayed the United States Army Air Force insignias below their wings. All were painted in olive drab and they made a fantastic sight. Little did we know then that these C-47 Skytrains would become a common sight in our local sky.

At the rear of the factory there was a strip of grass between the railway and the factory wall. Parked on this grass was an engineless de-Havilland Don with its wings removed and placed on the ground close by. I would think that it was one of several that were never given engines and on completion were to be used as training airframes. The Don was one of the less successful of de-Havilland aeroplanes. This one belonged to Newbury's Number 211 Squadron, Air Training Corps. It had been placed there by Mr Gerald Opperman who was also an A.T.C. officer. An A.T.C. sergeant named Bill Hartland who worked on the aircraft fitters took it on himself as being in sole charge of this airframe. Bill soon after joined the R.A.F. as an air gunner and unfortunately got the chop. One day while I sat down and had my lunch break, I then made a sketch of this Don. I will speak more about this Don in a later chapter.

It was in 1942 that I joined the Newbury & District Spotters Club. I became member number 51. All of its meetings were held in Elliotts of Newbury's Albert Works canteen. This was a furniture factory. After the war this firm got its name known in the aviation world when as well as manufacturing furniture, it manufactured sailplanes and training gliders. It's most known was the EoN Olympia high performance sailplane. It was of wooden construction and glass gliders had then to be invented. It also got known for its powered aircraft, the Newbury EoN registered G-AKBC. This aircraft they had based on R.A.F. Welford and they used it to tow their gliders. It became a common sight in the sky over home. During the war, furniture manufacturing ceased and the firm went over to aircraft production. According to what I have been told, they made parts for some of the following aircraft, deHavilland Tiger Moth, Airspeed Oxford, Miles Martinet, deHavilland Mosquito, General Aircraft Hamilcar and the Airspeed Horsa. They did make complete nose sections for the Horsa and as a Horsa rudder was later hung on the factory wall, I would take it that they made these as well.

Now getting back to the Spotters Club. Its president was Mr H. C. G. Buckingham who was the managing director of Elliotts Albert Works. Also on the committee was Mr Don Fratter. He was in later years to be my group's officer when I joined the R.O.C. (Royal Observer Corps) as a post observer. Don could tell some good stories, once you got him wound up. It was after my service in the R.A.F. that I was to work for Elliotts and take mid-day meals in that canteen. Later on in years when as an observer in the R.O.C., it would be to this canteen that I would come whenever we had a cluster meeting. Every fortnight on a Thursday I would purchase my Aeroplane Spotter from W. H. Smith's and this I always looked forward to. I remember how annoyed that I got when their supply of these papers got reduced and I was one of those unlucky ones that they cut out.

It was during one of our lunch hours that lots of unidentified troop transport gliders were released from their tug aircraft over Greenham Common Airfield. These would have been Airspeed Horsa Mk.Is. They were to become a common sight in the days to come, but this was the first time that we had seen them and we did not know what they were. Shortly after this they were removed from the official secrets list. Several of us climbed up on to the flat roof of a rear air raid shelter so as to get a better view of them.

On the 10th of February 1943, Newbury had its third air raid. Fifteen poor soles in the town lost their lives. All of this was due to one lone raider. This was a Dornier Do217E that had two shades of dark green on its upper surfaces and was all black beneath. For the record, it carried the code letters, F8 + AN. It machine-gunned the streets as it dropped its stick of bombs across the railway. The target must have been the road bridge over the railway as all the busy traffic from north to south used this during those days. If it was this bridge that it aimed at, then it missed it. As it flew from south towards the north it released its bomb load leaving a trail of devastation and destruction. St. John's Church, a portion of the Council School, a row of alms houses were all left in ruins. Other properties received damage and one bomb failed to explode. Having done its damage it then turned and headed in the direction of our factory. It was then not so likely to have done much more damage as its bomb load had gone. These can only be dropped the once. The way that our factory operated during a raid was this. As soon as the local siren sounded, red lights came on in various positions in the factory where they could be seen by all. The production was kept going. Raid spotters would then take up their appropriate station on the roof and around the outside of the factory. Those on the ground had an Anderson bell type shelter in which they could dive into after they had sounded the close alarm. For the main working force, brick shelters were built into the corners of the factory. I do not know how safe we would have been in them had the factory been hit. Each worker was detailed as to which shelter he or she had to make for. In the event of an enemy raider being sighted, a hooter would sound and we would shut down our machines and make for the shelters. In the past the hooter had sounded and all had been well. This time we heard the bombs as we shut down the machinery and were about to make for the shelters. The spotters when challenged as to what type of plane that it was then all gave different identifications. I had always wanted to go raid spotting. I had asked and had then been told that they had sufficient. I had been refused. After this raid, they then came and asked me. The siren did sound once or twice after this and along with Mr Norman Hopkins who was a member of the R.O.C. I did get to stand by an Anderson shelter, but there was never any more enemy activity, I had missed the lot.

LOCAL WARTIME ACTIVITY

Aircraft recognition became one of my main interests. I was forever on the lookout for fresh aircraft types that I could add to my sightings. I suppose that I had become a bit of a mechanical twitcher. In order to see different aircraft at close quarters, on some weekends I would cycle to various airfields to see what kind of aircraft were stationed there. I had started doing this back in my school days. At Greenham Common in the summer of 1942 there were some olive drab painted Douglas C-47's that belonged to the U.S.A.A.F. 51st Troop Carrier Wing. These we could walk right up to and the American guard chatted to us as we walked around them. Having cycled to Aldermaston, I found that the airfield had many Martin Marauders parked on it. As I have never seen any reference in books as to Marauders based there and that my wartime notes no longer exist, I am unable to say as to which bomber group it was that they belonged to. On an early cycle ride to R.A.F. Andover, I was to find some early helicopters. These were Sikorsky R-4B Hoverfly Mk.I. They could not have flown all that far as I never got to hear of any person saying that they had seen them over the Newbury area. Perhaps my pushbike had a greater range than what they had. One of these still survives in the Hendon Air Museum. Also on Andover there were a few Westland Lysanders. I had not expected these aircraft to look so large as they did when seeing them for the first time at close quarters. A visit to Hampstead Norris, now spelt as Hampstead Norreys, I was to see a line of Vickers Wellington Mk.IIs just on the other side of the hedge. On a later trip to Ramsbury, Airspeed Oxfords were flogging the circuit.

It is now nearly seventy years ago since I logged what I saw in those wartime skies. All that I can do now is to revert back to my wartime memories. On going back to my school days, there were quite a lot of Fairey Battles in the air. Many of these would have then been based at Harwell and Abingdon. Armstrong Whitworth Whitley bombers were to be seen with either inline or radial engines. Number 10 O.T.U. (Operational Training Unit) at Abingdon operated some of these. Later on, we were to see Wellingtons from Harwell and Tiger Moths from Theale. Aldermaston, Greenham Common, Membury, Ramsbury and Welford were to become the home of the U.S.A.A.F. Troop Carrier Wings. Their aircraft were, Curtiss C-46 Commando, Douglas C-47 Skytrain and Douglas C-54 Skymaster. Other U.S.A.A.F. aircraft often seen were Cessna UC-78 Bobcat, Stinson L-5 Sentinel Piper L-4 Grasshopper, Lockheed P-38 Lightning, Republican P-47 Thunderbolt and North American P-51 Mustang. Occasionally, Boeing B-17 Fortress and Consolidated Liberators would fly over. Waco CG-4A trooping gliders were assembled from out of wooden packing cases on Crookham Common. This being to the east end of Greenham Common from where these CG4A gliders would then be towed out to other airfields. Under the lend-lease the Americans used many of our Airspeed Horsa gliders. They also had Supermarine Spitfires Mk.Vs based at Membury along with some Piper L-4 Grasshopper Cubs.

Now that the Americans were occupying our local airfields, our sky was to become filled with their aircraft. They practiced a lot of night formation flying with their C-47's. They were quite a sight to see being lit up with navigation lights of red green and white. Also their exhaust flares were very visible. During the day, C-47s were often seen towing an Airspeed Horsa or one of their Waco CG4A's. Occasionally they could be seen towing two CG-4A's side by side. One of these towing two gliders for reasons I do not know, was forced to release its gliders. Both of the Waco's made perfect landings in two different locations. We lads had been given the word that a C-47 had just retrieved one of the gliders by the snatch method. The other one that was left was near the side of a field in the locality of Hoe Benham. As soon as we had been told this news we all made speed to get to this downed glider. I was with several other lads and we had got as far as the other side of the field in which the glider was in when the Douglas C-47 made its approach. We were on higher ground and so we looked down on the event. A line had been placed across the top of two poles which this C-47 had to make contact with. The approach was perfect and within seconds the Waco was snatched up into the air and was away behind the tug. It had been a very pretty sight to watch and I am glad that I never missed it. If only we had owned cameras in those days.

The DeHavilland D.H. 93 Don

The downed Waco CG-4A

Another thing that happened and I believe that it took place on a Saturday afternoon. I had arrived home from work and was having my mid day meal. There became a scream of aero engines to a very high pitch that was immediately followed by a sudden silence. I rushed out of the house and into the garden where father was working. He then pointed to the west. I was in time to see a parachute and a wing that was falling like a dead leaf. I had just been too late to see the main wreckage fall. A Lockheed P-38 Lightning had been in a power dive and had broken up in the air. One of its wings had broken away and I have now forgotten which one that it was. I seem to think that it was the starboard, but of this I am not certain. It had also lost its complete tail unit which would have had its serial number displayed on it. This tail unit was missing having broken off at the small ends of each boom. Father said that the pilot had dropped quite a long way before his chute opened. He also said that the falling aircraft had come very close to the parachute as it made its way to the ground. Mr Norman Hopkins, the chap I was to accompany when raid spotting lived in the small hamlet called Benham Burslot. It then contained about five cottages and a farm. All of these buildings no longer exist and the place has been removed from the map. Norman was a member in the R.O.C. and he also witnessed this break-up. He was ninety degrees to the crash site as to what we were and he also remarked on how close the wreckage had become to the descending pilot. This being so, he must have had a close shave. Later, we walked across the fields to go and have a look at the main wreckage. We were to find the aircraft up-side-down in the middle of a ploughed field. There was a strong smell of petrol and it is a wonder that it had not gone up in flames. Several people were there having a look and there was no military guard on it. The missing wing and tail assembly must have come down some distances away in other fields. This Lightning was painted all over in a gloss bright blue and could well have been a photographic version. I was later told that a chap had picked up the pilot's helmet and that it had some blood on it. A most likely cause of this crash could have been through it encountering compressibility problems. These Lightning's were noted for this and the R.A.F. had rejected the type and turned it down.

One sight that will stay with me for the rest of my days was the mass take-off of those Skytrains and each one having a Horsa glider on tow. D-Day had arrived. Our hamlet of Wickham Heath was in the circuit of R.A.F. Welford. This was the American base with their allotted station number 474. These glider trains were circling and formatting above us and the sky was full of them. They had all been freshly painted in those black and white striped D-Day markings. The air was vibrating with the sound of so many aero engines. Across the Lambourn Valley one could hear the many Pratt & Whitney engines being given full throttle as they laboured to get their fully loaded aircraft and gliders off of the ground and into the air. Right over our heads one Horsa glider started to pitch violently fore-and-aft. This then broke the tow line close behind its tug which then trailed back underneath the glider. This Horsa then dipped its nose and the last we saw of it was as it glided down behind Ownham plantation. The C-47 held its position in the formation and carried on without its glider. We were to find out what had gone wrong. It had been loaded with a vehicle and trailer. The two had separated and the trailer had then run up and down inside of the fuselage. If it had stuck in the tail, then we would have had a Horsa down on top of us. The glider pilot was very lucky as he pulled off a safe landing on the other side of Boxford village. Dad, who was in the Home Guard, then got to hear all about it. The Yanks tried to recover it and in so doing, they ended up by sawing the wings off of it. Having watched this spectacular event, it was then back in doors and to listen to the radio to find out where they had all gone to.

There had been very many military manoeuvres taking place in the air and on the ground. Also there had been a big build up of troops in our area. It had been a big working up ready for D-Day. Those wooden packing cases in which the Waco gliders had been transported in from America had been put to good use. Many of them had been removed from Crookham Common and taken to Sole Common woods. These woods were filled with American service men and they made good use of them by constructing buildings out of them. They even made a cinema, and they allowed some of the local children to go in and watch the films. All of these troops seem to leave these woods over night. Once these troops had all left, the local farmers were visiting these woods with their tractors and trailers. Many of these small local farms could then be seen with a glider box building added on to it.

As there had been so many American service men in our area than our own service boys, they then chased after our local girls. These American lads were paid more money than our service boys and they also had better material for their uniforms. They did not have to do much chasing. Our girls just fell for them and the good times that they could afford to give them. The saying at the time went, 'They were over paid, over sexed and they were over here'. Hardly any of our girls would look at us fellows and not being in a uniform we stood no chance. It was impossible to compete with them. One girl who was an evacuee that I went to school with was not at all fussy where she did her courting or who saw her at it. She soon became a very young mother, and a lucky strike for her, she became a G.I. bride. These letters G.I. stood for General Issue, and this is what she got. There was another girl who lived in Speen who enjoyed spreading her legs. Every evening as regular as clockwork she would cycle up to Wickham Heath where she would then meet up with her yanky G.I. As soon as they had met up, they would then make for the nearest copse. Their woodland position was always a dead giveaway as she would prop her sit-up-and-beg bike against the nearest tree. Judging by the disgusting mess, paper wipes and the number of French letters (condoms) that they both left behind them littering the woods having finished their session, it is wonder how she could still manage to sit the saddle on her four mile ride home. Sex seemed to be the only thing that these American guys were living for and our girls made double sure that they did not go wanting. Perhaps they looked upon it as giving comfort for the troops. Well it takes two to perform a sex act. After these American troops had left these girls must have become love starved.

At Sole Common camp the Americans practiced erecting dummy aircraft. These could be seen by the side of a field which adjoined the wood. From time to time there was a row of these stick and cloth aircraft lined up by this woodland. After the war, there became a large rubbish dump in a pit down in Sole Common woods. It was in this pit that an Austin Seven Ruby that I had owned for spares finished its days. Just after the war, there was placed in this pit the complete tubular nose frame from a Waco CG-4A glider. We boys then got a fancy idea that we could make some motorcycle front forks from this tubing. We spent an all afternoon with hacksaws and then came home with a few bits of tubing. Come another day we returned to obtain some more bits of this steel tubing. To our utter amazement, this nose section had been completely dismantled and broken hacksaw blades were everywhere. We must have given some other people the idea that this tubing could be useful.

On D-Day, many of the Americans that were stationed close to our home embarked from Aldermaston, Greenham Common, Welford, Membury and Ramsbury airfields. There was still plenty of other wartime activity taking place that was not all American. It was before the Americans came into the war on the 13th of August 1940 and I was nearly home from school, when an enemy incident occurred. Some things did delay us at times as we ambled our way home. One interest that had just been happening was watching a Latil timber tractor winching out tree trunks through the undergrowth. This time it was watching a steam roller gang tar spraying the road. The chap who worked on the tar pot heating up the tar always ruined his clothing. He had got round this problem by getting children to take him old cast-offs that their fathers had finished with. For some clothing he would in return take your photograph. After he had taken your picture he would then dip it in a chemical solution to process it. His prints always came out in a mirror image and they had a metal foil backing to them. The air raid siren had sounded and while I was nattering to this chap there came the sound of exploding bombs. This Mr steam-roller man then pushed me under his four wheeled living van. All in his best intensions I am sure. Had I not quickly crawled back out again, it would have robbed me of my only one sighting of a German raider in the air. This was only a fleeting glimpse as it passed through the bottom layers of the low clouds. Our British fighters were after him and so he had jettisoned his ten small bombs in Elcot Park killing a few unfortunate cows. I was then only twelve years old and I failed to identify it. All that I could remember was that it was twin engined and it had those black crosses under its wings. No sooner had Gerry gone when a Hawker Hurricane dived out of the clouds only to enter them in the same direction that the raider had taken. I do not know if he got away, but our boys were after him. The bombs that were dropped at Elcot were not the first of the enemy activity that had occurred in the Newbury area. The air raid siren had first sounded in anger just after midday on June the 25th, 1940. Throughout the war it was to sound 244 warnings. Newbury got off lightly when compared with the damage to many other towns, but Hermann Goring did send his Luftwaffe into West Berkshire and it made its presence felt. I will now give a quick run-down on most of the enemy action that took place at Newbury and around its district.

1940 was to be the year in which the most number of raids occurred. July the 3rd, a daylight raid on Thatcham. Fifteen H.E. (high explosive) bombs were dropped. The Great Western Railway was blocked for two hours. July the 28th, a Heinkel He 111P had got in to difficulties to the south of the town. Its crew then bailed out over Great Penwood. Left to its own devices, it glided down only just missing Woolton Hill House and slid across the lane that led to East End and finished up in the bottom of a cottage garden. It then destroyed its-self when it went up in flames. This Heinkel had carried a crew of five and several of these had roamed the woods before they were caught or had given them-selves up. The fifth chap had been wandering around for nine days. He was finally escorted to the police station by Lady Buckland.

Continuing with 1940, August the 13th was when those bombs that were jettisoned on Elcot Park. August the 16th, a raid at Thatcham. Colonel Urquhart was killed from Thatcham House. August the 19th, five bombs were dropped at Leckhamstead. August the 21st, was a daylight raid at Thatcham, six bombs were dropped. August the 26th, a workman was killed on a morning raid at Harwell. September the 2nd, there were many H.E. and incendiary bombs dropped in the district. September the 3rd, three bombs damaged some cottages in Newbury Street, Kintbury. Ten bombs were dropped in a line between East and West Woodhay. September the 16th, two ladies were killed in a daylight raid at Pamber Heath. Towards the end of September, more H.E.'s were dropped at Brimpton, Hermitage, Highclere Park, Marlston, Thatcham and Wasing. November the 7th, was the first bombs dropped on Newbury. An oil bomb on Goldwell Park, two H.E.'s at Speen. There were 40 incendiary bombs dropped within the borough with one landing on the Parish Church roof. Incendiarys were also reported as falling at Curridge Green and at Highclere. There was damage to some council houses by an H.E. at Ashmore Green. November the 13th, a raider was brought down by fighters over the Aldwoth-Blewbury downs. Its crew of three were captured single-handed by an Aldworth farmer. November the 18th, two bombs were dropped at Chieveley. November the 28th. Bombs were dropped between Deanwood and Foley Lodge which killed two horses. This ground is now a golf course. Our grandfather was living in Foley Lodge Cottages at the time. As soon as our Mother heard the news she was on her bike and got to Foley like a shot out of a gun. Grandmother was staying in Newbury at the time at her other daughter's house. Nobody got hurt but it blew all the furniture away from the walls. December the 3rd, a house on Bucklebury Common was destroyed by a bomb, its occupants were trapped in the debris. December the 11th, there was a bomb dropped at Beenham. December the 15th, an unexploded bomb had crashed through Lady Acland's home and it embedded beneath the house while she was holding a party of ten at Cold Ash. There were also three other unexploded bombs dropped on Ashmore Green. December the 19th, Greenham and Sandleford were straddled by bombs. December the 23rd, a Kingsclere home guard was killed while he was on his way to assist some injured people in a blast damaged cottage. It was not to be a very happy Christmas for some. December the 30th, one hundred incendiary bombs were dropped at Compton.

There was not so much enemy activity in 1941. On January the 19th, there was bomb damage at the Post Office and other properties at Newtown. February the 26th, there were a shower of incendiaries in the areas of Great Shefford, Fawley and Wantage. Newbury had its second air raid. Six H.E.s were dropped at 1.20 pm after the siren had sounded and all of them fell on open ground. Later on, another raider machine-gunned. All of this occurred on a Wednesday afternoon which for Newbury was its half-closing day. Between January and March there had been bombs dropped at Beedon, East Ilsley, Peasmore, Stanmore and Thatcham. April the 4th, four H.E.s dropped at West Ilsley. April the 9th, three bombs dropped on Newbury Race Course, one of them failed to explode. Three bombs hit a runway at Hampstead Norris airfield. April the 18th, two 250 kg bombs fell at Enbourne in Craven Park. Two more bombs were dropped between Nalder Hill and Stockcross falling in open ground. These two I will always remember due to a squirrel. It had been caught in a gin trap by a rear leg that was close to the bomb craters. It had pulled this trap from out of its tunnel. I intended to hit it with a short piece of stick and to put it out of its misery. Due to its location in the bottom of a hedge this squirrel managed to sink its front teeth into my right thumb and it held on. This then gave me a poisoned arm. After I had managed to get him to leave go, I then left it to carry on suffering in that trap. When those craters got filled in, a good Austin Seven car was buried in one of them that had belonged to Mr R. Sutton. April the 20th, a decoy airfield at Stanmore drew ten H.E. bombs. April the 22nd, two parachute mines killed several cows at Padworth. May the 3rd, ten H.E.s dropped at Sulhamstead and Ufton Nevet and two more near to Tyle Mill. May the 6th, an army convoy was machine-gunned along the A.4. Great West Road, near Theale. May the 12th, ten H.E.s and over fifty incendiaries were dropped in the Hampstead Norris area. September the 20th and 21st, Stanmore decoy airfield attracted ten more H.E.s and they all fell in open ground.

1942 was a quieter year. April 25th, eighteen H.E.s fell between Middle Farm and Park Farm, Lambourn. One of them was an unexploded, and they all fell on open ground. February the 10th, Newbury's third air raid when that Dornier Do 217 did so much damage. April the 23rd, two H.E. bombs fell west of Stancombe Farm, Lambourn. November the 1st, a lone Junkers Ju 188 flying in low cloud crashed into Walbury Camp, Combe Hill. I was cycling home from work and the siren had sounded. Having just passed through Stockcross village I heard that unmistakeable uneven engine noise of a German bomber. It sounded as if it was flying west along the Kennet

Valley. I then heard the crash that was followed by the sudden silence. It had previously been in combat and it had been too low to clear the high ground. If it had been a few more feet higher it would have got away with it. The following day I was cycling home again when an R.A.F. Queen Mary met me along the A.4 Bath Road in Newbury. This was by, what was then, the Wessex Sports Ground. The only identifiable portion of the wreckage which it was carrying was the tail assembly which had snapped off. This had the wiggled lined camouflage and the swastika painted on it. One part of that enemy raider was not on that transporter, this was the tail wheel. I was working one day at a cottage in East Woodhay when I said to a fellow, 'That's a nice wheel that you have in your barrow'. 'Yes' he said, 'It is puncture proof'. He then told me on how he had won it, to use his phrase. 'It had rolled down to the bottom of the hill when a German bomber had crashed into the top.

The Queen Mary and the JU 188 wreckage

By 1944, the enemy action had died right down. Hitler now had a war on two fronts. March the 14th, H.E.s and incendiaries fell at Chadleworth. The districts first flying bomb exploded in a wheat field a half-a-mile north of Shaw House. I have also been told of another of these buzz-bombs that was led in a field near the junction of the A.4 and the Stockcross turning. If that was so, then I do not know how and when it had got there and also without exploding. Another of these flying bombs was to blow a crater thirty feet deep in a field which was a half mile from Combe Gibbet. Some of these V.1,s that had found their way to West Berkshire could well have been launched from flying aircraft. All of these wartime activities that I have just mentioned, I have gleaned from other peoples records and so I cannot vouch for their accuracy.

Just prior to the war, unfortunately I do not remember in which year, there was a very strong showing of the aurora borealis (northern lights). It gradually came up from the north and it eventually covered the whole sky a blood red colour. We children stood with our mates father, Mr R. V. Simmons at the top end of our gardens by a white five-barred-gate. He then told us that he considered that it was a sign of things to come and of mass bloodshed. How right he was. Many times later on we would all stand together by that gate and from here we could see the blitz of London and Southampton lighting up the sky. From here we would stand, or sit on that gate and watch the many searchlights. When they managed to locate an aircraft it would light it up white. We always took an added interest when our two locally based searchlights came into play. The nearest to us was at Coombesbury, about a mile distant. The other one was at Winding Wood. This one would have been three to four miles away as the crow flies. One memory that will always live with me was the sound of so many high flying raiders with their unsynchronized engines as they flew over in the night sky heading north. The next day we were to hear when we turned on our radio sets that Coventry had been flattened. This was on the 14th of November 1940. Another of my wartime memories was when I was at Cold Ash and we watched hundreds of bombers from daylight to darkness as they made their ways high in the sky on a one thousand strong bomber raid.

We watched the searchlights

A far more pleasant sight was very early in the war. The old biplane Imperial Airways airliners would fly low over our homes, and when I say low, I mean low. I remember that we saw both of the Short L.17 Scylla Class. These were G-ACJJ "Scylla" and G-ACJK "Syrinx". We also saw several of the Handle Page H.P.42 s, but I now cannot remember which of them it was that we saw. I know that you could see the pilots sat at their controls because they were that low. We used the phrase, hedge-hopping in those days. It was as if they were flying from one land mark to another. If they had continued on their headings then they may have terminated their flights at Hurn. A mate of mine now deceased, Alan Francis, who lived at Bratton near Westbury, once told me on how he had watched one of these low flying airliners. It was a Handley Page H.P.42 Hannibal Class. It was flying very low and under a low cloud base. Near Erlestoke, its captain was then faced with high ground in front of him. Alan said, 'All engines were fully opened up and it disappeared into the cloud'. It must have got away with it as no H.P.42 s were to crash in

Wiltshire, but Alan remarked, 'I would not have been surprised if there had been some tyre marks on the top of that hill'. Although at that time we did not know what these lumbering airliners were doing, I have since learnt of their activities. At R.A.F. Harwell there were numbers 105 Squadron and 226 Squadron equipped with Fairey Battle Mk.IIs that formed number 72 Wing. They were flown out to France as a part of the Advanced Air Striking Force. Those old biplane airliners were used to fly the ground crews and their equipment to France. Their route would have taken them via R.A.F. Andover. Those Battles were soon to be shot out of the sky as they stood no chance against the German Messerschmitt fighters. There were many aircraft that met their fates by flying into high ground in stuffed clouds during the war. As I write this, I am now not sure if it was one or two Boeing B-17s that flew into Heavan's Gate on the Highclere Estate. I was once told that it was two of them but on reading how a lone survivor came back and recognised the tree that he had found himself under, I am now not sure if it was one or two. I do know that 50 m/m ammunition could be found on that hill for years afterwards.

Imperial Airways liners flew low over our home

In those days the army were always busy practicing ready for the real thing. One could wake up to find that tanks were hived up just inside the woods as they took part in manoeuvres. You might also be woken up by very loud bangs in the night. One night there was one ear splitting bang that woke every one up. For days after this the military were combing the whole area. We did not know what they were looking for, but my guess is that they never found it. This also happened early on in the war as Dad was still then a gamekeeper. In the middle of a field he found a very large chunk of jagged alloy metal. It had obviously been blown out of an aircraft. Looking around he then spotted another piece. He brought the largest piece home and shown it to my family. My brother Dick and I then went back with him to the place where he had picked it up. Together we then followed the line to that second piece and as we entered the woods we found other pieces. Together we took all of this metal and handed it in to the Stockcross village policeman, P.C. (Jimmy) James. This then made its way to some authorities, and neither or us ever heard any more about it.

The inside of my membership card for 1942-43

Jimmy was a good policeman and he policed his patch well. I recall the time when on a Sunday morning he caught Freddie Kempster and myself sitting up in an oak tree just inside the wood about one hundred yards from the road. Jimmy had heard us talking and had come on into the wood looking for us. He just could not understand why two boys wearing their best cloths should be sat up in a tree. Perhaps he was never a country boy himself. He would not let us walk back through the wood to my home. Instead he escorted us all the way back by the roads. Dad being the keeper had given us permission to play in that part of the wood. The estate had asked him to keep people out of their woods. P.C. 'Jimmy' was only doing his job and we respected him for that. This could never happen today. No policeman would patrol the countryside on a push bike. They would more likely than not, be motoring along that road and doing over the legal limit of 60 mph in a police car. Later on in life and after I had got married, due to the difficulties of finding a cottage to rent, we were living in Stockcross with my parents. I then owned an Ariel Red Hunter motorcycle with a sidecar that was registered JB 8843. This I had to garage two houses away. One night I had forgotten to garage my outfit and had left it on the by-road outside of my parents' gate. The next day Jimmy stopped me. He then offered to buy me a bundle of candles. Now that is the proper way to police. I was to make sure that I never forgot to garage my combination again, and I also respected that policeman who was stationed in the village to protect the community. Over the past years, successive governments have made cuts in our police force in relation to the growing number of citizens. Ever so many small police stations have been closed. This has caused the bobby to loose touch with his public. It is no wonder that crime has increased. When I was a lad and also when I first started shooting, a shotgun could be kept in the corner of a living room. Often there was never a need to lock up your home. If you wanted to shoot with a shotgun, you went to the local Post Office and bought a shotgun licence. This cost you just ten bob (ten shillings, now 50p). This small sheet of green paper gave you the right to shoot vermin, rabbits, pigeons and hares, but not game. If you did not know how to shoot, you then simply read the back of the licence and it told you how to swing the gun and go about it. You did need to have permission from the owner of the ground that you were shooting on. Why cannot it be like this today? The reason is that it is because our police forces have been allowed to dwindle so that the law has not properly been policed.

Now let me go back to those bangs that happened in the night. Another shattering bang that woke up all the people in the neighbourhood was caused when two Armstrong Whitworth Albemarles collided. They were both filled to the brim with bods and this happened over the village of Winterbourne. Their wreckage was scattered over a square mile and it all fell on open ground. The next day, we boys got on our bikes to go and have a look. I remember seeing the rear glazed end of a fuselage with parachute silks draped over it. We picked up a small piece of the wreckage and this we found had human remains on it. We did not like what we saw and so we did not go looking for the other aircraft.

To end this chapter I have got to tell you about our German spy. Well this is how we referred to the fellow. Down by the A.4 Bath Road at the bottom of Nalder Hill Road is Bradford's Farm. It being unusual as the farm buildings have a clock tower. This farm is now the estate office. During the war our army had commandeered these farm buildings. One night, Lord Haw-haw as we called him had broadcast in English that this clock was so many minutes fast or slow, I cannot now remember which it was. Now at the top end of Nalder Hill Road at Wickham Heath, we kids would then play on what we called the common. It was in the thickest of the bushes that we found a young man camping. If he had not been a spy then he might have been a deserter. We told our parents and they informed the police. Whoever he was, he was soon gone.

One of our evacuee boys, Ken Challenor, was to loose some fingers. He had picked up what he thought was a toy mouse and it exploded. We have wondered since, did that chap that we found plant that by the road side? You were never to know what you might stumble upon next in those very active wartime days.

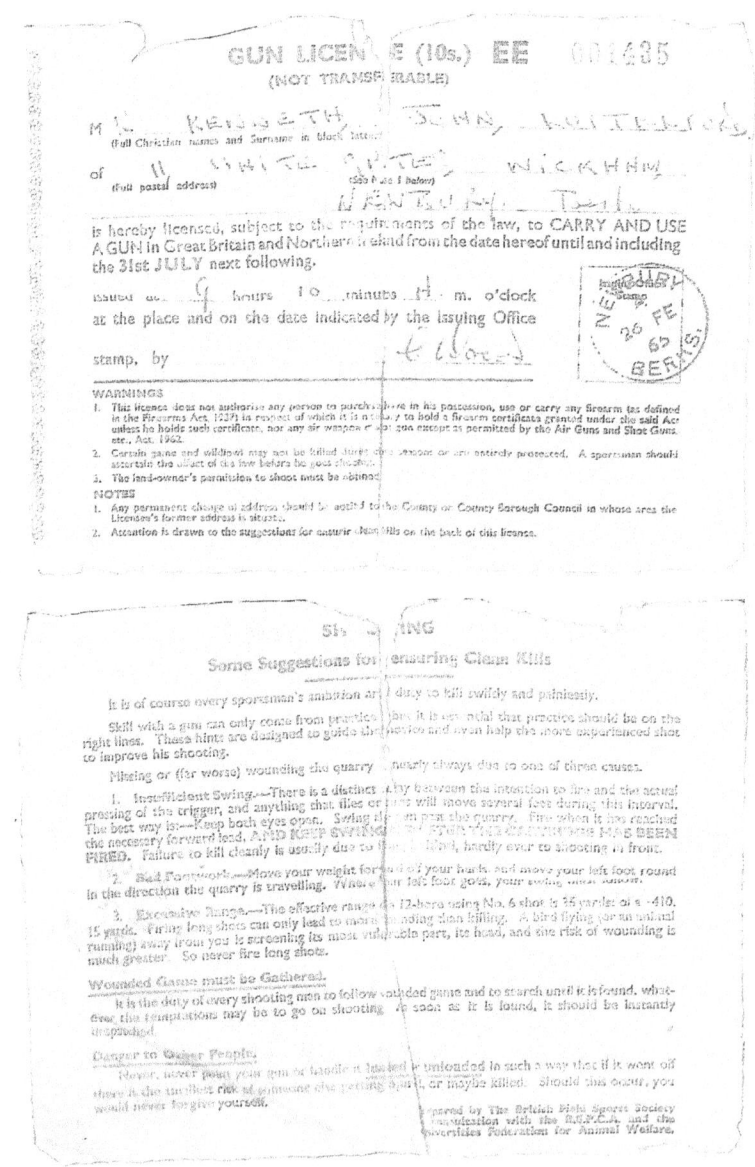

Both sides of a gun licence

A TASTE OF SERVICE LIFE

For several Sundays in succession, Desmond Newport and my-self had cycled together to Greenham Common airfield. Once there, we would position ourselves as close as we could to the end of the active runway. In doing this, we were on the side of the Newbury to Kingsclere road. This road was still being used by the public and it cut across the western side of the airfield. In so doing, it separated the two black hangars from the flying field and the main camp. There since has been enough history made on Greenham Common that a whole set of volumes could be written about it. The airfield that we then visited was constructed just after the start of the war. Before the war it had been covered with one mass of thick heather with a few small clumps of stunted scots pine trees. One pathway that I can remember ran through this heather and had started close to a place called 'The Ark'. Today it would have been in the vicinity to where the Americans once kept their cruise missiles in those thick large bunkers. After the war this airfield reverted back to common land for a short period. From here on at weekends we would go and fly free flight two-stroke diesel powered model aircraft. Sid Roberts brought along a large model with a rectangular fuselage. It was radio controlled and in those days the radio only operated the rudder. This was the first time that he had flown it. He flew it in circles that gradually got smaller in their circumference. It did not do the oozelam bird, but it spun in when over our heads. We all had to take to our heels including Sid himself. Needless to say, Sid's model had smashed its self to smithereens. My brother Dick had an aircraft that he designed and built himself and it flew very well. He was very lucky in not having his plane trampled on. All good things have to come to an end. This common then got extensively built on when it became a Nato base that was used by the United States Air Force (U.S.A.F). Their SAC (Strategic Air Command) then operated some of the following types of aircraft from it. Douglas C-47's, Boeing B-47 Stratojets, Boeing KC-97 flying fuel tankers and later Boeing KC-135 Stratotankers. Luckily there was never a serious accident with these as the approach to the two mile runway was over the southern end of Newbury town. Later there were General Dynamics F-111's. We had to put up with the noise from these while the Americans were making such a fuss about the noise from our Concorde. Peace women and air displays have also formed a part of this common's history. This airfield has now reverted back again to common land, but it will never be the delightful place that it was before the war.

When Des and I cycled to Greenham it was then the home of Number 15 P.A.F.U. (Pilot Advanced Flying Unit). They were equipped with many Airspeed Oxfords mark Is and IIs. There were far too many of them for us to count. Also on their strength were two Avro Anson MK.Is and one solitary Avro Tutor biplane. Situated close to the active runway, we then spent many a happy hour watching these Oxford trainers going about their business of circuits and bumps. This was doing a take-off, flying a circuit and doing a landing. We did see one or two dicey landings, but never any mishaps. Now also meeting every Sunday morning on that airfield were Newbury's Number 211 A.T.C. (Air Training Corps) squadron. So what did we do, we joined them and then paraded on Sundays with them. One corporal cadet was an old playmate of mine. Our grandfather on my mother's side was the head gardener at Foley Lodge. This is now a country hotel come a conference centre. Corporal Bruce Bateman's father was the chauffeur at Foley and they lived next door to our grandparents in a pair of cottages. It was to Foley Lodge Cottages where mother would take us on many weekends and so it was that Bruce and I would spend many happy hours playing together. Later Bruce was to see some active service in the R.A.F. when he flew in Halifax bombers with Bomber Command.

Now good old Bruce pulled his rank. He said, 'I would like these two new cadets to be given some air experience. It was agreed, for as soon as we had been given a meal in the mess which I remember finished up with peaches that was then a luxury, Bruce then escorted us two lads to 'B' Flight. We still had not got our uniforms and so we were dressed in our civys. 'B' Flight was at the Greenham School end of the aerodrome. We both had to draw harness and parachutes from a store and then we were taken to one of those Oxfords. This one had the serial number BM826 and it had been made by the Percival Aircraft Company. The pupil and instructor were first in and we then followed them from the door on the port side. The pilots settled themselves down and we were instructed to sit on the main spar behind them. This ran through the centre of the fuselage. There being nothing to strap us in with. Bruce then waved at us as we were taxied out from the dispersal pan. Eventually we got to the active runway. The pilots then did their checks, turned their heads to make sure that we were OK. The throttles were pushed forward and we gathered up speed down that runway. The aircraft lifted into the air and we found ourselves airborne for the very first time in our lives. It had only been a couple of weeks ago that we had been watching these Oxfords taking off from close to a runway. Now we were experiencing it for ourselves from the inside of one of these yellow bellied trainers. We flew out over the village of Brimpton and then turned north and then west as we flew the circuit. We flew over Siege Cross. I did not know it then, but much later on in life I was to spend many happy hours there with two Tiger Moths. We looked down on Thatcham and then my place of employment, Opperman Gears. We could now see across that railway line at the busy Newbury Race Course which had now become a mass of railway sidings. Seen in the lower end of the bombed Council School grounds was that de Havilland Don that had once stood at the back of our factory and close to the air raid shelter. As we passed over the southern end of Newbury town we could see the bomb damage and the line that the Dornier had taken. It was now our first circuit completed as we took our turn to run in for the landing. We had experienced about three of these circuits when we were asked if we had had enough, or, if we would like to go round again. 'Yes please' was our reply and so away we went again. I had now really and truly got hooked on flying. Now I was sat on the port side and Des was sat on the starboard. On our very next landing approach, an extremely loud horn bellowed into my left ear. We did not land but carried on with another circuit. We made many more of these circuits and each time as we made an approach this horn would blare out. We did eventually land and taxied back to the dispersal pan. It was only then, that we were told that there had been an undercarriage problem. From the starboard nacelle, fluid could be seen dripping down on to the tyre. They had got us safely down, but they never told us how close we had come to using the silk or on making a belly landing. It was a common sight to see an Oxford in the circuit with one undercarriage leg dangling. We were told that we had been up for about an hour and so this yellow belly had given us both our first hour in the air.

We paraded on Greenham Common many times, but I was never to get another flight from there. In one of the two black hangars the erks were working on one of the Ansons Cheetah engines. The one we were shown was stripped down and it had burnt out valves. An angry Chiefy (flight sergeant) told us that it had all happened due to a pilot trying to get more out of it than what it was capable of performing. Twice I had been given flying chits for Oxford flights but due to the pressures of work, I was unable to use them. I had very much wanted to experience night flying, but both of my parents point blankly refused to sign the authority chit. Some night flying practice was also undertaken in daylight. Pupils had to wear special goggles and sodium flares were lit on each side of the runway. By October 1943, all of these Oxfords had left Greenham and it then reverted back to the U.S.A.A.F. where it then became their station number, 486.

Nearly all of the Waco CG-4A troop carrying assault gliders were taken in their wooden packing cases to Crookham Common which was the heath land to the eastern end of the busy Greenhan airfield. These gliders were assembled there and tested, and from there they were flown out to other locations. At one time they were assembling about fifty a day. It was during one of the winter gales that many of the assembled gliders got caught by the wind and were blown across the airfield.

Now I did say that I would say more about the A.T.C.s Don in another chapter. That Don that got parked in the Newbury school grounds got blamed by many in the town as attracting that raider. What rubbish, we could not bomb accurately and nor could the Germans either. The orders came, that the Don had to go. On one Sunday morning we were all to parade and we were told that each of us should bring with him a sledge hammer or an axe or some similar tool. What we had to do was to smash that Don into pieces. It had got to be destroyed. They intended just saving the cockpit area. This had to be taken to a large house up the old Bath Road where it was then placed. The A.4 bypass now passes over that spot. No parts of that Don were ever to resurface. I now wish that I had kept a small portion from it. Maybe an auxiliary fin from under the tailplane. Only a few Dons saw any service. A batch of these became engineless airframes and were used for instructional purposes. What was said by de Havillands is that the Air Ministry had asked too much from it. This made the Don to become too heavy. A maker's brochure also said of the Don, 'The least said about it, the better'. All that I can say about it now is, 'Thank goodness that it was only a Don'. It carried the service serial M1284. I do not know for certain, but this number may at one time have been 1284M. That would have been a maintenance series suffix that was issued to non flying airframes. The unattached wings had an L series serial. I have since lost my records as to what that number was. De Havilland D.H.93 Don's were all allocated in the serial block L2387-L2436. Only about fifty of them were built and of these, only twenty-eight of them of them were delivered as completed aircraft. The rest became instructional airframes. All of those that were airworthy were grounded by the end of March 1939. I have often wondered what A.T.C. Sergeant Bill Hartland would have thought, when we destroyed that Don. He had guarded it so much when it was at Opperman Gears. Destroying that Don was not the kind of way that I would have wished to have started off when working on a de Havilland aeroplane. Well any aeroplane for that matter. There came an A.T.C. summer camp in the September of 1943. For this I had to take a week off from my work with no pay. This camp was not that very far away from Newbury. It was at R.A.F. Harwell. Today Harwell airfield has become a nuclear research establishment. Back in 1943 it was the home of number 15 O.T.U. (Operational Training Unit). Harwell's aircraft were the Vickers Armstrong Wellington bombers. These could be seen dispersed all around the airfield. The only other type of aircraft that were there was a small detachment of Handley Page Harrow transports. These all belonged to Number 271 Squadron. A few of these still retained their front and rear gun turrets while some of the others had been modified by having their turrets replaced with streamline fairings to their backs and fronts . A few of those that had been modified had also been given extra side windows. Once modified, these Harrows were then dubbed with the name, Sparrows. These Handley Pages were all dispersed near to the station's bomb dump. This was on the opposite side of the A.34 road and in the vicinity of 'The Horse & Jockey' pub. The Harrow first entered R.A.F. service in the mid 1930's. It was one of the first of the new monoplane bombers. The very first of the new monoplane heavy bombers was the Fairy Hendon. Hendons entered the R.A.F in 1936, but by 1939 they were all removed from service. The Harrow joined the R.A.F. in 1937 and it was followed in 1938 by Handley Page's Hampden.

Then, in 1939 the Vickers Wellingtons were first issued to Bomber Command. Now in 1943, all of these remaining Harrow and Sparrows were being put to good use in the transport role. These Harwell Harrows all carried the code letters YS. One of these was K7000 and its code letters were YS-S. While I was at this camp, this aircraft had its fore and aft turrets. At a later date it also got modified into a Sparrow. It was in this form that I made a solid wooden model of it. One year I loaned this model to a squadron reunion that was being held in Down Ampney.

Now there was something about these Handley Pages that was majestic. No sooner had they opened up their throttles then up came the tail and they seemed to float into the air as they lifted off. I expect that we were seeing them when lightly loaded. We were not to know it then, but in just a year's time, most of those Harrows were to be lost in France while they were being used to evacuate many of our wounded troops. One of the jobs that they were often given to do was in moving squadrons from one place to another. I remember watching one of these flying across the airfield with an exhaust flare on its port engine. Our billets were on the eastern side of the A.34 Newbury to Oxford road. To enter the main camp we had to go in through the main gate which was a few hundred yards along that road towards the north and on the opposite side of the road. Also on the opposite of this road to our huts and just close to the hedge was the perri-track (perimeter, outer taxi-way). Wellingtons would use this and we would not bother to go out and look at them. If a Harrow came along, the cry would go, 'There's a Harrow coming' and we would all rush out to take a nice close look. These Harrows had a very strong appeal to us lads and so we requested our A.T.C. officers to try and get us some flights in them. Our officers did try, but they were told that the work which these Harrows were doing took them down to the south coast. They would not let us fly in them in case they got bounced on by any enemy raiders. All of the Harrows were shadow shaded in brown earth and dark green on their fuselage sides and upper surfaces. Below they were painted in a sky blue.

On one of our camp days, the station received three visiting aircraft. These were lined up on the grass. We cadets were allowed to go and have a look at them. Two of them were Halifax bombers. I have now forgotten what marks that they were, but I do remember that each one had a different kind of nose. One was of the more solid type while the other had a full blown transparency. Both of them had later type noses than the one that is preserved in the Hendon Museum. The other aircraft was a de Havilland D.H.98 Mosquito Mk.PR.IV. It was camouflaged with its upper surfaces in a grey and dark green while it's under surfaces were in a lighter shade of grey. It carried the serial DZ596 and a single code letter U. It had probably flown in from nearby Benson and it certainly took our attention.

Each morning armed with our mug and eating irons (knife, fork and spoon), we were marched for a few hundred yards where we enter the station by the main gate. We passed the guard house and were fallen out at the airmen's mess hall. We were now experiencing the living conditions of the airmen. In this very pleasant atmosphere we joined the queue of airmen for our meals and then sat down at one of the long tables. One then filled ones mug up from a tea-urn that often also had bromide mixed in with it. After you had finished your meal you then returned your plates as you left by the outside door. Just on the outside of the door there was a steam heated galvanized tank in to which you dipped your mug and eating irons. My weeks stay here was to be a very happy one. We were shown around the hangars, given films in the station cinema. We were shown how to arm bombs, pack parachutes and many other trades. They introduced us to the link trainers and the bomb aiming trainer. We were given lectures, one of which was not to divulge anything that we had been told or had seen. Especially about some of the later marks of Wellingtons which were being prepared for tropical service over on the north-west side of the airfield. These could be seen leaving Harwell freshly painted in tropical camouflage. I now know that these Wellingtons were making a short flight to Harwell's satellite airfield, Hampstead Norris. From here, these Wimpies as the Wellingtons were affectionately known, would be flown out to the middle-east. They would be ferried out, sometimes two at a time across that notorious Bay of Biscay on their long haul to Gibraltar. This was their first stopping point after leaving England. Many of these Wimpies never made it as they got jumped on by Junkers Ju 88's. Germany had a good idea as to what was going on as they had targeted Harwell and Hampstead Norris.

Steaming into Stockcross

USAAF Welford's D-Day over Wickham Heath

```
         A I R  T R A I N I N G  C O R P S.
                    (NEWBURY WING)

The undermentioned Cadet has permission to be flown as a passenger
                 DAY
during the      NIGHT    of the period indicated hereon only.

Number    608        Rank   Cadet      Name   Rutterford

Period    20.6.43         0900 h.

UNIT STAMP
                                  AUTHORITY:-  [signed] F/LT.
           17.6.43                     O.C. Newbury Wing,
                                       Air Training Corps.
```

An unsuccessful chit for an Oxford flight from Greenham Common

It was here while at camp that I was given my second flight and this was in a Wellington Mk.I c. DV871 and coded KK – S. This logged me thirty minutes on Friday the 3rd of September. I was then 15 years old. Having drawn a parachute from the store, I was driven out to a Wellington that was sitting on its dispersal apron. I then climbed a six stepped ladder under the nose of the bomber and was directed over the main spar and down the belly of the aircraft to the rear turret. I was told whatever I did that I was not to tread on a portion of the fabric as this was only for an emergency exit when in the sky. I had to leave my parachute just inside the fuselage. The chute if I had had to have used it I would then have to clip on to a harness that I had to wear, this on to my chest. The two turret doors were opened and having climbed in to this Nash & Thompson turret they were then shut behind me. I was then separated from the rest of the aircraft. The engines were then started up and the aircraft became a living creature that was eager to fly. Now I was to experience the solitary life of a tail-end-charlie, but I did not have any intercom. The Wimpy moved off and it gave me the sensation on being dragged across the airfield backwards. I could hear and feel a loud clang-clang-clang that came from the retractable tail wheel. This old Wellington had seen quite a bit of service and was fast becoming clapped out. It had seen many raids over enemy territory and when it was once station at R.A.F. Wing it had taken part in one of those one thousand bomber raids. Sir Arthur Harris had called on his O.T.U.s when he made up that famous number when in launching these extra large raids. At last my pilot had found the runway and had lined up on it. The throttles were pushed forward and the airframe shook all over. Brakes were then released and sitting in the tail I then became airborne before my pilot. The runway was soon slipping away beneath me and it soon disappeared into the distance. When you start to enjoy yourself, time then flies, literally. Flying over the airfield gave me the opportunity to see just how well it had all been camouflaged. I looked down on our billets and could see all the other parts of the station where I had not been taken. My short flight had been local and out over the Ilsley Downs. All too soon we were losing height as the aircraft made back for the runway. I then became the last person in the aircraft to touch down as the tail wheel lowered. Thinking about it, I must have flown a little longer than the others in the aircraft. Along with the crew we were then driven back to the main station. I then had to return my harness and chute back to the store. I had very much enjoyed my short flight and I had not given any thought to the horrible task that this bomber had been made to perform. My next job was to locate and to join the rest of my mob.

As I have previously said, the firm that I was working for were manufacturing many control columns for these Wellington bombers. While at Harwell, I then had the opportunity to look in several cockpits of these Wellingtons. In each one I was to find the little stamp mark that had been placed on these control columns in our factory. This being a very small circle with the letters OG standing for Opperman Gears. This was the inspectors stamp after he had passed them as serviceable. Also in this circle there was a number. By this method this control column could be traced back to the factory that had made it. It was while I was on my way to the mess that I got clobbered by an erk (ground mechanic). He was busy working on a Wimpy all on his own when he was in need of some assistance. He was as what was known as, an airframe waller. I do not know what he was doing, but he needed me to work a wobble pump in the belly of the fuselage. Activating this pump would have been the first time in my life that I had ever done a job on an airworthy aircraft, even though that I did not know what I was doing.

While at camp we were taken to the gym (gymnasium). This was the place where you were to expel any surplus energy. One thing that I well remember was slipping up backwards on a smooth wet slippery floor having just taken a shower. I went down with a wallop which gave me a bump on the back of my head and a headache. The worst thing was that I could not then dry myself as I could then wring the water out of my towel. Like our billets, this gym was situated on the outside of the main station. I thoroughly enjoyed my week's camp at Harwell and it was while I was here that I entered my first public house. It was the Rose & Crown at nearby Chilton village. In order to have gone to camp I had had to put in a certain number of parades at that bombed Council School. Living way out in the country this had not been easy, but somehow I had managed it. I had enjoyed seeing all of those Wimpies and had also had endured the noise from many of them from those that had been flying throughout the nights. Both the Wellingtons and the Harrows were cloth covered airframes and both types were powered by Bristol Pegasus engines. There had been the odd Rolls-Royce Merlin powered Wellington there. These were Mk.IIs. Those tropical Wellingtons were powered by the more powerful Bristol Hercules engines.

It was back to Harwell again that I went for my third flight. This was on the 23rd of February 1944. For this I had to take a day away from work which cost me the loss of a day's pay. We cadets were given our air experience in a de Havilland D.H.89A Dominie. This was in V4724. Actually it was a pre- war Dragon Rapide that had been impressed into the R.A.F. When it was in civy-street it had been registered G-AFNC and it had served with The Aircraft Operating Co, Ltd. It was to survive the war and to be re-civilized when it was sold to Belgium where it became, OO-CCD.

On arrival at the station we found that this Dominie had been flown in especially for our squadron's convenience. The pilot in command then operated it from a taxi-way. This bod that was about to fly us was in a hell of a hurry. So much so that he point blankly refused to sign any of our log cards. He complained that he had not been given enough time in which to do so. Two very short circuits being non electrical were made in just five minutes flat each time the aircraft had been unloaded and loaded again with a fresh load of bods. This bloke could not get his air-bus driving duties over quick enough. It had not been worth loosing a day's pay and the war effort for such a short flight. For me it was just the chance to log a different type of aircraft. It was my fist flight in a de Havilland aeroplane. Little did I know then that this would be my first of many. On another day away from work we were given a bus outing to R.A.F. Odiham I have now forgotten the date, but it could well have been in the February of 1944. Had I have been given a flight on that day then I would have logged the date.

We arrived at an airfield gate only to find that no persons that were on guard duties there knew anything about our visit. Our bus was pulled over to the right side of the entrance while our officer was allowed to go in to get things sorted out. We sat there in that bus waiting for near on half an hour. At last our officer in charge returned and we were driven in on to the airfield for a few hundred yards. The bus was parked up and we were formed up into three ranks just inside the nearest hangar. Standing there facing the outside we noticed what looked like snow drifting across the sky. What we were seeing was smoke. A Mosquito had crashed through those wooden gates on to the same spot where our bus had been parked. It killed the guard that had just let us in and the crew of two in the aircraft. We were told that it was due to an engine cut on take-off. We had missed being in that crash by only about a couple of minutes at the most. If we had not been moved when we did, then Newbury would have lost about thirty-two air cadets as we filled up a thirty-two seat coach. I would then not have been here writing this and the Newbury Weekly News would have had something to write about. At lunch time, we passed back through this entrance while we were on our way to the airmen's mess. The place was one mass of ashes and foam. One engine had tried to bury its-self into the bottom of a large oak tree. The only recognized portion was the complete tail assembly. It had snapped off and was just over a wire fence and so had escaped the fire. The aircraft's serial number was on this, but I have now forgotten what it was. It was while we were making our way to the mess that one of our cadets picked up an aircrews identity tag and he handed it in to the new guard that was placed on duty.

As I have just said, I did not log the date. In order to try and find out more on this crash I bought a small book. It was called, de Havilland Mosquito Crash Log and it was compiled by David J. Smith. In this paper back it listed a No. 400 Squadron's Mosquito MM277 as on the 20th of February 1944 as having overshot the aerodrome and having to go round again. On going around again it killed two people. Now three people had been killed and so I did not take this to be the date of our visit and the crash. I wrote to "Aeroplane" asking for any information. With thanks to Mike Packham of Welwyn Garden City, he answered my question in, 'Information Exchange', "Aeroplane" January 2004. In this he states that it was a Mosquito PR.XVI, MM277 of 400 Squadron. It had overshot while landing and crashed into No. 2 guardroom killing an airman and injuring a service policeman along with the crew of the aircraft. The crew were, R.C.A.F. pilot Flt O. P. Alexander and WO, J. Cosoff and they were buried in Brookwood Military Cemetery. All though this gate was some distance from a runway, I would now take this aircraft to be the one that nearly got us. I cannot visualize two Mosquitos crashing through Odiham's gateways. We could well have been at Gate Two as I would have thought that Gate One would have had a brick built guard house and not a wooden sentry box. They say that a miss is as good as a mile, that is just as well as the death toll would have reached thirty-six. Of this happening we were told to keep our lips tightly button up and so it never made the Newbury paper.

We were escorted through some of the hangars. In one of them, several North American Mitchell IIs were undergoing maintenance. They carried the No. 180 Squadrons code letters EV. Some airframe erks then invited us cadets to take a look at the inside of a Mitchell. I was one of those inside when it did not please an angry chiefy (hangar flight sergeant). Those erks should not have invited us in as the aircraft was trestled. Also on that day we saw Hurricanes and Typhoons plus some other types which I have now forgotten about.

One day I cycled to grandfathers at Crux Easton. On the Woodcott Downs there was a bombing range. From along the Woodcott Road I stopped and watched some Mitchells that were bombing on that range with practice bombs. At the sides to this range were two brick built watch towers, of these, the southern one still remains. When the range was in use some red flags would be hoisted. In March 1945, the airframe of Airspeed Oxford 5087M being ex R6345 was placed in the centre of the range as the target. There was one crash that occurred there while on bombing practice and it was a Mosquito which was unfortunate by having a wing fold. It was quite possible that the Mitchells that I watched could well have been those from Odiham. There was also another bombing range in our district. This one was on Wellbotom Down between Upper Lambourn and Uffington. Several Wellingtons had misshaps while using this range and I believe that gerry also added a few bombs to it, but they would not have been practice bombs.

My second A.T.C. summer camp was at R.A.F. Wing in Buckinghamshire. In later years it nearly became London's third airport. If it had, it was to be given the name, Cublington. Our week's camp was in the September of 1944. Once again I had to get in a certain number of parades in order to be allowed to attend. Again I found this very difficult, but once more I just managed to do so. Wing was then home to No. 26 O.T.U. and they were equipped with Wellingtons and Hurricanes. The front gun turrets had been removed from some of these Wimpies and their noses faired over. We were told that it was because of what was being fitted under these fairings was the reason that we were not allowed to go into any of the hangars. One night we cadets were just getting our clothes off and about to climb between the sheets when several WAAF's poked their heads through the open windows. They were searching for places where they could bed down some Canadians. A lot of Canadian crewed Halifax's had lobbed in. For some reason they could not get back to their own airfield which was most likely in Yorkshire. Due to a shortage of billets, several of them were placed in along with us. Now these boys had obviously had a rough time having done many 'ops (operations over enemy territory). These lads were bomb happy and having got back safe again they had gone on the booze and who could blame them. Before long, bundles of hay were coming in through the windows. One chap had decided on having an outdoor crap. In the darkness he had chosen a spot that was a bed of stinging nettles. This poor chap was going around the hut and everyone was expected to inspect his bum. This he was blaming on poisoned ivy. Having had a skin full to drink he very likely could not have felt the pain in his rear end then. Later on I bet he felt it. In the morning the hut was in a hell of a mess and the R.A.F. were very apologetic. We lads felt very sorry for those boys.

During my weeks camp I was given two flights in Wellingtons. The first one was on the Monday and late in the afternoon. It was in a B Mk.X being LN221 and coded WG – Q, Q for Queenie. Along with another cadet named Lewendon who's father owned an art shop in Newbury, we were driven out to the dispersal by a WAAF in a six wheeled Fordson crewbus that had hinged double rear doors. We were to find this Wimpie with both of its Hercules engines already running. The ladder was lowered from beneath the nose for the second time for the benefit of us cadets. We were instructed to line ourselves up with the fuselage and to approach the bomber from dead ahead. This way we would not damage those revolving propellers. This aircraft was going up on an air test. Its pilot was F/O Bowells and he now had us two as passengers. I was instructed once more to make my way down to the rear turret while Cadet Lewendon, lucky chap was invited to sit next to the pilot. This aircraft had no front turret as this had been replaced by a fairing. Once down at the rear end I then left my chute in the fuselage and settled myself down behind the gun mechanism. This was a Frazer Nash turret and half of the Perspex protection had been removed. This had been done so that the gunner would have had a better chance of seeing an enemy fighter before it became too late. Being late summer it was not cold and I had perfect visibility as I watched Wing airfield slip away into the distance.

The remaining bombing watch tower

Harwell's Wellington DV871 and Harrow K7000

We were being flown at about 3,000 feet and I was busy looking out at the ground below and admiring the lush green countryside. I then saw a flight of camouflaged Tiger Moths speed from quite close underneath us. They then, at what seemed a record speed, vanished into the direction from which we had just come. Never since have I seen any Tiger Moths that appeared to have flown that fast. It was if they had been placed on a video and then played fast forward. I have often wondered if they had seen us coming or our pilot had seen them. Two towns were flown over and I have no idea as to which they were. Aylesbury and Leighton Buzzard were the two nearest towns to Wing.

It was on this flight that I first experienced a 'G' force. I think that I would be correct if I claimed it to have been my first aerobatic. That is, if one considers that a Wellington was capable of doing such a thing. The bomber was suddenly slipped into a corkscrew and I had no idea that it was going to happen as I did not have any intercom. It happened so suddenly that I will never know if it was a 'corkscrew starboard go', or a' corkscrew port go'. Which ever it was, this Wimpie was much lower afterwards. This was a manoeuvre that was often practiced by bomber pilots so that they might have a chance to get clear of searchlights or night fighters. My arms became too heavy to lift and for a few seconds I felt locked in my seat. I thought to myself, 'Damn good job that he did not decide to do that while those Tiger Moths were coming beneath us'. The skies were crowded during those wartime days. This pilot had given us some proper air experience and I enjoyed every minute of it. I think that we missed our evening meal in the mess. I remember that we found it a rush to catch an old blue bus that took us into Leighton Buzzard for the evening.

My second flight there was in a Wellington B Mk.III with the serial BJ598 and coded PB – L. This was on the Friday and our camp was coming to its end. Both of the codings BP and WG were used by No. 26 O.T.U.'s Wimpies. Again I was driven out in a Fordson crewbus but this time it was with a full crew. I squat down in the fuselage just to the rear of the main spar and the aircraft was filled by its crew. The pilot was having instruction and the crew were obliged to come along. I could not see outside of the aeroplane and it was like riding in the centre of a crowded bus. Sat next to me, one of the crew had his head buried in a newspaper. He then kindly let me borrow his head phones. This made it a little more interesting as I could then here the instructor giving his pupil instructions and could feel the aircraft move accordingly. When we entered the bomber the weather looked dull and dismal. On clambering out, it was then raining cats and dogs. The skipper that signed my log card was K. W. Simpson and the flight had lasted for one hour and ten minutes. This then became my last official flight with my A.T.C. No. 211 Squadron.

Now in 1946 I was expected to work overtime. By the time that I had finished my work I became as black as a night bomber. Cast iron dust is dirty stuff. Then after work I had that seven mile cycle ride home. It did not give me enough time to get cleaned up and into uniform and cycle back to Newbury. I was not able to attend parades like many of those townies with cleaner jobs. Due to this, I was not able to get in enough parades to be allotted flying chits. I felt that it was time that I did some flying. Many other cadets were attending more parades and were then getting flying. This they were getting from Transport Command who were then based at Membury now that the Americans had left it. All of my mates had now been called up and I was due to be called on any day. My only mate who also had not yet received his call-up papers was Dougie Lawrence. He was also in the A.T.C. only he was in the Thatcham No. 1866 Squadron that shared this number with Hungerford. Douglas was also a metal turner and in later years he became a Mayor of Newbury. Like most of my mates that I once had, he is also no longer with us. Together we decided that we would put on our uniforms and cycle to Membury and try our luck at getting a flight. This we were successful in doing.

Having arrived at the airfield we were told to leave our log cards in a flight office and to collect them when we returned and this we did. We were then given a serial number of a Dakota and we set off to find it. Find it we did. It was in a hangar with its cowlings off and it was going nowhere. Back to the office we went. We were then given another number and this time we were in luck. This Dak' was a C Mk.IV with the serial KN442. And it was coded WF – F. The letters JF were on the front of the aircraft. With scattered snow over the ground we left our bikes and enjoyed a thirty minute flight down to R.A.F. Stoney Cross in the New Forest. This Dak' was camouflaged and had the metal paratrooper bench seating down each side of its fuselage. One thing that I do remember is that after we had got past the Inkpen hills there was no more snow. Little did I know it then, but in June 1994, I was to fly again in this same Dakota. This time it had been sold and took up the registration G-AMPZ and was in the ownership of Air Atlantique. Gone were those metal benches and it was now fully upholstered with airline seating.

On Stoney Cross airfield we were to see many Short Stirling C Mk.Vs. These were all in polished metal finish and had got to be known as Silver Stirlings. One of which looked most odd with one of its main undercarriage legs collapsed. This one was on a hangar apron. There was also a handful of Dakotas there. Crews had been flying these down to Stoney and then all returning in one aircraft. This was also another half hour flight back and it was in a C Mk.III serialed KG550 and coded 8P – C. This one was fitted out with airline type seating. On arriving back at Membury, we were to find that the Flight Office had closed and so we could not retrieve our log cards. Mine eventually found its way back to the Newbury HQ. A kind cadet did manage to get his hands on it and returned it back to me. I was now looked upon as being a naughty boy. A letter was sent to me requesting that I must hand my uniform back forthwith. This I did not do, but I gave it back to them just as soon as I obtained my call-up papers. No one came looking for me and I was determined that it was not going to stop me from joining the Royal Air Force. I was to hold on to that uniform for another three months. There was a large board that was in the Newbury HQ that had all the names on it of the cadets that had made it into the R.A.F. My name was never placed on it. Much later I was to pal on with a member in the Calleva Flying Group. He was Peter Trask and he was at that time an officer in the Newbury A.T.C. He had been told about this board and he said that this board had mysteriously disappeared. I for one was not sorry when he told me this.

REGISTRATION OF BOYS AND GIRLS OF 16 YEARS

MINISTRY OF LABOUR & NATIONAL SERVICE

THIS CARD is an acknowledgment that you have

(I) Registered under the Registration of Boys and Girls Order, 1941; and

(II) Produced/Surrendered your National Registration Identity Card on attaining the age of 16 years.

If your new Blue Identity Card is not issued to you at the time of registration you should apply for it as soon as possible at the local National Registration Office for the address opposite, producing this acknowledgment.

If you are asked to produce your Identity Card before you obtain the new Card, you should produce this acknowledgment.

YOU SHOULD KEEP THIS CARD CAREFULLY.

1. Full Name (Surname in BLOCK letters)
2. National Registration Identity Card No.
3. Home Address (in full)
4. Nationality: British/Alien.

Official Stamp and Date
For N.R.O.

(i) Identity Card produced and surrendered.
(ii) Identity Card produced and returned to holder.
(iii) Blue Identity Card issued.

E.D. 431C

Delete whichever is inapplicable

P.T.O.

Registration—Why?

You are anxious to do what you can for the country at this time and the Government have required you to register, so that they may help you to find the best way of fitting yourself to do your duty as a citizen and of assisting the present national effort.

Are you among these?

Large numbers of boys and girls of your age are already giving up much of their spare time to different kinds of training or public service, as members of various organisations—whether Clubs, Guides, Scouts or Brigades, or helping in Civil Defence. Many boys too are preparing for future military service as members of the Cadets or Air Training Corps, or by serving now with the Home Guard. If you are already playing your full part in any of the above ways, keep on with what you are doing.

If not—then what?

You may, however, not yet have taken up any such training or service. Possibly there are good reasons for this. You may be fully employed for long hours on war work and giving all your energies to it; you may be devoting your spare time to continuing your education after working hours, or if you are a girl, you may be helping in the home.

Some of you, of course, are still at school and your time is pretty well filled up. Your job is to get on with your education; your Headmaster or Headmistress will tell you if there is something more you might do.

That extra bit.

But it is the "bit extra" that counts and everyone in these days wants to do his utmost. Now that you have registered you will get a letter from your Education Authority asking you to come along for a chat with someone who can tell you the various ways in which you can lend a hand in your spare time. If you have not up to the present signed on for some sort of useful training or service, it will be your duty to respond to this invitation.

It is for you to choose.

You will be free to choose from among the opportunities that may be open to you in the neighbourhood where you live. The Government are confident that, given the chance, you will want to do anything you can to help now and to prepare for the future. It's up to you.

Ministry of Labour and National Service,
London, S.W.1.

Both sides of my registration card

My call-up papers

Top: my medical card, below: my pay book

I BECAME A ROOKIE

Apparently I had been reported to the A.T.C, s HQ by a Newbury corporal who had been flying officially at Membury on that day. Douglas had been OK as he had belonged to a different squadron. A month previous to my Membury excursion I had become eighteen. I had been expecting my call-up papers to come any day. This was early in the February. As it happened, my papers never arrived to the middle of June. I entered into the services on the 2nd of July and I returned my uniform back personally on the 1st of July. As far as I was concerned, I was still Cadet Number 2603 of B Flight in Number 211 Squadron at Newbury. No way did I intend them from stopping me from enlisting in the Royal Air Force, the army was not for me. In my eyes, going flying like I had done had shown a keen initiative. It was people like Douglas Bader that had disobeyed an order and so writing off an aeroplane and nearly himself as well was the stuff that Brit's are made of. I felt a little saddened that in Newbury's eyes that they had treated me like being a rebel. Since then I have spoken with several people that had got themselves flights with the U.S.A. and just for the asking. I now regret that in those days that I did not do this myself.

While speaking of obtaining flights from Membury, I will relate one flight that the late Frederick Giddings had and he did not have to go asking for it. Fred wrote a book on Membury and he kindly let me have a copy. It was a private book and he never got it published. I will here take up his story just as he had written it. He was at the time a school boy in the Lambourn School when he and another boy had played truant.

As a true country boy, a day off to go rabbiting, either to earn money or to supplement the family larder, was still irresistible. It was during one of these days off when Jim Puffet and I were over by the Eastbury Grange, that one of the often seen Piper Cubs (L4) aircraft from Membury flew low and slow over us. Waving our jackets in a form of a greeting, we were amazed as the Cub turned into the wind and landed beside us and its pilot climbed out and stepped down. 'What are you boys doing?' he asked.' Rabbiting' we replied. 'Shouldn't you boys be at school?' he next asked. 'Yes' Jim replied. 'Say, how would you two like a ride in the Cub?' he asked. 'Yes please' was the answer. So aboard we both climbed squeezing into the rear seat, within a short time we were in the air. 'Great' we thought as we were flown over Lambourn. Shortly afterwards we were landing at the Membury Airfield, where the pilot called over another service man who was in a Willys Jeep. We were told to get in, which we both did, and then much to our disgust we were taken to our school and then to Mr Clarke. Ouch! That was one aircraft trip that these boys never forgot.

After my Membury affair, life for me grew rather dull. The zest had gone out of it. Douglas who was a little younger than me had been called up into the Royal Navy. Fred Davis another mate of mine had also been called up. Not into the three services, but as a Bevan Boy. He was put down the coal mines at Oswestry. This he did not like one bit, but he was lucky as he got transferred into the army. He was a very tall lad and I would think this may have been the reason for his transfer. Here was me left in that factory with all of my mates gone, no girls worth looking at and expecting my call-up papers every time that the postman called. These papers never came. On the 6th of June, I had an uncle return home from serving out in the middle-east. The next day was the start of the Victory Celebrations. These finished on a Monday with a carnival and a dance in the town's drill hall. I went to the welcoming home party and tried my best to live up to the celebrations, but life for me was dead. Many chaps were now leaving the services fast, but I was still waiting to go in, but when.

On one day at Oppermans we each received a slip of paper in our wage packets. This told us how much income tax that we had each paid. I then realized that I was getting far less money than all of the other chaps. This upset me, and so I approached Charlie Mankin who was the shop foreman for a rise. He point blankly refused to give me one. He then told me that in his eyes I had been slacking. I stormed back to my lathe and Sid Roberts who was working the lathe next to me then asked how I got on. 'I would not stand for that', said Sid. 'Go down and see Mr John Opperman in the offices'. This I did. Mr John was very fair. He gave me a week in which to earn some bonus and if I did then he would give me a rise and back date it. I then got my rise. After this, Charlie then made my life hell being as I had gone behind his back. I was working in misery and I mentioned it to my parents. They advised me to leave and so I gave in my notice. Now it was that my troubles started. I could not manage to find work. Chaps were leaving the forces fast and I was still waiting to go in. I could not stand this waiting any longer with my parents keeping me. I got on the phone and spoke to the Reading recruiting office asking them why it was that I had not yet received my calling up papers. This then got things moving. They then became concerned because if I did not hear from them within a week, then I would be forced to take another medical. Within that week my letter came. It was on a Saturday morning, June the 22nd and my date given was the 2nd of July. My destination was Padgate, Warrington. Good show, I could now relax, Padgate was for the R.A.F.

Tuesday the 2nd came and I said farewell to my family and set off with the travel warrant which they had provided. My journey took me as far as London on the old Great Western. To some of the bods, GWR stood for 'God's Wonderful Railway'. To us service types it became known as the, 'Go When Ready Railway'. I then had to continue on the London, Midland & Scottish, the LMS. To us it was to become the 'Lousy Mucky & Scruffy. The services had nicknames for the other two railways. The LNER was the 'Late Never Early Railway' and the SR was the 'Slow Railway'. Although for me this was my first long trip of what was to be many, a note in my diary stated that I arrived at 3 pm. The first thing that the Royal Air Force gave me when I reached my destination at Padgate was a FFI (Free From Infection medical examination), We were later to refer to these as Short Arm Inspections. It did do some good as one chap was lead away feeling very sorry for himself. Once we had got our bedding sorted, we then made for the mess. Later on in that evening then found most of us in the station cinema. Having got us behind the wire fence of Padgate we were not to be allowed to go out again. The main reason was, not that they could not trust us, but we were in the kitting out stage. They did not wish to have their men parading the streets of Warrington in half civy and half service clothing. Once that they had got us into full uniform they had to be sure that we were good enough to act the part. Because of this, we were made to stay behind the wire fencing during our short stay at Padgate.

1946 was the only year in my life that I had kept a diary. I now wish that I had done this throughout my service career as I would then have had more notes to refer to. As I am able to refer to this diary, I can give you a full account of this short stay in Padgate. I am commencing this on Wednesday the 3rd which was Day One. I spent eight days here and was then posted to R.A.F. Wilmslow on Thursday the 11th.

Day One. Took intelligence trade test. Started to get my pay book. Lots and lots of waiting around. Evening to the camp cinema. Saw the film, "Irene".

Day Two. Ration cards. Got my pay book. Had X-Ray. Put into C Flight. To a show.

Day Three. In to Warrington in a troop lorry with two loads of kit bags. The WO in charge of our party of five gave us a half hour in the town. Received my kit including uniform. Had photo taken for identity book. To camp cinema. . Fitted webbing.

Day Four. First pay. Fitted webbing. Saturday being a half day. Sing song in No. 3 NAAFI.

Day Five. Sunday. Listened to Forces Favourites in No. 1 NAAFI. Layed around on the grass. To the station cinema.

Day Six. Had trousers altered by the camp tailor. Parcelled up my civy clothes. To the station cinema.

Day Seven. Sent of parcel. Fatigues in bulk stores on the boot counter. My chance to throw boots at others. To see a play in the gym that was called "George & Margaret".

Day Eight. Had service identity cards. Were given another FFI. This followed by fatigues for talking.

Thursday the 11th of July we were all marched down to the Railway Station in Warrington with our new kitbags rammed full and resting on our shoulders. Here we all boarded a train to R.A.F. Wilmslow in Cheshire. This was the drill training camp where I was about to perform my square bashing, and as they put it, to get my new number dry. This number, and it was a number that was in a series that was only allocated to ex A.T.C. cadets was 3085376. This number was to become firmly imprinted in my mind.

My first flight, BM826 with a u/c problem

I GOT SOME IN

In a strange way, I grew to like Wilmslow. Although all of the time that I was there I was longing to get away from it so that I could be on a permanent station with less bull. I think that my liking for Wilmslow was due to the amount of team work. One took great pride in this and always tried to do one's best as your team had to be better than the others. You were always self conscious of not letting the other chaps down and so you always aimed at doing your very best. Also, it was while I was here that I became more use to mixing with the opposite sex. Whatever it was, I was never given enough time in which to get bored, and so I found it to be a happy station.

That very same day that we arrived on camp they issued us with our training rifles. These polished lumps of wood and iron had been issued to numerous airmen before us. In the past, every piece of them that would loosen had been so done. This was so that when they were slapped while performing drill they would then create an exciting noise. Well this is what the drill instructors thought. We were all introduced to the station barber who was not allowed to run out of work. His job was to make sure that we still had just a little hair showing on our heads when we left his hut doorway. Once I was made to undergo two hair cuts on the same day. Boy, how all of that BS (bull-shit) made your hair grow.

On the very next day we were introduced straight into square bashing. This was then followed up with four lectures. These included the subject of VD (venereal disease). Well a chance of having sex would have been a fine thing. It was while I was here that I received a letter from Dad, bless him. It was a written letter on how to behave myself and not get some young lady into trouble. I had never been given any sex education at home and I think it must have given my parents some second thoughts. After these lectures and what time was left of this day we were told to use in cleaning up our huts. We had thought that they were brilliant, but they told us that they were dirty. Not just dirty, but filthy.

Each hut had a large metal coal bunker and these had to be burnished bright. The floor to be so polished that you could see your refection in it. Broom handles and table tops had to be scraped with razor blades and you did not have to make a dust while you were doing it. The life was hard and I think that it became much harder after all of that lazing about that we had been made to endure at Padgate. We all got stuck in and we had too, and looking back on this life it did not do any of us any harm. Our first week at Wilmslow ended with the MP's (military policemen) searching through our huts and kit bags as some bod had reported that his watch had been stolen. We were later to refer to these MP's as snowdrops as they all wore white headgear. At last, and by the Friday evening we had become trusted airmen. This our very first pass out of the camp. This, the chance for us to go down town and display our uniforms to the locals. Not that they would want to look at us as they had seen the likes of us over and over again. We did find a pup or two and for some of us, the Rex Cinema. But woe-betide any of us who were over a second late while returning through those guardroom gates.

I had set my heart on becoming a good airman and was bashing the square with the rest of the mob when I suddenly became poorly all over. I reported on sick parade as I did not feel at all well. I was made to continue with my training and I then felt much worse. Once more I joined the sick parade and marched down to the medical centre. This time the MO (Medical Officer) ordered me to stay in my bed. Due to all of the hut BS, this upset the rest of the chaps as they were not keen on me being there. Nor also were WO Harvey and Corporal Holt that keen on me being there. I then came out in a bright red spotted rash and this then did give them a reason to get concerned.

The MO, the camp doctor was sent for. He then diagnosed that I had caught scarlet fever and had me shifted into the O.I.D.H. which was in a rear corner of the camp. I believe that these letters stood for, Observation of Infectious Diseases Hospital. I was then told that I had become most unpopular with the rest of my billet as they had been looking forward to their first leave on the August Bank Holiday. Due to my infection, they had all been confined to camp. I was never ever to meet up with any of these chaps again. Hard luck boys.

The R.A.F.'s remedy for scarlet fever was for me to stay confined to my bed and to be waited on by hand and foot by pretty WAAF nurses. Life was now not so bad after all. In this isolation hospital I was placed in a small room which I had to share with another chap who had gone down with the same bug, but he had come from a different training wing to me. After spending a week or so in bed we both started to lose our spots, but they kept us both in bed for twenty days. After this bed period they had us out of bed and on our feet. During this second stage we then had the company of a couple of WAAFs who were in a similar condition as ourselves. Eventually this hospital decided that we were over it and so they sent all of us packing on ten days sick leave.

I arrived home for a late tea on the 20th of August. This being my first leave, I then set out to enjoy showing off my new uniform and enjoy meeting old friends. On my ninth day at home, my brother Dick went sick and the doctor was called to visit him. Dick had gone down with scarlet fever and the doctor instructed me to ring up my R.A.F. station at once. I then went to the telephone kiosk and made a trunk call to Wilmslow. They just said that it was a coincidence and ordered me back to camp. Well we did not think that it was a coincidence, but back to camp I had to go. I then had to leave my mother to nurse Dick and my own family could not mix with other people. It was not until after a month later that I chanced to meet up with the other guy that had shared the isolation along with me. He had only just returned from his sick leave. He had gone home like myself and had given this bug to his sister. Now that hospital had not cleared us. They should have given us throat swabs. These we never had. The R.A.F. did not want to know and our families should have been compensated, but how can you beat an organisation like the military services.

Now back at camp I was mixed in with a hut of bods and ordered to be the hut orderly. I was then given duties to perform in the cookhouses and stores as I was placed in Pool Flight. This until a fresh intake came in that they could team me up with. Eventually I was joined up with a new bunch of boys from Padgate. These boys had brought with them a very odd character and he had lived in Warrington and so he was never issued with a rail warrant to go and join up like the rest of us. He was either very thick, plain right stupid, or trying very hard to work his ticket. Whichever it was, we were very thankful for him. Though this might not have been the case, for the unfortunate lads that had to share the same hut with him. The drill instructors made a habit of picking on him and while they were doing this, they then left the rest of us alone. Also it often gave the rest of us a jolly good laugh. This chap's name was Smith. Living in Warrington he had got to know Padgate very well and so every night that he had been there he had found his way out and back in through the fence and had slept at his home. Because of this, those chaps had given him the title of, 'Mr Smith from Blackymoor'. Apart from bashing the square, we also had to do some rifle and brengun firing on the range. For this we were issued with serviceable rifles from out of the armoury. Somehow, Mr Smith had managed to obtain for himself an extra live round. With this and his drill rifle, he managed to place a hole through his hut roof. This did cause quite a stir, but things grew much worse when he started throwing his bayonet across the room.

For the second time, I got stuck into my square-bashing. On most days, very low flying aircraft would pass over our heads while we were being stood to attention. I was always eager to look up at them and so I had to move my eyes without moving my head. They were up on air tests from Avro's aerodrome at Woodford. The types seen were, Ansons, Lancastrians, Yorks and the then, new Tudor Mark Ones. Also in this Avro's circuit was the prototype Tudor Mark Two, G-AGSU which was very long in the fuselage to the front of the wings. It was the first of the British stretched airframes. A long nose on an airliner was then something quite new. Down in the town one day I was waiting in a bus queue for Macclesfield. I then got talking to a couple of chaps that were stood to the front of me. They then told me that they had been flying in 'SU and they were surprised that I knew its registration letters. A year later on the 23rd of August 1947, this Tudor was taking-off from Woodford when it pranged. It ended up destroying its-self with its long nose under water in a pond. This had been caused through aileron reversal, a thing that is often not associated with large aeroplanes. It happened all the same. The crew of four were all killed. Two of these poor souls were Avro's chief designer Roy Chadwick who had designed the Lancaster bomber. The other was the firm's chief test pilot, Bill Thorn. When I read of the sad news, I then thought of those two chaps that I had spoken to in Wilmslow. I still wonder if they may have been in that ill-fated crew of four.

Each week we had a BS night. This was always on the night preceding the hut inspection. Bull could never be allowed to be relaxed as all weekend passes depended on not having a dirty hut. To give you just one instance. If a match stick was found between the floor covering and the hearth to the stove, then you would have a disgraceful hut and you would all lose out on having week-end passes. Apart from all of this, kit and bedding had to be folded just so. Razors were to be kept spotless and even if you had to shave with cold water. Bayonet scabbards and boots had to be black leaded and polished so that you could see your face in them. You also had to blanco your webbing and keep all of your buttons and cap badges shining bright. Also, the brass ends to your webbing.

As the weeks rolled on, so we got better at our foot and rifle drill. In between sessions on the square we would partake in the following. Range firing, film shows on VD and not pleasant to look at, short arm inspections, dental parades, aircraft recognition, kit inspections, hut inspections, gardening around the hut which included white washing the kerb stones. On some periods we were handed over to the P.T.I.s (Physical Training Instructors). These were known to us as muscle bound heroes. If not given general PT, we could be made to do the assault course or be taken out of camp along some country roads on a run. No way were the R.A.F. soft with us, far from it.

Evenings if we were not writing letters or doing bull, we would spend our time with a walk down town or go to the NAFFI (Navy Army Air Force Institute) where we could purchase our sweet ration. Then there was the Y.M.C.A. (Young Men's Church Army) and then our favourite, the WAAF NAAFI. This we were only allowed to visit and I believe it was only on one night in the week. I did for a short time walk out with a WAAF named Doris. Both of us being in uniform, made us be that extra careful on how we behaved. She was to pass-out from her square bashing and was posted to Staverton in Gloucestershire where she became a police dog handler. I was left bashing the square. Very often if you had dated a girl you could then find yourself placed on fatigues in a cookhouse. It did not matter how good one was, these fatigues could not be escaped from all of the time.

Some week-ends one could be lucky and obtain a thirty-six hour pass. With a seventy-two, one could get home. After bashing around for weeks we finally had our pass-out rehearsal on Number Three Square. These squares were sacred ground. Woe-betide any person caught walking over one. This was followed by another short arm inspection. On the following day, Wednesday the 16th of

October we had our pass-out parade and on the same square. This was then followed by a pass-out dance in the NAAFI in the evening.

The following day and I was transferred back into Pool Flight. This they told me was because I had not come from Padgate along with the others. This had caused me to miss my posting. I now found that now I was back again in Pool Flight my life was just that little bit more relaxed. I had to parade a little later than the others each morning and here I was then informed as to which section of the station that I would perform my working day. More often than not I was sent to the WAAF clothing store where I found the girls and the lads to be a very friendly bunch. All of the new WAAFs at that time did their elementary training on the WAAF Wing at Wilmslow. My duties here was checking and packing female clothing. I remember that one of my jobs was counting packets of sanitary towels, enough to keep the WAAF Wing dry for months.

It was not always to the WAAF store that I would be sent even though the store had asked for me. I was still billeted in with a square bashing mob and had to do my share of BS, but compared with the rest of my hut mates, I was now respected as being an old hand. One morning when I paraded I was detailed along with another chap to go to the HQ of the WAAF's Training Wing. We were then taken to an empty hut and our job was to dismantle and remove some double bunk beds, These spaces then had to be replaced with single beds. We were busy with this task when there was a large scamper on each side of the hut. It was a fine sunny day and several of the hut windows were all open wide. In the huts on either side of us, the girls had been given a limited time in which to change for PT. We quickly decided that our best plan was to lay low as we did not wish to be mobbed by a large crowd of angry girls. Together we both got to the centre of the hut, but we could not resist an occasional peep. We then saw sights that we had never seen before. I knew every stitch of clothing that these WAAF's were wearing as I had handled most of them, but I had never handled what they were moving them from. For one week we had several days out of camp. We were hired by a farmer. Our job was picking up potatoes and mangel-wurzels and these days made a pleasant change from the normal camp life.

Life had now gone quiet for me on the camp. I had now gone out and met up with a girl who was living at Alderly Edge. On most evenings I would go off camp and meet up with her. We had grown very fond of each other and it was with a sad heart that I left Wilmslow when my posting eventually came through. I had been chosen to be trained as a F.M.E (Flight Mechanic Engines) a trade which would have me working on aircraft. On Saturday the 14th of December, I hoisted my kitbag on to my shoulder and set out for the railway station and my journey to R.A.F. Cosford in Shropshire.

TRAINING TO BE AN ERK

The very first thing that I noticed as the train pulled into Cosford station was that there were many aircraft dispersed on the airfield. Many of these were Avro bombers that were painted in the Tiger Force colours. These were white on the upper surfaces and black on the under surfaces. Had the war on Japan not have ended when it did, then these would have been used to drop bombs on Japan. This G.W.R. railway line and its station separated the airfield from the main camp. As I gazed out of the carriage window I thought to myself, that this looked more like an R.A.F. station. Having arrived on a weekend, all that I was immediately concerned with was finding some place that I could get my head down and a safe place where I could leave all of my kit. Having got myself temporarily fixed up, I then set out on the Sunday afternoon, to explore the local town of Wolverhampton. Having nearly got myself flattened by a trolleybus which crept up silently behind me I was to find that most of the younger folk seemed to collect them-selves around Dudley Street. Here I got chatting to a Scottish airman and together we went for a jug. Jock and I then rounded the night off at the flics. I remember doing this as the film which was being shown was called, 'Tailspin'. It was all about young American women in pre-war days racing specially designed close circuit racing aircraft. The theme tune to it was 'Beautiful Ohio'. Much to my surprise, I have never seen this film shown on the television.

On the Monday morning I reported for duty at the Wing Office. Here I was again automatically placed temporarily in Pool Flight. It was then suggested to me that if I had any outstanding leave that I should fill in a form and bang in for it. They then put it to me that once my flight mechanic course had started that there would be no more leave for another six months. I banged in for nine days privileged leave and had it granted. One useful thing was done before I set out for home and this was to get issued with a set of tools that I was to use while taking my course. It was then home on leave which took in all of the Christmas. The new-year though was to be taken at Cosford. On the last day in December I had to make my way back there on the good old G.W.R.

From here on I am not able to write so fully on the rest of my conscripted service as from then on I never kept a diary. Perhaps that was just as well. On our first week we were taught the right and the wrong ways of filing metal. For all of that week we were each stood at a bench reducing the size of a piece of metal. Never ever draw the file backwards, we were told. Having eventually achieved a degree in flatness, I was never ever to use a file again during my service career. The first three months of this course was taken in large workshops on the camp side of the railway. The second half of the course was taken on the other side of the railway over on the airfield. That portion of the airfield is now the Cosford Air Museum.

One evening I had escorted some girls home to Walsall on a bus. In so doing, I got back into Wolverhampton too late so missing the last train back to Cosford. To be caught going in through the main gate after time was a punishable offence. The only alternative was to break into camp hoping not to get caught doing so. Jankers had to be avoided at all costs. I walked to the outskirts of the town where I then met up with two other guys that had also landed themselves in the same situation. Together we were all in luck at this late hour as a car pulled up and gave us a lift. Back in those days, people would stop and pick up service men and it was quite safe to do so. Our next problem was that our lift had taken us to the wrong side of the airfield. The moon was up and it was shining nearly as bright as day. Together we managed to get over the fence as we broke into the airfield. We then had to run from aircraft to aircraft while trying to keep within the shadows. Having got past all the aircraft, we then had to run the gauntlet across the wide open space of the airfield. This airfield was patrolled and we did not wish to be eaten by Alsatian police dogs. We succeeded in this and also in managing the airfield fence, but we now got chased by some railway staff. We eventually managed to shake them off and now we had to break our way into camp. Then by creeping from the shadow of one building to the next, we made it back to our own billets. Were those girls worth all of that trouble? Not on your Nellie. One thing was for sure, we had put to good use what we had been taught when running those assault courses.

It is now sixty-five years ago since my Cosford days and my memory is not as good as it use to be. I am now not too sure as to the orders in which the subjects were given to me while on that course. Come each week we would move from one subject to another. Some of these subjects were; The general workings of an engine. 'Hands up, all of you that know how an engine works'. Up went my hand along with many others. 'From now on you will forget all that you think you know and you will learn it our way'. All the same, my little bit of knowledge was to hold me in good stead. Arithmetic was another subject. I remember this welsh sergeant who had lived all of his life amongst the city bricks taking the wee-wee out of me because I had been a country dweller. He had the gift of doing sums and I didn't and so he delighted in continually calling me a swede, the rotten old so-and-so. We had a week on the Rolls-Royce Merlin, the engine that powered the Spitfire, Hurricane, Lancaster, Mosquito and Mustang. Not to mention many others, such as the Beaufighter and Wellington. We had a week on Bristol engines, or was it two? The Pegasus with its poppet valves and the Hercules with its sleeve valves and junk heads. I believe that we had the Armstong Siddeley Cheetah. I do know that we had a full week on Frank Halford's de Havilland Gipsy engines. The four cylinder Major and the six cylinder Queen. One week was given to mags and carbs (magnetos and carburettors). It was then that we learnt that there was far more to aircraft carburation than what there was to motorcycles. These had built in things like boost and altitude capsules, ant-gee devices, carb heating. There were also accelerating pumps and slow running cut-outs. I do not know how it all came about, but I came top of our class on this subject. Another week was spent on props and C.S.U.s (propellers and constant speed units with their ancillary equipment). To wind all of this up, we were then given just one week on jet engines.

Now although the jet engine had just seen a limited war service in the Meteor Mk.Is, to the air force it was looked upon as being spanking brand new. Nearly all of their aeroplanes were still being pulled along with windmills to the fronts of them. Some people seemed to think that this fan like thing was placed in front of the pilot just to keep him cool. This was partly so, just see that propeller stop going round and you could watch that pilot start sweating. All of the way through this course we had been kept to our own bunch of lads. In our bunch, we knew that we had one intelligent guy who had served with a team that had helped in developing the jet engine. I seem to think that it was with Sir Frank Whittle, but I may now be wrong. It may have been with de Havillands or Rolls-Royce. Whichever it was, he had told us that when we got on to jets he was going to tie that instructor up in knots. We had all waited for this, and sure enough this bod came out asking our instructor questions that he could not answer. Frequently the instructor said, 'I will try and find out for you and let you know later on'. Halfway through the week the instructor tumbled that this chap knew more than he was making out. The cat was let out of the bag and for the rest of the week our pupil was teaching the instructor and we all became good friends. The only engine that they had to show us was a Rolls-Royce Welland. This engine owed its origin back to the early Whittle engine. I believe that it was a reverse axial-flow.

Of all of these subjects, the ones that I found to be most interesting to me were the mags and carbs and the week on propellers. The propellers that we were given tuition on were, Fairey, Rotol and de Havilland. The later were very good propellers but they were far more complicated.

I was now very much enjoying my most interesting life at Cosford. On most weekends I could obtain a thirty-six hour pass. This was from the Saturday lunch time until the Monday morning. By then you had to be present if you did not want to get AWL (absent without leave). At this time my girl friend had left her employment in Alderly Edge and had gone to live with her mother at Sale. Our relationship had started to become serious. On alternative weekends I would make my way north to see her or south to my home at Wickham Heath. Money was short and so I would always hitch-hike on my ways going, but I would only trust to the railways to get me back to camp in time. With the hitch-hiking, I would often map out different routes. This then gave me a chance to see a bit more of the country. Hitch hiking south was not that easy until I had got past Birmingham. I had a better chance of changing my routes when travelling north. As my girl friend was living in a small house, I would hop on a late bus into Manchester and stay the night in a YMCA hostel. I would then travel back to Sale on another bus early in the morning. This hostel was situated between a railway station and Piccadilly Square. Nearly every time that I made my way to it I would be accosted by prostitutes who would grab on to my arms. There was also a problem of getting off to sleep as the city trams would rattle on late into the night. They would also wake you up early in the mornings. It was not always prostitutes that accosted me. On one weekend I ran right out of luck while travelling south. I had reached Oxford and it had got very late. In those days, all of the traffic that was travelling south went through the city centre. I approached a chap as he came out of a pub and asked him if there was a service men's club in the city where I could dig in for the night. This lying git told me that his route home took him very close to one. I then tagged along with him and had walked quite a distance before it came to me that he had a touch of the gay gordons.

During the following winter months, England became gripped in severe arctic conditions. Many of the service camps became frozen up. Cosford became one of these. All of the huts, ablutions, workshops and cookhouses were fed with steam from large boiler houses. This severe weather proved too much for these steam systems to cope with and the whole place froze up with devastating results. It broke many lavatory pans and wash basins and it must have cost our government a small fortune in repairs. There was only one solution that our government came up with and this was to close these stations down and send all the service personnel home on freeze-up leave. Towards the ends of our freeze-up leaves we would tune our ears into the wireless set as many of these camps were being given extensions to the leave periods. My time came when I was to travel back to Cosford. I had got as far as Reading Railway Station when news reached me that Cosford had been given a leave extension. Due to this bad weather there were no buses running out to my home from Newbury, and so I legged it. I was back on Shanks's pony when the local squire, Mr R. (Toby) Sutton came along driving his ex-wartime jeep with his chauffeur sat by the side of him. The jeep pulled up and Toby offered me a ride in the back. Mr Roland (Toby) was a grand fellow but he had lacked discipline in his childhood and had been given several private tutors. Like many of the well-off gentry, he had become a little eccentric in his behaviour. You could not wish for a better bloke, but he still liked playing around while others of his age would put their hands at more serious things. Where most people might attend a function in a car, he more than likely might roll up driving a tractor. Having climbed on board, we first had to call at his house. He then promised to drive me all the way to my home. Chapel Road at Wickham Heath was well known for always getting completely blocked with snow when we had bad winter weather. He just had to try it. We soon became snow-bound well past the height of the headlamps.

We all jumped out into snow that was up to our waists and his chauffeur and I spent about a half hour while Toby thoroughly enjoyed digging his jeep out. I could have walked home quicker, but he did do as he promised, he drove me all the way home. After a terrific cost to our country, Cosford and all the other military stations were repaired. I then returned to complete my course.

Having completed stage one, we then had to tackle stage two. This was held on the other side of the railway on the airfield. This I found was to be the most interesting part of the course as we were now working on aeroplanes, even though they were never expected to fly. As plans had already been laid down for the starting of the next intake at a certain date, this part of our training was rushed and cut short. So much time had been lost due to all of that bad weather. Our route on to the airfield took us across a rail bridge. Had we had known it was there, then it might have saved us from having to have climbed two fences and have been chased by railway personnel. On the camp side of this bridge was dumped a complete unpainted airframe. It was a short nosed Bristol Blenheim Mk.I. Cosford also held courses for F.M.A.s (Flight Mechanic Airframes). This would have been one of their discarded instructional airframes that had been removed from their workshops. This made me wonder what other interesting airframes that may have been lurking away in some of their large sheds. If only that Blenheim could have survived and had been placed in the now, Cosford Museum.

In one of the training hangars were some Bristol Beaufighter Mk.Xs. Every week their engines were dismantled and then reassembled by a fresh lot of trainees. Our turn came and together we tackled the job. On completion, we then found that we had a problem. A quantity of nuts had got left over. While some of us were discussing what action we should take as we felt that we should not throw them away, one intelligent lad had solved the problem. He had removed several sparking plugs and had fed them down the plug holes, job done.

From the Monday to the Friday of each week we were kept hard at it while learning to become F.M.E.'s. On a Saturday morning we would start the day with a colour hoisting parade. After marching off we were handed over to the P.T.I.'s. This could be a trek over the assault course, a run around the roads, exercises in the gym or a combination of these items. On one of these Saturday mornings I was busy doing exercises in the gymnasium with the rest of our intake when I had a disaster. We were ordered to perform wheelbarrows. I became a wheelbarrow while another bod held my legs. Each wheelbarrow was told to try and knock down another wheelbarrow. This not being an easy task as when you remove one hand from the ground you tend to fall over yourself. One fellow walloped me on the upper arm in such a position that it gave me an acute muscular pain. A fresh order was given, to up on our feet and start another jumping exercise. I had started doing this, and that was the last that I remembered until I looked up to find that a P.T.I. was sitting on top of me and was pinning me to the concrete floor. The rest of the bods were forming a circle and the P.T.I. and poor old me were in the centre of it.

I was then told that I had just had an epileptic fit. If I had, then that P.T.I. should not have been pinning me down. I now know that I had fainted and in my mind I was still doing the exercise. I had passed out due to that pain and it had given me a pain as I now had a head ache where my head had walloped the concrete. Another lad was then detailed to escort me down to the station sick bay where I was to see the M.O. At the sick bay the M.O. then called me into his surgery and asked me what had happened. He then sent me back out and then called in my escort. This chap was then sent back to the gym and I was told to go back to my hut and lay on my bed for the rest of the day. Apart from a bit of a head ache and a bump on my bonse due to it being bounced on concrete I was feeling fine. My weekend pass had already been issued to me and it would have been a crying shame to have wasted it. As soon as 12 O'clock came, I was out of that gate and hitching a ride towards Newbury. Cosford being a very large station it had several mess-halls along with their cookhouses. Every so often one of these would be taken out of service for a spring clean. All of the airmen that had been using that mess would be diverted to what we called, The Cookhouse in the Woods. At the time of my down-fall, this cookhouse in the woods was where I had to go for my meals. It was such a long walk so early in the morning that I had skipped breakfast. This might also have been a contributing factor, but no way would I tell the M.O. that.

While working on the airfield it gave you the chance to look at aircraft as they flew over. It was now only a couple of years since the war ended and very many things still needed more time in which to get back to normal. B.E.A. (British European Airways) were having to make do with what aircraft that they could lay their hands on. They did have some Douglas Dakotas and the Vickers Vikings had yet to come into service. In order to make up their numbers they had got hold of some Junkers Ju.52/3m tri-motors and named them the 'Jupiter Class'. Whereas the Douglas Dakota had just served the Allies as a troop transporter, so the corrugated metal clad Junkers had served the Luftwaffe as their troop transporter. These Jupiter Class airliners became a common sight in the skies over Cosford. They then all carried large registration letters across and below over both wings. One of these was aptly registered G-AHOG.

Towards the ending of our course we had to do some engine run-ups on an old all night black Beaufighter Mk.I. This one still had the flat tailplane. No sooner had I sat down in the cockpit and they had me out again. Things were being rushed. We were scrubbed round doing various engine starting which should have included prop swinging and marshalling of aircraft. This was a pity as it could have been useful to us and would have been most interesting. All of this was due to the time that had been lost while the camp had been frozen up.

We all passed the course and there had been no failures. One or two had achieved extra high marks and were to be sent straight on to a fitters course where they could then become Fitter 2.E's. For this it meant another six months bind. I not being a regular was thankful that my markings had not been too high as I was looking forward to putting all of my training into practice. I was now looking forward to being posted to an operational squadron be it, fighters, bombers, transports or seaplanes. We had handed back our tool boxes and we were all stood on an end of course pay parade. At the same time we were all being given end of course leave when my name was called out. I was then ordered to fall-out and to stand to one side. A bunch of papers were handed to me and I was told that I had to report to the station hospital on the following morning.

Cosford's hospital was situated just across the other side of the road from the main gate. Once established, I then became an out- patient. I was allowed to wander out anywhere that I liked within reason. While hospitalised, I had to wear a white shirt with a red necktie. I palled up with a chiefy named Flight Sergeant Edwards. The weather was fine and together we would stroll out and visit various local places. One of our walks took us to the historic village of Boscobel. For this I have a date, it was on Thursday the 19th of June, 1947. Here we were to discover a bit of old English history. We walked to the 'Royal Oak', a tree in which it is said that King Charles II had safely hid in from Oliver Cromwell's men. There was a very old house called 'Boscobel House'. This ancient place was open to the public and so we had a guided tour where we were shown its secret panels. Well, they were secret once upon a time. There were passages to a chimney and an attic hiding place. I do not know if it was haunted, but it gave me that impression. There was also a nunnery that we walked to that Oliver had blown the roof off. Oh-boy, that man did do some destructive damage in his time.

Then came the day when I was provided with a rail warrant to go to London and back. I had to report to a large house that was owned by the Air Ministry. Here they gave me some E.E,G. Treatment. I once knew what these letters stood for, but I have since forgotten. I do know that one of the E's stood for Electrical. I had to sit in a cubical while lots of electric leads were positioned over my head. It felt as though they were placing me in an electric chair. They then made some tests on me and back to Cosford's hospital I went. I was then allowed to continue with my walk-abouts until my test results were sent from London. Much to my relief, I was then told that there was nothing wrong with me. It had been the only time in my life that someone had told me that I had had a fit. I was then discharged and sent off packing on my end of course leave.

With my leave over I then returned back to Cosford where once more I was placed into Pool Flight. All of those fellows that I had taken my course with I was never to see again. I was told that they had all been given overseas postings, but to where, I never found out. Due to my escapade in the gym, I was to receive a home posting. The closest that they could post me was to R.A.F. Colerne in Wiltshire. When I asked all the rest of the lads if they knew where it was, none of them knew. Several of them thought it to be in Northern Ireland. They all must have been dreaming of Colleens. As it turned out, it was just north-east of the City of Bath and high up on a plateau. It was also on the very north-west corner of Wiltshire in the stone wall Cotswold country.

Since then I have put the clock back by making visits to the Cosford Air Museum. This I first did with a Tiger Moth owner, Ted Lay and some of his friends. It was nice to walk around so many old aeroplanes. When I was stationed there I know that on the field there was Tiger Force Lancasters and there may have been some Lincolns. This I am not now sure about. Here in the museum they did have an Avro Lincoln. It was RF398 and the museum staff reckoned that it was haunted. We were told that things had moved around in that aircraft when the museum was closed. We were also told that several people had taken tumbles from it without hurting themselves. It had also been said that the temperature in certain parts of that aircraft had been colder than in any other part of the building. One of the staff thought that the restless spirit may have come from some wreckage of a Spitfire that was once placed under the Lincoln. Also here and was painted with the British civil registration G-AFAP was a Junkers Ju.52/3m. Both of these aircraft reminded me of Cosford as it was when I knew it. Try as hard as I could, but I was not able to picture the training hangars. Mind you, several decades had gone by since then. On crossing that railway bridge and looking through the rear gate the wooden huts looked just the same as I had remembered them. Long gone was that shining metal Blenheim Mk.I, but I could still picture it there. Since my visit I have now been told that all of these wooden buildings have now been replaced with new brick built buildings.

My mother and my wife in the snow, Chapel Road, Wickham Heath

The Royal Oak and a Jupiter Class

Boscobel House

Cosford's huts. Seen from the rear gate

A FULLY FLEDGED ERK

The first thing that I noticed as the train was making its way south towards Bath was the red hop leaf pub signs of the Simmonds beer houses. These signs being local to my home, and displayed on the 'Nag's Head' at Stockcross. I had been posted to No. 39 M.U. (Maintenance Unit) which belonged to No. 41 Group. It was generally know as a Spitfire M.U. as it handled more Spitfires than any other type. This was a maintenance unit and not a squadron, but there was nothing that I could do about that. Having arrived at Bath Station I was to find that the aerodrome was some distance out from Bath City and that it was situated on a plateau at the top of a very long steep hill. This hill was known as Banner Down and it was on the north-east side of the city. There were two maintenance units in residence. These were No.39 and No.49. Reporting to the station HQ, they informed me that I was to be placed on the roll-call of 'Prod B' hangar. The Prod standing for Production. I was to be billeted in a hut on the satellite camp at Thickwood. For my journeys to and fro I was to report to the station cycle store and draw for myself a pushbike. Such was the state of affairs that I was forced to take a WAAF machine, or else walk. I plumped for that WAAF machine. This old bone shaker was to get me around where ever I wanted to go. This included trips out to local pubs. Being a ladys mount it was very low geared and was to prove useful when negotiating the many steep hills that were local in that part of the country. Every road that led to Colerne and Thickwood necessitated climbing at least one steep hill. The only pub that there was, with a ride on the flat, was the 'Six Bells' in Colerne village. To us erks, it was always referred to as 'The Clangers'.

Being a country born boy, I settled in at Thickwood like a duck taking to water. Or should I say, like a pigeon taking to a wood. No more bull, well not the kind that I had been use to. It became a far more relaxed life than what the other erks were living on the main camp. These chaps were living in centrally heated 'H' block two storey brick barracks. We even had our own small NAAFI that we could cycle to. None of us seemed to bother with girls, not that there were any local ones. But if you had found one, nobody would have stopped you from bringing her back to the hut. Of course, you would have had to share her with the rest of the blokes. Now that I was here, I was too far south to be able to make any journeys up country to Sale. Thickwood was just a small encampment that was situated amongst the dry stone walls and it was over a couple of miles away from the main station. I now became a country airman. It was not all honey though. One could often get very wet and cold and you had to make that bike ride before you could eat your breakfast. In times of poor weather you then had to re-clean your boots before you went on parade. All of this we took in our stride and we would never consider swapping with any of the bods that were living on main camp.

Production 'B' Hangar stood next door to another hanger which was Production 'A'. Between the two there was a tarmac taxi-way and each hangar had a concrete apron. When all of the hangar doors were fully opened you could then see into each hangar. Both of these hangars were close to the side of the old Roman road that was known as the Foss Way. In the Roman days, this road ran between the City of Bath and the City of Lincoln. This Foss Way just clipped the north-western side of the airfield. Every time that one of our kites flew it had to taxi for a short distance along this ancient roadway. This same road was also used when- ever we pushed a Spitfire to the firing butts. It also had to be crossed each time that a compass was swung. If the armourers wished to take the fighter to the butts we would have to stop working on it. Us engine and airframe wallers were then needed to help push the kite there. It was while the cannons were being fired on the butts that I had been asked to push the button that fired them while the armourers had been busy out on the wings. Not many people can claim to have fired the guns of a Spitfire, but at the time that I did, I did not give it a second thought. It was just another job that I was expected to do.

Production 'B' was basically a Spitfire hangar. The only aircraft that were worked on inside that hangar while I was there were Spitfires. On the east side in the hangar were a row of double staged Merlin engine Spitfires. On the opposite side the row of Spitfires were divided between Merlin powered and the Rolls-Royce Griffon engine Mk.XIVs. In the top left hand corner there was always placed a Mk.IX which we could rob for spare parts. These aircraft were dubbed as 'Christmas Trees'. In the side annexe to the hangar behind the row of Merlin engine Spit's there were stored many wooden wings. These would have come off of Miles Masters or Martinets, or both. I never did get to know where the rest of those aircraft were stored. I expect that they were around in some other hangar on the station. On the opposite side being the west side, the hangar had an out-building. I believe there was a boiler, though in the winter it got damn cold. There was Chiefy's den, the hangar office, the ablutions and the bonded stores. I was to be kept strictly working on the Merlin engine Spit's. Most of them were Mk.IXs, but occasionally a Mk.VIII or a Mk.XVI would join the row. The only times that I had anything to do with the Mk.XIVs was when a loud cry of Two-Six was given. If I was not doing a job in which I could not leave, then I would be expected to help in pushing it to where ever it had to go. The only time that I did have anything to do with Griffon engine Spits was at the ending of my service. A row of Spitfire F.22's were placed half way down the centre of the hangar. These had to have their wings removed as they were to be sent elsewhere by road for some mod to be carried out on them. We had to bend our backs under them to take the weight as the airframe wallers removed them. Coolant pipes were cut through and boy, were those wings heavy. We then got to hear that these mods had already been done. Someone had slipped up. These trestle Mk.22s which were in the PK serial range and they were still in the centre of the hangar when I left.

All of these weary war-worn fighters had been flown into this MU. Many had been delivered by A.T.A. (Air Transport Auxiliary) pilots. These were a mixture of men and women who were often referred to as 'Anything to Anywhere' or, 'Ancient Tired Airmen'. Now that they were at Colerne, they had been placed in out-door storage. Their engines had been inhibited and all over they had been sprayed in a thick lanolin. Their cowlings had been taped up to try and keep the rain water and dampness from getting in. We did not make or assemble any Spitfires, the meaning of the word Production being quite different. My job here at Colerne was to help in making these old fighters airworthy again. When made airworthy, they were then sold off to overseas foreign air forces and so to help our government recoup back to the treasurer a little of the large losses that had incurred during the war. I did once find a double U2 battery size torch that was designed to clip on to a waist belt. Unfortunately it was of little use as it had rusted solid. It had been on the top of the engine and would have most likely have been there when the aircraft was flown in. This then proved to me that a vast amount of dampness had managed to get under those cowlings.

Now back in the hangar they had to be inspected by the U.I.D. (Unit Inspection Department). They would then consider all of the jobs that were needed doing to them. At the same time they would take in to account the number of hours that the aircraft had flown since its last major inspection. All of these jobs that were in need of doing were then written down on a form that was known as the 1860. As each erk completed a job he would then sign against it on this form. This would then be countersigned as being inspected by an N.C.O. (non Commissioned Officer).

After each aircraft had had its 1860 completed being fully signed up and having past its engine ground running, it would then be air tested. Finally, it would be sprayed over in a mat camouflage scheme. The upper surfaces being a grey and dark green, while the under surfaces being all grey. Whichever country that it was being sold to it would then be given its appropriate markings, but it would retain its RAF serial on each side at the rear of the fuselage. Each aircraft was given yellow to its outer wing leading edges. During the time that I was there, most of the Mk.IXs were sold to Turkey. A few of the others went to Denmark, Holland and South Africa. All of the Griffon powered Mk.XIVs went to Belgium. These had the teardrop type canopy, but there was one odd one. This was RM802, it had the early hood with built up rear fuselage. These Mk.XIVs looked very impressive with their five bladed Rotol props. Their engines were always started up by using a Coffman cartridge starter. All of the Spitfire Mk.IXs that left us for Turkey had their wings clipped and they were fitted with under wing bomb release gear. For their ferry flights they were fitted with belly slipper tanks that would give them a greater range. I once had a list of all of the aircraft that I had worked on. Over the years this has got lost. There is a possibility that some of these Spitfires may have since been restored and have been brought back to this country and are flying today.

Nearly every Saturday morning we would start our day with a colour hoisting parade. After this we would clean up around the camp, but if work had got beyond schedule, then it was back to the hangar. As a rule, come mid day and the rest of the weekend was our own until being present at the Monday morning hangar roll call. Down close to the apron where we paraded stood a couple of Avro Lancastrians in out-door storage. One of these was VL969. Later these two were taken out of storage and sold. No 49 MU dabbled in these and one of them did depart Colerne wearing very crude civil registration letters. One day I had a chance to nose into one of the grass covered blister hangars. It was chocker-block with Tiger Moths minus their wings. Each one was camouflaged and they stood on their wheels with their noses on the floor and their tails high in the air. They completely filled that hangar and I do not know where their wings would have been stored. I would make a guess that most of these would have eventually have found their ways on to the civil market.

On the northern side of the station was No 49 MU. I never did get over there to see what they got up to. On rare occasions they would fly a Lancastrian or a Mosquito. Every time that one of their aircraft flew it had a long way to go before it got to the flying field proper. Their test pilot would half fly and half taxi the aircraft over some of this distance. On walking or cycling up from main camp to our hangar one would pass several rows of stored war-worn Lancasters all parked nose to tail. You then crossed an open grass area. Should you hear a roar of aero engines, then it was as well to take a good look, as a Mosquito might be heading in your direction with its tail in the air.

Towards the Marshfield side of the aerodrome was a large long area which was generally spoken of as, 'Down the Field'. Here there were rows and rows of Spitfires in open air storage. Among them was the odd early one. One of these was P7350, a Mk.IIa and she now serves with the R.A.F. Battle of Britain Memorial Flight. She is the only flying survivor that took part in the Battle of Britain. As the oldest airworthy Spitfire in the world it is now thought that she was the 14th Spitfire built at Castle Bromwich, Birmingham and would have been flight tested by Alex Henshaw. During that famous battle she served with No 266 and No 603 Squadrons. Due to combat with a Messerchmitt Bf 109 she was forced to crash land. I believe that the repaired bullet holes can still be seen. She was rebuilt and flown into No 37 MU on the 15th of November 1940. This being only three weeks after her crash landing. From here she was to serve with No 64 Squadron and the Central Gunnery School. She then went to No. 57 O.T.U. and from here she was flown into No. 39 MU where she was then relegated into outdoor open air storage down the field. The R.A.F. then sold her to Messrs John Dale, Ltd. They had the foresight, and immediately gave her back to the R.A.F. so to be placed in an air museum which was housed on Colerne station. Here she was painted in a poor paint scheme and I once photographed her on a Battle of Britain open day. Eventually she was restored back to airworthiness and became G-AWIJ on the British civil register. Going to Duxford she became a movie star in the well known film, 'The Battle of Britain'. After her completion of filming she was presented to the R.AF's B.B.M.F. (Battle of Britain Memorial Flight). Another Mk.II down the field was P7490. This old girl was left in a rather poor state with her cockpit hood open. I must confess that I helped myself to her engine data card. This black paper card I still have. Down this field there was a Spitfire Mk.VII which had very pointed wing tips for high altitude flying. Standing close to this was a Miles Martinet Mk.I. The Spitfire was MD107 and the Martinet was JN435 and coded QK-6. This I know because I photographed them both.

On the south-west side of the airfield it had become a grave yard of Lancaster bombers. They had all made their last flights into Colerne and they were parked around the edge of the airfield awaiting their fate. All of them were Merlin powered. Many of them had faithfully brought their crews home from over enemy territory, and perhaps with wounded or dead on board. Below their cockpits they carried their operational displays. A painted bomb for every trip that they had made over enemy territory. Those of their crews that had survived were now most likely in civy street as their old aircraft stood here awaiting the scrap-man's torch. Most of them were in bomber black, but mixed in with them were some that had been painted in the white and black Tiger Force colours. Some other Lancasters which were just stood around were mat white all over while others from Coastal Command were painted in sea grey, green and pinkish tones. In the far south-west corner of the airfield where the village and the Foss Way roads met, a contractors firm was busy cutting up these old girls. One day they had a mishap and all the fire engines rushed off to give them assistance. A young lad had flicked a fag-end and it had landed on or in a petrol tank which had been lined up along with others. I expect that after this he would have been a lot more careful.

For some reason, we had become short of nuts for screwing down the cam covers on our Merlin engines. These nuts were a quarter inch B.S.F. (British Standard Fine). Two of us were detailed to cycle round the airfield and to try and obtain some of these nuts from one of these Lancs. It was no good taking them from Packard built Merlins, they had to come from British built engines. I have now forgotten how we climbed up to these engines, but we must have managed it by walking up inside of the fuselage. We then had to remove the top cowlings but I do know that we succeeded in obtaining these nuts. In many of these old birds the fuselages were strewn with old maps. Search as I did, not one of them was of England. All of them were of foreign soil. On looking back, I now wished that I had pocketed a few of them.

Our neighbouring hangar, Prod 'A' also worked on a few Spitfire Mk.IXs. One of theirs was BS125 as it formed a background for one of my photographs. This old Spit would most likely have started its flying career as a Mk.V and at a later date to have been converted into a Mk.IX. For my photography I had bought myself a 127 Kodak vest-pocket camera. This fitted into my tunic pocket. Film was nearly as scarce as rabbits eggs. I had got to know a photographic shop down in Bath. He had obtained some ex R.A.F. panchromatic film. With this he reloaded spools for me. Sometimes I achieved some good pictures and other times, not so good. It was a gamble that I had to take. Prod 'A' also turned out the occasional Lancaster. One of those was RE187 as I photographed another erk standing by its tail. Film was then in very short supply and I found it most difficult to take photographs of aircraft. Just as soon as I got my camera out, other airmen would rush in hoping to be on the photograph. I would then have a photograph of a lot of bods with hardly any aeroplane. Prod 'A' hangar carried out a lot of work in preparing the then new silver-grey Gloster Meteor F. Mk.IVs ready for entry into squadron service.

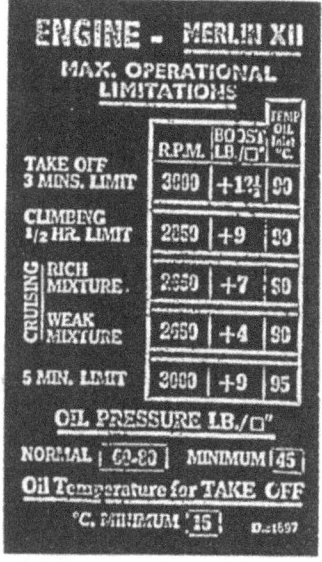

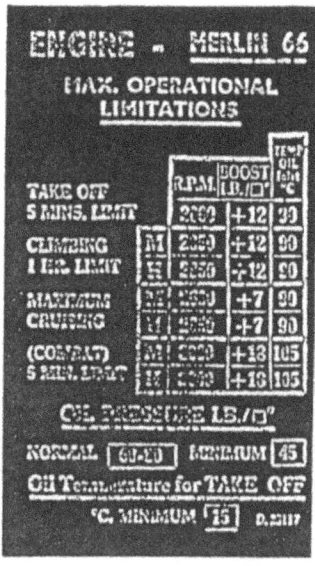

The original cards were from the following

1. SPITFIRE Mk II.   P7490.
2. SPITFIRE Mk IX.   NH539.
3. SPITFIRE Mk XIV.
   May have come out of MV378.

The Marks IX and XIV cards were changed as they were conssidered dirty. P7490 probably got broken up for scrap.

A set of three engine data cards as were placed in Spitfire cockpits

Our test pilots name was White. I have now forgotten what rank he held, but we erks had dubbed him as Chalkie. Not to his face mind. He did not get to fly that often, but when he did he made sure that he enjoyed himself. I am not sure, but he may have flown for No 49 MU as well. When ground running an engine, in order to test it, our Spits were always bolted down to metal eyes in the concrete aprons that were provided for this purpose. By using s special strap that passed over the small rear of the fuselage it held the tail down. From this rear anchorage a special harness went under the aircraft to secure and chock the front wheels. Whenever an air test was flown, the aircraft was made ready for the pilot and normal chocks were used. During the run-up, several airmen would be detailed to lay over the tailplane in order to hold it down. This was far from being a pleasant job and it was to be avoided if at all possible. I became one of the unfortunate that was laying with my tummy over the tailplane and trying to kiss the port elevator while Chalkie was pushing his throttle through the gate with my back to the slipstream. Up came the tail and the R.A.F. had me airborne for the only time in which I served with them. My toes were leaving the ground and I thought to myself, this is it. I expected to be blown under with my head denting the concrete. Fortunately for us on the tail, the bod with the fire extinguisher waggled his aileron vigorously and Chalkie pulled back on his knob. If he had not done this, then the Spit would have nosed over and bits of propeller would has flown for miles. That is, if it had not jumped the chocks. It has never ceased to amaze me how a tail could lift so while being blanketed by human bodies. Having completed his air test and giving us a zoom low down by the side of the hangar he then came in and landed. We met him as he got to the Foss Way and then escorted him back to the hangar. 'Flies like a bird', he said. Although we erks had to keep our thoughts to ourselves, we all agreed that he nearly took off like one as well. Chalkie then handed me his parachute and instructed me to place it on the wing and close to the cockpit of next doors Meteor F Mk.IV, RA441. Which was parked out on the grass while he popped into Chiefy's den to sign up the Spits paper work.

Chalkie then took to the air in the Meteor. This time it did not take off like a bird, but neither did it land like one. He flew around for a while and all looked well until he was making his landing. He made his approach and lowered the flaps. These worked alright as they were worked by a hydraulic system. Having touched down he then had a brake failure. The brakes on the Meteor were operated by compressed air from a bottle in the fuselage. This should have been kept fully charged by a Heywood air compressor which was driven via a shaft through the main spar from off of the port engine. But something had gone wrong. As the end of the runway drew near, Chalkie then took action by leaving the runway in a wide sweep across the grass to port. His starboard wing then removed a length of chestnut fencing and at the same time the right wheel left a mark only six inches from a sheer drop which was a cut-out layby where the Bath buses stopped. Having just negotiated this hazard he brought the Meteor to rest with the front of the fighter sticking through a low hawthorn hedge. Surprisingly, very little damage was done to the Meteor. Chalkie had then got out of his cockpit and was standing looking at the aircraft when the C.O (Commanding Officer of the station) pulled up in his car. This then set a wave of ripples in motion as the crash crew who were on duty at the other end of the runway never turned up to offer him their assistance. They had watched him landing and then they had lost sight of him due to a humped brow in the centre of the runway. They had thought that he had made a normal landing. The C.O. was not so amused. I was later to take-off from this same runway in a Handley Page Hastings, but more on this in another chapter.

Produce my camera and the erks would clamber for a snap shot

The only time that I became airbourne whilst in the R.A.F.

One day we at Prod 'B' had a failure while one of our Mk.IXs was having an air test. Having got into the air the engine temperature gauge went off the clock. Chalkie made a half circuit and brought it back in. Jock with his David Brown tractor was sent out to the middle of the airfield to retrieve it. The trouble was traced to a thermostat that had gone u/s (unserviceable) which was down in the port wing root. Little things like this could happen and the trouble had not shown up on the ground running. Well, that is what air tests were for. A rumour then circulated around the hangar that one of our Spitfires had crashed at Blackbushe. Many of us had signed up after doing jobs on it and so the news gave us funny feelings. Later we were to learn that the ferry pilot had come in to land with his brakes full on. Whatever happened after I do not know, but we never saw that Spitfire again.

Come most weekends I would make my way home to Wickham Heath. It was impossible to travel up country as the distance was too great. My relationship had grown too serious with that girl and I was trying hard to cool it down. I was still writing her letters and at the same time trying not to make them so lovey-dovey. It was a shame as I had become very fond of that girl, but life as it was became very wrong. There was no way that I could afford to marry her and I was not yet ready for marriage. Eventually I would get demobed (demobilized) and the last thing that I would wish to do was to live in the City of Manchester. She was now living with her mother having not got a father and I was looking forward to living back in the countryside. At the same time, she should have been enjoying her young life and not brooding over me. It had become a very difficult situation.

Travelling to and fro from home at weekends was proving difficult to say the least. Although I had been granted a home posting, rail services between Newbury and Bath were poor and busses would not link up. I was also faced with no transport that could take me between Newbury and Wickham Heath. I tried hitch-hiking, but this was no good. There were so many other servicemen on the roads from Melksham, Compton Bassett and Yatesbury that it completely dogged all of my chances of getting lifts. Also it was a much harder job when I had to make my return journey. From Colerne each week, there was a special London bus. I could only use this if they had failed to fill it up. I would then only pay half of the full fare. In order to get back to camp I then had to walk a mile or so down a lonely road during the early hours of the morning. I finally solved all of these problems by using my own cycle.

A little cycle mileometer fixed on my front wheel spindle told me that the distance from the hangar doors to my home via Ford and Chippenham was exactly forty-five miles each way. It was far longer when on most weekends I would cycle first into Bath in order to obtain my films and photographs. On my way home I always made a stop for lunch at the White Horse Cafe at Cherhill. Returning back to camp would have me jumping out of bed at a quarter to three in the morning and then on to my pushbike. On some of my journeys back to Colerne I had been faced with strong westerly winds and on one night it was a gale force wind facing me all of the way. There were times when I could nearly go to sleep while riding a pedal cycle. On another night I was forced to ride the Marlborough Downs in a thunderstorm. It was far from pleasant being the only person around for miles on a metal bike. From the time that I left home I had been watching this thunderstorm creeping closer as I made my way up through Savernake Forest. Having travelled several miles west of Marlborough there was one almighty bang with instant lightning. I had reached a metal telephone kiosk and I slung my bike down and took refuge in it. Having waited for five to ten minutes I was to see no more lightning. It had been like watching a firework display that had ended up with a colossal bang. On one of my returns I had to stop and mend a puncture. Fortunately the moon was up. I did not carry tyre levers, instead I carried my eating irons, knife, fork and spoon. With these I was then ready for a breakfast in the mess if I could reach camp in time. These eating irons then doubled up for tyre levers. On the weekend of my puncture, I had forgotten to bring them. I was forced to improvise. I kept a kitbag D-handle with a lock around my saddle pillar. This I used to keep my bike locked safe when on main camp. By using this D-handle I managed to remove my tyre and mend that very fast puncture.

Returning back on one weekend the bulb had blown in my lamp. On most of my journeys back I would ride without using any lights. This was because it reduced the drag that my dynamo gave as it operated from the side of my rear tyre. Late Sundays and early Mondays there was very little traffic on the roads. Roads were then narrower and far more twisty and the lights and sound of a vehicle could be detected long before it reached you. I would only light up as I cycled through the towns. In the centre of Calne I was always stopped and challenged by a policeman. I never got to see the same bobby twice. This night he tried to pull me because I had no lamp, a bulb had blown. In the end I got him to relent, but he told me, if I got stopped again in Chippenham, then it was working when I had left him. I always had to be back for the hangar roll call and I never failed to make it. By now, we Thickwood erks had been forced to move on to main camp. I seldom had time to call in at Thickwood and so it made no difference. We soon got use to the comfort of the H-blocks. No more of that messing about with coke stoves. I had handed back to the cycle store my faithful WAAF bone shaker and I now used my own cycle between the billets, the mess and the hangar.

We did have our little hangar mishaps. One chanced to happen as we were nearing the end of a working day. Most of the erks had crawled into their little private holes as the hangar had gone quite quiet. I was sat on the starboard wing up against the fuselage with my legs hanging down over the leading edge and doing not much more than nattering. To the front of me and placed by the side of the engine was a steel stepladder. Standing on one of the bottom steps and facing me was an erk named Money and he should not have been there. Settled comfortably seated on the top of these steps was an engine bod named Colin Orchard. That was his name if my memory serves me right. Colin was busy telling us on how he flew Fairchild Argus and some Tipsy B.2's on some of his weekends. As he did so, he rested his right elbow on the starboard cam cover. To my surprise, the nose of the aircraft started to sink downwards. Had we have had the gumption, we could have jumped down and stopped it. I regret that this we did not have. We were that dumb struck that we just continued to watch it happen. Within seconds the steps got buckled as the spinner continued to make its way towards the hangar floor. The aircraft then came to rest on two of its four blades of the Rotol propeller. I think that the name Rotol came from the first part of Rolls-Royce and the last part of Bristol. No longer could I remain seated and so I was tipped off of the wing and came to rest on my own two feet. I cannot remember what happened to Money, but as the steps collapsed they took Colin with them. On picking ourselves up we were most astonished to find that the hangar was no longer quiet. None of us were hurt and around the kite was a ring of bods with chiefy Sadler pushing his way through them and making his way to us.

The riggers had trestled the Spit and had failed to put the correct number of round washer type weights that they had tied around the rear of the fuselage. The riggers tried very hard to blame us, but it had been their fault for not correctly trestling the aircraft properly. We then blamed them. The Spitfire had tilted on a couple of ball type jacks which fitted into sockets under the wings. Fortunately for all of us, the Spit had stayed on these jacks as the undercarriage was in the retracted position. Normally we engine bods were busy with our own jobs and we did not pay too much attention as to what the airframe boys were up to. The tail had gone up into the hangar roof. A rope was found and then slung over the tail and the fighter was returned back to its even keel. Both of the propeller blades had bent right round without snapping and they had prevented the kite from leaving the trestles. The only damage was to the prop which now had two slightly curved blades. The U.I.D. kindly said that it was u/s anyhow and that it had to be changed. Certainly, after this there was no doubting its lack of serviceability. In other words, there had been a hush up, though it could have been very nasty indeed.

Should we have decided to go into a town, then it was into Bath City. To return back to the aerodrome the long winding steep hill of Banner Down had to be negotiated. I have never been one for bricks and mortar, but if there was one city that I grew to like, then it was Bath. It is now a tourist attraction and people visit it from all over the world to see its Abbey and the Roman hot springs. It is a very beautiful city with its centre in a hollow and its many streets set on hills. It has old mellow stonework that is mixed in with the greenery of many trees. At night, it can be viewed from above from the many surrounding hills. The stone, the greenery and the street lighting give it a charm which is all of its own.

The city ran a fleet of old pre-war Bristol single deck buses. Very few buses had been built since the war except for a small number of utilities. These had mainly been single deck Bedfords. Bath's buses had aged and had seen a lot of hard work being that they had operated in very hilly country. One night there were so many of us airmen waiting to get back on the last bus that the company were forced into providing a relief. Both of these buses became over filled. As ours moved out of the bus terminal it became clear that ours was suffering with a very sick engine. Not all of its pots were functioning properly. I did not expect it to get up Banner Down and from there on we would be forced to walk. To my utter astonishment we got about a quarter of the way up there before it conked. It was then that the other bus passed us and all the bods on it were cheering us like mad. Our driver was not to be beaten as he placed it in reverse and restarted the engine. Then he let it build up all the revs that it could muster and let go the clutch. This way we made quite a few yards before it stopped again. Many many times he repeated this trick and eventually we limped over the crest of that long hill. A little further along the road and we passed the other bus that had also broken down. Further along the road were its passengers that were all footing it

Back to camp. Now it was our turn to cheer, and boy, we gave them a loud one. This episode must have played hell with the clutch. It did not say much for Bath's transport and in those days there was no M.O.T testing. It made one wonder just how safe that those buses really were. If they were not that likely to go, then how likely would they be in being able to stop.

The first Spitfire that I worked on was a Mk.IX, MA592. One of the jobs that I had to do was to tighten the large retaining nut that kept the propeller on. This on the morning after the night before. This required heaving on a very long and large spanner. Every time that I heaved, then so did my stomach. Thanks to a chap named Meadwell who kindly heaved for me so that the propeller was fitted nice and tight. Strange as it may seem, this was probably the last one that I worked on and it was partly due to me. I had removed the flame traps to wash them out as I had been instructed. It was then found that the stores did not hold any special tab washers for replacing them. I was not allowed to use the old ones and so the Spit was sheeted and placed outside the hangar. These washers were ordered but they took many months to arrive. Now that they had arrived, I then commenced working on it. Well if it was not the last, then it was one of the last. This Spitfire was sold to South Africa and it was given orange centres to its roundels. If it had served with the S.A.A.F. (South African Air Force) for another couple of years, then these centres would have been replaced with orange springboks.

Mk188 is towed away for a compass swing. It had served with No.64 Squadron as SH-R

The hanger nosedive

There then came a time when some bright spark gave us all individual jobs to do. Prior to this, each person would do all the jobs that needed doing on a single Spit. There may have been two of you at it depending what needed doing. Each person was given his one particular job to do. As soon as he had completed it on one aeroplane then he would move on to the next. As some jobs took longer than others, I thought it to be a very poor system. The job that was given to me was to renew all the clips and hoses on the coolant system. I then had to replenish it with fresh ethylene glycol of a 30/70 mixture. It was during the winter months and it was a sod-of-a-job. Our hangar doors faced north and south and at times the wind would whistle straight through one door and out of the other. Often I had to lay on my back on the cold concrete floor for hours on end. First I had to remove the plates from inside at the tops of the radiator covers. Then one had to grope with arms into places where they were'nt made to fit. By the use of the screwdriver I removed the old rusty Jubilee type clips and prised off the old hoses. This then let cold stagnant fluid run down your sleeve. Then you had to replace these items with new ones. What you really required was a set of long thin arms that would bend in the middle.

Our engines were started with the use of a trolly-ack. This was a two wheeled hand cart which contained charged up batteries. A lead from this had to be plugged into the starboard side of the engine. When one got the thumbs up from the bod in the cockpit, you then pressed on a button on the trolly-ack. Having got the engine turning over, you then walked up between the wing and the revolving prop to remove the plug and its lead. The first time that our engines were run it would require numerous strokes by the chappie in the cokpit on the ki-gas priming pump. The engines would not run properly until all of the inhibitor had been burnt out of them. Until this had been done it made for bad starting. With either an exhaust or a carburettor fire occurring, the drill was to keep bashing away until the engine started. This way you would either suck the flames in, or blow them out. The result of this was dirty red flames burning from the exhaust stubs and they were not that far from the uncowled fuel tanks where one sat on the top of the other. With one eye on the extinguisher and the other on those flames you would hope that you never had to use it. As it happened, we never had to use an extinguisher on an engine fire.

We had got over this stage of events and my sergeant, Sergeant May was sat in the cockpit giving the engine some gun while I was stood with the extinguisher at the wing tip. I was surprised to see what I thought was white smoke coming from close below the fuel tanks. Grabbing the fire extinguisher and shaking the aileron all at the same time, I was thinking that's funny, smoke should be black. I then noticed milk coloured liquid running along the ground. As my sergeant shut the engine down, so the cockpit became engulfed in steam. One of my hoses had blown. I then expected to get a rollicking, but all he said to me was, 'get on and replace it, this is why we ground run so that any faults will show up now and not in the air'. I have since wondered if this might have been that same aircraft that had had that failed thermostat while on its air test. When testing a fuel system, any leak would require draining the tanks. This 100 octane was not used in the aircraft again. It got used up by swilling it over the engines to remove the sprayed on red lanolin. Thinking about it now, this had been a risky business as one spark could have caused a hangar fire. We just did as we were told and never gave it a second thought. The hangar electrics were far from perfect as I found out for myself. On the walls of the hangar were some handles where one could wind down some multi-electric plugs. The floor of the hangar was wet with condensation when I went to plug a wander lead in. The shock that I got nearly knocked me off my feet.

One duty that we could not help being roped in for was the station security patrol. This duty was patrolling the airfield throughout the night. We had in charge of us a duty sergeant who would send us out on bicycles in pairs. I am not sure now, but I believe they armed us with a truncheon and a whistle. If it was not these, then it certainly was'nt firearms. We were given several hours of patrolling and several hours break. There was no NAAFI breaks at these late hours. About half way around the peri-track (perimeter aircraft taxi-way) there was a discarded fuselage from a General Aircraft Hotspur training glider that had a serial on it in the BT range. This then became known to us all. It made an ideal place in which to catch up with a bit of shut eye. One could only do this while the other bod was keeping guard. Well any way, who would be daft enough to try and steel an old Lancaster that was up for the chop. Should we hear or see anything that looked a bit suspicious, then we would be off to investigate, or run the opposite way. On the other hand, should we see lights of an oncoming vehicle, we would then both wake up and cycle off in different directions as it could well be the duty officer. One night we did have some fun. The officers mess had thrown a party and a wagon load of females had been guests to this party. They had got themselves pee'd up to their eyebrows. They had set out in the wrong direction and were circling the peri-track and could not get off of it. Between us we had the delight in arresting them. To be truthful, to be alone amongst all of those old Lancs in the dead of night was quite eerier. With the bit of wind, some of them tended to creak. Many of them may have returned bringing dead airmen back with them.

Later this duty got stopped and we lost no sleep over this. They replaced us with S.P. (Special Police) dog handlers. And I for, one would not then had wished to have gone roaming on that airfield at night. It was around this time that we had a few WAAF's posted to our hangar. As they were all fabric bashers and the only fabric on our Spits was on some of the control surfaces, they got put in the hangar stores. I for one enjoyed chatting up a nice one, but I never got around to dating her. We only had them for a very short time. As there was nothing much that they could do, it would have been for them just to spend their time until they had got fresh postings through.

During my time with Prod 'B', the only other aircraft that we had other than Spits was a Lancaster. This was a late one being TW923. It sat on the grass to the front of the hangar. There was no room for it inside as the Spits took up all of the floor space. I did do a job on its inner port engine, just enough to place my signature on the Lancs 1860. As all of our Spitfires only had one seat and Chalkie claimed this, we erks never got a chance to fly. Our Lanc only made the one test flight before it left us. This was on a Friday afternoon. Most of the N.C.O.'s had found themselves a place on board including my old friend Corporal Robins. Robbie was one of the old school and together we got on like a house on fire. In those days a pound was a pound and each week Robbie would always borrow a pound note off of me without fail. He just could not sort himself out, but he never failed to pay me it back. I would then place it on one side in my wallet ready for him to borrow on the next week. This he would use for his coach fare to London. He was like a person that must keep his clock ten minutes fast so that he would not be late for work. In return he would loan me kit on kit inspections and would often do me other small favours. For a ride in that Lanc, he was not able to help me with. We erks did have the last laugh on them, Some local fog came down and our Lanc was diverted away to another station This then stopped our N.C.O.'s from getting away on that weekend. While on the subject of N.C.O.'s, we did have one sergeant who got posted to us who was very short and tubby. He was that short that he could stand up in the wheel well of a Spitfire. Like those WAAF's, he also did not stay with us for long.

One day I was instructed to go before an officer. He then informed me that I had been selected to attend a fortnight course at the de Havilland propeller factory at Lostock near Bolton in Lancashire. I argued that I did not think that it would be of any help to me, or to them, and perhaps I should not go. He then told me that I was being sent and that was the end of the matter. I knew from when I had my F.M.E.'s course that D.H. props were very complicated. As it turned out, it was the best fortnight that I had in my whole R.A.F. service.

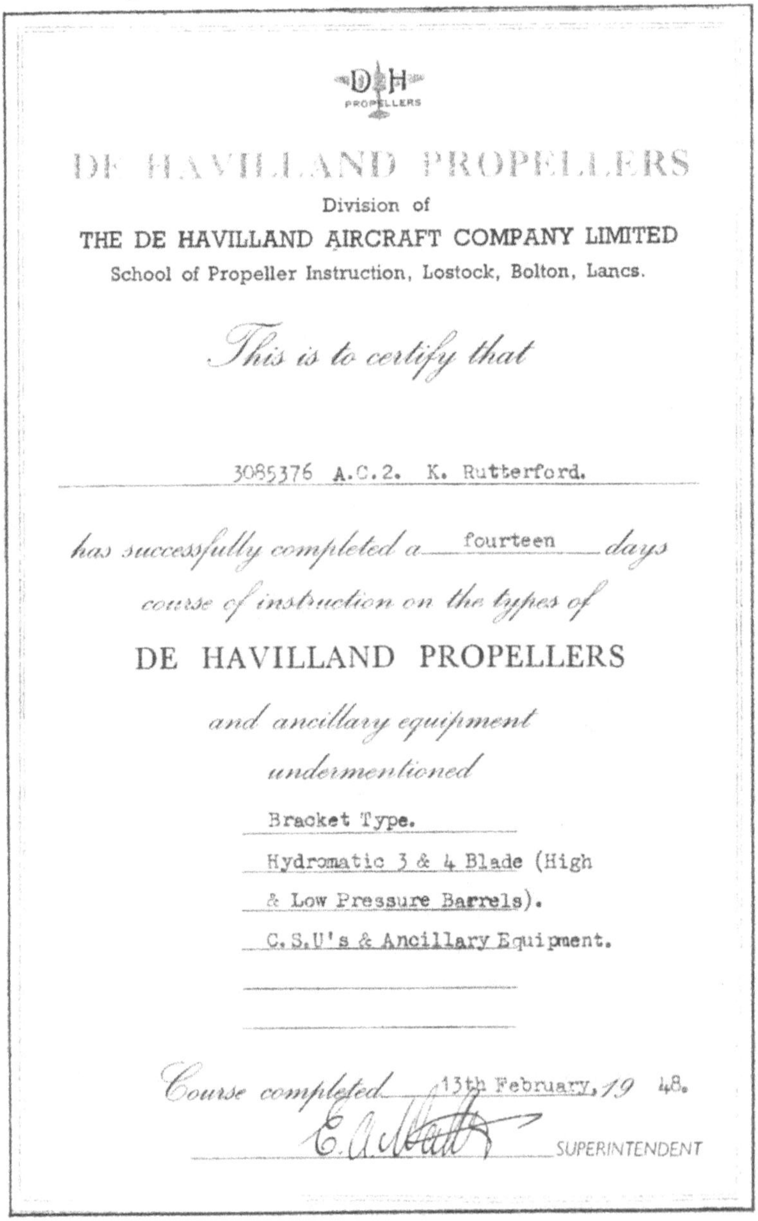

DE HAVILLAND PROPELLERS
Division of
THE DE HAVILLAND AIRCRAFT COMPANY LIMITED
School of Propeller Instruction, Lostock, Bolton, Lancs.

This is to certify that

3085376 A.C.2. K. Rutterford.

has successfully completed a fourteen days course of instruction on the types of

DE HAVILLAND PROPELLERS

and ancillary equipment undermentioned

Bracket Type.
Hydromatic 3 & 4 Blade (High & Low Pressure Barrels).
C.S.U's & Ancillary Equipment.

Course completed 13th February, 19 48.

SUPERINTENDENT

My very proud certificate

Spitfire Mk IX MA592

Spitfore Mk IX NH539

Lancaster TW923

While on this course I was to spend my 20th birthday. The de Havilland Propeller Instructional School was held at their Lancashire factory. I was billeted along with some other R.A.F. personnel in a civy hostel which was named, 'Highways Hostel'. This was in Euxton, Lancashire. To get to Lostock we had to make a double bus journey each day on the Ribble Transport. The food was very good at the factory and at the hostel and we did not go short. The mid weekend came and I had prepared to go to Blackpool along with the others. On going into the hostel, I was handed a phone number and was instructed to ring it. It was my old girl friend and I must have mentioned that I was going on this course in one of my letters. She had been ringing around Lancashire until she had found me. I did the only thing that I could and that was to go to Manchester and see her. That night I think that I broke her heart, I was never to see her again. I was still very fond of her and I felt sad and awful over our parting. I had told her a white lie, this was that I had another girl friend which I had not. Fate had brought us together, and it was fate that had torn us apart. I am afraid that I did not handle the situation as well as I should have done.

That visit to Manchester was the only thing that marred this course. Perhaps it had been meant that I had to go there and that is why I had found myself selected for attending that course. I got stuck in and completed my fourteen days with de Havillands'. On our last day there they showed us over their factory. I remember seeing propeller blades spinning round on a lathe while they machined the root end and wondering how it was that they did not fly out from between the centres. I became very proud of myself as I obtained a certificate. With this I was told that should I go for an engineer ground licence in civy street, it would then have covered me on working on de Havilland propellers, and all of their ancillary equipment. There were about two dozen of us taking this private course and I was the only erk on it. I was an A.C.2 (Aircraftsman Second Class) at that. All of the rest of the chaps on that course were either N.C.O.'s or officers. It was only two or three of us that had done well enough to be given these certificates. My certificate stated that I was now covered on deHavilland propellers and their ancillary equipment and undermentioned were, Bracket type, Hydromatic 3 and 4 blade, High and low pressure barrels, C.S.U.'s (constant speed units) and their ancillary equipment.

When I got back to Colerne I was given my A.C.1. (Aircraftsman First Class). I Had developed fears that they might send me off on my own working on deHavilland propellers. These were fitted on Lancasters. It was all very well having that piece of paper to wave, but without any experience behind me I found it quite frightening. As it happened, I was never to see another de Havilland propeller again.

I settled back down to working on Spits and enjoying the NAAFI breaks. I was sent before a board where they made me up to L.A.C. (leading Aircraftsman). I had got my props. They then asked me if I would like to sign on. I had not settled, going home each week had made me long to be back in civy street. I refused. Now on looking back, I very likely made some silly mistakes. I should have taken the bull by the horns. That certificate that I had, I should have made use of it. Maybe if not working on props, but had tried to get a job working on aircraft, perhaps with de Havillands. I also had that chance to sign on and enjoy aircraft and to leave with a good service pension. Maybe, I could have got married and lived in married quarters. Anyhow, it was not to be. Since then I have also made many more mistakes in my life. I guess that we all have made a few. One cannot put the clock back. As it was, there were no aerodromes close to Wickham Heath and my country home was calling for me.

The Highways Hostel, Buxton

I GOT PLUCKED

'Roll on demob', or 'Speed on demob'. These were the cries often spoken of amongst us conscripted airmen and it never failed to annoy the regulars. At long last my release date had arrived, and there was a corporal S.P. on Colerne Station who was also due for release at the same time as myself. As he had a higher rank than I did, it was he who they trusted to carry the paper work that had to travel along with both of us. Though his rank had been higher, I had been drawing more money than him as my trade had been worth more. Not to worry, we were both happy and on our way out of the mob. We were heading back for good old civy street.

Together, we journeyed by train back up country. This time it was to No. 10 P.D.C. (Personnel Dispersal Centre). This was at Warton, near Kirkham in Lancashire. Here on August the 12th 1948, I was given my Class A release and this then automatically relegated me into the Reserve Group G.1. This then meant that should our country be faced with any future hostilities, they then had the right to call me back into the R.A.F. As I have never been informed that I have been released from this group, then officially, I am still tied to the R.A.F. Due now to my age and poor health and owning a disabled badge, I would not think that I would now be of any use to them. Since leaving the services I have now learnt how to swing a prop though it might not have been to the air force's standard. This I could still do, but in my state of health I would sooner leave it to a younger person. Not that the R.A.F. has many props left. Most of what they now have will be kept as wall decorations. Although I was never called back into the mob, there had been many times that I had dreamt of being called back in there again.

I said my goodbyes to my snowdrop and we both set off on our own individual ways to choose our new civilian clothes from the large clothing store. Having spent quite a time in kitting myself out with a new pinstripe suit and a trilby hat, etc, I then came out of the stores at the opposite end carrying a very large brown cardboard box with my new hat perched on the top of it. No longer did they throw the gear at you like they did when I entered the service at Padgate. Having collected my last travel warrant, pay and other bits of paper, I then loaded myself into a garry (R.A.F. trooping lorry). As it filled right up, you were then taken on your last official ride to Preston railway station. Low and behold, who should jump in next to me was my snowdrop.

The garry then dropped us off at the station and it was then that we found out that we had both missed out on some good trains that would have sped us on our ways. There was only one thing that we could do and that was to wait for some later trains. Together we walked out of the station until we found a nice friendly pub. I have never been one of those that worried about the licensing laws, but this place stayed open till well into the afternoon. We kept on drinking some very expensive brew that they only sold in half pints at a time. I then had a funny feeling coming over me, as like, I have drunk far too much. The landlord also suggested to us that he thought that he had sold us enough of the stuff. Corporal Snowdrop then tore the stripes off of his tunic, this to the surprise of the rest of the customers. 'Dink up', he said, 'We only get demobed once in a lifetime'. On continuing drinking, I then began to feel back to normal again. The pub then shut its doors and together we made our way back to the railway station. Staggering along with our large cardboard boxes and tit-for-tats I felt fine.

I saw Snowdrop away first on his journey home to Wales and then I had to hang about for my own train to take me home via London. My train came in and I clambered on board stuffing my large box and titfer up on the parcel rack. Now I was faced with a long journey and a change of railway station in Smoke (London). As this express train picked up speed it began to rock as only the L.M.S. could. Looking out of the carriage window I then discovered that all of the things that were supposed to have been stationary were now moving about. I then came over, well, horrible. This decided me on making a move. I opened the compartment door and once in the corridor I then dropped down on all fours and then set a course for the end cubical which I entered and bolted the door. I then new nothing more of my journey until I was well past Crew, and on my way to Smoke. Some idiot was banging like hell let loose on the door. After this rumpus had died away, I then opened the door and crept back to my compartment. My box and hat were still perched up on the rack, but all of the faces in that compartment had changed. My inner side now felt like a sewage works as I got off of the train in Euston Station. My nearest Y.M.C.A. was at Paddinton. With a great effort I arrived there and this was at the time before the bear. The rest of my journey on the G.W.R. I was not able to take until the following morning. That first night that I had arrived at Colerne the lads had got me pissed. I now had left Colerne in the same way. No matter, I was now a civilian once again.

BACK ON MY BIKE

In the Air Force I felt that I was no longer a free man. The R.A.F. had ruled my life. I had been conscripted into the services and I had been forced to go. Perhaps if I had signed on in the first place, or had served far away from home, then I may have had different feelings than what I had. Due to so many American service men around my home, I had not been out with any female company until I had been called up. I then got very fond of a girl and had then been moved far from her and all of these things had made an effect on me. My parents though far from rich had given me a good home. I had managed to get to my home on most weekends from Colerne. I had longed to be back there again with the woodland just outside of the back door. Now that I was demobilized, I now felt free again. I had been given demob leave and I made sure that I was going to enjoy it. With hindsight now, on looking back, had I had set off and found a job in aviation, then my whole life could have changed. As it was, I got back on my bike and visited aerodromes and other places. I had got use to long distance cycling and this form of transport cost me nothing. I enjoyed my last leave and I did not look for a job until my leave came to an end.

I did not realize it at the time, but in myself I had become a very unsettled person. Due to the way that I had left Opperman Gears, I did not attempt to go back there. Thatcham Mills was about as far as I was willing to cycle for work and so I got myself a job there at a firm called Croppers. They made cardboard boxes for many other firms. Cornflake manufacturers were the kind of people that these boxes were produced for. I now had gone out with a few girls, but it was from here that I started to court Daphne who eventually became my wife. Daphne was working on the cutters and creasers and I was working on the litho section. Here I worked on printing presses and learnt how to mix up ink colours. I stuck this job for a year and then I started to move from one firm to another. I did eventually go back to Oppermans, but they used me for cheap labour. I then had a year with Vickers at their Supermarine Works at Shaw where they gave me the number SW.288. I was still unsettled and I moved on again. Eventually I settled down with the Newbury furniture makers, Elliotts of Newbury. Here I learnt how to work with wood. Before I had learnt how to turn, drill and mill with metal. I would have stayed with this firm if they had not put me on a large wood sander. The chap that had worked it had broken his wrist and they were forced to find another operator. They chose me. I did such a good job on it that they refused to take me off of it. I was working under artificial light and there was no suction plant to remove the wood dust. Health and safety had then to be invented. Every time that I blew my nose I filled my handkerchief with wood dust and this dust also clogged in the corners of my eyes. This going on I realized was not good for my health and so I looked for an outdoor job. This I found with the General Post Office on G.P.O. Telephones. With them I worked on the over-head construction and spent quite a bit of my time working up poles in the countryside with my head up with the leaves on the trees. This firm later became P.O. Telephones and finally B.T. I am now as I write this an ex British Telecom worker and drawing their pension.

Having now given to you a quick run through of my working life, I will return to the time of my demobilization. It was in late summer and I would take rides out on my bike. I also started to do work on my little Triumph motorcycle NV 4132. I did get it back on the road for a short time and then I let a Reading firm work on my engine. These people bounced the crankcase assembly and after that it became scrap metal. The frame and wheels I let a fellow have and he turned these into a grass track racing machine. With this Triumph I had taken my first driving test up in Reading. I knew that the examiner had taken a disliking to me as he kept on referring to my wobbly rear wheel. Needless to say that he failed me and so it was back to my trusty pushbike that I got around for the next year or so.

Several times while on my last leave I would cycle to Aldermastom aerodrome. It would have been a good place to have looked for a job had it not have been so far away from my home. Perhaps if I had had that motorcycle on the road, then I may have done so. Unfortunately for me it turned into a non starter. This place was later to become the A.W.R.E. (Atomic Weapons Research Establishment), or as some others have said, 'Arrive Weary Return Energetic'. It had been a wartime airfield which had been cut out of the evergreen woodlands. It was intended to be used as an O.T.U. America then came into the war and so it became their Base No. 467 in 1942. It then became home to P.47's, P.38's and B.26's. In its final wartime days it was the U.S.A.A.F's (United States Army Air Force) home to the 434th T.C.G. (Troop Carrier Glider). It was one of several airfields in the south in which the Americans took-off from when setting out for Normandy on D-Day. Now as I made visits to it on my trusty cycle, the Americans had long left and it had become a civil airline training school. The Ministry of Aviation had taken it over.

Having arrived at Aldermaston airfield, I would spend several hours watching the flying and they did quite a lot of it. Air Service Training had quite a variety of aircraft based there. Three aircraft that I know of by their registrations and this because I saw them through my viewfinder were, Douglas Dakota G-AGFX, Avro York G-AGNN "Madras" and Avro Lancastrian G-AKTB "Star Glory", This Lancastrian was painted overall in a two tone blue colour scheme and it carried the markings of B.S.A.A. (British South American Airways). It was the prettiest Lancastrian that I had ever seen. I had developed a hobby of photographing different kinds of aircraft but in those days my trusty Kodak vest pocket camera had no zoom. Because of this, many aircraft that I photographed only came out as small distant subjects. Because I always carried a camera, Cliff Lovall then referred to me as 'Ken the Camera'. Most of the aircraft that were using Aldermaston I could not get close enough to take good photos of them. Also to be seen in the circuit were Avro Tudors and Airspeed Oxfords. As I remember these civil Oxfords, they had purple fuselages and engine nacelles with white flying surfaces. Their registrations were applied right across both wings as in the pre-war days and they did look nice. Parked on its own and close to the road was a Handley Page Halifax B Mk.VI, RG726. It was still in its bomber black and I took a couple of photographs of this. In these days there was no colour photography, film was hard to get and it was all in black and white. I do not know what became of this Halibag. The chances are that it ended its days at Aldermaston, or it may have been flown out to some scrap dump like Southend in Essex. If only the powers to be had had the foresight to have saved it. A Halifax should have been flying with the B.B.M.F's (Battle of Britain Memorial Flight's) along with the Avro Lancaster PA474. Well I suppose one could say the same about the Hampden, Whitley, Wellington and Stirling. At least, this one was still there well after the ending of the war.

On a Sunday the 22nd of August 1948, I set out from Wickham Heath very early in the morning for the Isle of Wight. This was the first of two of my cycle rides that I made to there. An air display was being held on Somerton Airfield at Cowes. I took my trusty Raleigh cycle across the Solent on one of the old red funnelled paddle steamers. I enjoyed my trip across the water and it gave me a rest from pedalling. The old paddle steamer ran very close to the R.A.F. Sunderlands that were moored off of Calshot just before you reached the spit, not a Spitfire. One of the Sunderlands that my camera recorded was RN302 and coded TA-H. At Calshot there was a captured Blohm und Voss six engine German flying boat. The motors which powered this flying boat were twelve cylinder liquid cooled diesels. Actually they were six cylinder, having two opposing pistons in each of these long cylinders. Each engine drove a three bladed propeller, and each engine had a geared driven supercharger. This flying boat was painted overall in a mat-white and I believe from memory that the engines were painted in black or a very dark grey. It carried R.A.F. roundels and a red code letter R. Later it had its port outer engine removed. A novel feature of this flying boat was the outer wing floats. They were positioned mid-way between the outer engines and the wing tips and each was in two portions. One portion of each float retracted inwards while the other portions retracted outwards. To me, this looked to be a cleaner and stronger idea than the floats used by Shorts' on their flying boats. It would also have cut out some drag. By the spring of 1947 it had been beached close to the castle. I now found that it had gone and I expect that it had been dismantled and scrapped.

This trip to Cowes was the first air display that I attended. I had previously taken a very long train journey via Reading back to Bath when I looked in at Woodley Aerodrome on a Miles Aircraft open day. This had been a more look and enjoy day than a flying display. Most of the civil aircraft had been painted in cream-yellow with red registration letters and trimmings. I can remember amongst the many aircraft present that there were two M.5 Sparrowhawks and an all red M.57 Aerovan that might have belonged to a flying postman. Also there was a long row of camouflaged M.33 Monitors. These were target towing aircraft and I wonder if they ever got delivered to the R.A.F. Film was then in short supply and unfortunately on that day I had an empty camera.

Having collected my bike off of the boat I then continued my journey inland up a hill to the aerodrome. The trouble with cycling was that by the time that I arrived, the flying display was nearly over. The first thing that I saw as I neared the airfield entrance was the de Havilland Gipsy engine Dragon II G-AECZ fly across the road in front of me as it came into land. It was then owned by the Wiltshire School of Flying and was based at Thruxton. It was silver overall with red registration letters and wheels and it was selling joy flights. Later in the day I bought myself a ride in Morgan Aviations cream and red trimmed Auster J/1 Autocrat G-AIBS. This cost me 10/- for ten minutes, being a bob a minute. On looking back, I now wished that I had plumped for a ride in that Dragon. It had served during the war as AV982. It was later sold to Ireland and was registerd EI-AFK. It then became well known as it now masquerades as Aer Lingus's first aircraft EI-ABI "Iolar". Since then it has been registered as EI-ABI(2). I now doubt that I will ever get a ride in this old girl, but as yet, I have not given up hope.

On the field I was to find many pre and post war light aircraft. There were two de Havilland D.H89A Dragon Rapides and two Supermarine Walrus aircraft. One of these was painted a dull yellow colour and it might have belonged to United Whalers, Ltd. The other one was pushed into a corner with faded paintwork and military markings with folded wings. Elliotts of Newbury were present with their Newbury EoN G-AKBC. How I wished that I could have hitched a ride home with them, but I had got to cycle it. I expect that they would have been fully loaded anyhow. Some of the aircraft that I took photographs of were as follows; D.H.85 Leopard Moth G-ACTJ. I have seen it reported as being in a black livery. When I photographed it at Cowes it was in a dark green with a lighter green and white and it looked very smart. The D.H.87B Hornet Moth G-AELO was then in a metallic light blue. This in later years was to be the first Hornet Moth that I was to have a ride in. This on the 24th of August 1994 with Mark Miller at a de Havilland Moth Club event being then red and silver. I took two photographs of Tipsy B.2 G-AFKP. It was in an electric purple and aluminium colour scheme. The Hawker Tomtit G-AFTA was present in a dark blue and silver with its registration letters spread across both wings above and below. It is now seen in military markings where it is a part of the Shuttleworth Trust collection. There was a spatted Miles M.14 Hawk Trainer being an ex R.A.F. Magister. Also present was the Miles M.18 Mk.3 G-AHOA that was fitted with a greenhouse type cockpit. An all red Proctor III being G-AKWJ. An Auster J/2 Arrow and Autocrats G-AGTX and G-AGVM named "Virgin Minx". One aircraft present that was not British was a Piper Super Cruiser G-AJGY. This was in a light yellow and red. There were many others, but these I did not record.

The Newbury EoN was a regular sight flying over our home. Elliotts then kept it on R.A.F. Welford and here it had the whole flying field to its self. The firm used it for towing and delivering their gliders and sailplanes. Its familiar sight in our sky was to disappear when it was destroyed at Lympne on the 14th of April 1950. It took-off without its pilot and with a sailplane in tow. Later when I was to work for the firm I saw its remains in one of the large sheds. Many worst wrecks than that, have been rebuilt today. Also there was a part built second EoN. I expect that they both got broken up and helped in feeding the boiler house fire. G-AKBC was a pretty little aeroplane and it showed promise. It first appeared in a light sky blue with dark blue registration letters when it was flown with a Blackburn Cirrus Minor engine. In June 1948, it was given more power when the Cirrus was replaced with a de Havilland Gipsy Major 10. It was then given additional dark blue trimmings with its name placed below the cabin. Many years later I made a visit to the Berkshire Aviation Museum at Woodley. I was very surprised that they had nothing to speak of from Elliotts of Newbury. It was such a pity that this museum had not been started sooner when some of Elliotts items from their Albert Works in Newbury still existed. I also expect that all of those stored Master wings that were in my hangar at Colerne most likely finished up in a large bonfire.

I was now faced with the long haul back over the North Hampshire Downs. Having passed through Newbury, now in the darkness I was very weary and I can remember that it took all of my effort to push my cycle up Speen Hill. I did cycle to some other places, Blackbushe and also to the 1948 S.B.A.C. (Society of British Aircraft Constructors) Show. One photograph that I took on that day was of a Junkers Ju290 that was dumped in the bush, this the vegetation on the airfields outskirts. This photo I dated as 11/9/48.

Walk-about in the Farnborough bush

MOTORCYCLES & PHOTOGRAPHY

Eventually there came a time when I said goodbye to my faithful Raleigh cycle. Now as I write this, for the life of me, I just cannot remember parting with it. I guess that it had to go in order to make room in the shed for the motorcycle. Altogether I have owned a dozen different motorcycles which included two Vespa scooters. I have ridden them for thousands of miles both as solo and with sidecars. Both methods I thoroughly enjoyed, and yes, I did have a few near scrapes. The makes that I once owned, and they were all second hand, were, Triumph, Calthorpe, B.S.A. (Birmingham Small Arms), Ariel, Zenith, Ambassador and the Vespa scooters that were manufactured by Douglas. Well over a half of them were pre-war machines. The two that I derived most pleasure from was the Calthorpe DP 9614 that I named "Constance" and the Ariel Red Hunter JB 8843. Those two bikes along with a 250 cc B.S.A. CFC 841 were to see me through my courting years.

The old Calthorpe I bought off of my mate Desmond Newport for £20 and it was to serve me well. Des sold it when he bought for himself a reconditioned ex WD (War Department) 350 cc side valve Royal Enfield. My other mate Dennis Simmons also bought one of these at the same time. This I borrowed during the time that he was overseas performing his army service. They were good bikes, though not as fast as my old Calthorpe. Mind you, having the quicker foot change, they were often to leave me behind as I had the old fashioned hand change.

Now just a little bit about "Constance". I used her and then took her off of the road for the Ariel. We boys then had fun with her stripped of her mudguards and lighting dirt-tracking in the wood between the fir trees. Later after this I was to put her back on the road again. She had an under-slung Burman gearbox. When I bought her the case of this box had been damaged on the drive side and a lay-shaft was held in a specially built fix bush to the outside of the casing. This bush gave way and I then rode her for thousands of miles with a jubilee clip holding the bush up in its rightful place. Eventually I did manage to get another gear-box casing and with the help from Burmans' I renewed the box. Burman's slogan was, 'Geared for good going' and I was never let down with gearbox trouble. "Constance" was the same age as myself to the month and being a 1928 model. She had been built new with electric lighting and her mag-dyno was constructed all in one piece. Her carburettor was of all brass and was made by Amac. Both of her push rods were in cased in one tube and this made many people think that I had an over-head camshaft job. She was a 350 cc o.h.v. model named 'The Popular'. What showed her age were her Druid type front forks and her wedge type petrol tank with its T-handle filler cap. She did get through some oil as she was built with a total loss system. The speed in which you used the oil was regulated by an adjuster on the Pilgrim oil pump. This I would adjust for if I was doing some fast motoring, ie 60 m.p.h, or if I was only pottering about. On my way to a Farnborough air-display I had kept this oil regulator high so as to compensate for the crankcase pressure. On leaving the S.B.A.C. show the police held up a large bunch of around fifty or more motor cyclists that were waiting to get out on to the main highway. There then became a lot of horn blowing behind me. I looked back to see why and one chap then shouts, 'Hey you, turn it up, what d' ya' think ya' have got there, a disell'. Connie had layed a thick blue smokescreen that the Red Arrows would have been proud of. All of the other bikes were hidden from view behind this thick curtain of smoke. I was forced to re-regulate my oil pump.

It was with "Constance" that I started my courting. I was on my way home from Daphne's home at Lambourn in the early hours of what was then, a Monday morning. It was brilliant moonlight when I entered some thick fog that had drifted up from off of the Lambourn Stream. I kept my headlamp on full beam. Had I had used the parking light, then all might have been well. I pranged into a steep grass bank on the junction of the road that leads down into East Garston village. The next thing that I knew was the bike and I were laying up this bank with the hot cylinder steaming from spilt petrol that had come from the tank filler cap. I was very lucky that she had not gone up in flames. Once more in my life I was very lucky in this way. This other event I will mention in a later chapter called 'Roman Tigers'. The headlamp rim complete with its bulbs and reflector had left the lamp and had rolled down in to the field. The front mudguard had arched its-self and its large diameter exhaust pipe had parted at the joints. I had not hurt myself until while still dazed I fell off the bank. The church clock down in the village kept striking as I got things back together again. I wired the headlamp up with a wire across the top of the petrol tank to the battery and I replaced the exhaust. As I slowly rode her back home, each time we came to a bend she would wobble.

Come the afternoon on that Monday I was booked in for a driving test in Reading. Daphne was wanting to ride on the pillion. Once home, I went in doors and came out with a torch and inspected "Constance". What I found was that one top fork link had snapped in two. The other one was arched up in a curve. I motored into Newbury very slowly where a friend of mine, Wilfred Bevan who worked in a motorcycle shop managed to find me two more front fork links. These then replaced the damaged ones and with my L-plates fixed to the front of my broken headlamp glass, I then continued on to Reading where I then passed my driving test for Group G, motorcycles. If that examiner had tumbled, I feel sure that he would have found some excuse to have failed me.

This old bike was to take me to many air shows. Also to many airfields where I would go just to take a few pictures of some rare aircraft that may have been, perhaps as rare as my old Calthorpe, the last of its breed. One of these was at White Waltham on the 29th of May 1950. Here, Bond Air Services were selling rides in their deHavilland D.H.86B Express G-ADVJ. She was sprayed silver overall with a darkish green trim. Having Daphne with me, and to have gone up in her would have cost me double and so it was that I kept what little money I had in my pocket. Many times since I have wished that I had not been such a miser. I have since flown in many more deHavilland types than any other and the majority of these have been in Tiger Moths. Like that old D.H.84 Dragon G-AECZ, if only. If only I had flown in that Eighty-Six. The type now is an extinct and is a dead breed.

The S.B.A.C. Farnborough show in 1948 would have been one that I cycled to. That year the deHavilland D.H.108 Swallow Mk.III, VW120 landed. This single jet engine tailless aircraft so enthralled the crowd that hundreds of people broke ranks and swarmed on to the airfield to take a close look. One could not then see the Swallow for people. I then took this opportunity to walk out on to the aircraft park and to obtain a few nice close-ups of other aircraft. I was then one of those persons who could not afford a camera with a zoom or an extra long range lens. To many of my aviation friends, thanks to Cliff, I have now become known as, 'Ken the Camera'.

I must admit that I enjoyed every early Farnborough show that I went to. The 1949 show was inspiring. During the week I had rushed out from under Cropper's factory roof to view the Bristol Brabazon Mk.I, G-AGPW as it made its way towards Farnborough from Bristol. At the weekend I then went there to see it at close quarters for myself. It was the largest landplane that was completely built in Britain. Apart from giving a lot of employment to the workers at Bristol, it did very little else other than destroying a village and giving Filton an extra long runway. The runway was lengthened to 2,750 yards. In order to do this the village of Charlton was demolished and a road was diverted. On the Brabazon's first flight, Bill Pegg lifted it off at just 833 yards. At a cost of £3 million it was designed just to carry 100 passengers across the Atlantic. It was powered by four pairs of coupled Bristol Centaurus eighteen cylinder air-cooled radial piston engines. Needless to say, it never saw any service and it was broken up along with its sister airframe.

Some other aircraft at these early shows were the two Armstrong Whitworth A.W.52 Flying Wings. They were both white overall and each was powered by two Rolls-Royce jet engines. One had Nenes and the other had Derwents. Geoffrey Tyson flew along upside down in the Saro S.R.A.1 jet flying boat fighter TG263. Downside up flying was his speciality. The Avro stable flew the prototype all white Vulcan bomber with some colourful Avro 707 deltas formatting each side of it. Even Elliotts of Newbury were there with their Newbury EoN and Olympia EoN sailplane. They also had a Primary and Baby glider on show. All of their aircraft were of wooden construction. There was the Short Sealand prototype G-AIVX with high mounted engines, it was resplendent in a rich cream and green. A Short Solent flying boat made a low pass and the Saro Princess flying boat G-ALUN was to fly for less than one hundred hours and then it was cocooned in an out-door storage. It must have flown far less than this when it made its low pass over Farnborough. It was never to fly again and was broken up along with other unfinished airframes. If only Aquila Airways Limited had been allowed to have had them. The writing was on the wall. Flying boats were no longer liked as they used up sheltered water which wealthy owners of luxury yachts were making use of.

In those early years of Farnborough, the dominating aeroplanes were Canberras and Meteors. Each year they would be shown in a different mark or as test beds. The old four engine piston Avros would be present with some Merlin engines removed to be replaced with new development engines. The Merlins if they still had them would be shut down and they would then fly on their new developing engines. They had become flying engine test beds. Vickers Armstongs had developed the world's first pure jet airliner. This was the Nene Viking G-AJPH. Each time that it took-off it would burn away a portion of the runway leaving behind it a pall of smoke similar in colour to that of my poor old "Constance". After its most glorious beginning, it was then sold to Eagle Airways who had it converted into a Viking Mk.1b Freighter with a large cargo door. Vickers also converted one of its Viscounts with two Rolls-Royce Tay jet engines. As it had a tricycle undercarriage it did not burn up the tarmac. But oh, how those wings flexed. The Viscount was to become one of our best selling airliners. Although I enjoyed watching all that flew here, it was British built and it made one feel proud. There were some monstrosities such as the large Cierva Air Horse with its tri-rotors. Also the Blackburn & General Aircraft Limited's G.A.L.10 Universal Freighter WF320. I never then dreamt that one day I would fly in its successor, the very useful Blackburn Beverley. Then there were some other aircraft builders that were new to aviation. The Portsmouth Aviation's Aerocar Major G-AGTG being twin engine and twin boomed. The all magnesium constructed Planet Satellite with its V tail and rear propeller. This one never was to fly. Two show stoppers were the first in service deHavilland D.H.106 Comet prototype G-ALVG and the Armstrong Whitworth's Apollo G-AIYN. This was powered by four Armstrong Siddeley Mamba propeller turbines.

If only, and I find myself keep on saying, if only. If only Britain had not tried to lead the world by building too large before she had got herself financially back on her feet. It is true that sales of wartime Tiger Moths, Magisters and Proctors were killing the market. Also from America were the Piper Cubs, but light aircraft did not require such large development costs as did airliners and jet fighters. Miles aircraft did show what could be done. The deHavilland D.H.60 Moth had shown the way following on from the First World War but the lessons had not been learnt. A few of those impressed aircraft were now finding their ways back on to the civil market. The Miles Gemini, Messenger and Aerovan had proved successful until the firm went pop. They were all of wooden construction and the Americans for one were now starting to build their so called spam cans in metal. It was obvious that this was the way to go. Our aircraft industry had the knowledge and the ability to manufacture sophisticated aircraft but they lacked the finance to see their projects reach fruition. deHavillands did start off well with their Comet airliner but unfortunately they were to lose out when disaster struck them. It had been a big gamble and this had caused them to have lost their lead.

It was in 1954 that I went to my last Farnborough show. This may also be the same year that I witnessed my two U.F.O's (Unidentified Flying Objects). This event I will come to in the later chapter, 'Seeing is Believing'. This was to be the year that Farnborough turned sour on me. Due to this I never went back there again until a year or so ago. I was to fly over it though in a Westland Wessex helicopter and of this I had no choice. I had taken a young work mate, Tony Bosley with me on the pillion of "Constance". We had decided to arrive there early so that we could take as many photographs of the display aircraft before it got crowded. We were some of the first through the gates and we succeeded in obtaining some nice pictures. Having arrived early we then found that we had some spare time on our hands. To help pass this time away we decided to go walk-about into the Farnborough bush. At that time there was quite a lot of it. Our so doing was to see if we could come across any old discarded relics of interest. Back in 1948 I had seen and photographed the hulk of that Junkers Ju.290A whilst walking between the gorse bushes. There were many others then doing likewise as my Junkers photograph clearly shows. This time we found such an interest. It was a rusty old V.1 doodlebug that was minus its flying surfaces. It was laying on its side along with some other rubbish. Having decided that, well yes it could be worth a photograph, we then stood on top of what looked like a short section that had been cut out of a Lancaster fuselage and then took our photos. We had just clicked our cameras when two army brown jobs wearing red lids and mounted on a couple of horses turned up. They then told us that we should not have been there and that the reason that we had got there was because these two idiots had both decided to take lunch together when they should have been patrolling the area. In other words, they had both neglected their duties. These horsey bods then arrested us and we were both marched off to a brick building. To the side of where we were and several hundreds of yards away in the distance was a wired scrap metal pen. This pen contained cut-up scrap metal alloys in sizes that a man could handle. I would think that it was destined for a scrap metal merchant. These twisted alloy pieces I could not make out from which part of an airframe that they had come from. We were then told that this pen contained some of the metal that was the remains of the deHavilland D.H.110 that had crashed during the previous S.B.A.C. show. In their eyes there was a possibility that we may have photographed some of this. What if we had, the daily newspapers at that time had shown this aircraft breaking up in front of the crowds. Hundreds of people had taken photographs of it. Having been interrogated, they then confiscated our films. We were not searched and so we kept some of those we had used in our pockets. Our cameras were empted and the films from out of them were confiscated and they took our addresses. We were then given a pass out to walk down the town so that we could purchase some more films at our own expense. By the time that we returned we were far too late to secure a good place to watch the flying display and so we decided to go and watch what was left of it from what was then known as, up on the hill. They did at a later date process our films and send them back to us, but with no apology. Mine was the first exposure on a new film and all that I got was that one frame of that flying bomb.

We had been subjected to bureaucracy and military red tape that was entirely due to their own negligence and making. All of this had been at a cost to our selves. For me, this had completely ruined my day. It had been a pathetic incident that they had put us through. These Farnborough shows were becoming more and more geared up to the heavy aeroplanes. I myself always preferred the lighter side of aviation, and also, the older the better. Out of those Farnborough shows that I did go and see, my most liked display was Ronald Portious in the little Aiglet Trainer G-AJYW. This does not mean that I did not enjoy any of the other displays. To me, all flying is interesting. That incident put me right off of going to Farnborough and I have never been to another S.B.A.C. show since.

"Constance" was to serve me with transport to other air days including many trips to the V.A.C. (Vintage Aeroplane Club), but more of that in the next chapter. There was the one time when she did let me down. This had been on my first visit to Old Warden to view the Shuttleworth Trust. On her pillion I took my brother Dick who at that time was on leave from the army whilst serving in Germany. This would have been before my last visit to Farnborough as the dates on my photographs were the 20th of May 1951. We had gone to look at old aeroplanes and we were a little disappointed that only a few were on show. Roped out on the grass were their, only three old timers. These were the Bleriot XI Monoplane that was new in 1909, the Deperdussin Monoplane that was new in 1911 and the Blackburn Monoplane that was new in 1912. We also saw their Sopwith Pup N5180 that had once been a Sopwith Dove G-EBKY. We could look at several old veteran motor cars and a large collection of old farm tractors which looked as though they had all been painted from a very large pot of green paint. Two other aircraft that I took photographs of on that day were the Miles M.17 Monarch G-AIDE and the Piper J-3C-65Cub G-AJDS. This cub was aluminium overall with blue registration letters and chequered aluminium and blue rudder. There were a few other visiting aircraft and along with them was a Tiger Moth. As Tigers were then two a penny, this one escaped my camera. More is the pity now.

Having seen all that we wanted to see, we then walked back to the field where "Connie" was parked on her rear stand between many motor cars. We had looked upon enjoying our long ride home to Berkshire and enjoy the fresh green countryside. I went to kick-start my old Calthorpe only to find that things had gone solid and I could not turn her engine over. It did not take me long to trace the trouble to the mag-dyno which was situated to the front of the engine. Not known to us, the mag portion had run hot on our way to Old Warden. This had melted the shallec or whatever it was. As it had cooled off, so it had set solid. My thoughts were, if it had worked when we got here, free it off and it should work again. First I had to completely strip down the dynamo half before I could start stripping down the magneto half. I was busy doing this when a chap came along and offered me the use of his hammer. It was the only tool that he carried. I felt sure that he must have motored down from Birmingham. I soaked the offending armature in petrol and it free'd-up. I then had to reassemble the unit and retime the ignition. The engine ran sweet again and we were one of the last to leave the field. It then rained on us for the rest of our journey home. This I did not mind as it helped in cooling that magneto.

After a while I replaced "Constance" for the Ariel Red Hunter JB 8843. When I bought this bike she had an upswept exhaust pipe and a 350 cc engine with semi-open rockers. By the time that I sold her I had started a family. She had then been given a new frame and had a 500 cc engine and was bolted to a sidecar. After I had got my own home, my old Calthorpe had resided in a lean-to at my parent's home in Stockcross. They wanted her moved and firewood had been placed all around her. On moving her, the water had run down on her and the rust had done quite a lot of damage. I then advertised her for sale in Exchange & Mart. A chap came down from Ealing, London, who already owned an old Calthorpe car. I then let him have it for £2 including an old brass bulb horn as he promised to restore her. Many is the time now that I had wished that I had kept her. I could easily had dismantled her and placed most of her up in the attic. I more or less gave her away and that was that. Many is the time since that I have dreamt that I still had owned her, only to awake very disappointedly. Oh what fun we could have had with her at vintage rallies today.

Myself standing by the Spitfire Mk IX, RR182 destined for Turkey

The Newbury EoN from Elliotts of Newbury

My photograph of that flying bomb

THE VINTAGE AEROPLANE CLUB

When that fortnightly paper, 'The Aeroplane Spotter' ceased publication, a group of very interested people formed a club called 'Air-Britain' and I believe that it is still active. Back in the 1950's having then left my service in the R.A.F. behind me, I then joined this club. Every fortnight they would issue a four page news letter called 'British Civil Aviation News. I always looked forward to receiving this and it was like receiving the old 'Aeroplane Spotter' all over again. I now cannot remember why I came out of it, but at a guess I expect it was all due to a lack of funding. Often I have thought of rejoining, but it is just one more of these things that I have never got around to doing.

Having been demobbed from the Air Force, I now started searching around for some interest in aviation. This I found when I joined The Vintage Aeroplane Club as an associate member. It got referred to as the V.A.C. for short. This club had been formed by two people, Captain Ron Gillman who was a senior captain with B.E.A. (British European Airways) and David Ogilvy. At that time Ron Gillman was flying Viscounts along with Captain Fred Terry who I will write about in a later chapter called 'Roman Tigers'. David Ogilvy was to become better known for all of the good work which he performed with the Shuttleworth Trust at Old Warden. It was at the end of 1951 that the wheels were set in motion by a gathering of owners of pre-war light aircraft when they held a meeting at White Waltham. The V.A.C. was then formed. It also offered an associate membership for enthusiasts of these old pre-war aeroplanes. I joined them and I attended an air display at White Waltham in 1952. I also introduced this club to my young workmate, Tony Bosley. Together we would travel to V.A.C. events on "Constance", and I do not think that we ever missed any of them. These were nearly always held at either Denham or White Waltham and they utilized those two aero clubs, club rooms.

Around about this time, many of the pre-war light civil aircraft that had survived the war due to one means or another, were now finding their ways back on to the civil register. These aircraft then became candidates for the V.A.C. As Tiger Moths, Magisters and Rapides were two-a-penny , and having been in production during the war, they were not considered as eligible for membership. Even so, a few of them did take part in some of the events. Ron Gillman was a part owner of a 1932 vintage Avro Type 616 Sports Avian G-ABEE. This he had helped in its restoration. Due to her registration, she became known as 'Old Gabby'. It was always a pleasure to watch Ron making a short landing in this old Avro. He would side-slip this old biplane right down to the ground and then land off of with a very short run. The run was so short that even a Fieseler Storch would have found it hard to have emulated. I have seen my old departed friend, Captain Fred Terry make similar landings in his Tiger Moth G-ACDJ. In fact, I have seen him do it while sitting in his front cockpit. Perhaps both of these captains had been given some early tuition by Captain McIntosh who had gone down in aviation history as 'All Weather Mac.' All Weather had been noted for making over a half-dozen force landings on the run between London and Paris. He had flown twin-engined ex World War One, Handley Page 0/400's. Most farms in those days generally had smaller fields. One now wonders just how many of those force landings might have been made after gliding across the English Channel. The old 0/400 would have had a lot of drag built into it. Ron Gillman was one of those people that were a Clark Gabel look-a-like due to his neat thin moustache.

For my journey to Denham, I would head off in the direction of London up the old A.4. No one had thought about motorways in those days. I would turn north once through Slough and take the A.412 to Uxbridge. Tony was nearly always occupying the pillion. Most of the club's events were for members only, but on a few occasions, the public were invited along. The flying events had items in the programme such as balloon bursting, or chasing about the sky after cascading bog-rolls. There was also flour bombing competitions. On the 17th of October 1954, at Denham, the club had a set-piece that was floated on the grass to the front of the club house. It was a battleship that was constructed from a pile of large cardboard boxes. A fellow was placed on board to record which aircraft had made flour bomb hits on this boxed battleship. An over enthusiastic chappie flying a Miles Hawk Trainer III failed to hit the thing with his flour bombs. He then climbed and turned and made a kamikaze attack and then ploughed through the top most boxes which then became airborne in several directions. The ship's captain ducked down in order to keep his head and as fast as he could he abandoned ship. The Miles Hawk was given a red flare and a hell of a rocket once he had landed. As this offending aircraft was an ex wartime Magister, he may not have been a club member. I have now forgotten. It had been very dangerous, and I am pleased to say that it was an isolated incident. Most of the V.A.C. events were held at Denham or White Waltham, though one did start at Denham and finished off at Panshanger. This was the home of the London Aeroplane Club.

An Avro Type 638 Club Cadet came on to the market. It was powered by a de Havilland Gipsy Major I engine and it had served during the war as a communications hack with the seaplane firm, Saunders-Roe, Ltd. The Vintage Aeroplane Club then purchased this as its own aircraft. It cost the club £75. It then cost the club as much again in order to obtain a C of A (Certificate of Airworthiness). Full members were then entitled to fly this old biplane for the price of £1. 10/- (£1. 50p) per hour. I never did get to fly in it. Not that I did not wish to, but I was running a motorbike and courting Daphne and it took all of my pocket money. I just kept on putting off until it was too late. I had missed the boat, or plane as you might say. Tony did get to fly in 'HP along with his pilot, the 'Mad Major', 'Under the bridges' Major Draper. Not under any bridges though, while he was flying in it. I was at that time up in the little Aeronca 100, G-AEVS. Twice I was to fly in 'VS and I believe Tony flew twice in 'HP. We just flew with the pilots that we had been told to go along with.

Our club had invited other light aircraft to invade us at Denham on the 14th of February 1954. On this winters rally, any visiting aircraft that arrived without being photographed from the air were given a free lunch. The Aeronca that I was flying in was resplendent in an overall primrose cream-yellow with saxe-blue registration letters and leading edges. Her registration letters were applied across both wings in the pre-war style and she did look nice. Mike Dibble flew me and I was armed with my old faithful Kodak vest pocket camera. This was on the day of that battleship. Any would-be raiders that managed not to get photographed from the air and then made a flour bomb hit on the battleship was then given a free lunch. There were eight of us defending aircraft and seven raiders attacked. Mike was keen to get as high as possible without us rubbing noses with any Northolt airline traffic. Apart from searching the sky for raiders, we had to keep our eyes open for airliners. If we spotted a raider, our small little two-seater could then gain an extra bit of speed in a dive. We only had a two-cylinder 36 h.p. engine up front. As we never saw a raider, I never got to find out what a dive in an Aeronca 100 was like. Mike spotted a friend down on the ground and he waggled the wings. I was invited to handle the controls and this was the first time for me to be able to try my hands on controlling an aeroplane in the air. A picture of this aircraft is in the front piece to this book.

The second time that I got to fly in her she had been re-sprayed all over in red and had been given white registration letters. I did not think that she looked so nice in this darker colour scheme. This time I was only armed with a notebook and pencil and there was no cardboard to be bombed. We flew around for forty minutes and patrolled our sector until 11.30 am. The only aircraft that we saw were the defending Piper Cub G-AIYV and the Club Cadet 'HP in which Tony was flying in. The Spartan Arrow G-ABWP then formatted on us as we made our way back for the landing, but my camera was down on the ground. That should have taught me a lesson. Conditions then got very turbulent and my young pilot then decided to fly over the Denham wood at full power and then to keep his landing run as short as was possible. He did a very good job of it. This was on the 17th of October of that same year. I may not have flown in that Club Cadet, but at least I had enjoyed the comfort of an enclosed cabin during these winter flights.

Tony and I had palled up with a friend who worked at Croydon Airport named, Trevor Cheeseman. Trevor had invited me to have a look around Croydon and I had accepted his invitation. He gave me a tour of most of the hangars and I did obtain many interesting photographs for my own collection. These photographs I dated 29th of July 1953. Three of the aircraft that I clicked while looking at them through the view finder were the civil Ansons. These were the Avro Type 652A Mk.I, G-AIXV that belonged to Transair. It was being used as a freighter and was silver overall trimmed with blue. It was unique having a turned nose cone. G-ALUM was another Anson Type 652A Mk.I. The other one was an Avro Type 652A Srs I, G-AGZT that was owned by Channel Air Services. It had its registration displayed across both wings in the 1930's style. Another aircraft that comes to mind that I photographed on that day was the Lockheed Model 18 Lodestar, N9949F. I now remember, I had taken Daphne with me as I had photographed her standing by this aircraft. Also there was the Lockheed Model 12A, G-AGTL. This was a light pea-green with dark green letters. Hid away in one of the hangars was the Short S.16 Scion Junior G-AEZF. Now that I have deviated into the past, I will mention just a few of the many other aircraft that I photographed while taking rides to airfields on my Ariel Red Hunter.

So here goes, 20/7/52 D.H.85 Leopard Moth G-ACMN at Thruxton; 31/7/52 Avro Tudor Mk.4s G-AGRF, G-AHNJ, G-AHNK, G-AHNN at Hurn; 6/8/52 Avro Lincolnian G-ALPF at Southend; 31/8/52 Avro Tudor Mk.2, G-AGRY at Blackbushe; 4/4/53 D.H.95 Flamingo G-AFYH at Redhill and on the same day, Consolidated P.B.Y.5A Catalina (Amphibian) VP-KKJ "Namnagani" at Blackbushe; 20/6/53 Miles M.7A Nighthawk G-AGWT, D.H.85 Leopard Moth G-ACMA, Miles M.2F Hawk Major G-ACYO, Percival Q6 G-AEYE, all of these at Southend; 9/7/53 Boeing B-47B-46-BW Stratojet 12271 at Fairford; 25/7/53 D.H.89A Dragon Rapide G-ALAX at Eastleigh and on the same day, Short Sunderland Mk.III G-AGEU "Hampshire", Short Solent G-AGER, Short Sunderland MK.5 PP162/G-ANAK, Short Sandringham G-AGKX, Short Seaford Mk.3 G-ANAJ, most were dismantled shells on Hamble Beach; 27/8/53 D.H.83 Fox Moth G-ACCB at Thruxton, 12/2/55 D.H.98 Mosquitos Israel Air Force 4x3182 and 4x3186 at Blackbushe; 22/7/56 D.H.98 Mosquito PR Mk.34 G-AOCK ex NS753 and Percival Vega Gull G-AEYC at Thruxton. These were just a few of the many.

Having deviated, I must now get back on track. Tony and I were at Denham on the 2nd of August 1954. We had been with Trevor who was not keen to join us as we made our way over to a Proctor that had turned up to try and sell some joy rides. This Percival P.28 Proctor Mk.I, G-AIHG was being flown by a very pleasant lady, Mrs Jackie Moggridge. Neither of us had flown with a lady pilot before and so we both handed her over our ten bob notes. I sat on Jackie's right hand side and so Tony had the back all to himself. Jackie was there to sell rides for her boss and I do not think that she had much trade and it was also on a Monday. We stooged around between five and six hundred feet and we both enjoyed our little flip. During the war Jackie had been an A.T.A. (Air Transport Auxiliary) pilot. Or as it was said, A.T.A. stood for 'Anything To Anywhere'. She had flown many aircraft types which had included, Liberators, Lancasters, Mitchells and Spitfires. At the time of our flight she was waiting to hear about a job of ferrying Spitfires out to the far-east. Of this she would not divulge any more. During 1957, Jackie published her flying story in a paperback called 'Woman Pilot'. It was a Great Pan Publication, No G239 and it cost when new 2/6d (15p). It is nice to be able to say that I have flown with that very nice distinguished lady pilot. Now having read her book, I know of some of the excitements which she experienced while flying out those far eastern Spitfires. Such a pity that she did not mention me in her book, but then, who would want to do a thing like that. Since then, I have seen her on the television in several programs on the A.T.A.

The Kamikaze attack

Some of the items that would be printed in a programme at a public V.A.C. event would be as follows. A formation of the V.A.C.'s aircraft. Often it would be the two Avro's, G-ABEE and G-ACHP and de Havilland's own nicely restored D.H.60 Cirrus Moth G-EBLV. It was then painted in a dark yellow with dark blue. Another formation was from the Hawker stable at Langley near Slough. They would put up three aircraft that were all painted in a nice shade of darkish blue with gold letters and trimmings. These were the Tomtit G-AFTA, the Hart G-ABMR and their Hurricane Mk.IIc G-AMAU "Last of the Many". Yes I do know that it was produced during the war, but we considered that it was a candidate for the V.A.C. Civil Hurricanes were always few and far between. One event that was always a pleasure to watch was a mock dog fight between the Hawker Hart G-ABMR and the Gloster Gladiator G-AMRK. So that this event could be staged, I have known the time when there was a whip-round towards the petrol. G-AMRK was then silver overall with red registration letters. This Gladiator was restored by Vivian Bellamy by using parts from another Gladiator N5903. I photographed this one in his hangar at Eastleigh on the 26th of July 1953. I was later to have a flight with Viv around the rocks of Lands End in a Cessna 172A, G-BAAL when I treated my youngest son Alan to his first venture up into the air. We had hoped to have flown in the Rapide G-AIYR but no others would come along and help in filing it. Hawkers were then flying their little Cygnet G-EBMB. It had first flown in 1924 when it was entered in the Lympne Trials. Now while performing in the V.A.C. events it was powered by a Bristol Cherub III engine. Both the Cygnet and the Hart were later presented to the R.A.F. Hendon Museum and the Hurricane got to fly in the 'Battle of Britain' film and ended up in the Battle of Britain Memorial Flight. The Gladiator is now with the Shuttleworth Trust at Old Warden.

Aeronca G-AEVS and "Constance" at Denham

The club did get into air racing. On the weekend the 3rd of May 1952, at White Waltham they held the West London Trophy Race. Then from Denham they held a two day event on the 1st and 2nd of August 1954. On these dates it included the Chiltern Hills Air Races. I was one who was allowed to take photographs of some of the entrants as the starters flag was lowered.

The year of 1956 was the undoing of the V.A.C. On the first day in that year, those trees in that wood at Denham claimed the Avro Club Cadet G-ACHP. She had got caught in a freak squall of wind. With the loss of its aeroplane, the V.A.C. just folded up and this was because the club had lost its Club. A similar thing was to happen with the Calleva Group in later years when they lost their Tiger Moth G-AJHU. This I will speak about in the chapter to come called 'Roman Tigers'.

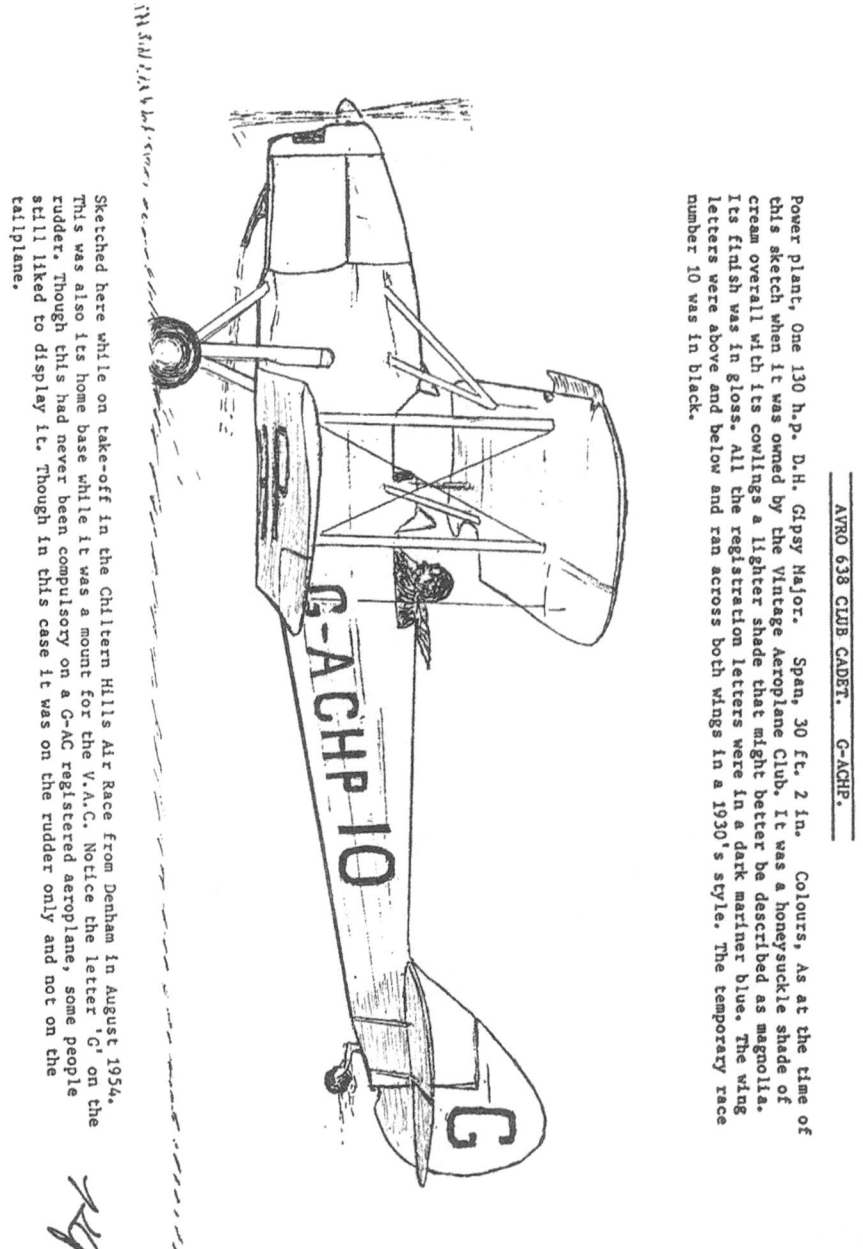

AVRO 638 CLUB CADET. G-ACHP.

Power plant, One 130 h.p. D.H. Gipsy Major. Span, 30 ft. 2 in. Colours, As at the time of this sketch when it was owned by the Vintage Aeroplane Club. It was a honeysuckle shade of cream overall with its cowlings a lighter shade that might better be described as magnolia. Its finish was in gloss. All the registration letters were in a dark mariner blue. The wing letters were above and below and ran across both wings in a 1930's style. The temporary race number 10 was in black.

Sketched here while on take-off in the Chiltern Hills Air Race from Denham in August 1954. This was also its home base while it was a mount for the V.A.C. Notice the letter 'G' on the rudder. Though this had never been compulsory on a G-AC registered aeroplane, some people still liked to display it. Though in this case it was on the rudder only and not on the tailplane.

FOR THE HISTORIANS

For the sake of the historians, the painters and the model makers, I am here listing many of the aircraft that could be seen at Denham. White Waltham and Panshanger in the days of the V.A.C. an awful lot of water has gone under the bridge since then and so I am not sure of all of the old aircraft which had V.A.C. membership. I am placing an asterisk * by those which I believed to have had membership. Some of these aircraft were just visiting while others were residents to the airfields. In those days the photography was in black and white and so many of the colours may now have been forgotten.

AERONCA C.3. G-AEFT. Dark blue and silver. Extra cabin windows. Believed current.

AERONCA 100. G-AEVS* for colours see in chapter. Believed current.

AERONCA 100. G-AEWU* Darkish red and silver.

AUGUSTA BELL 47G.

AVRO 616 SPORTS AVIAN. G-ABEE* Silver overall with dark blue cowlings and letters.

AVRO 638 CLUB CADET. G-ACHP* Two shades of cream with dark blue letters

AUSTER J/1 AUTOCRAT. G-AGXG.

AUSTER J/1 AUTOCRAT. G-AGXU.

AUSTER J/1 AUTOCRAT. G-AGYO.

AUSTER J/1 AUTOCRAT. G-AJXS

AUSTER J/2 ARROW. G-AJAM. Silver overall with red letters.

AUSTER J/5B AUTOCAR. G-AJYV. 'Blue Sky'. Silver overall with mid blue letters.

AUSTER J/8L. G-AMYI.

AUSTER 5. G-AJAK. Silver overall.

AUSTER 5. G-ANHS.

AUSTER J/5F ANGLET TRAINER. G-AMTB.

B.A.C. DRONE. G-ADPJ* Vivid blue fuselage with slight lighter blue flying surfaces. The registration letters and U.L.A.A. on the rudder were in black.

BLACKBURN B.2. TRAINER. G-AEBJ* Polished metal and silver. Maroon letters and struts. Believed current.

CHILTON D.W.1. G-AFGH. Was in Denham hanger.

COMPER C.L.A.7. SWIFT. G-ABUS. 'Black Magic' Gloss black overall with golden yellow letters and trim.

COMPER C.L.A.7. SWIFT. G-ACTF* Silver overall.

DARK KITTEN. G-AEXT* Red fuselage with silver flying surfaces. Believed current.

DARK KITTEN. G-AMJP. 'Mole Catcher'. Similar colours to XT above.

DE HAVILLAND D.H.60 CIRRUS MOTH. G-EBLV* Fuselage dark yellow with dark blue. The flying surfaces being aluminium silver.

DE HAVILLAND D.H.60G GIPSY MOTH. G-AAWO* Red fuselage with silver flying surfaces. Believed current.

DE HAVILLAND D.H.60G.111. MOTH MAJOR. G-ADHE*

DE HAVILLAND D.H.80A PUSS MOTH. G-AAZP* Silver overall with red letters and cowlings.

DE HAVILLAND D.H.80A. PUSS MOTH. G-ABDF* Shortly after making it's first appearance at Denham it had a fatal crash taking it's crew with it.

DE HAVILLAND D.H.82A TIGER MOTH. G-ADIH. Silver overall.

DE HAVILLAND D.H.82A TIGER MOTH COUPE. G-AIZF. Silver. Light blue letters.

DE HAVILLAND D.H.82A. TAXI TIGER MOTH. G-ANSA. Deep red and silver.

DE HAVILLAND D.H.85 LEOPARD MOTH G-ACMA*. Silver overall with black letters. Believed current.

DE HAVILLAND D.H.85 LEOPARD MOTH. G-AIYS* Silver and blue. Believed current.

DE HAVILLAND D.H.87B HORNET MOTH. G-ADNB*

DE HAVILLAND D.H.87B HORNET MOTH. G-ADND* Dark blue and silver. Believed current.

DE HAVILLAND D.H.87B HORNET MOTH. G-ADNE* Believed current.

DE HAVILLAND D.H.87B HORNET MOTH. G-ADUR. Silver with yellow and black. The London Aeroplane Club.

DE HAVILLAND D.H.87B HORNET MOTH. G-AEET* Red fuselage and wing registration. Silver flying surfaces.

DE HAVILLAND D.H. 89A DRGAON RAPIDE G-AHGH. Silver with red letters.

DE HAVILLAND D.H.94 MOTH MINOR. G-AFNI* Red overall with cream letters.

DE HAVILLAND D.H 94 MOOTH MINOR. G-AFNJ* Silver overall with black letters.

DE HAVILLAND D.H.94 MOTH MINOR COUPE. G-AFOJ. Silver overall with yellow letters. The London Aeroplane Club. Now in the Mosquito Aircraft Museum.

DE HAVILLAND D.H.C.1 CHIPMUNK. G-AJVD. Metal finish with yellow letters piped with a black edging. The London Aeroplane Club. Believe it still exists.

ERCO 415C EROCOUPE. G-AKFC. Metal finish with red lettering.

FAIRCHILD F-24W ARGUS. G-AIYO. 'Grey Dove'. Based at White Waltham.

FAIRCHILD F.24W ARGUS. G-AJSN. Bright blue with yellow cowling letters and struts.

FAIRCHILD F.24W ARGUS. G-AJSK. Silver overall with red letters and trim.

FOSTER WIKNER WICKO. G-AFJB* Dark red and silver.

GLOSTER GLADIATOR. G-AMRK* Silver overall with red letters and spinner.

HAWKER CYGNET. G-EBMB*. Cream fabric with black letters. Now in R.A.F Museum.

HAWKER TOMTIT. G-AFTA* Royal blue overall with gold letters and trim. Now with the Shuttleworth Trust as K1786.

HAWKER HART. G-ABMR* Colours as TA above. Now in R.A.F Museum as J9941.

HAWKER HURRICANE llc. G-AMAU 'Last of the Many'* Colours as TA above. To the B.B.M.F as LF363.

HILLSON PRAGA. G-AEUT* Silver overall with mid blue letters.

HIRTENBERG H.S.9A. G-AGAK*. Silver overall.

MILES M.2L HAWK SPEED SIX. G-ADGP. Deep cream-yellow overall with maroon letters and trim. Believed current.

MILES M.11 WHITNEY STRAIGHT. G-AERV. 'Anky Sim'* Silver overall with light blue letters and trim piped with black edging. On the nose an alloy swan.

MILES M.14 HAWK TRAINER 111. G-AFBS. Silver overall with royal blue letters and trim. Denham based.

MILES M.14 HAWK TRAINER 111. G-AJZH. Denham based.

MILES M.14 HAWK TRAINER 111. G-AKKW. Denham based.

MILES M.14 HAWK TRAINER 111. (COUPE TOP). G-AKRV.

MILES M.17 MONARCH. G-AFCR*

MILES M.38 MESSENGER 28. G-AGPX. Panshanger.

MILES M.38 MESSENGER G-AKAO.

MILES M.38 MESSENGER. G-AKBO.

MILES M.65 GEMINI 1B. G-AFLT. Silver with dark blue trim and white top to fuselage.

MILES M.65 GEMINI. G-AJWS.

MILES M.65 GEMINI 1B. G-AKHJ. Silver overall with dark blue letters piped with red edging.

MOSSCRAFT M.A.2. G-AFMS*. Cream overall with red letters and trim.

PERCIVAL P.6 Mew GULL. G-AEXF* Broken and in hangar at White Waltham. White overall with black letters.

PERCIVAL P.16A. Q.6. G-AHOM. Silver overall with dark blue letters. Captain Percival flew into Denham in this while a V.A.C. event was being held.

PERCIVAL P.28 PROCTOR I. G-AIHG. Silver aluminium with dark red letters and spats. Flown into Denham by Jackie Moggridge.

PERCIVAL P.28 PROCTOR I. G-AIWA. Silver overall with dark green letters.

PIPER J-3C-65 CUB. G-AIYV. Silver overall. Denham based.

PIPER J-3C-65 CUB. G-AIYX. Silver overall with blue letters.

PIPER J-3C-65 CUB. G-AKAA.

SAAB 91.B. SAFIR.Sk.50. 8-91123/23. Silver overall with Swedish military markings. Was at Panshanger at the time of a V.A.C. rally.

SPARTAN ARROW. G-ABWP* Cream and bright blue.

TAYLORCRAFT PLUS D. G-AHAI. Denham based.

TAYLORCRAFT PLUS D. G-AIIU. Silver overall with dark blue letters and nose cowlings. Denham based.

TIPSY B.2 TRAINER. G-AFSC*. Silver and red. Believed current.

TIPSY B.2 TRAINER. G-AFWT* Yellow overall with black trim and letters. Believed current.

The charter ticket for G-AWCH

MY CHANCE TO OBSERVE

With the demise of the V.A.C, my aviation interests took a downward turn. To combat this, I took to motoring to air events and airfields where I continued to build up my collection of different aircraft photographs. By now I had pensioned off my old trusty Calthorpe "Constance" and I was riding an Ariel Red Hunter, but it was still a pre-war machine. Sometimes I would take Daphne on the pillion and at other times I would ride out on my own. Typical of the ride-abouts that I made was in July of 1952 when I called in on Hurn and took my pictures of the four Avro Tudor 4's that had been placed out to grass. These were, G-AGRF "Elizabeth of England", G-AHNJ "Star Panther", G-AHNK "Star Capulet" and G-AHNN "Star Leopard". One other of my excursions was when I made a trip to Redhill with the purpose of obtaining some photographs of the last remaining de Havilland Flamingo prior to it being broken up and sold to the scrap-man. This was in July 1953. On my way to Redhill I made a stop at Blackbushe. Here I managed to get a nice photo of the Consolidated PBY-5A Catalina amphibian VP-KKJ "Namnagani". Her colours were black and white. Whenever I made a ride out to Blackbushe, I never failed in finding something fresh that I could add to my collection. Typical aircraft types were, de Havilland D.H.90Dragonfly, Vickers Vikings, Lancasters, Yorks, Piston Provost, Tudors, and many American service types.

In the February of 1954, Daphne and I got married. We had to start off by living in caravans. It was not then possible to rent a house for love nor money, well not British money. The Americans were back over here once again on Greenham Common and also on Welford's old airfield. This was now becoming an ammunition arsenal. All of the Americans required a lot of housing. They were paying treble the price to what we British could afford in rented accommodation. The local landlords made it quite clear to us that they would not rent out their properties to the likes of us British working people. We rented caravans in three different sites. Daphne then fell on our first child, Linda. My parents then suggested that we should move back in with them. No way could we manage to put money down on a house and so we continued to try and find some rented accommodation. Eventually a gamekeeper friend spoke up for us to the lady that was managing the Elcot Hotel. She agreed to let us rent the old bothy that was to the rear of a large garden wall. Before we could move in we had to clean it out from dirt and cobwebs and decorate the interior. First nettles had to be cut down in order to get to it. This we did along with my parents help. We bought our new furniture and were about to move in. The lady agreed not to take any rent off of us until we were actually living there. First, we were taking along the new floor coverings prior to the arrival of our new furniture. When we got to the bothy door we then found a note placed in it. It said, something like this, 'Due to her solicitor, she could not then let us rent this bothy'. All of our new furniture then had to go into storage. Camp Hopson in Newbury could not believe us until we showed them the note. They were very good to us and they gave us free storage. This incident caused me to have a nervous breakdown. An old friend of mine from my A.T.C. days , Frank Benson, along with his wife Joyce had managed to rent a house in Highclere. In a one roomed dwelling attached to their home lived an old lady who owned the property. This dwelling became empty and thanks to Frank we were able to rent this dwelling. Here we lived for the best part of a year and it was with thanks to Daphne's mother's rent collector that we managed to get a new council house in Thatcham. We now had our little daughter Linda. Here we lived for a year or so and then exchanged council houses with a family at Wickham.

Now while living at Thatcham, I decided to look for a new interest in life that had aviation at its roots. I then joined the R.O.C.(Royal Observer Corps). The post crew that I joined was in a Lema Cluster with its post located at Cold Ash. The role of the R.O.C. during the war years had been aircraft reporting. Now due to the cold war it was rapidly changing to nuclear detection. This meant in having to man an underground post and report on nuclear bursts and fall-out levels. It was still thought that enemy aircraft could sneak in low under the radar net and so the above post was also retained. Due to this, aircraft recognition was still on-going. At that time I knew most of the light aircraft when I saw them. Now I had to get to grips with the larger heavy metal. Within the Corps I found a little of what I was looking for. That interest in aircraft which was also shared by the others. There was comradeship and the pride that was taken in the running of the post.

Not so long after I had joined, I then made my council house exchange from Thatcham to Wickham. This was from the east side of Newbury to its west side. This then got us back in the same location as where our parents lived and also back into the countryside. Cold Ash was about twelve miles distant and so I transferred to the R.O.C. post at Shefford Woodlands. This was always known as the Hungerford post as it was crewed by that town's people. It was in the same Lema cluster of the four posts. Our head quarters was No. 14 Group with its centre at Winchester. We were on the outer northern side of our group and our boundary met up with the Oxford Group. My new post was Lema Three. This post like most of the others, was situated on very high ground in the Shefford Woodlands area and it was much closer to my home than the others that came from Hungerford. On one evening of each week, we as a team, would meet up in a pub in Hungerford. Here in a private room we would sup ale as we got our heads down in to the training. Several times each year we would be expected to take part in exercises. We then had to man our post full time while these exercises were taking place. The aircraft reporting role was now on its way out. Each post had its underground chamber that had been built at quite a high cost to the government. Nuclear reporting of bursts, be they air or ground, and the decay rate had to be reported over a land line.

With the dropping of the two atomic bombs on Japan, I now realized that nuclear weapons were here to stay and that they were not going to go away. Now that they had been invented, there was no way that they could be done away with. Like earthquakes and volcanoes, they are here and one has to try the best methods of living with them, and that was the way that I approached nuclear weapons. Myself, I do not like the stuff. I look upon it as being dangerous and I am not a lover of nuclear power stations. Having these, then leaves behind that nuclear radiation which future generations will then be forced to live with. As an individual there is nothing that I can do about it than except that is now with us and to try and find the best ways of living with it. That was my frame of mind when I joined the R.O.C.

The powers to be then decided that each cluster should have its own radio post. This made sense as land lines could easily be destroyed with a nuclear attack. Our post was the one that was chosen in our cluster to operate the radio. We would then take all of the information from the other three posts on the cluster and then report it through to the centre on the radio. The other two posts on our cluster that I have so far not mentioned were Great Bedwyn and the Newbury post which was at Wash Common. The chief observer of this Newbury post was Charlie Baxter who was a work mate of mine. One thing that I was never very happy about was that in thundery conditions we had to raise a high radio mast. We were situated on the highest open ground and this aerial led down into our underground bunker. Had we had received a lightning strike, it could have been curtains. Mind you, if we were in a nuclear war, a lightning strike to a post would amount to nothing. It nearly came to that with the Cuban crisis, but thank God, no body pressed a red button. I have never been one to quote the Holy Bible, but in the New Testament in the book of Acts, Chapter Two, and the verses 19 and 20 read. 'And I will show shew wonders in Heaven above, and the signs in the earth beneath; blood and fire, and vapour of smoke: The sun shall be turned into darkness, and the moon into blood, before that great and noteable day of the Lord come: Could this prophecy be referring to a nuclear disaster, or some act of nature such as Yellowstone National Park erupting'?

It is not my intention here to write on what might happen to the earth or on the workings of the R.O.C. My intention is to tell you about some of the enjoyments that I derived from being an observer. Once every year we could attend a summer training camp. This was always held on an R.A.F. station. Often on one that was having a period of under care and maintenance. Each year these camps would be held in different parts of the country. While here at camp training, it gave you the chance to regain the living life of the serviceman. We were nearly always given an afternoon off in the middle of the week and the summer evenings were all our own. I also enjoyed taking my own transport and enjoyed the chance of being able to get out and to see some fresh countryside. My other hobby that I have always enjoyed was the collecting of old shotgun cartridges. I have written several books on this subject. These old cartridges that are collectable are those with paper tubes that were sold by gunmakers, gunsmiths and ironmongers that carried their firm's names. While in these different locations, I would usually obtain a few of them which I would then be able to add to my growing collection.

One year I rode all of the way to Lancashire on my Vespa scooter. On another year I rode all of the way to Norfolk on my Ambassador 175 cc motorcycle. I remember this bike well due to one happening. I was motoring on it from Reading to Ashamstead in the dark along small country lanes to visit a gamekeeper friend. I came upon a right angled bend and as I shut down quickly, its two-stroke engine stalled. Its fire had gone out and with it the lighting as it had what was called direct lighting. This caused me to end up through a gateway and to fall off of the bike in a very muddy field entrance. Again I have side tracked and so to get back to my R.O.C. days. Riding that Ambassador home from my camp at Binbrook in 1961, I decided to have a break by making a stop at Kidlington, now Oxford Airport. I had previously made a visit here with my brother Dick on the 21st of May 1949. Then we had journeyed there by bus and together we had flown in a red and silver Dragon Rapide G-AKSL. This had been Dick's first venture up into the air. That Rapide had belonged to Goodhew Aviation. I parked my bike and had a walk round. This being in the good old days before the terrorists changed things. People would then welcome you to have a look around in their hangars. As I was in uniform, I was at once offered a ride in a brand newly imported Cessna 175B Skyhawk. This was G-ARMR and a Mr Braithaite its owner was busy impressing a friend with his new purchase. At this time, this new Skyhawk had not yet had its registration published in the new lists of registrations that were printed in some of the aviation magazines. Sitting in the rear its owner flew us to Hempton where there was a disused airfield of Barford St. John. Once here, the owner then let his friend make three approaches. Barford had started out as a R.L.G. (Relief Landing Ground). It got used by aircraft from Kidlington and Upper Heyford during the war. It was to see such aircraft types as Oxfords, Mustangs and No. 16 O.T.U's Wellington Mk.IIIs. These were then followed by Mosquitos. The Gloster Aircraft Company also used it to test its prototype Meteors. While here they were known as Gloster F.9/40's. These were DG204, DG205 and DG206. Also tested here was the Gloster E.28/39 Pioneer W4041. On our way back while over Blenheim Palace, the home of the Duke of Marlborough, Mr Braithwaite turned round and offered me a cigarette. This was the first time that I have ever smoked in an aircraft, and I also believe, the last time as well. This he lit by pulling out a glow lighter from the instrument panel. I then enjoyed a fine blend of freemans in comfort and luxury. I speak of this because aeroplanes and naked lights have never gone together until then in my world. The R.A.F. had brought me up never to smoke in the close proximity to bowsers or aircraft, or in any hangar. These training camps were very helpful and most interesting. They were also as good as having a paid holiday.

Another enjoyment that came my way through being an observer in the R.O.C. was being given air experiences. This was something that I had never been given while serving in the R.A.F. They had considered it to be unnecessary. Ever since my first flight in that Airspeed Oxford I have always faithfully logged every minute that I have been flown in and the type of aircraft and its registration. If my home was to go up in smoke, one of the first things that I would try and rescue would be my flying logs. The aircraft types that I flew in whilst in the R.O.C. were, Armstrong Whitworth Argosy, Blackburn Beverley, Bristol Britannia, de Havilland D.H.106 Comet C.2, Handley Page Hastings C.2 and the Westland Wessex. I never did get to make it in a Lockheed Hercules. I am not going to describe every flight that I had while in the Corps. In order to show you the enjoyment of having these flights I will just refer you to the last four of them that I had while wearing my R.O.C. uniform.

A date had been set to one side in August 1965 for our post to go flying. In order to do this we had each given up a days pay. To make sure that we got a flight, Don Fratter our officer had arranged that we pay a visit to Odiham in the morning where we might obtain a helicopter flight. He then arranged for a visit to Lyneham in the afternoon where we would stand a good chance for a flight with Transport Command. This way we might not lose out as we would stand a chance of flying from one of the stations. In that morning we obtained a helicopter flight. Unknown to the R.A.F. we fast motored from the centre of Hampshire to the north of Wiltshire where we then succeeded in obtaining a flight in a Comet.

When we arrived at Odiham, we were to find that we were not expected. This then brought floods of memories coming back when I last visited Odiham while in the A.T.C. Their squadron of Wessex helicopters were due to leave on that day by going off on a detachment. Later on we were to see them formate and leave. Rather than disappoint us, Head Quarters Flying Wing then laid on a special flight of fifty minutes in their Westland Wessex XR524 that was coded F.

We boarded the chopper on an apron-pad and from this we took to the air and were flown off in an easterly direction. R.A.E. (Royal Aircraft Establishment) Farnborough was hovered over. It was then closed for flying as the runways were under repair, not that this could have stopped a helicopter. After reaching the Hog's Back, we did a rate one turn and flew back to Lasham. This became a very interesting flight as our pilot gave us a full demo' on the helicopters capabilities. At one time we were windmilled down towards the top of an overland power grid pylon. As we drew very close, the power was restored and away we went. Later the Wessex was banked so steeply that we looked straight down at the ground below through the open doorway. Winding off our ride, when back at Odiham, we were then flown across the airfield sideways and in both directions and then finally backwards. The next thing that happened was that our pilot landed us facing up on a very steep bank but he held plenty of power to the main rotor. From here we were flown low across the field and back on to the pad from which we had started from. With a little hover, we were then settled back down and the two Rolls-Royce Gnomes were shut down. We thanked the crew as we had all thoroughly enjoyed the experience. Now as we had all previously been taught, if you are lucky enough to have a leave form, then you should make good use of it. This we did by setting out for Lyneham and so to make good use of the rest of our day.

We arrived at R.A.F. Lyneham where we were booked on a 150 minute flight in the de Havilland Comet Mk.C.2, XK699 "Sagittarius". Nick-named by her crews as "Tear-ass", and not for nothing. As I write this, that Comet is now the gate guardian for R.A.F. Lyneham. I once obtained a special permission to go to the station and photograph her. A brisk walk across the Comet Bay and we located and boarded the aircraft. For the take-off, we sat in rearward facing seats and then fastened our seat belts. We took-off in daylight and headed west for Cornwall where we were flown to St. Mawgan. Our Comet then did some touch and goes by flying in over one coast and then flying out over the other. While on our return, somewhere over Somerset, we all experienced an extra large bump. It was the largest bump that I had ever experienced in the air. I was standing at the time and it gave me a pain in the rear of my neck. We had been given the freedom of the aircraft, but once back at Lyneham we were instructed to sit and to buckle up our seat belts. The rest of our ride then consisted of circuits and bumps.

Our first circuit was made by passing over Calne and then Swindon. Little did I know then that one day I would be living down there. On the first two circuits, just approaches were made. The engines being given full power as we zoomed up into the darkness again. Sitting in the seats we were very conscious of the enormous thrust which those four Rolls-Royce Avons were poking out. It was now quite dark as we looked out over the lights of Swindon with the wing tips just visible in the moonlight. A beacon was flashing out the letters 'HV' in morse, this being Hullavington. After the fourteenth circuit we finally came in for a landing. By now we were all tired and a little hungry, we had been well satisfied and by the time that we had reached our homes we had all had enough for one day. All the same, we all had thoroughly enjoyed our selves.

The Handley Page Hastings was about to be taken out of service. It had given Transport Command many faithful years of service by plying around the globe. All of our post had never flown in a Hastings and we wished to do so before it became too late. Together we mentioned this to our officer who did not say yes and he did not say no. He kind of encouraged us to try and get a flight for ourselves. As the Hastings were based at Colerne, and this had been my old station, it fell on me to act on behalf of our post. I picked up pen and paper and wrote a letter addressed to the C.O. (Commanding Officer) of my old station. Well, when I was demobed, they did say, look in again sometime. My letter could not have been too bad as I got a reply from the C.O. He invited our crew to a visit of the station. I also took along with us my work mate Charlie who was the chief observer on the Newbury post. We all then enjoyed one hour and ten minutes flight in the Hastings C.2. WD485 of No. 36 Squadron.

Together we arrived at Colerne on the 26th of June 1967. We were then given a tour of the station. This included their air museum and a brand new Lockheed Hercules that was at the M.U. From here we were taken to the operations room and here they showed us that we had made their flight board. This was marked up as 'A Special R.O.C. Flight'. The R.A.F. bus that had been allotted to our party for the day took us out on to the airfield where we drew up next to our Hastings WD485 that had been written on their flight board. This C.2 was parked in a line of others of its breed which included a few C.1's.

The take-off was from that short runway which had a hump in the middle of it. This was the same runway in which Chalkie had experienced his trouble in the Meteor RA441 about twenty year ago. This hump made it impossible to see the other end of the runway from the flight deck of the Hastings when the aircraft had arrived at the holding position. Both of our pilots remarked that for them, that this was the first time that either of them had flown from it. We took-off into nice clear visibility. This old Hastings trundled along at a nice steady speed at a height that was most enjoyable to enjoy the scenery below us. We were invited to pay visits to the flight deck just two at a time. Our flight took us west as far as Chivenor. Flying westward we kept just in land and in sight of the coast. We then did a one hundred and eighty degrees turn to starboard where we were kept just out to sea so that we could enjoy the beauty of the cliffs and the coast line. The colours in the sea due to the sun and the shallows in the water were most beautiful. We could also enjoy looking out across Exmoor. As our pilots put it, we must not joy ride out over the new Severn Bridge and so our Hastings swung south and back over the land. It was then that our captain called up London's Heathrow over the radio and identified us as a four engine piston. This was to make sure that we were well clear of any airline traffic.

All too soon and we were back on the ground at Colerne. I for one was very pleased to have been given this chance to fly out from my old station. Also to be able to view it all from the air. We all had found the Hastings to have been a very pleasant aircraft to fly in. It had served our Air Force well as a flying tramp, and we all felt sorry that it was being taken out of service. Together we agreed that between ourselves, the income tax money that we had paid to the treasury had been very well spent. We then thanked our R.A.F. party and F/lt Sully for taking us. My guest Charlie Baxter had borrowed a large old motor for the occasion and into this we piled for him to drive us back to Hungerford.

Had our flight in that Hastings had cost the treasury too much money? Shortly after this we were all presented with some sad news and it came almost overnight. Due to defence expenditure cuts, our post was to be closed down. We had been given the chop. We had all received limited payments for managing the post and a mileage allowance. All of us were fully trained and we had given a lot of our spare time in order to be trained. Not one of us on our post were that concerned about receiving payments. We would all have willingly have carried on without them, such was the pride in our post. As it was, we were sacked and made to leave the corps. They may have thought that they had killed off our post, but they had not. We still continued to meet for over a year in the same pub with thanks to the landlord and the landlady. We forgot all of the nuclear stuff and just took enjoyment by taking it in turns to provide aircraft recognition tests while we enjoyed a beer. The breathalyser test had not then been thought of. We may all have downed a few pints but we always drove home safely. Our meetings only came to an end when a few of us moved too far away. From now on only one post had been saved out of every cluster. There was no longer any clusters as you need more than one to form a cluster. From out of our Lema Cluster, Charlie Baxter's post was the one that they kept. It was such a pity that a club had not been formed on a country wide basis. There were hundreds of bods who like ourselves that had been thrown on the scrapheap. We could have retained many of our skills and done many other things like taking airline flights to overseas events.

The official logic if that is the right word, was that now only the nuclear side of the business was going, then they could have a coarser network. By widening the network, posts would now be twenty to thirty miles apart instead of about ten. In so doing, they then managed to get rid of many sound underground posts and to keep a few that were plagued with dampness and water problems. Another sickening thing was that at the same time as they made this decision, they had been advertising over the television asking for more staff. With the cuts in the post network they then required more staff in manning the centres. Being one of the outer clusters we stood no chance. At the time of the chop, many of us had already arranged with our firms for the time off in order to attend the coming summer camp. We were then told that if we wanted to, that we could still go. This we debated between ourselves and so we decided to go. In doing this, we would then get a chance to put our views at the top. We were then to be sickened by what we saw and what we were told. We should not have gone. All of those in those posts that had been struck off must go. Those who's posts remained could stay, but even they had to cut their manning staff down by numbers. On the Newbury post, Chas who was the chief observer had the unpleasant job of saying who it was that had to leave on their post. Camp had normally been a very friendly place where one met up with other observers from all over the country. There was a very sad atmosphere about this camp. Amongst those that were staying there was many untrained and scruffy. The likes of those who chose to wear light coloured socks. No thought or thanks had been given to the Red Spitfire types and the Chiefs who had spent hours in getting training material ready for the training evenings. They and we all felt that our country had hit us all a very hard blow below the belt.

We had all been sacked for being good boys. If it had happened today with a private firm, then there would have been eruptions. All of our paper work had to be handed back, but they told us that we could keep our uniforms. I do not know how many of us sacked observers made use of our uniforms, but I did and only the once. I have thought twice about putting this in print, but I now feel that it should go in. Many a good serviceman has been so because he dared to do something that he should not have done. That old saying, 'he who dares wins'. Not that I have been a good serviceman in my time, yet on the other hand, I have not been a bad one either. The incident that I am about to relate to only came about due to the way that I felt that I had been treated and on the breaking of my pride.

I worked along with Chas and I had managed to get him that Hastings flight when along with my post crew. Chas had got to know some of the aircrew at Lyneham and was getting a few flying trips while wearing his uniform without the Winchester H.Q. being aware of it. One day I said to him jokingly, 'Hey, don't forget that I still have a uniform. With this he took me serious and he was determined to pay me back for getting him that flight in the Hastings. This is the way that it all came about as I went along with him on one of his unofficial flying trips.

Wearing my R.O.C. uniform, I then met up with Chas and he drove me to Lynham in his old Bedford Doormobile. This event came about only a week or so after I had been stood down. The weather was getting ever so foggy as we crawled our way into Wiltshire. I was now without any official identification card, but then, what was the point in allowing us to keep our uniforms if we could not wear them. These were some of the many thoughts that was going through my head at the time. I was now getting second thoughts as we drove into that Transport Command station. Well I had to press on regardless as I had left it too late to turn chicken. At Lyneham we sat sipping hot cups of coffee as we filled in the blood chits. These we were made to do just in case there might be an accident. This also made a chill run up my spine as I decided that it would be the better of two evils to sign my proper name and my ex number. Chas had been using his own number and it had not got back to H.Q. for as far as we knew. Our flight was to be in No. 511 Squadron's Britannia XL636 named "Argo" and A' go she did.

We boarded the Brit with the rest of the crew at 10.45 am. By 11.00 we were airborne and in one hour and ten minutes we had reached Prestwick in Ayrshire. Here we did two fly-over approaches. It was then back south to Manchester's Ringway Airport where we performed two more of them. We then headed on south for Gatwick where on reaching it we did another couple of fly-overs. From Gatwick we then headed back to Lyneham by picking up the 'Green One' air-corridor. We then circled Swindon and landed back at 15.30.

On our take-off from Lyneham the fog had lifted, but it was still very dull. The first leg of this training flight was flown at around 15,000 feet. We looked down on a solid layer of cotton wool looking cloud while flying in brilliant sunshine. At one time a few of the Welsh mountains could be seen popping their summits through the cloud way over to port. We were served with coffee and on leaving Prestwick we were each given a pre-packed lunch box. On passing over the Pennine Range, they were not to be seen, but the clouds below us could be seen to be lifting over the very high ground. My thoughts then turned to Amy Johnson on her last ill-fated flight in that Airspeed Oxford. We had plunged down through those thick clouds each time we made those murky let-downs. For our crew they knew exactly where they were, Amy had stood no chance. The only time that we saw sunshine on the ground was in the vicinity of Gatwick. On leaving Gatwick we were back into the rolling clouds and Didcot Power Station being just visible through the cloudy haze off to starboard. On this leg I took a photograph of the aircrafts shadow that was portrayed on the top of the cloud layer in a peculiar rainbow coloured halo.

On the ground at Prestwick we saw a B.O.A.C. (British Overseas Airways Corporation) Boeing 707, a Dakota, several de Havilland Doves and a R.C.A.F (Royal Canadian Air Force) Star Fighter among the many other aircraft. At Ringway it was ever so murky. Among the many aircraft there, Tridents were noticeable. Blackbushe had many light aircraft and Farnborough had a Beverley and a Hastings. These two aerodromes we just flew over and they were just clear of cloud. Gatwick was filled with airliners. Boeing 707's, various four engine Douglas DC's, a B.U.I.A. (British United Island Airways) H.P. Herald, a Britannia and several Airspeed Ambassadors with G-ALZP on the taxi-track. There were far too many aircraft for me to take them all in with just two passes.

"Argo" was fitted out with rearward facing seats to the rear of her main cabin. We also shared this flight with ten Swindon A.T.C. cadets. Although they did not know it, they kept on bringing me back memories of those two flights that I had in those Membury Dakotas. Our Flight Sergeant A.Q.M. (Air Quarter Master) was a very nice chap, but all the same I just could not help feeling out of place all of the time that I was in the aircraft. As we departed the Brit', her engines were kept running and a fresh crew and some more passengers boarded her. Here we left her as we made our way back to Charlie's Bedford. We then sat drinking cocoa from a flask as we waited to see "Argo" take to the air again. At the start of her take-off run we both detected a weird noise. Her engines were shut down in a haste as she aborted the run. She then came to a stop and pulled to the side of the runway. Whatever had gone wrong it could not have been too serious as after a time she slowly taxied back to the Britannia Bay. Whatever her trouble had been, it could quite easily have happened at Prestwick or some other place elsewhere. I thanked my lucky stars for my flight and at the same time I vowed to myself that I would never risk taking another flight in an R.A.F. aircraft well wearing my R.O.C. uniform. In one way, this flight did me the world of good and it made me take a better look at myself. I now felt that the government had just been paid back for the way in which I had just been slung out of the corps. I now decided that the wearing of my uniform was well and truly over.

Some of us were still meeting in "The Royal Exchange" which was also known as "The Town Gate" in the October of 1972. On the 2nd, three of us decided that we would fly over our old post and view it from the air. These were Percy Cleverley who had been our chief observer and was a night operator in the Newbury telephone exchange, Martin Munday who then worked in A.W.R.E. at Aldermaston, and myself who dug holes for telephone poles, and then planted and climbed them. We motored to Blackbushe where we chartered the Cessna 172 G-AWCH from Yellow Bird Air Taxis, Ltd. These people were known by their next door neighbours as 'Rentacrash' and we were about to find out just why. This did not stop us booking the Cessna and they listed our flight as 'Photography'. On this flight we had one hour and ten minutes in the air.

I sat to port in the front while Percy and Martin filled up the rear. Our pilot, Phil Cardue then flew the aircraft from the starboard seat. By doing this, it gave Percy and myself the chance to open up the windows so that we could use our cameras. These windows opened upwards in a Piper Cub fashion. As we were taxied out, I started to record our trip on a cassette recorder. This was to become a failure as I had placed it too close to the firewall where the engine noise was very pronounced. Turning the aeroplane on a compass pad, Phil then went through his checks before we made for the active runway. Permission was granted for Whisky Charlie Hotel over the radio and at the same time, Phil asked me if I would like to try my hand at the take-off. I was sitting in the normal pilot's seat and being dead keen, I just could not refuse the offer. As it happened, dead might have been the correct word for it, for had we had pranged, one wonders what the Accident Investigation Branch would have made of my black box tape recording. This was as near as we came to renting a crash. This Cessna was fitted with push-pull control wheels. Phil instructed me to pull back at a certain given airspeed and at the same time he did not tell me how hard and how far back that I had to pull on this control wheel. He had told me that he would correct any swing with the rudder pedals. At the reached airspeed of 65 knots I then pulled back on the wheel as instructed, but far too much. As we rotated I then kept my eyes on the clouds ahead. The result was that we had an all up weight simulated take-off of a B.A.C. Lightning in a Cessna. After this our good friend thought it best that he would do all of the flying himself. After all, this is what we were paying him for. I must admit that I learnt a valuable lesson from this incident and I am sure that he must have learnt himself a lesson as well.

Reaching 1,250 feet, a course was set towards Reading. Here the M.4 Motorway was picked up where Phil followed this as far as Theale, the place where during the war there was once an E.F.T.S. (Elementary Flying Training School) with many Tiger Moths on its charge. Now it was all water filled gravel pits but at least there was still one hangar there. From here our pilot flew by Bradshaw following the old Great Western Railway via Thatchan, Newbury and then Hungerford. Flying down this Kennet Valley, Martin then spotted a silver Tiger Moth in a field on the eastern side of Thatcham. This was G-AJHU that belonged to the Calleva Flying Group. When this Tiger was spotted, I then had no idea that in days to come that I would join this group and get to know that Tiger intimately. This I will speak more about in the chapter 'Roman Tigers'. Our Cessna then lost some altitude and I took my first look at her from the air.

I took my first photographs at Thatcham and we took several more as we circled Newbury. This was the first time that I had photographed our new telephone exchange from the air. Unfortunately we had picked a very dull day and the farther west we flew so the haze got thicker. It was certainly not a day for taking pictures although we did the best that we could. Due to these bad conditions our photographs were very far from good as what was to be expected. Over Hungerford we made a similar excursion of the town and then headed north to view our old post site. Having reached it we circled low, but there was no longer any person down there to log us. The visibility worsened and I then got us lost in trying to find Wickham. The viz had got that bad that you could not see across a field. I soon found out where we were when the Nato U.S.A.F. bomb dump was spotted below us. This was Welford, Wickham was then found by following the M.4 Motorway. Again we got lost as I tried to find Wickham Heath. If I had had control of the aircraft myself it would not have happened, but our pilot would keep swinging off to port all the time. Photography was useless. From Stockcross Phil then spotted the A.4 road and made for it. Jimmy Fairhurst's flying field at Shaw Dene came into view. There were several aircraft on the ground including a Beagle Terrier. Phil remarked that he would not mind landing there. We had not sought permission and so we did not suggest it. Our local survey completed, a course was set across country with some kind of radio aid from Blackbushe. Back at Blackbushe I noticed that I was not offered to help in the landing. Yellow Bird Air Taxis, Ltd then extracted £14 from us and we considered that we had been given good value.

From here we then motored on to London's Heathrow where we had a look at the bigger stuff. I have often wondered what Percy and Martin really thought about my attempt at a take-off. This was the very last time that we ever flew together. Now both Percy and Martin are long gone and so is my old work mate, Charles Baxter.

Hastings WD485 taking-off over the hump

THE RETURN OF UNCLE SAM

Daphne and I had found it very hard to get our own home up and running. We had also started our family. Finding a home where we could at last settle down had been very difficult to say the least. The Americans had snapped up every rented habitable property in our area. During the war they had commandeered all of our local girls. They had swept them of their feet with their yanky charm, posh uniforms, fat pay-packets and giving away nylon stockings. As it was generally said at the time, they were over paid, over sexed and over here. Due to all of this, then it is of little wonder that I and many others like me had began to feel a little anti American. A work mate of mine named Brian was killed when riding his motorcycle to work across Snelsmore Common. The American was at fault who was motoring to the Welford camp. Before he could be brought to trial, the base shipped him back to the States and his parents never received a penny. Incidents like this did not help for having good relations.

Working on telephones, I had often to work on the American bases of Greenham Common and Welford. I got to know several of the American servicemen and they all turned out to be nice guys. Many of the problems were not of their making individually. These problems had been brought on by their military. The majority of the American servicemen were very easy going. One must remember that if it had not been for America, then we may never have defeated Hitler.

The U.S.A.F. (United States Air Force) S.A.C (Strategic Air Command) had first brought their B-47 Stratojets to Fairford in Gloucestershire. These were early models and I went along to have a look at them in the August 1953. Whether or not I should have taken photos of them I do not know, but I could not resist poking my camera lens through the chain link fencing. I photographed three of them and their numbers were 12230, 12269 and 12271. They had nine JATO (Jet-assisted Take-off) solid fuel rocket units mounted in each side of the fuselage between the wings and the tail. Once discharged, they then had to be carried as so much dead weight. Later models were updated and fitted with thirty-three JATO units on an external metal frame. Once used, these racked frames would be dropped after the take-off. I was never to see any of these used at Greenham Common and I would not have wished to have been around when all of these framed harnesses and bottles fell out of the sky.

The first time that I knew of the Boeing Stratojet was when I saw the pictures of it in one of the late Aeroplane Spotters. These fortnightly aeronautical newspaper journals first came out in the early 1940's and continued up until 1948. When I first saw that XB-47 in the Spotter, little did I then realise that these would become stationed close to my home and become a common sight in our skies. When based on Greenham Common airfield and we were living at Thatcham, they were to wake us up when they fired up their six under-wing podded J-47-GE jet engines in the middle of the night. I have to say that they were very impressive being streamlined like a fish with thirty-five degree swept back very flexible wings. These wings carried double engine pods inboard and single engine pods outboard. The undercarriage was of the bicycle arrangement being in tandem which retracted into the fuselage. Braking utilized deceleration parachutes. These they would release after they had turned off of the runway. On take-off and as they took to the air, each engine would leave a trail of black smoke. Before this, I have only associated this with steam engines and dirty diesels.

It is not my insension here to write a history of Greenham Common. This would take a set of volumes on its own. As Greenham Air Base was then just over a mile away from our home as the crow flies while we were living in Thatcham, it is only fitting that I should give it a mention. This airfield was not the same as the old wartime one from which I first took to the air in an Airspeed Oxford. That one started to go back to nature until the government decided to use the site again for a NATO (North American Treaty Organization) base. It was then completely redeveloped having only one large long runway of 10,000 feet that extended into Crookham Common. I am not sure when the first American aircraft arrived on the new base. All that I can do here is to refer to my old spotting notes. To do this I have first got to separate them from other civil aircraft activities. About fifteen Boeing KC-97 Stratotankers were in residence between April and July in 1956 and numbers 2681 and 22684 were the last of them to leave. Between the October and December of that year, about fourteen Boeing B-47's were flown in and one carried the number 36231. After these had left and up until the March of 1957, there came another fourteen KC-97 Stratotankers. About half of these were fitted with long range under-wing tanks. Number 3170 was one of them. Now as I like C-47's and Dakotas, I can tell you that in the January of 1956 that there were ten of them based on Greenham. For the historians they were 0-292111, 0-311548, 0-315773, 0-349567, 0-292916, 0-315219, 0-315541, 0-315558, 0-330717 and 31532 which had a red tip to its fin and a red trim tab on its rudder. There was a trim line down the fuselage and it carried the blue spangled S.A.C. band around the centre of its fuselage. In the March of 1957, three more C-47's were in residence. These were 0-4883, 0-24214 and 0-315645. Also there was a Douglas C-54 being, 0-50555.

From then on and in the 1960's, several hundred B-47's must have flown through this base. They would arrive and depart three at a time. On each visit they might stay for a fortnight or so. As soon as three had departed, then three others would fly in to replace them. There were two distinct types of these B-47's. No sooner had they landed, than they would be refuelled and bombed up and fitted with the JATO harness. As they bombed each aircraft up, shields were then placed around so that no person could see the bomb or bombs that they were being loaded with. Once in a while they would practice a red alert and it was said that the crews were not to know if it was a practice run or the real thing. Thankfully they were always called back to their hard standings before they would need to fire up those JATO rockets. It was also said that just as soon as an aircraft had been made ready, it had then been briefed on to a set target that it had to attack.

Over the years, very many aircraft movements have taken place at Greenham Common. Most of their flying had been accident free. In February 1963, a B-47 number 32134 crash landed on the air base with no bombs on board, or so it was said. It had been on route to England from Lincoln, Nebraska, and it had been air refuelled over Goose Bay. One of its crew used an ejector seat near ground level and was killed. The other three in the crew were taken to the base hospital. It may have been just as well that they did not have many flying accidents because the western approach to that two mile runway was over Wash Common. This was over the high ground which was to the south of Newbury town and it was suburbian. If a KC tanker had dropped down on one of these southern housing estates and had gone up in flames, then flaming jet fuel would have flowed down into the town and there would have been a major catastrophic disaster. I well remember the day when we were digging a new trench to bury a telephone cable. The machine accidentally cut through another cable that we did not know was there. It then put their officer's mess out of action and this was on the outside of the base fencing. Their alarm was set off and a long convoy came our way with its lead vehicle having a large white board across the front of its cab that was near as high as the cab itself. Painted in large red letters were the words, 'Disaster Control'. If one of their flying tankers had gone down on the western approach, I fail to see what this convoy could have done about it.

On Friday the 28th 1958, they did have a major disaster on the base. From the top of Shaw Hill, Newbury, which was on the north east side of the town, I was to watch this disaster unfold. I was working along here with the cable gang. Three B-47's had taken-off and had flown away which was normal procedure for them. Shortly afterwards, one of them was heard returning. With my interest in aviation, I stood up on the high road side bank along with our brick box builder, Charlie Buxey. To the front of us it was grass fields. Today it is all housing estates. Together we watched this returning six jet bomber. Where we were standing we were looking south across the Kennet Valley and Greenham base was just over the horizon on the opposite side. I said to Charlie, 'Hell, he,s dropped his two wing tanks'. 'They are not tanks, they are birds', said Charlie. With that two enormous columns of red flame rose up into the air for two to three hundred feet. 'You were right said Charlie, they were not birds'. From where we were standing, we could not quite see what these tanks had hit as the base was just over the brow. With this, the whole gang stood up on the bank and watched. Whatever had been hit it was burning well. We should have got down behind the roadside bank in case there had been any large explosions, perhaps nuclear. Instead we just stood there looking across the valley in utter amazement. Well we were two to three miles distant.

The B-47 that had returned had developed an overheated engine. It had been told to return and to drop these tanks on the overshoot to the runway. Instead, these tanks fell in the centre of the airfield. One fell on a parked Stratojet and the other went through a hangar roof. I do not know, but I expect that this bomber would have been too heavy to land with these tanks full. I did not know until then that these wing tanks were detachable. This B-47 should have landed. Instead it was told to make off for some other airfield. One tank had fallen on a parked Stratojet and the other had gone through the roof of a hangar with another B-47 in it. One B-47 was burnt out and another, number 20256 was damaged by heat. It was said that the B-47 Stratojet that had been destroyed was not bombed up. Nothing was said about the heat damaged one. These military powers do like to indulge in cover-ups. Years after, there became a lot of cases of leukaemia in a local part of Newbury. This was in the area where that smoke had drifted. I still think that there was a possibility that the one outside of the hangar could well have been bombed up. The American servicemen so it was said, were leaving the base in all directions and in so doing they were hampering our emergency services from getting in. As soon as an aircraft had arrived at Greenham, screens were quickly put round the bomber and then as soon as it had been made ready, it was allotted a given target should it needed to have been sent. With the large number of nuclear bombs on that base, there must have been enough of them there to have destroyed the world as we know it. And all for what purpose. Had there had been a nuclear explosion then it would not have bared thinking about. The hangar doors were blown off and one chap who was in an office on the top of the hangar roof was said to have slid down breaking both his legs. If there had been a nuclear explosion, might it have triggered off Aldermaston and Harwell? At the time the press made headlines such as, 'Bomber strafes its own base'. Myself, I think that this was as close that I have ever come to a major disaster and I could quite well understand some of the concerns that those Greenham Piece Women had.

On the brighter side, with my interest in aircraft spotting, I did log a few of the many interesting aircraft that had flown into Greenham. Some of these were, Two Globemasters, 1153 and 3005 on the 17/7/56; B-36, 21355 on 21/10/56; Globemaster, 1148 on 28/10/56; Gloster Meteor, VM452 approaches on 9/4/57; B-29, 0-462081 on -/9/57; B-36, 92720 on 5/9/57; B-45, 0-7035 on the same day; Vickers Armstrong Varsity, WL637 low passes on 6/3/59; All white Handley

Page Victor, XA931 on the same day; Some KC-135's in 1960; C-54, 0-49054 and C-47 on 20/4/60; B-52F, 60588 on 15/8/60; On a lighter note, Olympia Sailplane 93 on 17/8/60; KC-135, 63637 on 27/11/60; B-52, 80253 on 14/11/60; B-52, 70070 on 8/1/61 with a tall fin; Lockheed T-33, 11625 on 22/6/61; N.A. Harvard, KF314 on 3/8/61; B-58 Hustler, 12059 "Can Do" record breaking. These were just a few of the many visiting aircraft and it should give you some idea as to the amount of aircraft movements that took place when this base was active. One day, and I have failed to record the date, I was one of several of us that were working by the side of an aircraft hard standing when the Boeing 707 'Air Force One' was taxied in to it. How I would have liked to have had my camera with me. When working on the airfield we had to have an armed guard with us. Cameras were definitely not allowed.

There is one song that suits the Americans fairly well, and it goes like this. Anything you can do I can do better, I can do anything better than you. And like anything you can build, I can build bigger, I can build anything bigger than you. And, yes they could. One day I was watching one of their large C-5A Galaxys as it was flying along very tight below a solid cloud base. I found it fascinating to watch. It was scraping the bottom of the clouds as it went on its way. In so doing, it kept on picking up portions of cloud. These small portions would then stay on the top of this large transport and be carried along for a short distance. As this cloud built up, it would then roll off the back of the aircraft. This was something that I have never seen happen before or since.

Prior to the arrival at Greenham Common of the G.L.C.M's (Ground Launched Cruise Missiles), Greenham then became home to some extremely noisy General Dynamics swing-wing F-111's. At this time America was telling Britain and France that their Concorde was far too noisy to land in the States. While they were doing this, Newbury, Thatcham and their local districts were having their piece shattered from the noise that these swing-wing jets were making. May I here make it clear that I had my own thoughts on those cruise missiles being housed in bunkers on Greenham Common, but these I do not wish to share with you.

Whenever we had to work on the actual airfield we could only do so while being escorted. We were not allowed to be let lose alone on there. While working on the main camp we were then given the freedom to be on our own. When on this NATO base you were as good as being in America. Over the years since the airfield of World War Two, very much of our underground telephone plant had got lost. In some places the ground over it could have been built up by as much as twenty feet. Often it was far cheaper and quicker to abandon the old and provide all new. One day we were searching for our plant. You had to try and find it first before you might come to the conclusion that the search was hopeless. It was just one of those days when our guard kindly offered us some help. He called in an electrically operated dozer that had four large wheels with balloon tyres. The Americans set it to work and as it dug deeper it formed a very deep basin in the ground. All of a sudden its electrics caught fire and it sat in the bottom of the basin. The Americans then retrieved their damaged dozer and we never did get to find our missing plant. At the time it reminded me of our black Labrador crossed collie woofer named Fred. One night he had got into next doors garden and had found himself a hedgehog. This prickly creature worried Fred and so he started moving round in circles as he dug at the ground all around this hedgehog. This being in the centre of our next door neighbour's garden plot. The hedgehog rolled its-self into a ball and as Fred dug, so the hedgehog rolled into the centre of a basin which Fred kept digging. The next day our neighbour was to find this large up-turned dome in his garden with all of the soil distributed far and wide.

On another occasion we were working just outside their east gate. At this time, the base had contractors in who were burying huge tanks for fuel installations. A well dressed chap wearing a bowler hat pulled up at the gate guard hut driving a big black limousine. He obviously wished to see some other person who was working on the inside. As the guard was speaking on his telephone, this chap spotted the person who he wished to meet just inside the gate. He started to walk over to speak with this other man and had strolled for about twenty yards inside. It was obvious that this chap was of the same firm as he also had a big black limo' with a number plate which was about one digit away from his own. Within seconds, and he was surrounded as several jeeps pulled up. He then had guns pointed in to his front and his back. His bowler was then removed and the contents of his pockets placed into it. He was then bundled off in a jeep with a gun still sticking in his ribs. We did not see him until very much later in the day when they brought him back and dumped him in his car on the outside of the gate. We learnt a valuable lesson on that day, never ever to take any liberties with those American guards. Once on the inside of that fence you were no longer in Britain. You were as good as being on a military station in America.

On the 19th of July 1956, the air base was open to the public. I enjoyed that day, and on this event one was allowed to carry a camera. There was a fine line-up of U.S.A.F and R.A.F. aircraft. I cannot now remember all of them. Those that I took photographs of were as follows, Armstrong Whitworth/Gloster Meteor NF.14, WS750 coded W; Boeing B-47e Stratojet, 12404; Boeing KC-97g Statotanker, 22692; Fairchild C-119F Packet, 18252; Blackburn Beverley, XB267 of No. 47 Squadron, Abingdon; Handley Page (Reading) Marathon T.11, XA273 coded C; Hawker Hunter F.4, XF320 coded R; North American B-45 Tornado, 7083 code BE-083; North American F-86D Sabre, 24101 coded FU-101; Percival P.56 Provost T.1, WV665 coded B-P; Republic F-84F Thunderstreak, 26667 coded FS-667.

To wind this chapter up I am quoting from the American base newspaper the Greenham Herald dated Monday, October 28, 1963. Greenham welcomed a B-58 Hustler crew after they had made a record speed and distance flight. A S.A.C. B-58 crew claimed an international super-sonic speed distance record October 16th completing an 8,028 (statue) mile flight from Tokyo to London in an elapsed time of 8 hours, 35 minutes. The B-58 was assigned to the 305th Bomb Wing, Bunker Hill AFB.

The Hustler super-sonic bomber streaked through the starting gate at Tokyo, after taking-off from Okinawa, and passed over Japan, Alaska, Northern Canada, Greenland and Iceland, before landing at R.A.F. station Greenham Common. Five aerial refuelings by S.A.C. KC-135 tankers were accomplished along the route. The B-58 passed through the London gate at 2;34 p.m. London time, 8 hours and 35 minutes after passing over Tokyo at 5;59 a.m. London time. The average ground speed for the flight was 938 m.p.h.

Crew members of that record setting bomber were, Maj Sidney J. Kubesch, 33, El Campo, Tex., aircraft commander; Maj O. Barrett, 32, San Antonio, Tex., navigator and Capt Gerald R. Williamson, 26, New ORLEANS, La., Defence Systems Operator. The previous Tokyo-to-London record was held by an English Electric Canberra crew in 17 hours, 42 minutes on May the 25th 1957. The Canberra averaged 335.2 m.p.h.

Now this NATO base is long gone. The local council decided to break-up that long runway. What they saw was a profit in the concrete rubble. They should have been made to have left that runway only if to be used in an emergency. Failing that it could have just been covered over with soil. Should our country ever have a cause to need it again then it would still have been there. It would not have taken a bulldozer long to have reclaimed it. Hungerford always had cattle roaming on their common. Newbury had to do the same. There was never any cattle on it prior to an airfield being built there. In pre-war days it was a very beautiful place clad all over with purple heather where the town folk could walk its many footpaths between the heather and also take picknics.

A B-47E Stratojet lands on Greenham Common

UP IN YOURS

Although the R.O.C. had given me opportunities to fly in those large R.A.F. aircraft, I still felt that I needed another outlet so that I could get myself into the air from time to time. I still made odd trips to airfields where I continued to add to my photographic collection. The sad thing today is that I still have hundreds of black and white negatives of several sizes and it is not easy to find any person who can still print them at a sensible cost. One trip that I made was to Thruxton in my little Austin Seven OD 9120 named Odette. At that time there was a row of civilized Mosquitos that had been put out to grass until they all rotted away. I managed to take a photograph or two of some of them before things got too bad. On that day I bought a joyride in the prototype Thruxton Jackaroo G-AOEX. I sat my little daughter Linda on my knee and this then became her first flight in an aircraft. As I am writing this, that old Jackaroo is now in the ownership of Arthur Christian who has been working on her for many years. There is every chance that one day she will fly again, but by the speed of the progress, I may not still be around to see it. Our eldest son Clifford had his first flight along with me at Blackbushe in the Piper Tri-Pacer G-ARCU. Our next eldest child, Bobby went along with me in the deHavilland Heron 1B G-AOXL when we made a visit to a Battle of Britain day at R.A.F. Benson. Although I had stopped visiting Farnborough, I nearly always would attend a Battle of Britain air display. Back in the fifties and sixties, many R.A.F. stations around the country would open up to the public and put on a show for the public. Today they cannot afford to do so. They would also be pushed to find enough pilots and aeroplanes. What sad times it is that we now live in, it makes me wonder why we ever won a war and also for what. In those days I had travelled as far south as R.A.F. Andover and as far north as R.A.F. Waddington to enjoy a Battle of Britain display.

Many is the time that I have felt like kicking myself, this for never having tried harder to obtain a flight in a flying boat. Especially as they used to operate off of the Solent. In the August of 1976, the Short S.25 Sandrinham VP-LVE "Southern Cross" that belonged to Antilles Air Boats made a visit to Poole Harbour. It had been flown there by Captain Charles Blair who did us the honour of letting us people enjoy this old boat that he had flown to England via Ireland form the Virgin Islands. For the week that he was at Poole he had planned on selling joy flight around the Isle of Wight. This way he would have given many British people the pleasure of flying in this historic flying boat. At the same time it would have helped him in financing his visit. At last here was the opportunity for me to fly off of the sea and in a four radial engined flying boat. Well that is what I thought, but it was not to be. The captain did manage to make one or two of these flights just after he got there. On that coming night, the "Southern Cross was vandalized. A plug had been unscrewed from one of her floats and she had nearly capsized. Who would have thought that you would have needed to have placed a guard on a civil aircraft. A new plug then had to be made and all of the sea water pumped out of the float. This put her out of use for most of her weeks stay. I very much suspect that the vandal was a boat owner. I never got to hear of any person being charged for doing that damage. I once had a bitter experience of having my small car vandalized in a car park while I was attending a deHavilland Moth Club's banquet in Stevenage. My car was a Citroen Dyane with a soft top. The vandal had slit the roof and the seats and twisted everything that he or she could not break off. All of my tools were stolen and also some of my clothing. The only thing that they did miss was my camera and photographic gear which was in a black box in the rear on the floor. I know how I felt over that incident, and so I can quite well visualize how Captain Blair must have felt over his float incident.

It had been announced that on the Saturday the 28th of August that the "Southern Cross" was to depart from Poole for Ireland and I would think that this would have been for Foynes on the Shannon. I then motored down to Poole just hoping that I might be lucky enough in getting myself a flying boat ride. Several other people had got similar ideas as well as myself. I also was aiming at getting some nice coloured photographs and of this I succeeded in doing. Having arrived at the harbour, we were then told that Captain Charles would make a few pleasure flights before he departed. I joined the queue and the flying boat filled up. Due to all of those people that like to muck about in small boats, the harbour master would not give him any permission to let him fly from the sheltered waters of the harbour. The captain taxied out to the sea with his first load of passengers. When he got there, he then considered that the sea was too rough and so he returned back to the quay and unloaded them. I had been stood on that quay waiting to be on the next flight. Obviously Captain Blair had made the right decision, although it proved to be very disappointing for me. Like a few of the others, we never even got to have a ride in her. I did later on in that day take a boat trip out into the harbour to the flying boat where I was able to take some nice pictures of "Southern Cross" both from the inside and also on the outside. The harbour authorities did then clear a stretch of water in the harbour for him to make just the one take-off, this for his return to Ireland.

I found it pathetic that our country that had been so rich in aviation had acted the way that it had. Had it had been foul weather during the week, those people with their small boats would have been only to pleased to have kept their boats tied up. Surely they could have given up just a little portion of the harbour for this occasion. In pre-war days, Short 'C' Class Empire flying boats had flown our Union Flag worldwide. Short Sunderlands had flown thousands of hours during the war while protecting our convoys so that we could then enjoy the freedom of peaceful living. B.O.A.C (British Overseas Airways Corporation) together with Aquila Airways Ltd, had also flown our flag post-war. Our country should only have been too pleased to think that Captain Blair had decided to visit our south coast where these grand old boats had once been made and flown from. They should have made him welcome with open arms. Charles was a grand old fellow who sadly past away now several decades ago. I was very pleased that I was able to meet him. I am sorry if I offend those seafaring people of Poole, but I do think that you behaved very badly.

The deHavilland D.H.83 Fox Moth G-ACEJ had languished for a while at Walkeridge Farm, Hannington. It had arrived there for Cliff Lovell to tidy her up and to give her a new lick of paint. When she had arrived she was silver overall with red letters and struts. Cliff had sprayed her in a new colour scheme of black and silver with gold letters and trim. These new colours were suppose to have been the same as those that were once worn by the second production Fox Moth G-ABUT that had romped home by winning the 1932 King's Cup Air Race. These may have been the correct colours, but on looking at several old black and white photographs, I am now not quite so sure.

An air test was scheduled for Wednesday the 23rd of June 1976. For this I took a day's leave from my work so that I could be present and take a few pictures. Cliff needed to make a trip to Thruxton to tank her up. As there was a spare seat, Cliff very kindly invited me along for the ride. There was no front seat fitted in the small cabin and so I sat by the side of Ron Souch and we faced forward. It was a nice warm summers evening as we took to the air and flew down to Thruxton in company with the SIPA 903, G-BDKM. This pleasant little trip lasted about twenty minutes. The Fox was nice to ride in and was extremely quiet. This was made possible by the long exhaust pipe which extended way back beneath the passenger cabin. I was able to look back through a small inner window between the rear of the cabin and the pilot's cockpit where I could see that Cliff was also enjoying himself.

On reaching Thruxton, the SIPA landed first and we then followed it in. While here, I took a stroll down the long row of picketed aircraft to see what was there. One aircraft that had eluded my camera was the Sokol M.1C, G-AIXN. This I then added to my collection of photographs. Ron and I then took a stroll down the side of the grass runway while Clifford took 'EJ up on his own. Flying just outside of the Thruxton circuit he then tried a stall or two so that he could see just how well the aircraft handled. We two then just layed back on the grass and took in the sound of that beautiful old aeroplane.

For our return trip I had arranged to aim my camera at the SIPA. This I did. When I had finished, I slid the little curved window along, poked out my left arm and stuck my thumb up. It was then that I discovered that time can really fly, literally. I then felt my watch leave my wrist with an accelerated velocity. My first thoughts then were for the tail of the aircraft, more than what they were for my missing time piece. As it turned out it had missed on hitting the aircraft and I never got to hear of anybody suffering from a timed headache. Somewhere deep in the lush green of the Hampshire countryside there may still be a watch. Perhaps someday a person with a metal detector may come across it, but I am sure that it will have stopped ticking by now.

As we flew over Popham we were waved at from below by Jim the airfields owner. This was a good enough signal for Cliff to take the Flying Fox in for a landing. For the short distance from here back to the farm I exchanged seats with the lady passenger of the SIPA. This then gave her a chance to ride in the Fox and for me to take some air to air pictures of the Fox Moth. Once more, sod's law stepped in as the film in my camera jammed up and tore. For some reason, every time that I had been fortunate to try my hand at air to air photography things had gone wrong. Half of my troubles had been through not owning an expensive enough camera, or was it just due to those gremlins. When I had arrived at that farm hangar on that afternoon the Fox Moth was having the last touches of gold sprayed on to her cowlings. Then all of the masking had to be removed, pushed outside on to the apron, wings unfolded, dusted down and the propeller fitted. It had been like a dream that I had been given the chance to have a flight in her and to have been the first person to take pictures of her wearing her new colour scheme. Four days later she was to make her first public appearance at Old Warden wearing her new silver, black and gold.

On the 17th of August 1982, a visiting aircraft at Old Warden crashed and came to rest on the top of this Fox Moth, Echo Juliet. Both aircraft became torched when fire broke out and the occupants in the other aircraft lost their lives. Although the Fox was then destroyed, I did get to fly again in her as G-ACEJ many years later. I will explain all about this in the later chapter, 'The Aircraft Restorers'.

Four months after my ride in the Fox Moth, I called back at Walkeridge Farm. I had got to know Arthur and Ruth Christian long before Cliff Lovell had decided to have his workshops there. I had first got to know Cliff when he had a small workshop on Blackbushe. Arthur was a farmer with a keen interest in aviation and many other old things that were mechanical. I first met Arthur when I had to do a job of work there while employed by the General Post Office Telephones. At that time he was the owner of the one and only single seat light aeroplane, the Taylor Watkinson Dingbat G-AFJA. Later he was to sell it and then still much later on he was to buy it back in a crashed condition. One day he hopes to restore it but that Jackaroo G-AOEX has got to be finished first. The Dingbat was a home built aircraft that was well described in Richard Riding's book 'Ultralights' with its book reference being, ISBN 0-85059-748-X. It was, and still is, powered by a 30 h.p. Carden-Ford water cooled engine. Most one-off home built aircraft of the 1930's disappeared during the war years, but not the Dingbat. It just got passed on from one owner to another. The Carden-Ford engine was heavy for the amount of power that it gave out having been a conversion of a car engine. This then made the Dingbat a bit underpowered. Having said this, the little Chilton Monoplane which was also described in Richard Riding's book flew, and still flies very well with this engine. Suffering with a poor power to weight ratio, Arthur who being built like me was not the lightest of persons, but he did manage to fly it. I also had a chance to speak with Roy Nerou about the Dingbat as he was also one of its many owners. Roy is now very much into the Chilton monoplanes. The late Bill Hardy once told me on how he had flown it. All that I can remember of Bill talking about it was that he was very pleased when he managed to get it back safely on the ground again. When in Arthur's first ownership, 'JA's colour scheme was a primrose-yellow overall with sax-blue registration letters. These were applied in the post-war style. Arthur kindly gave me permission to go all over it with a ruler and also a Piper Vagabond which he once owned. From these measurements that I took I then made two G.A. (general arrangement) drawings. These I am including here in this book. Arthur gave me a flight around the Kingsclere area in his all white Vagabond which was still carrying the French registration F-BEBL. Well it was all white when I first got into it, but it was later to change colour. This was my very first flight in a Vagabond. After much juggling between us, we finally extracted this high wing side-by-side two seater out through its new hangar doors. Both of us being large blokes, there was then no more room to spare once the cabin door were shut. I think that you will find that it was their little Vagabond that saved the Piper Aircraft Company just after the ending of the war. All the same, it was not quite such a tight fit as being in an early Cessna 150. After my flight, Arthur then took a lady friend of his family up for a quarter of an hour. When first extracted from its hanger, 'BL was all white with red trim and black letters. After its second landing it had changed colour. It was now a shade of brown that looked as though it had been camouflaged with white streaks. Every cowpat on that field must have splattered it. Arthur then called out his wife Ruth and between the four of us it took us over a half hour to bring it back to white again. If there is one thing that is better than red dope for sticking on fabric covered aeroplanes then it is cow muck. In later years I was to spend hours removing up-turned dung heaps from the lower wings of Tiger Moths on a level with the undercarriage. Captain deHavilland's team did not design any mudguards for their Tiger Moths.

On Sunday the 10th July 1977 I had my first glider flight. It turned out to be the shortest flight that I have ever made. Because of this it was one of the most interesting. Like my first powered flight in that Airspeed Oxford, it was not taken without some troubled problems. This short flight was taken at Thruxton. The glider which was selling flights was an ex A.T.C. training glider. It was a Slingsby Cadet TX Mk.3. It was known in the civil field as a Tandem Tutor. This craft had no British civil aviation markings, but it bore the B.G.A. (British Gliding Association) number, BGA 1559. The actual time in the air was between one and two minutes. Altogether with the many preparations it took on nearly a couple of hours. You may quite well ask, was it all worth it, and my answer was yes. For this most interesting experience it cost me 75p. As I have just said, like my first powered flight it was not without its problems.

Having joined the queue, it was then that I noticed that things were not going right. The winch snarled up and this broke the wire in several places along the ground. Having waited for over an hour, my turn eventually came. Some more delays then occurred, as I squashed myself into the front cockpit, I then had to extricate myself back out again. This cockpit must have been tailored around a small A.T.C. cadet, it certainly was not intended to fit me. It gave me an inferior complex, like, that I had become as fat as Hermann Goering. I was not then, but perhaps today, yes. All of this was because Peter the pilot had noticed that his car had gone missing. A search of the airfield located it and it was retrieved. Again I squashed myself back into that tiny cockpit. I was then ordered to strap myself in though it would have been near impossible for me to have fallen out unless my tight fit had broken the glue seems. I feel sure that those sides must have bulged.

Having tidied up the cockpit of loose straps we were now at last ready to fly. Peter in the cockpit behind me, then gave the command, ' take up slack'. Alan who was kindly assisting was sitting in the car which was now back at its rightful place. He then flashed a signal to the winch operator using the cars headlamps. The winch was at the other end of the gliders grass runway. These glider flights were taking place to the side of the powered runway. This was then followed by the signal,' all out'. With this the wire rope tightened and the glider accelerated up the field at a rapid rate of knots. With such a terrific speed we overtook the tow rope. I thought to myself, 'this is most interesting' as the safety catch was slipped and it aborted us some eighty to a hundred yards from our starting point. 'That was far too fast', said Peter. 'The trouble is that the winch operator is new to the game'.

Out again I had to get out and I was sure that those cockpit sides were getting wider apart. Together along with the rest of the helpers we then man and woman handled that glider back to the starting position. A Mini-pickup, Ute, if you are an Australian, retrieved the rope and for the third time I squeezed myself back into that minute cockpit. Those signals were again repeated and once more we sped along the grass. This time the glider reached between five and six hundred feet when there was a loud bang and a jerk. This was the report as that rotten cotton, well wire rope had broke again close to the glider. The glider jumped in the air on being set free and Peter levelled out and through the stick to starboard so making a very tight turn and an approach back to where we had started from. In such a very short space of time I found it nice to be able to hold a quiet conversation out in the open between the two open cockpits. 'Too damn fast again and also far too slow at the start', said Peter my pilot. 'We should have made well over 800 feet if all had gone as it should have done'. It was the gliders nose pointed down and level out as the skid slid along the tarmac and back on to the grass, and that was my first glider flight.

Mine became the last flight of the day. Peter had released the broken end of the towline and this then became lost in long corn which was growing by the side of the gliders runway. On these flights, one is expected to join in with the fun of the ground handling. These were the jobs like, lowering or lifting the wing tips. Also, running along and holding the wings level at the wing tip until the air took over. After another three quarters of an hour, the missing end to the wire was found. Peter then decided that he had flown it for long enough for that session and so no more flights took place.

Saturday the 13th May 1978 was a date given in the deHavilland Moth Club's newsletter for a summer rally at Colton Aviation with the Chipmunk Club. All deHMC members were invited along. I decided that it could be a good day out and so I set out in the direction of Cambridge in my old Simca van. On this I clocked up over a hundred miles each way by motoring across country and it was well worth it. This event was held on Little Staughton Aerodrome. Having arrived, I was very surprised not to see any Tiger Moths on the ground, but I did get to meet some other interesting people in the aviation world. I had taken along with me some of my albums of photographs of deHavilland aircraft. While I was showing my albums to a bunch of pilots I asked them if there was any chance of me getting a ride in a Chippie. One of the gents then said, 'Yes, I will take you up just before I depart'. Though I did not know it at the time, this kind gent was Ralph Steiner who was a founder member of the Chipmunk Club. This was the reason why his aircraft was parked by the side of the display hangar and not along with the many other Chipmunks. Because of this, he then told me that he would be one of the very last to leave. I then went back out on to the airfield where I took several coloured photographs of the Dragon Rapide G-AGTM that had been freshly painted as a Domine NF875. It had just been restored by Coltons and was now wearing Royal Navy markings. It was soon to leave for a home at Duxford. At that time I did not know it, but in the future I was to win a ride in it by doing a competition in 'Aeroplane Monthly'.

I arrived back at the hangar at 17.10 to find that a disco was moving in and that a row of cars had parked down each side of the taxi-way. Soon after, this Chipmunk was manhandled from nose to tail and with a little bit of car bouncing. After all of this performance I then though that I would have lost my ride, but Ralph was true to his word and he kept his promise.

I was strapped into the rear seat and plugged into the intercom. The prop was then swung, the hood pulled back and we taxied out. Ralph then called up the tower on the R/T stating, 'About two circuits and a landing for Mike November'. We taxied up on the left hand side of the runway to the take-off end. Here we waited until that Rapide had got out of the way. Ralph then applied a little flap and then we were off. The flaps were then fully raised as we climbed out over the other end of the runway. During that day, I along with another fellow, had quickly decided to lie down flat when a Harvard did a very low beat-up to the side of that runway. Just after turning on to the downwind leg I was surprised to see the Chippie G-BBMX hanging in the air just to the rear of our starboard wing tip. Again, if only, but my camera was back on the ground. When would I ever learn? After about a minute the stick was pulled back in 'MX and we were left on our own again. Ralph cavorted me about the sky with banks, climbs and dives in all directions. He then said, 'Would you like to go over the top'. I then replied, 'Yes please', and with that the top of the canopy was showing green fields as we reach the halfway stage of a loop. It was then just one fast beat-up along that runway close to where previously a Harvard had done likewise and we came in for our landing. I thanked Ralph for giving me such a delightful experience as we climbed out of the aircraft. I did like that Chipmunk and it had been great fun. I found it to be a very pleasant aeroplane with plenty of zest. I had plenty of room in it and the high seating gave excellent visibility all- round. It was well worthy to carry the name, de Havilland.

I had a surprised telephone call on Saturday evening the 25th of June 1978. It was Tim Williams on the phone and he was inviting me to travel with him to Old Warden on the following morning in his Thruxton Jackaroo G-APAM "Myth". A display was being held and the deHMC had been invited. I had already made previous arrangements to travel there with my late pal, Tony Woollett. This was to get up very early in the morning and drive down the M.4 Motorway to Wokingham where I would E.T.A. (Estimate Time of Arrival) by 08.00. We were then to travel on together in his car. A quick phone call to Wokingham soon re-arranged things. This then gave me a lay-in in the morning and to arrive at Tim's house by 11.00.

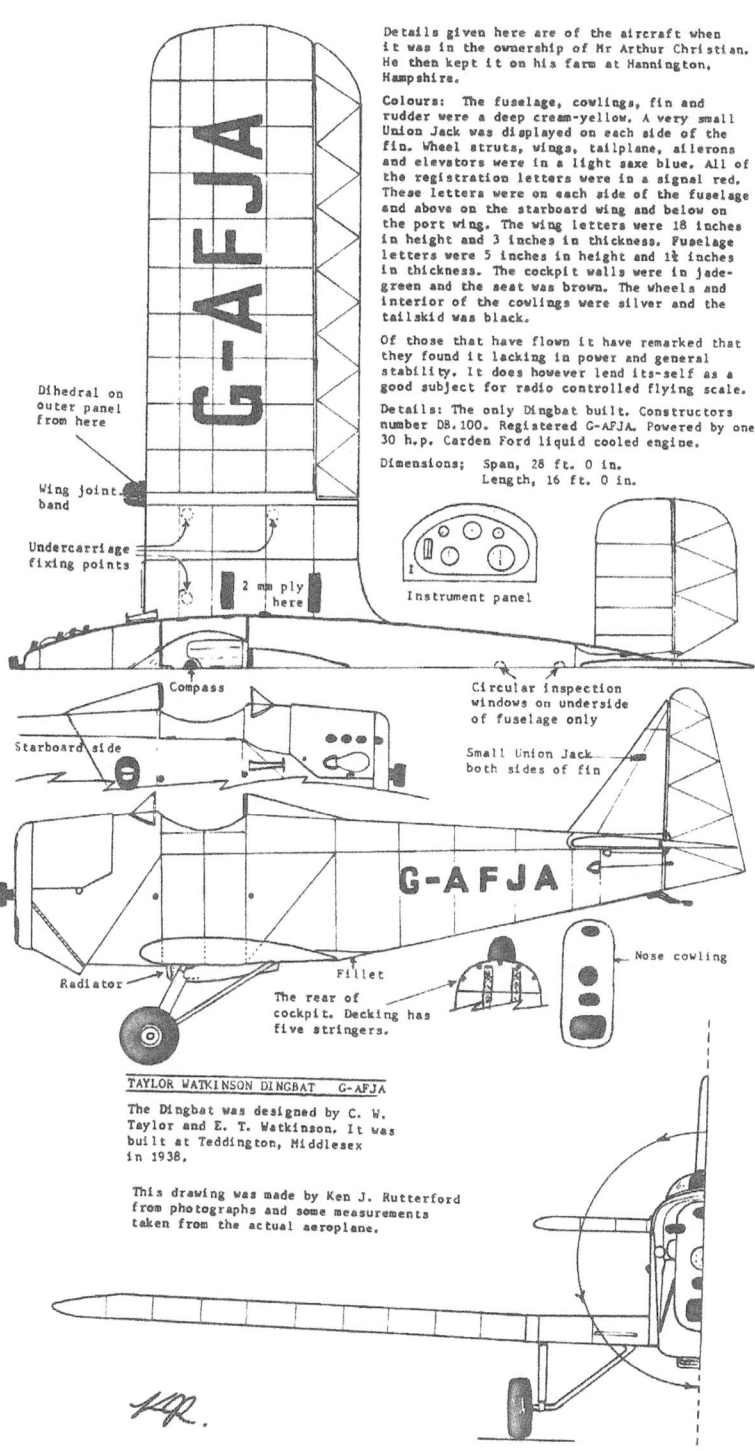

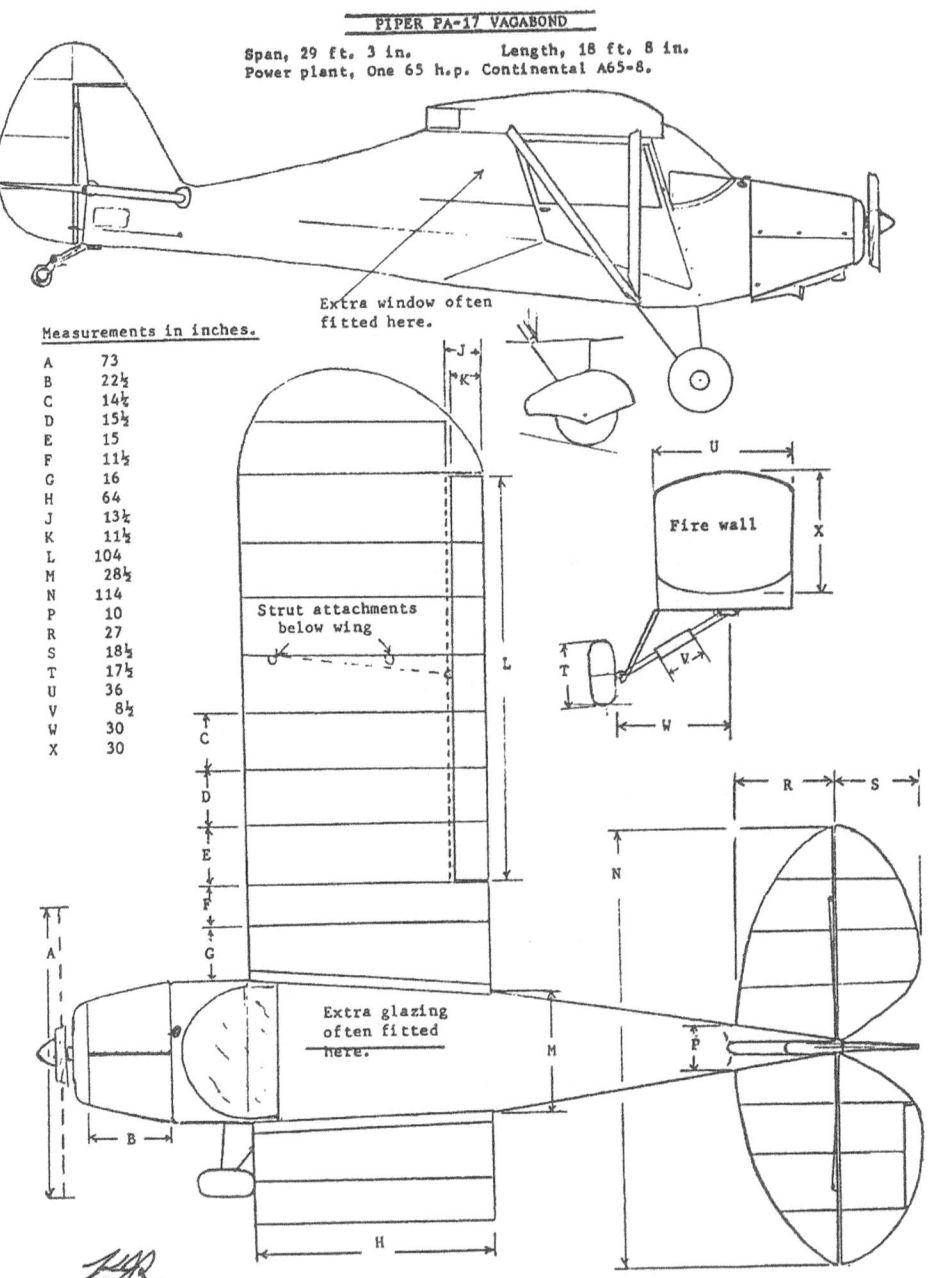

The morning brought with it a fine, but very cool day. There was a strong blustery wind that threatened to blow us off of our desired course. I arrived before Timmy was quite ready. He had been quite busy trying out a new launching trolley that he had constructed for a man powered aircraft that was being built up on Greenham Air Base. Here would have been another little bit of interest if one was to write a book on Greenham Common. I then gave Tim a hand with a forty-five gallon drum of aviation spirit. This drum was then tipped over and into the boot of his little Citroen Dyane. I know that we did not transport it far, but I had never ever carried anything as heavy as this in mine. Together we both ran round to the front to get in before the motor had a chance to decide to sit down on its backside. In the past when pole testing, we had carried forty-five drums of creosote in the rear of a Morris Minor and that had made the rear springs inoperative. A slow drive was then taken to the field where the 'Roo' was patiently waiting for us. The drum was then tipped back out again as the little car gave a large sigh of relief. A hand pump was screwed into the drums bung-hole and the aeroplane was given its drink through a rubber hose. This was a much quicker method than the one which we were using when refuelling at Thatcham. Tim then checked over his trusty biplane that all of it was still there and working and that no one had stolen any of it. Walking out into the field he then threw several handfuls of fresh cut grass into the air to satisfy himself into which direction he should make our take-off run. The decision made, he then returned back to his Roo.

I then loaded myself into the rear left hand seat and Tim swung the prop from the rear. By 12.30 we then left this undulating field and we were soon passing over my home as Tim set a course towards the Chilton Hills. We should have been at Old Warden by13.00, but we made it by 13.45. I seem to remember that Timmy was one of the last to arrive at Hatfield when the Moth Club held that Famous Grouse Rally. Tim was typical me, I could never arrive anywhere on time. We were the last of the visitors to fly in and my pal Tony had began to think that something had gone amiss and that I had missed out. This was my first trip in his Jackaroo. I found her to be noisy but comfortable. Conversation had not been possible and we both wore earmuffs. The visibility had been good but we had passed between a couple of squalls near Aylesbury.

This old Roo was once owned by Sheila Scott and the white coverings which she had made to cover the seat were still there. It had been her who had named it "Myth", this standing for 'Female Moth'. Tim had retained this name and it was painted to the front on both sides of the fuselage. The colours of "Myth" were a custard yellow all over with red trim and red sunburst flashes being painted across the wings. Tim had told me on how he had been flying along when he was suddenly formated on by two Stamps from the Tiger Club. One off each wing tip and both having a similar colour scheme. It was a pity that there had not been another aircraft present with a camera so that this formation could have been recorded. As a Jackaroo, G-APAM is no more. She is still very much around and I have since had a ride in her with Marcus Barton, but she has now reverted back to a Tiger Moth from which she once was. She now wears Tim's Puss Moth's blue colour scheme, but her name "Myth" has been retained.

John Pothecary of Redwing and Comper Swift fame had asked Tony Woollett if he could put on a display of his 1/36th scale scratch built civil aircraft models on Saturday the 26th of May 1979. This at the 'Air South Garden Party' that was to be held at Shoreham. Tony agreed and took along with him his boxed collection of model aircraft that he had constructed out of polythene plastercard. I first met Tony when at an air display on Greenham Common and at the same time a Consolidated Liberator flew over which surprised both of us. Since then we became firm friends as we both shared the same interest of pre-war civil aircraft. Now, Tony is no longer with us. In the past I myself had done a little scratch building of 1/72nd scale models of aircraft. On making some of them, I have had to thank Tony for showing me some of the methods that I was to use. Tony kindly invited me along with him to Shoreham and also to assist him in keeping a close eye on his models once they had been placed out on display.

By 06.45 I was motoring east along the M.4 Motorway and making for Tony's house in Wokingham. The weather was far from good. I then left my motor at Tony's home and together we set off for Shoreham in Tony's car and with a boot full of boxed models. The further south that we motored, so the weather became worse. By the time that we approached our destination, it had gone very dark with heavy bursts of rain and the wipers were working flat out. Some of the tops of the hills were obscured by low cloud. Tony remarked to me, 'The only aeroplanes that we are going to see today are the ones that we are bringing with us in the boot'. I had to agree with him.

By mid day, we had got all of the models displayed and to our surprise, then out came the sun. The passing storm had blown completely away and the cloud base had lifted. Clive Shaw a young confident experienced pilot was about to set out on a navigational competition and he had asked John if there was anyone who would like to go along with him for the ride. John then kindly agreed to keep his eye on the models and to let Tony and myself go flying. The aircraft was the Piper Cherokee 180, G-ASIL. Tony sat in the front with Clive and I had the rear to myself. By 13.45 we were airborne and quickly made height to 2,700 feet. Clive then made an attempt to fly the course and he kept me occupied by handing me a piece of paper to mark the turning points on. It had started out as a nice trip, but as we kept on flying so the wind picked up speed and it was gusting at over forty knots. Our turning points were, the Duke of Norfolk's residence, some lock gates, sand and gravel pits, a windmill, sewage works and followed from there with the set course that should return us back to Shoreham. We flew this to the best of our ability and we just managed to return back to Shoreham before the weather got very angry. The only other aircraft to take-off in this competition was a Cessna and it did not complete the course. The wind then wound its way up to forces eight and nine on the Beaufort scale. Clive managed to land us by landing us in the shelter of the hangars and once on the ground, the Cherokee was wheeled into the shelter of one of them. The remarks on the competition form went, Ken who flies in Tiger Moths had to poke his head through the roof. Tony who makes very nice models could not navigate for all of the toffee that he sells, plus what a lot of rubbish, etc, etc. Tony's job was being a rep' for a confectionary firm. We had both enjoyed ourselves and Tony's models had helped in saving the day, but oh, what a bumpy trip.

Another flying display was held at Old Warden on Sunday the 24th of June 1979. This was on the same day as the Greenham Air Tattoo which was being held on my doorstep. I had decided that the lighter and older aeroplanes were for me and so once more I set out early in the morning for Wokingham. I then travelled for the rest of my way along with Tony. This time we were blessed with better weather, though not perfect. Back nearer to my home, the Greenham event had been dogged by heavy rain showers and it had kept their gate takings down.

It was while I was nattering to Charles Coote, a fellow Moth Club member who had painted pictures of many old deHavilland aeroplanes, when Tony Haig-Thomas came on the scene. I had previously told him in a conversation that I had an ambition to fly in all of the deHavilland aeroplanes that I could possibly manage. As I am writing this, I still require to obtain rides in a Moth Major and a Moth Minor to complete all of the active Moth types. 'My Leopard is due to fly in a few minutes', said Tony. 'If the pilot agrees, then you can go along for the ride'. How could I refuse such a sudden offer, especially as Cliff Lovell had phoned my home for me to go over to

Walkeridge Farm to give me the chance to fly with him in this very aeroplane. This had been back in January and on that very day I had been away at the Wembley Model Engineering Exhibition.

I thanked Tony H-T, and left Charles to go and find the Leopard Moth G-ACLL and its pilot. Lema-Lema was being flown by Angus McVitte and he had just stepped out of Shuttleworth's de Havilland D.H.51, a large two-bay biplane named "Miss Kenya". Angus was a most experienced pilot. He had to be, for only the very experienced and trusted pilots were allowed to fly the Trust's aeroplanes. Angus had collected many aircraft types in his logbook. Some of these were Mosquitos, Valiants and Comets as well as those old aeroplanes in the Shuttleworth's collection. 'I have never flown a Leopard before', said Angus, very apologetically just as though anything might happen, 'But you are quite welcome to come along for the ride'. After our ride in the Leopard, he then said, 'I have only to fly the Hornet and then I will have flown all of the Moth types'. It would not have surprised me if at some time in his flying career in the past, he may well have flown the D.H.103 Hornet a twin-engine derivative of the famous wartime Mosquito.

I clambered into the rear seat along with a few engine spares and placed the little leather tongue through the buckle of the lap-strap. Angus then sought a swing and this had the Gipsy Major turning over at about 800 r.p.m. We taxied down the long grass runway and here I took a snapshot at a Chipmunk that was holding ready to take-off. I did carry a camera on some of my flights, but then I never managed to use it for air-to-air photography. It was always to be, sod's law. Angus did a few checks and then we were off. 'What terrible ailerons', said Angus as he shook the pole from side to side. I know that it would never have been quite like that in a Tiger. 'Let's see what she stalls like', he said. He then throttled her right back and then raised her nose. I then had a feeling that she did not wish to stall, but she must. 'Ah there she goes', as the Leopard dropped a wing, and I now cannot remember which one that it was, Angus was too quick for her. Terrible ailerons or not, he took charge as the Leopard tried hard to turn over on to her back and before a spin could develop. He then moved the stick forward and back. 'Just trying her stability', he said. Then, 'I wonder what she glides like'. Down went a lever on the right hand side of the panel, this then turned those undercarriage fairings into the slipstream so forming a simple air brake. 'Yes I do think that it helps a bit he said', while he kept the A.S.I. (Air Speed Indicator) at just over fifty knots that this Leopard had stalled at. 'I think that we had better take it back, such a pity though, but they may miss it'. There is a pilot down there who is waiting to take it to Duxford'. It was then back to Old Warden where I thanked Angus for letting me share his first experiences with the D.H.85. Angus made a nice soft landing and for my first ride in a Leopard Moth I had been treated to a flight which only a test pilot could have given. I now had a good idea as to what a Leopard was like in the air. The type D.H.85 had been one of Sir Geoffrey deHavilland's most favourite aeroplanes. This one, LL had the flat sided fuselage which only a few of the first production models had. At the time of my ride in her she was in an all blue colour scheme. Tony H-T was later to sell her and I believe that the new owners then broke her.

In the spring of 1980, The Amy Johnson Flying Display was held on Paul Airfield at Kingston upon Hull, to give it its full title. On May the 3rd, I motored the 274 miles non-stop in my white Simca van to go and enjoy it. I left my home in Berkshire at 20.00 and kept the wheels turning until I arrived at my destination at 02.00 in the early hours of the morning. For the rest of the darkness I bedded myself down in my van. This is where a van could score over a car. It was now Sunday morning and by 09.30, I was on Paul Airfield. By 10.00, and I was up in the air in Southern Joyrides Ltd, silver Dragon Rapide G-AIDL. This was one of the last airworthy D.H.89's that I had never had a chance to inspect through my view finder. I was soon to have this matter put to rights. This old biplane was in a beautiful condition and its interior had been recovered in a blue rexine cloth. At this time in the morning the crowds had yet to arrive. Mike Hood, the Rapides pilot along with his wife had flown up from Biggin Hill on the previous day in order to sell joy rides at £6 a time with five minute flights. I was then about to enjoy £24's worth of free air travel.

As I got my photography gear out, Mike was about to run up his two Gipsy Queen engines. He managed to get the starboard engine turning over on the aircrafts flat battery. It then point blankly refused to turn over the port engine. It was then that I waded in and offered my services by giving him a swing. Now many times I had swung a Gipsy Major engine, but these only had four cylinders. Now this Gipsy Queen had six of them. I then soon found out that in swinging a six was a complete new ball game. Those two extra compression strokes came round more quickly. I kept on swinging and at one time it had nearly started as it chugged over for a few revolutions. It then wetted right up and although we could have tried sucking out, Mike decided to look for another battery. This found and with some very long jump leads we then had both of the Queens running under their own power. Mike knew of only one way of putting some life back into that duff battery and that was the expensive way of taking her aloft for a while. For all of my efforts, he then suggested that I might like to fly around the area with him.

The weather was fine, but at the same time it was dull and cold. I found it nice to be back in a Rapide again having flown to Scotland in one on the previous year. More on this flight in the chapter, 'Ye'll Tak' the High Road'. With the cabin all to my-self I stood nattering and looking out over my pilot's shoulders as the grey clouds came down to meet us. I did not know it then, but in three years time I would again fly in Delta Lema with another Mike, Mike Janaway when together we took a trip over our country's capital city.

We had stooged around over the Humber Estuary where we had gazed down on its cold grey waters. Back on the airfield and as I climbed out, I was to meet up with my pal, Tony Woollett. Tony had loaned some of his model collection to Hull City. Later in the day I was to look at the internal display which had a lot of Amy's old items placed in it. Tony had made a special model to 1/36th scale of Amy's old deHavilland D.H.60 Gipsy Moth, G-AAAH "Jason". This was the aeroplane in which she had flown out to Australia. Tony had also included the spare propeller whish she had had lashed to the centre cabane struts. He had also painted on the drift lines to the lower wing. Like my flight in that Leopard Moth, Tony had once more arrived on the scene just too late to obtain a free ride. I had tried hard to ring him very early on at his hotel. Every white Hull telephone box that I had tried had been out of order. This was long before the coming of mobile phones. Being a telephone engineer myself, I was not very impressed with Hull's telephone network. In the end, I did manage to get through, but by then, Tony had left his hotel and checked out.

Miranda McKay called to me across the fence as I was making my way to my car and then for home. This was at Old Warden. She wanted to know if I had taken any good pictures at the Woburn rally as they were in need of some. Mike Vaisey along with his father Ted who is now long gone, was there also. Mike had previously said that he would take me up in his Sixty Moth on a day when the conditions were quiet. I had not forgotten this as I had yet to obtain a ride in a D.H.60Moth. I then asked him if the conditions were then quiet enough. 'Sure', he said. With this I then had twelve minutes in his red Moth G-ATBL and every one of them was worth counting. Getting into the front cockpit on a D.H.60 Moth was not quite the same as doing so in a Tiger. One has always to be so careful when entering strange aeroplanes as they have to be made extra strong where it matters, but they can be quite fragile in other places. With the Sixty Moth you need to be extra careful. The rear flying wires have to be stepped over and above you is the fuel tank. To butt this is not good for your head and it is not all that good for the tank either. With the Tiger Moth you can enter the front cockpit from either side by using the wing walks. With the D.H.60Moth, the majority of them had a long exhaust pipe fitted to one side or the other. This depending on which type of engine was fitted. You could then only enter the front cockpit on the opposite side to that long exhaust pipe. These pipes got very hot and they could burn the flesh. Once settled in the cockpit that exhaust could warm the side of your face. That was the way that it was in that era. Now take the old five ton Foden steam wagon. I can here you now thinking, what has a steam wagon got that is common to an aeroplane. In the case of the Foden, the driver had one leg outside and the other one up close to the firebox and this depending on the side of the steerage. As with the D.H.60, depending on the side of that exhaust, one side of the body was kept warm while the other side of the body was kept cold. One day while at Old Warden, Cliff Lovell gave me a circuit in his American built D.H.60 Moth, G-AAMY. It was fitted with wire wheels and the high pressure tyres. Shortly after this ride, Mike gave me a circuit in his D.H.60G Moth G-ATBL and it was fitted with the large low pressure wheels and tyres. The difference on the ground was enormous. One could quite well understand why so many people changed to having the low pressure tyre wheels.

deHavillands made Sixty Moths with two types of fuselages. Some were constructed as a plywood box while others had metal frames being fabric covered . The D.H.82 Tiger Moth had the metal frames but its cousin the radio controlled Queen Bee had the wooden fuselage. The Tiger Moth was developed from the D.H.60 so that the instructor had a clear escape if needed from the front cockpit, the wings were staggered rearwards. I believe that I am right in saying that the only Moth types that could not fold their wings were the two Tiger Moths. The D.H.71 Tiger Moth racer come experimental aircraft, this being a monoplane. The other was the biplane D.H.82 Tiger Moth trainer. These wings could not be folded unless you pranged it, and then they could be made to fold, but more on this in the next chapter, 'Roman Tigers'

'Aeroplane' and as it was known as before, 'Aeroplane Monthly' is a magazine that I have contributed to for many years. I received from Richard Riding, then its editor, a letter. It was dated the 3rd of October 1983. 'Ah deHavilland', this letter started off. I expect that you will be delighted to learn that you have won an hours flight in the Russavia Dragon Rapide. This was the same aeroplane that I had taken a set of pictures of on the day of my Chipmunk flight with Ralph Steiner. The letter went on, Your correct entry to our 'Ah deHavilland competition was one of the lucky eight to be pulled out of the editorial hat, well done. The flight will take place from Duxford Airfield at around 11.00 a.m. You will have to pay the normal entrance fee of £1. 20p, but this will be refunded once that you are inside the airfield'. I never did receive that refund, but as I was given cups of hot coffee on such a bitter cold day and plus an extra ten minutes in the aeroplane, who in their right mind would grumble about that. This letter went on, 'Make your way to the Russavia office which is located on the ground floor of the control tower. You will be met by Mike Russell and myself'.

The day, or I should say, the night before this Rapide flight was our Calleva Group's annual dinner, and more on this in the next chapter. On this occasion it was held in the 'Three Swans Inn' in Hungerford. Daphne had gone away to Blackpool on a coach for that weekend and so it found me putting myself to bed at gone one-o-clock in the morning. I then had to get myself up before six so that I could reach Duxford in time for that flight on the following morning. That evening in Hungerford I had kindly been offered two chances of flying up to Duxford in a Tiger Moth. Bill Hardy in our group's aeroplane and Peter leCoyte in his own Tiger Moth G-JOA/T5424. It is not very often that I have turned down a chance to be flown in an aeroplane, but on this occasion I did just that. I could not see them getting up in time to fly me after all of the alcohol that had been consumed at such a late hour. It would have been nice to have been the only person to have turned up by air, but yes, I certainly did the right thing on this occasion. Perhaps I might have taken one of their offers had it had been in the summer time. Also I had given my son Bobby the chance to go with me. I was also very doubtful that the early morning fog would clear away in time. I do believe that both of these pilots were pleased that I had refused them after it had all sunk in. It being after the dinner-do and all. As all of that Sunday turned into a most bitter cold day, that early flight would have been a freezer. In the end, Bob decided not to come with me.

I set out from home in my VW camper at 07.30. I then followed as near as was possible a ruled line that I had drawn on my map. First it was to Wallingford in order to get across the River Thames. From then on it was via, Wendover, Dunstable, Luton, Hitchin, Letchworth, Baldock and Royston. There was not so much fast traffic on the roads in those days. I was to arrive ten minutes before my E.T.A. Here I was to spend another twenty minutes before anyone would let me on to the airfield or to their museum. I had endured an extra cold ride as there had been a sharp frost. Having an air cooled engine. What little heat there was came from the heat exchangers at the rear. By the time it reached the front there was hardly enough of it to keep the windscreen defrosted. Perhaps I would have been warmer in a Tiger Moth or I should have driven all of the way there wearing my flying-suit and helmet. Had I had flown up by Tiger Moth then I think that my pilot and I would have been like solid lumps of ice and that is how cold it was. Any how I arrived frozen. Once inside the place I walked to the control tower where I was spotted by Richard. He and several of the others had not been stopped from entering the airfield. Perhaps I should have taken that letter with me. Richard then led me to a nice warm room where I started to thaw out. Here I was introduced to the rest of the lucky winners as I started to feel my fingers again while drinking a piping hot cup of coffee. Yes I would have been frozen stiff in a Tiger and would have had to have been lifted out of the cockpit. I had done the right thing.

We were then all instructed to take a good look at a map with our route marked on it. A thought then came to me, 'Hell, I hope that our pilot is not expecting us to navigate for him'. A very stiff questionnaire was handed out to each of us and it was not printed on cardboard either. The bottom of this was sealed up and we were told that we were not allowed to open it and to look at the prize. Some of the passengers filled theirs in during the flight. I chose to fill mine in once I had got back on the ground. By then, I hoped that my brain might be back out of cold storage. Having landed I then made for my camper and the atlas and I started to fill it in. I then thought that perhaps I ought to get myself back to the flying control. I then found out that all of the other papers had been handed in and were being marked. I did not complete the thing, but I think that my answers would have been around average. The prize turned out to be a ride in their Tiger Moth. Needless to say that having not returned my form I stood no chance. It was to be that I was not to fly in a Tiger Moth on that day at Duxford. I do not think that any of the other contesters had been offered flights in Tiger Moths on that day.

The Russavia Collection had put on show its new acquisition, the B.A.C (British Aircraft Constructors) Drone, G-AEDB. It was finished in a dark blue with red outlining to its letters which were displayed across both of its lower wings. This beautiful little aircraft was parked to the front of the tower. Once inside the Rapide, I just had to click at it with my camera through a window. I then took a rear seat and the person that sat on my left hand side was Ernie Cobb who had motored up all the way from Bristol. We had become a plane load of gents without any female passengers.

Captain Mike started his starboard engine first and then followed on with the port and this shook the airframe into life. By 12.00 we were leaving the grass and heading out in a westerly direction. Turning towards the M.11 Motorway and then on down towards Stansted Airport where the Rapide made an approach and flew along a lighted runway. It was then on to Broxbourne. From here we flew to Hatfield where Mike circled the place. It was then on to Cardington where Mike used the two large sheds as a pylon in an air race. From here it was the return back to Duxford. We were landed at 13.10 and our ride had taken us over many other places of aviation interest such as Panshanger and Salisbury Hall of Mosquito fame. Altogether we should have seen about forty places that had seen aviation history. I do know that Radlett and Stag Lane were two of them. Many of the others were once World War One and World War two airfields. It was all very well for any local people that knew their own area, but I would very much have preferred a nice running commentary given from the cockpit. This way we would all have known what we were looking at. I for one would have welcomed being shown where the Stag Lane airfield and factory had been. When Mike later asked, 'Any questions?' I suggested to him 'Can we go round again?' I can still picture his thought now, 'Some people are never satisfied' If only we had each been given a map with our journey marked on it would have made all the difference. That is what maps are for. If I had known what was coming, then I would have taken along my road atlas from out of my camper.

I am sure that we all enjoyed the flight, well I did. Sitting at the rear of the cabin it became obvious that most of the tighter turns were made with the rudder only, as the ailerons hardly ever moved. The Rapide had got a decent sized rudder. This was something that deHavillands could have increased in size on their D.H.86 Express airliner. In the rear of the cabin we had to put up with a very cold draught. This we took to have been coming from around the entrance door. Much later on when our ride was nearly at its end, one person noticed that there were some cabin air vents on the sides and to the tops of some cabin windows. Once these had all been closed up, it then started to get a little warmer. It had been a typical winter's day and although the cloud base had remained high, it had stayed dull and was bitterly cold. As we had flown over Old Warden, it was noticeable how rough the wind was by their windsock. Back at Duxford there was then quite a strong wind blowing and this put paid to the Drone flying.

The clear cut winner of the quiz was Stuart Howe who was well known at the Salisbury Hall Museum. So he should have been as he had flown over much of his home area. His prize was a Tiger Moth flight. We watched him take to the air in their G-MOTH. This Tiger had been made into a look-a-like of K2567, this being the R.A.F.'s first Tiger Moth. It had been given a stringer and fabric rear decking and straight down edges to the rear cockpit entrance doors. On much later Tiger Moths, these had been angled so that blind flying hoods could be fitted. There was also a foot well for ease of entry into the rear cockpit. I did not know though if they had fitted a Gipsy III in place of the Gipsy Major under the bonnet. All the same, she did look smart in her overall coat of silver. I think that it was such a pity that Richard Riding had been left behind at Duxford, he should have occupied one of the seats. As I write this it is now the late Captain Mike Russell. This competition had been well worth winning.

Daphne had been asking me to take her to Thruxton airfield on the 13th of May where a large out-door car boot was to take place. I was not that keen on going, but on that Friday night I had dreamt that I was present at an auction where there were several boxes and galvanized baths that were full of old shotgun cartridges. I had then woken up before I could find out if they had been sold. This then changed my way of thinking and so I took Daphne to that Thruxton sale.

Having spent far too much money on what I hoped were some good bargains, and all of them we could quite well have managed without, my interest was aroused on the other side of the fence and I had not seen any cartridges or old loading gear. On the active airfield side, gliding was taking place. With a little enquiring, I was told that I could have a gliding experience for as little as £12 with the Inkpen Gliding Club. For this I could have a ride in their all metal LET L-13 Blanik two- seater sailplane, BGA 1824. I would then be cast off from an aero-tow at 2,000 feet. It could then be possible to stay up there for twenty minutes. I then decided that as I had been asked to come to an airfield that I should have a basin full of this.

The Inkpen Club had been formed and had operated not far from their village of Inkpen. They had used the higher down land near Shalbourne. Due to much harassment from a few people who had complained of excessive noise from the tug aircraft, the club had been forced to make a move. This they did from the quiet downs to Thruxton airfield which already had far more aircraft noise and in a larger populated area. When they had operated from the downs of Shalbourne they had only had to fly over a few isolated farm houses. Thank God that we had people like these Inkpen flyers in our country in 1939 when we needed them. I then had a word with Daphne and she fell in with my arrangement, though she nearly might have had to have found her way back home on her own. Back to the other side of the fence I strolled. It was then kindly suggested to me that if I would like to fly next, then they would fit me into their roster and it would then save my wife from hanging around. I parted with twelve notes and awaited the return of their sailplane.

My pilot was Ivor Hughes who would make a very long trip to Thruxton just as often as he could. Filling out a form I then noticed that the date was the 13th. Jokingly, I said, 'Perhaps I didn't ought to fly'. This sailplane had tandem seating under a clear blown hood. I was then seated to the front in the cockpit. Ivor was busy giving me a hand with the seat harness when I detected a bit of a commotion. An EoN Olympia sailplane was stretching its glide as it landed just over and in front of our glider. Ivor had quickly left me. That Olympia had been at zero feet. 'I would have yanked you out but I had no time', said Peter very apologetic. The first thing that I knew was when that Olympia had landed close to the front of me and then I knew what all of the fuss had been about. 'That will be a brown trouser job', said Ivor. I then thought that this incident should have taken care of the 13th and so I settled down in the cockpit to enjoy my flight.

To the front of us and slightly to starboard stood our tug with its slack wavy towline laid out on the ground. This was the Bellanca Citabria, G-BDBH that was Registered to Master Gear Co Ltd. The name of the aircraft, Citabria had been derived from the word Airbatic spelt in reverse. As I looked at its registration letters DBH my thoughts automatically reminded me of one of the old Frank Garrett shotgun cartridges. This he had named 'The DBH' standing for, 'Deadly But Humane'. My pilot then climbed in behind me and handed me back my camera. It is as those gremlins of the air always decide to attack my camera if I decide to take it flying with me. The blind in my camera then stuck stopping me from seeing through my view finder. The long perspex hood was then fastened down and we became as snug as a bug in a rug.

A few instructions were given by my pilot to some of those on the outside and our tug then moved forward and the slack was taken out of the towline. Away went the Citabria with us trailing along behind it. I was not sure as to which one of us got into the air first. I then took some pictures with my faulty camera just hoping that something would come out. I was lucky as some things did. Trailing along behind the tug, it appeared to be jumping about all over the place as we groped skywards towards Andover. Obviously we had contributed to this illusion. At about 1,700 feet, Ivor then released us from the towline. Having become free, our tug then banked away to starboard and then lost no time in getting back down on to Thruxton's grass. We were now flying on our own, or be it, gliding.

Ivor then headed us out over some yellow fields of flowering rape. This he said could produce us some good thermal lift. This kept us gliding around at about the same altitude. I was then told that due to the rising wind, these thermals were streaking out. I was then handed the controls and this pleased me. I did not have them for many minutes as I was only too pleased to hand them back. Reluctantly I did so as I could see that we were sinking fast. I did not have my pilot's skills to retain our height. I felt sure that if Ivor had wanted to, he could have kept us in the air for much longer. As it was, I had jumped the queue and those other chaps back on the ground were eagerly awaiting the return of their sailplane. This flying time had slipped away quickly as we headed back for that Thruxton grass. This flight clocked me sixteen minutes in the air.

I had first called at Enstone Airfield when I had been making a journey to Stourport. There had been talk of our group's Tiger being based there should we have had to make a move from Thatcham. The only thing that I did not personally like about it was the distance that it was from my home. This was just over fifty miles each way. One thing that I did discover here was the Enstone Microlight Centre. This centre was well equipped with nice new aircraft and flying gear and was based in a nice new hangar. I made a close inspection of the various machines and they were all well designed and maintained to a very good order. This centre gave tuition on both types of microlights, the weight-shift and the three axis controlled. I nearly got myself a ride in the three-axis Dragon that was nothing like a D.H.84. It took on the appearance of a two-seater side-by-side Luton Minor. Due to the amount of flight bookings and on keeping my E.T.A. in Worcestershire, I never got this ride.

Tuesday March the 12th 1985 was a nice sunny day with very little wind. I had been promised several Tiger Moth flights but due to the time of year and the weather, none of these had taken place. With an urge to get into the air, I set out for Enstone. I arrived at this aerodrome which is in typical stone wall country where it would not be recommended to fly through the tops of any hedgerows. Here I made some inquiries about buying a flight in a microlight and I was told that I could have one in a weight-shift. This was because the only person who was free to take me at that time was a weight-shift man. I was then introduced to the Southdown Puma Sprint, G-MMVI. The letter M immediately following the dash indicated that it is a Microlight and not a Moth as was in Mike Russell's Tiger G-MOTH.

The Sprint was a British machine that was made in Portsmouth. It was constructed around a basic metal frame that stood on three wheels. Mounted on its apex was a large delta shaped flexiwing that was designed to pivot fore and aft and from side to side by the movement of a triangulated hand frame. It seated two in a very tight tandem position. Its power unit was of foreign manufacture having been made in Japan. It was a 440 c.c. air cooled Robin that drove a fixed pitch pusher airscrew. The throttle was an accelerator pedal that was fitted on the outer right on the footrest bars. These bars being linked so as to steer the nose wheel when ground handling. On the extreme left of the hand bar frame was a rubber bulb. This had been fitted so as to actuate the shutters in a camera that could be fitted to the port wing tip. On my flight I took my camera up with me. I took one or two shots, but these were not to have come out. The weather was that cold that my camera just refused to function.

My pilot who had been nominated to fly me was a young man and I believe that his name was Neil. Anyhow, I shall here continue to call him by that name. Although I had my own flying suit in my motor, Neil went inside their club room and brought me out a nice blue Ozee Thermal over suit. This I would very much liked to have kept. I then had to fit on an open faced hard helmet complete with a visor and integral built intercom. I was then instructed into the rear seat with my back up against the pylon tube. I looked back at the small propeller and noted that I would have had to have been extremely clumsy to have stuck a hand into it. A lap belt then secured me to the airframe as we both sat out in the open. Neil then took up his position in front of me and had it been any closer he would have sat on my lap. To the front of him was an altimeter, a compass and an A.S.I. To the rear of us was the engine which was started with a pull cord. Its exhaust was fitted with a silencer which it made for quiet running. With that wooden propeller revolving behind me we were off on a long taxi run in order to get to the active hard runway. I was instructed to let my feet go loose on the foot bar. This so that Neil could try and steer us a path between the many bumps and some extra deep potholes. The one thing about potholes is, that these are about the only things that are still being produced in quantity in Great Britain today. I soon got use to sitting within the metal frame. Eventually we arrived at the runway. From this a Piper Pawnee was operating as it was working some farm fields that must have been close to the aerodrome. No longer are these crop sprayers allowed to operate working over farms in Great Britain.

The small power-plant behind me sprang into full revs and we rose up into the cold air and very much like a gyroplane. Height was made up to 2,000 feet and the conversation in terms of strength was very good. This was by use of the intercom. Neil then demonstrated the microlight to me. Though it looked for all the world like a hang glider with an engine fitted to it, especially from a distance, it was far from being this. These are powered aircraft within their own rights. I was then told that this flexiwing was vice less and that they had never been known to spin. Having just been given this reassuring bit of information, he then performed some very tight turns. His turns were as tight as any that I had experienced in a Tiger Moth. I then asked him what the stall was like and so he performed two. The first was nice and gentle. On the second, the nose, if that is the correct word, dipped far lower and in the recovery as the engine was opened up, we climbed up near to the vertical. I thought, 'Oh hell, is he going to try and loop it'. From this he then levelled out. I found it surprisingly free from cold draughts in this nice warm suit and being sat so close behind my pilot. Dressed up in that borrowed gear I was kept nice and warm. Neil then told me that these flexiwings absorbed many of the bumps that could be felt when flying in a small fixed wing aircraft. I was given several goes of trying my hands on that hand bar. Each time I found that I managed to do some of the things wrong by moving in the opposite directions. This came about because the controls are reversed to that in a normal aircraft. This they termed as, three-axis. To make a turn to port the bar is pushed to the right, and for starboard, to the left. To lower the nose this bar is pulled back and to raise the so called nose it is pushed forward. Even on the ground the foot bar operate opposite to a rudder bar. To learn to fly one of these would be similar as to what Sir Geoffrey deHavilland had to do after he had first taught himself how to fly with the rudder bar working in the opposite direction as to the normal practice of today.

It took us about five minutes to lose our height for the landing. I was then given a second chance at controlling with the bar on the downwind leg. All too soon and we were back on that runway. It is funny how time always seems to fly much faster when one is enjoying one's self. We then had to hold off while three other aircraft, a Jodel and an Evans V.P.1. on the grass runway and for that Pawnee which was on the hard runway. I was then given a shot at steering it along the ground as we slowly made our way back to that nice warm hangar. This had given me a half an hour of sitting in that frame-work and with twenty minutes of this, up in the air.

Back in that hangar I happened to mention that I was dry and if they knew of any place where I could swallow a cup of tea. The girls in the office then offered to make me one providing that I could drink it without sugar. Having a nice warm drink along with the ladies, I then paid the £12.50p for my flight, plus a £1 temporary membership fee. I then asked them a few questions about medical fitness and insurance. I was now to be told that there was no insurance other than a third party just in case we had come down the wrong way and had made a hole through some person's roof. I had not been shown any of the small print prior to taking to the air, but if I had, it would not have stopped me from making that flight. In fact, had I had the money, and if it had been on my doorstep, then I could quite easily have got hooked on these microlights. Flying the trike as it is known was great fun. You are out in the elements and it is the next best things as to be flying with the birds. That flight then changed my feelings that I had about the flexiwing. I now consider that it is quite safe providing that it is flown within its limitations. Yes I know, this sentence can quite well apply to all other aircraft.

In this chapter I have described to you a few of the aeroplane rides that I have taken during my lifetime. Once up in the air I have often been given the chance to handle the controls and I have never refused. There was the time when I bought myself a ride in a deHavilland D.H.104 Dove from Kemble. My pilot was Nick Goff and he had flown with my old pal, Captain Fred Terry. Having been nattering to him prior to the flight I was ushered into the right hand front seat of the flight deck. The door was then closed that separated us from the passengers in the cabin. I was then able to feel the controls of the aircraft. ' Oh for the wings of a dove'.

I have told you on how I was once given some control of a take-off in a Cessna 172. I will now finish off this chapter on telling you of some control that I was once given on a landing in a Piper Super Cub. My brother Dick and I had gone to have a look at the old place where we were both born. This being, Sarson Wood, Amport. In that vicinity was Thruxton. As we both like aeroplanes, we decided to call in and have a look-see. Here we both bought a ride in a camouflaged Cub painted in American markings so that we could then fly over our birth place and to see it from the air. Dick took the first flight and I then went on the second. The Cub is only a two-seater. On my flight, I said to the pilot who was sitting up front, 'May I have a shot at keeping her level'. With that I was given control for the rest of the flight, other than the use of throttle. 'Can you see the airfield and the runway', I was asked. My pilot controlled the throttle and I steered her down towards the grass runway as we were knocking along at about sixty knots. At about thirty feet, and yes I can easily judge that height through climbing telephone poles for the latter half of my life, I said to my pilot, 'You have control'. With that he said, 'No, you are doing just fine'. I then brought her right down on to the grass. As our wheels rolled on, he then said, 'Right, now I will have control'.

"Southern Cross" VP-LVE in Poole Harbour

ROMAN TIGERS

Early on in 1976 my job of work took me to Siege Cross Farm which is just east of Thatcham. A chat with Mike Janaway who was then the son of the farmer brought up the subject of aviation. It was then that he told me that the farm housed two resident Tiger Moths. These were the Calleva Group's G-AJHU which was effectually known as 'Hotel Uniform' after her two last registration letters. The other was then the second oldest Tiger on the British civil register. She belonged to Captain Fred Terry who was a British Airways captain. Her last two letters DJ were alphabetically referred to as 'Delta Juliet'. Down at the wooden farm hangar she was simply known as 'Dee-Jay'. The oldest British civil Tiger Moth that was flying at that time was G-ACDC that was owned by the Tiger Club. Since then, G-ACDA has come back on to the register. In pre-war days, these three Tiger Moths were a portion of the fleet of The de Havilland School of Flying. The Tiger Club's DC has seen many rebuilds and so had Fred Terry's DJ. Prior to Fred's ownership, she had seen service on crop control duties working over farms and had once been extracted from some trees.

I was walked down to the hangar where I was shown these two biplanes. I must have shown a considerable interest as I was invited to attend the Calleva Group's next meeting which was then held in the Pineapple public house at Ashford Hill. This with, the chance of joining the group, and the possibility of becoming an associate member. I have always had a very soft spot for old de Havilland aeroplanes and here I was to find two of them that were nearly on my door step. In those days, all good aeroplanes had a certain smell about them. This was due to a mixture of dope, oil and leather, amongst other things. Both of these two old Tigers both smelt delightful, and what is more, I was accepted as an associate member.

And so it was, I became a member of the Calleva Group. I cannot express in words since that date in joining them, the enormous amount of kindness that was to be given to me from all of the other members, both the full-flying and the associate alike. This then gave me a fresh interest in my life as my interests had been lacking since many of us were sacked from the R.O.C. From then on I stayed as a member of this group until its demise in the late summer of 1986. After the collapse of the group, I then still stayed on at the farm in helping Captain Fred Terry in maintaining his beloved DJ.

These two Tigers share a field with herd of milking cows and from time to time a fresh bull would also be sharing the field with them. This I was never happy about, especially when the herd had to be driven to one side of the field so that a Tiger Moth could land back on to it. An alsation dog lived loose on the farm and this gave the group some security. This group was one of the oldest Tiger Moth groups in the country and it probably had during its life time, the largest number of members that went through its books.

At this point, I think that a few words about the group's history will be appropriate. For this I can do no better than refer to 'Notes for new members'. This was compiled by the late Bill Hardy who was the club's chairperson of long standing. It had been Bill that had held this group together through many difficult times and many people had often referred to it as, Bill's Group. But first I must say a few words about Bill. Although many people had given and had shown me kindness, Bill had given me more time and wellbeing in the group than any other person. Perhaps I felt this way about Bill as I was so often to work along side of him whilst working on the aircrafts Gipsy Major engine. In the event of any problems, then it was Bill that we all turned to. He was a professor from Reading University and his mechanical knowledge and ability was supreme. I always enjoyed working with him and I also enjoyed flying with him. The forward view when sitting in the rear cockpit is not the best. One day when Bill was sitting behind me, I shouted back to him, 'Helicopter approaching us dead ahead'. With this, Bill through the stick over. Later when we were back on the ground he gave me a compliment as he said, 'I do enjoy flying with you'. I do not know if it had been due that chopper that made him praise me, but I took it for what it was meant. It was not always praise though, I can remember him bellowing at me from the hangar as he donned his long leather flying-coat, I was sat in the front cockpit while the engine was warming up and I had let the revs build up a little high. That time his words were not so complimentary.

The Calleva Group was first formed in the autumn of 1961 at a meeting that was held in the Pineapple pub at Ashford Hill. During its time, it was to run for a quarter of a century. This first meeting was held by some of the staff at Aldermaston's A.W.R.E. This meeting had followed from an advertisement which suggested the forming of a flying group. This ad' had appeared in the 'A.W.R.E. News' in the October of that year. The original aims of the group, was to provide sporting flying for its members and at as low a cost that could be made possible. This had to be made consistent with a good operating standard. It was also decided that this group was to be run with as few rules as was possible. It was to dispense with any unnecessary formalities. The philosophy behind this being, that private flying was already shackled with a plethora of regulations which provided the ubiquitous Jack-in-the-office with every sort of opportunity his favourite word,' No'. It was decided by those who formed the original members group, that a deHavilland Tiger Moth should be bought.

When this group was first founded, Tiger Moth aircraft were not that hard to come by. Today they are very much sought after and are looked upon as vintage aeroplanes. They made their come-back and this to the thanks of one man, Stuart McKay a founder member and the dynamo of the de Havilland Moth Club. Also by people like the Newbury Aeroplane Company who have kept Tiger Moth owners supplied with rebuilt wings. These do tend to get damaged from time to time. And in my eyes the wings are the most important part of an aeroplane, Yes, I do know that every other part is just as important, but the wings have to be in a tip-top condition. Those first members of the new group adopted the name of 'Calleva' after the old Roman name for their walled in, Calleva Atrebatum. This was the woodland town of the Atrebates. It is situated to the east of Silchester Common and was once enclosed by forest lands by the joining of Silchester and Pamber forests. From here, the Roman roads went out in all directions like the straight spokes from the hub of a wheel. It is fun to be able to look at these in the fields as many of them can still be seen through the growing crops. The Calleva Group's first Tiger was G-AOJJ. They purchased it from the Wiltshire School of Flying at Thruxton just before the Christmas of 1961. The Wiltshire School of Flying was based at Thruxton. It was here that Calleva decided to base their JJ as its members were on excellent terms with the aerodrome management and hangar staff. With the help of the late Jack Haines, a really high standard of maintenance was given to their aircraft.

The Calleva Group had the misfortune to lose their JJ when it was spun in at Thruxton on the 9th of November when a member had got caught out by bad weather. He managed to have spun it in at Thruxton on the 9th of November 1963. Although then an insurance write-off, she was later to be rebuilt and owned by Ted Lay who painted her in an all yellow R.A.F. training colour scheme with the serial DF128. In this, Ted flew me to the Woburn Rally in 1987. Calleva then replaced JJ with the Tiger Moth G-APRX. They bought her from a gliding club at R.A.F. Bicester. RX then served Calleva well. While with the group it made a number of flights to France and Scotland. On the 13th of April 1969, an unlucky day, it also crashed. It was stalled into some trees at Compton Abbas just after it had taken-off. The groups third and final Tiger Moth G-AJHU that I got to know so well was purchased from the Dorset Gliding Club of Tarrant Rushdon. Her constructors number being, 83900 and she was ex T7471. She had been built during the war by Morris Motors at Cowley near Oxford.

Thruxton airfield where Calleva was based was taken over by a property development group in 1967. By 1971, its new owners were deliberately making life difficult for the flying groups which were operating from out of there. By the spring of 1972, the harassment had reached such a level that Calleva decided to look for another base and this is how it came to be based on this West Berkshire farm. The length of the chosen field was extended by cutting down a portion of an old orchard. This then became known to its members as The Overshoot. The field ran north to south and its northern hedge had to be lowered and laid. The wooden hangar on the southern side was completed in the autumn of 1972, and in 1975, the year before I joined them, it was extended so that Captain Fred Terry could also keep his Tiger Moth G-ACDJ there as well. These two Tigers then shared the hangar right up to the ending of the Calleva Group. After this, DJ stayed on a little longer.

Since the time that I joined them, the group gradually got more and more like the old Vintage Aeroplane Club. As one was a club, and this one was a group, there was a difference. In a club, things are often done for you. In a group, you are expected to do more things for yourself. The old V.A.C. had operated around the Avro Club Cadet G-ACHP with many other members owning their own aeroplanes. In the beginning, the Calleva Group was just its own Tiger Moth G-AJHU. It was later to have several of its members who owned or had shares in other aircraft. These were, Captain Ken Whitehead who would fly the Supermarine Spitfire Mk.XIV G-FIRE, Captain Fred Terry with his G-ACDJ, Peter leCoyte who had given his name to the registration of the group's HU, he had bought himself the Tiger Moth G-AJOA which he flew in the military markings T5424. Peter's Tiger Moth was pictured on an 11p Jersey postage stamp. Tim Williams then owned the Jackaroo G-APAM and was later to own that lovely old de Havilland D.H.80A Puss Moth G-AAZP. This he was to name "British Heritage". It was in this aeroplane that he and Henry Labouchere flew it out to Australia in the later end of 1984. If I had been the general manager of the Royal Mail, then this aeroplane would have been portrayed on a British postage stamp. I will relate more on this flight later on in the chapter 'Down Under'. There was the late Ben Cooper who Calleva always looked up on as being of a membership status. He then owned the Piper PA-20 Pacer G-BFMR and the 1930's Klemm L-25 G-AAUP named, "Cementine". He was later to own the Aeronca C.3, G-ADYS. She was always affectionately known as "Gladys" due to her registration letters.

Being involved with a de Havilland Moth aircraft, it was at a Pineapple meeting that Freddie Terry suggested that we all join the de Havilland Moth Club. This was a new club that had not been long up and running. Many of the group's members then decided to join this new deHMC including myself. This Moth Club which did, and still is doing, very much for members and enthusiasts of old de Havilland aeroplanes was very much run by Miranda and Stuart McKay. If any person rightfully deserved his MBE, then it was Stuart. This club has, and is, still doing very much for owners of Moth aeroplanes, not only in this country, but worldwide. Along with Calleva, these two very different organizations went along hand in hand as far as my aviation interests were concerned. For some of the pleasures that have I derived from these, I can do no better than describe a few more of the flights which I have enjoyed in old aeroplanes.

One Sunday in June 1977 found me working with a silver dope brush on Hotel Uniform for at that time she was out of commission. Fred had wheeled his DJ out of the hangar and was very kindly letting two or three of our group's pilots get their hands and feet back into the air. After Bill Hardy had taken his ride, Fred then took me up sitting in the rear cockpit for about twelve minutes. On most occasions I have usually flown in a front cockpit. Very many of my flights have been short ones, but most enjoyable all the same. One never wore a parachute as it was always recommended to come back to earth with the aeroplane. As we sped along the grass, the rain then started to tip down fast. Looking towards the Hampshire hills these had been clagged out of sight. Fred then pointed out to me the field in which he recently had to make a dead stick landing into. He had to pass under some power wires as he made this engine off forced landing. On Fred's request, I then chopped the throttle. He then made a practice dead stick landing back on to our farm flying field. Dead stick landings are very good things to practice. Like Fred had to do, one never knows when the unexpected can occur and then it has to be done for real. Between us we then wheeled DJ back into the hangar before her cockpits could fill up with water.

As I have just said, Fred had been met with just such an emergency. He had taxied out from close outside the hangar and taken-off with a gentleman friend of his. Well he was a friend before they had taken-off. Unbeknown to him, his clumsy passenger had knocked the fuel off. Fred having only just become airborne had made very little height and so he had not got any time to look around his cockpit. He rightly chose a field and into this he went. Once on the ground the trouble became obvious. As the take-off run was very restricted, Fred decided to fly his Tiger out without the weight of his passenger. His passenger then had to walk his way back to the flying field. I was not there on that day, but it was said that the sight of Fred turning back so soon without his passenger gave some of those working in the hangar a nasty shock. They were convinced that Fred must have inverted DJ and tipped him out. Freddie was not amused as the story was told to me. This was that his passenger had borrowed a pair of his flying boots and had then scuffed them out while walking back to the flying field.

Bill Hardy had always enjoyed flying on a Christmas Day. This when the conditions were suitable. It was in 1978 that he asked me if I would care to join him. It is not easy pushing the Tiger out of the hangar and preparing for a flight on one's own. I could not think of anything better and so it was that Hotel Uniform had the air under her wings all to herself while every normal person was busy stuffing them-selves with Christmas pud and the like. Between the time of arranging and the 25th of December, we had two inches of snow and a few foggy days. I had not expected to fly, but as Christmas came along, nature saw to it that we would not have a white Christmas. Christmas day was a nice one. The snow had all gone and the sun came out shining between the scattered clouds that through dark shadows over the landscape below us. There was not another aeroplane in the sky.

Over the years I have owned several old Volkswagen transporter campers. I did earlier on tell you how I could nearly have gone up in flames when I pranged on my Calthorpe motorcycle. I then said that I would later tell you how it nearly happened to me again, this I am now going to do. I was on my way to the hangar in my camper and was motoring along the A.4 road through Thatcham. In the rear of the camper standing on the floor I had a jerrican filled with five gallons of petrol to be used in the aircraft. Normally I never carried cans of petrol as there was no separate compartment like that of the boot of a car. Now these old VW's are not very warm vehicles at the best of times. They are air cooled, and I do like air cooled engines, but for warmth they can give out very little comfort in cold conditions. What little heat that there is comes from two heat exchangers. These are under the floor at the rear of the vehicle. This little bit of heat then has to travel without air assistance from the back to the front. By the time it has reached the front it is only enough to stop the windscreen from freezing. My line of thinking at that time was that if a Sentinel steam wagon could have a large fire in its cab, then why should'ent I have one also. After all, it was fitted out with bottled gas and a cooker. Between the two front seats I had fitted a small gas heater. It was a bowl type that screwed on to the top of a small gas cylinder. It was strapped in its location in a circular well so that it could not move. The heater was also lock-wired to the gas bottle so that it could not unscrew. I had decided that I had made it quite safe, but in this case I was very wrong. I was nice and warm and cosy and gave no thought to the petrol can which was way down at the rear. A stupid idiot then stepped out in front of me. At the same time another stupid clot driving the camper van made an emergency stop. That caused that jerrican to slide forward and land on top of that lighted bowl heater. I should also have secured that can of petrol. That became a lesson well learnt if ever there was one. Just how stupid one can be at the time and never realise it until it has become too late. If the lid on that can had been knocked up, then I would have gone up in a pillar of flame.

DJ over Uffington White Horse

Circling my home in HU

My phone rang early. Bill had told me that he intended to arrive early at the hangar by about 11.30 am. Would I please be there a little before and help in the preparation of our flight. I there for set out a little bit extra early and I was surprised to see that the aircraft was parked outside of the hangar and that all of the cows had been removed from the field. On the rear seat was a Christmas cracker and on this was written, 'A merry Christmas'. I closed the small back door up again so that Bill would find it and checked the oil and fuel. I then did a walk-a-round to check that all of the bits that should move could and those bits that were not suppose to move did not. How careful one always is with an aeroplane and yet one can jump into a car and hurtle down a main-drag without a care in the word. That is until something unbeknown happens like a flying petrol container.

Bill was dead on his E.T.A. and found his cracker. 'Har, two cigars', he said. 'Tis good of old Mike'. I then pulled on another pair of trousers over my existing ones and got the engine turning over with Bill sitting in the rear cockpit at the controls. The newly rebuilt Gipsy Major kindly started on my first swing and it sounded sweet in the crisp air. I then loaded myself, belted up the Sutton harness and plugged myself into the gosports. Up the field we taxied and then it was away into the crisp still air. Bill flew me west to Lambourn at around 3.000feet. As we passed over Jimmy Fairhurst's field there were four aircraft firmly on the ground. Again it was a Christmas lunch time and we must have been the only aeroplane up in the sky for miles. Airport towers would have been manned and I wondered what they may have thought if they saw our little blip on their radar screens.

On reaching Lambourn, Bill circled the place about three times while I shot of some film. Oh yes, it did all come out. Not a sole was to be seen anywhere and not even a horse. Thirty-five minutes later and we were back on the farm. Bill then arranged to fly off to Kingsclere and I would go home hoping that Daphne had got a Christmas lunch waiting for me. I would then motor to Bill's home in Kingsclere and arrive at around 15.30. This I did and we then set out together to the field that was known to us as, Bishop's Hill. Here HU was awaiting us. Once here we always picketed the Tiger Moth on the top of this curved hill under the lee of a tall hedge. One day we had landed and taxied to this normal parking spot. When we got out we were both surprised to find that we had parked the aircraft in the set out of a shooter's pigeon decoys. I bet that we were the largest bird that this shooter had ever known to have come in and land on them. Again I got HU's prop turning over. It was just a short hop back to the farm where we put Hotel Uniform away. I was then motored back to Kingsclere with Bill in his Bentley Four-and-a-half where I then picked up my old VW. That was a very nice way of spending a Christmas Day. By the time I returned home, it was teatime.

On the 15th of September 1979, Peter Trask flew me over to that famous field called Seven Barrows, near Litchfield, Hampshire. Alas, Peter is also no longer with us. It was on this very field that Geoffrey de Havilland had taught himself to fly in his Number Two Aeroplane back in 1910. My intension was to obtain some nice photographs of HU parked along the side of the de Havilland Memorial stone that at that time was situated just inside the field being on a parallel with the old A.34 road. Since then, this stone has been re-sighted due to the making of a dual carriageway. I had been keeping my eyes on this field and had noted that the crop had been harvested but the straw still remained. We then took a weeks holiday in Cornwall and when I returned I phoned up Peter and suggested that together we took a look at this field. Peter agreed and so together we set out for Seven Barrows to find that the straw had been cleared. This was on the Monday which was my brother Dick's birthday. We then found by reading this memorial stone that it was exactly sixty-nine years previous that Mr de Havilland had made his first historic flight.

We found this memorial stone nearly hidden with weeds. Together we went gardening by removing all of these grasses and wild flowers. Our next concern was to make sure that on this field there was nothing that could damage an aeroplanes propeller. Having satisfied ourselves that this field could be flown into, we then set off to locate Lord Porchester's farm manager, Mr Harold Vine. My memory is fast fading, well I am now in my eighties, and so I hope that I have got his name correct. He then gave us permission to fly Hotel Uniform into the field. It was our conversation and us taking note of the date on that stone that bore the fruit for the de Havilland Moth Club to hold their meeting a year later. This on the 10th of September 1980 commemorating the 70th Anniversary of Mr Geoffrey de Havilland's first successful flight that he made from off of this Seven Barrows field. The weather was not so kind on that day of the Moth fly-in as it blew with gusts up to gale force. I well remember digging the hole and erecting the wind sock and Stuart saying, 'Good. Now I have an airfield'. About twenty light aircraft made it on to that field and the majority of them were Moths. One Tiger Moth F-BGCS had flown all the way from France. There was a fly-past by a D.H.104 Dove, a D.H.106 Comet and a D.H.114 Heron. These three larger aircraft flew over in salute. Very many people came and although the weather had been most unkind. That day was rated as being a great success. I should have flown on that day had the weather had been calmer. As it was, I found plenty to keep myself fully occupied on the ground.

It was in the August of 1980 that both of these Roman Tigers were about to become non-flyers if their annual checks were not completed before a coming Wednesday. I had been giving Freddie a hand on his DJ on the Saturday and again on the following Sunday. Much work still had to be done before the visit of the licensed inspector. Having got most of the work up together, Fred suggested a ten minute air test. His comments were, 'The weather is now fine and should we fail the inspection, at least we can fly now. I had to agree with him, well I had too. Her cowlings were replaced and together we wheeled DJ out of the hangar. Fred then gave me a few instructions on the correct way to take hold of the pole. He then saw to it that I was sitting nice and comfortable in the front cockpit. He then starts us up with the first swing of the propeller and I catch her on this first with the ignition switch, all good stuff. The electric cow fence had been removed and by 15.15 we were up in the air. Freddie's voice boomed over the intercom clear and loud as he did not use the old Gosport speaking tubes. As we drew away from the field he then failed to hear my twittering voice and so the rest of the flight was in silence. As I was unable to talk with him I had to raise an arm up in World War One fashion. But not my arm with the time-piece strapped on to my wrist, by now I had given up on throwing away good watches.

As we flew on, Fred then made a simulated engine cut and approached a large field without making a landing. Heading north, he then kindly let me take over the controls. Not that one is likely to have to land an aeroplane should your pilot be taken very ill, but it is always as well to be given a little practice, just in case. I was then instructed to keep the Tiger's snout on the straight and level. After a bit of like, riding the waves and the rollers, I then managed to keep her nose pointed at one of Didcot Power Station's cooling towers. Fred had given me a very good explanation of ridings these so called waves in the air. It is like carrying two buckets of water. Should they start sloshing, then you have got to let them level out. I must here make it clear, that although Fred could not hear me, I could still hear him. Before I had got near enough to collide with this large manmade object, Fred asked me to do a rate one turn by using both stick and rudder. I think that I did a good one as I eased her nose up slightly so that I did not lose any height in the turn. After concentrating on my flying by keeping her nose on the horizon, I then found that I had lost myself in the air. Had I had been on the ground then I would have known where we were. Fred then said, 'Where are all of those aeroplanes'. Not that I was able to tell him, but I then knew exactly where we were as every house on the ground fell into its proper place. We had been over the old wartime airfield of Hampstead Norris. We were unable to have got lost as I had the nose pointing to a white Sony factory that had been built close to our farm flying field. For a few minutes we entered some cloud and Fred flew her on the instruments. Having come out of cloud then came Fred's booming voice, 'Are you strapped in'. Up went my thumb and down went DJ's nose for the start of a loop. A few stall turns followed and it was then back to the farm and the landing. Back on the ground at the hangar, Bill had arrived. DJ was now covered in cow muck and so we had to start cleaning her all over again. Both of the Tigers were to pass the licensed engineers inspections. That air test had been satisfactory and all of the work on the two aircraft had been well done.

A Thursday evening found me ringing Stuart McKay's telephone. The Moth Club was to celebrate the 50th year of the Tiger Moth and I wanted to be in on the act. It was to celebrate the first batch of Tigers that were flown from the factory to R.A.F. Cranwell in Lincolnshire. It was then that I was told that Hatfield had been closed and that the R.A.F. at a very short notice had given permission for this event to be started from R.A.F. Henlow. It was Miranda who answered the phone and in a few seconds I was told that Tim Williams had got a spare seat in his Jackaroo

'Myth'. A quick tinkle to Tim and I was told that I could occupy his spare seat, but, I would have to find other ways of getting back. I accepted Tim's offer, and so it was that I set off preparing to try and go barnstorming back to Hungerford where I was to leave my motor.

It had been decided at the monthly Pineapple meeting that the Calleva Group's members aeroplanes should all first congregate at Siege Cross Farm and then fly on to R.A.F. Henlow in a formation or a gaggle, depending on which. Tim suggested that I should arrive at his home by 09.00 and then pick him up in my little Citroen. I could then leave my car in his hangar-tent which was pegged out on the field where he was going to fly from. From this field we would then fly on to Thatcham where we would land and meet up with the other aircraft, Peter with his OA and Fred with his DJ and the group's HU. Our formation was scheduled for leaving Siege Cross at 10.00. Tim also told me that he had to pick up another passenger at Henlow and he would fly with us on our leg to Cranwell.

I set out for Denford where Tim lived in my small Citroen. The weather was fine with a weak westerly wind, but the cloud base was low and was capping the local hills. I picked Tim up as arranged and we motored to the field where his 'Roo' was tented in the corner of a large field near to Chilton Foliat. The tent was untied and "Myth" was wheeled out and my car driven in. While Tim went about his D.I. (daily Inspection), I retied the tent and removed some baggage. This was then loaded on to the aircraft and we climbed on board. To save on time, Tim started to taxi across the field and to warm up the Gipsy Major as he went. A flick of the magneto switches and, oh-dear, one mag was out of action. That would never do. The trouble was soon diagnosed to a broken spring on the contact breaker of the port magneto. To get the tools and another spring it was then a trip back to Tim's house. Once back at the flying field and the aircraft was soon made serviceable. The Jackaroo then took to the air and we made for Thatcham as we headed east skirting a storm which had just passed through. Having landed late on Siege Cross Farm we were to find that there had been a bit of bother. Peter leCoyte then landed in his Tiger Moth and Ken Whitehead and Marcus Barton were still busy preparing Hotel Uniform. Fred and his brother William were still tanking up their DJ. We were the first away and we were quickly followed by Peter in his T5424 while HU tagged along behind. One aeroplane remained firmly on the ground and it was Fred's. A couple of circuits of the farm showed that the prop had stopped turning and that the cowlings were raised. Due to a spot of unpleasantness that had just taken place with Joe Janaway the farmer, we did not land again. We just all waggled our wings and set a course for Henlow with T5424 and HU formated behind us.

At Henlow we were to find that most of the other Moths had got there before us. Apart from all of the Tigers, there were three veteran D.H.60 Moths. These were G-EBLV, the Hatfield based Cirrus that was being crewed by George Aird and his wife Lorna. These two people had previously crewed a Dragon Rapide to Strathallan on which I had been on, but more on them in the next chapter. The other two D.H.60G Moths were G-AAWO and G-ATBL. Also on the field were a gaggle of Hornet Moths. Captain Fred and Brother William as he was generally referred to, eventually flew in. They also had developed some mag trouble. The mag drop had eventually been cleared by changing all of the sparking plugs. I then bumped into Charles Coote and had a quick natter before attending the briefing. There was an aerobatic event taking place at Old Warden and so we were instructed to fly to the east of them and to keep out of their way. Six Tigers were then picked out and all of them had military markings. These were to fly out first. They were to fly in a formation and were to break their journey at Grantham which was then under army command.

Peter's Tiger was one of these and together they were to represent that first delivery of Tiger Moths to the R.A.F. Peter was later to tell me that they had been given champagne and cakes.

Tim then introduced me to our passenger who's name was Rod. He had applied for his seat through Stuart McKay. Stuart's wife Miranda, then loaded our luggage into the boot of a car. This then gave us more room and we were ready for the off. It was a pleasant ride and not too bumpy. On route we were handed a questionnaire which we were told had to be filled in. With eleven answers to be found it kept us busy. Tim had now fitted a long exhaust pipe to his' Roo'. This now made life a lot more quiet in the cabin and the exhaust note could now be heard barking along behind us. On route we passed over the other six Tigers that were parked on the ground at Grantham. As we rounded out for our landing on Cranwell, Hotel Uniform could just be seen following along behind us.

At Cranwell we were all marshalled on to a grass square at the rear of the college buildings. The wind was picking up again. Tim had forgotten to bring his picket irons with him and so he turned up with a couple of iron railings. The veteran Moth G-EBLV was given the sanctuary of a hangar and so it was that I was able to borrow a set of pickets from George. As there had been a few cancelations, then I was able to attend the banquet that was held in the College Mess. On the table at this banquet I found a medallion commemorating the D.H.82 Tiger Moths fifty years of service, 1931-1981 awaiting me. That was a lovely surprise. After our feast, I then joined up with several of the others on a conducted tour of the college which then ended up at the bar. Later I boarded a bus for Sleaford to the Carre Hotel. Here I had a double bed with a room all to myself. Lorna and George were also staying at the same hotel and I was to enjoy their company at the breakfast table. The coach then collected us at 09.30 and returned us back to the airfield where flying commenced at 10.00.

Tim was then away on a navigational exercise. I lost out with a toss of a coin to go along with him. While all of this was taking place, Peter leCoyte then offered me the front seat of his Tiger when he returned to Staverton, but he wanted to be airborne by 14.00. Rod Nicholls, our passenger from Henlow had suggested that all the Calleva aeroplanes should have their picture taken when flying in formation past the stately Cranwell College Hall with its Winking Willie. Over the past years, many flights of R.A.F. aircraft had been photographed doing just this. Permission to do this was sought and granted and it was decided to do this as soon as the navigational exercise had been completed. The question then came up, what to use for a camera ship. I liked the idea of getting some pic's as well and so I suggested the other Jackaroo G-AOIR. Maurice Brett then kindly obliged and so I had the front right seat and Rod who's idea it had been sat in the rear. I had struts, landing and flying wires to contend with. As it had been Rod who had suggested the idea, we gave him the best position. At the same time as we were preparing for this, Ken Whitehead was having problems with Hotel Uniform. For some time we had been plagued with the problem of the propeller working lose on the crankshaft. This had first come about when a member had flown her up north and he had let an engineer remove it as he thought that he could cure an oil leak. This he did not cure, but he also failed to fit the propeller back properly as he allowed it to ride on the key instead of fitting tightly on its taper. This old problem returned and so it was that HU that should have been the lead aircraft then stayed down on terra-firmer.

All that could have been done had been done and we were ready for the photographic sortie. Oh-no, now Rod had gone missing. Peter had a spare front seat and so he invited Marcus's girl friend along for the ride. Rod then turned up while I was chasing after some people to try and get some help for HU. Eventually we all got airborne except for Hotel Uniform which sat firmly on the ground. But why was Peter not holding his place in the formation? Fred was holding a nice position on Tim's tail and eventually a kind echelon formation was obtained and we took a few pictures. Peter was very soon back down on the ground and I knew that he was eager to get away. When we got down his aeroplane was there, but he was nowhere to be seen. It was then that we got to hear about his bad formation flying. His lady passenger in the front had been taken ill. She had put her head over the side and had thrown up and poor old Peter had copped the lot. This then delayed him a little longer. After the poor girls unfortunate sickness, Peter and Marcus had set to work washing the aeroplane and the flying kit. Eventually we started to roll for the journey to Staverton at 14.45. I then cried out to Peter that I had left my camera behind at some place. Having said this, I then located it under my rain coat. This I had fortunately brought along with me. My own flying kit was back at Chilton Foliat in my car. I had not required to wear it in the cabin machine. Peter loaned me that washed out helmet that smelt far from sweet and then as we taxied out, the strap broke on Peter's goggles and so we had to stop and do a swap. There can always be a something when flying in Tiger Moths. At long last, Cranwell was being left far behind us.

It was a nice flight, but at the start it looked as though it might cloud in. Having over flown Leicester, the haze then gave way to perfect visibility. I could then see for fifty miles or more, the radio masts at Rugby being clearly visible. It was a sheer beauty to be flying again in an open cockpit looking down on lots of ripening cornfields that gave the countryside a patchwork quilt effect. This is the delight that one can obtain when flying in an open cockpit. The dressing up and all of those other little things that can sometimes crop up is all a part of the fun. I am very pleased that in my lifetime I have been given the chance to enjoy them. At one time we came near to some parachutists and gliders where other people were enjoying being up in the air. This trip took a delightful one and a half hours. Cheltenham came into view and Peter by the use of his radio then started our let-down for Staverton.

Coming in on a metalled runway in a Tiger Moth was new to me. I awaited the crunch from the metal tail skid that never came. I had forgotten that Peter's Tiger was fitted with wheel brakes and a tail wheel. Every other time that I had landed in a Tiger it had always been on grass or something similar. With instructions given over the radio we taxied to the fuel pumps where the Tiger's needs were replenished with aviation fuel and oil. Peter then called up for permission to taxi and we then took a slow ride over tarmac to the hangar. We had made good time and we still had arrived before Peter's wife did with their car. Having flown me a part of the way across England, Peter then insisted on driving me back to Chilton Foliat where I had left my car. For this trip which I had not expected I was most grateful to Peter and his family. This was typical of the amount of kindness that had been given to me whilst I was a member of the Calleva Flying Group. For any work that I did on the aircraft or the hangar I received no pay and I would not have expected or accepted any. For the kindness shown and the chances of flying in Tiger Moths more than made up for this. I was treated as though I was a paying member. I had once suggested that a small contribution might be in order while at a group meeting. This they then rejected. That Cranwell gathering I had thoroughly enjoyed.

Bank holiday Monday in the May of 1982 found us enjoying a lay-in when the phone rang. Daphne thinking that it would be for her rushed down the stairs. No longer can I now dash down any stairs and I have since lost Daphne. As it happened, it was for me. Tim Williams was asking me if I would like a trip with him to the Henlow Gala. This was being held on R.A.F. Henlow and the Moth Club had been invited. That day had been planned for me to go over to Thatcham and to help Bill in placing a bit more of Hotel Uniform back together. Tim's kind offer over ruled this. How can any sane person turn down an offer of over two hours flying in the oldest airworthy Puss Moth G-AAZP. A phone call to Kingsclere and Bill then understood the situation.

I presented myself at Tim's by 11.00 and by mid-day we were lifting off from Folly Farm, Hungerford. The large flock of sheep that kept the grass short and shared the flying field were well trained. They were not like the Janaway's milking herd. As the Puss taxied out, they all as one, moved across to the east side of the field. This then left us with a clear take-off run. We were up in two thirds of the field on this very warm day and we followed the Kennet River and the canal where the Crafty Raft Race was in full sail. I had once before seen this event from the air when I had flown with Peter Trask in the group's Tiger. Tim then flew over the Thatcham farm which brought Bill out from behind the thick hangar curtains wearing his white overalls. Well I had shown up at Thatcham but it was more of a hindrance than of a help. We gave a quick wave and Tim then set off on his course for Henlow.

Our trip was pleasant but with considerable haze. Large white land marks showed up. One yellow glider was seen, but apart from that we saw no other aircraft. Having spent fifty-five minutes in the air we were now landing at Henlow. Several other Moths were there and next to follow us in was Peter leCoyte in his G-AJOA/T5424. Peter Trask along with his son, Ian had come by road. Captain Roger Bailey then landed in his very smart silver, black and gold spatted Puss Moth, G-ABLS. This then put two Pussies together on the ground.

Some very fine aerobatics were performed by a Zlin 50. Other aerobatics were performed by the Cranfield G-BCIT and a Pitts Special Biplane. Henry Labouchere was into his aerobatic display in his Australian built yellow Tiger Moth, G-BEWN. While he was performing, two Yanks invaded his airspace with a couple of their Fairchild-Republic A-10 rear jet ground support Thunderbolt II's. These are often referred to as, tank-busters. These aircraft when flying in this country seem to do so in pairs. Once when I remarked about this I was told, 'They have too, if one falls out of the sky, then the other one can see where it went'. Henry soon cottoned on to what was taking place and so he wisely spun down to earth and landed off of it, and that ended Henry's display. I was told that they had asked him if he would fly again later and that he had refused. If that was true, who could have blamed him as it had been a degrading and dangerous thing to have happened. The Airship Industries new and very expensive Skyship G-BIHN paraded its self. Five years later I was to fly in their Skyship 600, G-SKSC. I will tell you about this in the chapted, 'Mainly on the Lighter Side'. A touch of nostalgia was provided by a Hurricane, a Spitfire and a North American Mitchell. None of these three believed in hanging around for long and burning up the av-gas.

The show over, it was then for me another enjoyable flight back to Hungerford in that lovely old Puss Moth. This 1930's aeroplane I had seen stripped to its bare bones and I liked everything about it. The metal framed cabin fuselage, generous wing area, low drag frontal area, and its folding wings. D.H. had got it all right. If it could be put back into production today with a modern engine I feel sure it would find a market. On our way home in a hazy warm atmosphere we encountered some very fine drizzle. This caused a miniature rainbow to follow along with us for a few minutes. Having arrived back at Hungerford, three circuits were flown to herd that flock of sheep back on to the eastern side of the field. As yet, these sheep had not yet been fully trained for the landings. So far, Tim has given me five separate flights in his ZP. On this one that I took to Henlow, I was given a nice circular metal plaque. It is inscribed, 'de Havilland Moth Club 1982 Henlow Gala. To the centre is a plan view of the Tiger Moth G-ACDA. This old pre-war Moth was to be restored only to be incinerated when it got crashed and then hung in some high tension power wires. Since then it has once again been rebuilt. This plaque I will always treasure.

We were just about to push the Puss back into the hangar when in came Sir Patrick Lindsay in his Morane-Saulnier M.S. 500 Storch. This aircraft was a war-time French built version of the Fieseler Fi.156 Storch. Registered G-AZMH it was painted up in German wartime markings complete with a swastika. He made one of the shortest landings that I have ever seen with a conventional aeroplane. He had just flown down from Blackpool taking over two and a half hours having consumed about forty gallons of petrol. Alas, I had no film left in my camera as he would have made a perfect picture coming in against the back drop of trees. Sad that it is, Patrick is also no longer with us. He died of cancer and he fought the disease as well as he could. He was to be very much missed in the aviation world.

Wednesday the 2nd of June 1986 was that ill-fated day for the Calleva Flying Group. The Tiger had just been returned back to Siege Cross Farm after having a very lengthy stay away where it had just been given its new C of A. (certificate of Airworthiness). She was then looking at her very best and had been fitted with a brand new set of stainless steel landing and flying wires. A radio set was then about to be installed and approved. On that Wednesday it was wheeled out by a member who I will refer to as Mr BG (bad guy). Well I have to call him by some thing. BG had been a member of the group for just over a year. He had shown a great interest in working on the aircraft and in his flying. On that day, BG was told by Mike Janaway as he entered the field with a friend, that the conditions were not suitable for flying. The field facing north to south was being blown with a very strong gusting westerly wind. This strong cross wind made it most unsuitable for flying out of on that day.

BG had brought a friend along with him who he obviously intended of flying him regardless on that day. He should have had enough common sense not to have placed his passenger or the aircraft in such danger. It was such a pitty that he had not taken a leaf out of Captain Blair's book when he had returned the flying boat back to the quay and refused to fly his passengers. At the farm buildings, Mike had heard him start the engine, but he had thought that BG was only showing his friend the aircraft. This had not been the case, he had started a take-off run towards the north with his passenger and then aborted. Lacking every bit of common sense, he then started off on his ill-fated run towards the south. BG then started heading towards the farm house. As he tried to correct, that strong cross wind got under the starboard mainplanes and he was blown across the field. With the throttle wide open and the tail down as they roared across the field. If only he had chopped the throttle again, things might not have been so bad. Instead he gave it maximum revs and in a panic he had heaved back the pole. The result of this was that the poor old girl was asked to do what she couldn't. She was raced across the field with her tail dragging the ground until she hit the hedge and was then forced between two apple trees which destroyed her wings and undercarriage. She then came to rest facing the way that she had just come in a crumpled heap. BG had well and truly pranged her.

It could have been worse as ghosts might have walked that farm. This crash had only just missed hitting the wooden hangar in which Fred's DJ was housed. This, by less than thirty yards. As it was, nobody got hurt except for the occupants that must have suffered from shock. BG had not given any thought to his passenger or all the other members of the group, They had been patiently waiting for months for the return of their aircraft so that they could get their flying hours in. We had not been a club, but a group. All members should have at all times have considered the interests of their fellow members, but not BG. Hotel Uniform did not kill him, but I was surprised that none of the other members didn't do so.

Hotel Uniform had flown less than a dozen hours since being back at Thatcham with her new C of A. I was not present when BG pranged her. I was told all about it from Mike Janaway who sadly has now passed on elsewhere. They had stood in amazement as the aircraft made its fatal run and to start with they had thought that he was going to crash it on the farm where they were standing. I stood there in sadness for a minute as I looked at the ball of wreckage. Having a camera with me I then took a set of photographs. Just in case of any problems with the insurance people. Having done this, I then set to and removed what was left of her crumpled wings. The hedge had removed her under-cart. I also had to remove all of those new flying wires which were now bent up and buckled. Mike then went and got his tractor and with this we placed what was left of her to the rear inside the hangar. I wept, and I am sure that DJ did as well. Due to BG's doings, this became the ending of the once proud Calleva Flying Group.

This was not the ending for me down at the Siege Cross hangar. Fred still kept his beloved DJ there. Fred's brother, Brother William had moved down to the far eastern side of Kent and he seldom manage to travel to Thatcham. Fred and William had nearly always flown together. Now as I write this, it is the late Fred and William, like Bill and Mike, they have all passed on. Fred was also living quite a distance away in the Wye Valley on the English-Welsh border. Due to this, he did not fly DJ as much as he would have liked to have done. When he did manage to fly it, he shared his flying with Mark Peters and myself, Together, Mark and I helped him as much as we could with the maintenance on DJ. We seldom visited other airfields. An average trip might be to the Uffington White Horse and back, or something similar. Most of the time when flying with Fred he had me handling the controls. This gave me so much enjoyment and I believe that I had more of this enjoyment with DJ as to what I did with HU. Both of these Tigers did give me a lot of enjoyment and pleasure. At the end, and all good things have an ending, Freddie complimented me by telling me that I was flying the aeroplane quite well. In other words, the aeroplane was doing everything that I asked of it. I was also positioning the Tiger where it should have been in the sky.

There is one little story that I can now relate, but I would never have done it a few years ago. The Calleva Group had got permission to fly from several fields on the Will's owned estate near Litchfield, Hants. This was so that members could practice take-offs and landings without upsetting the Thatcham inhabitants. I have never been able to understand the average public. A low flying Tiger Moth, should one need to go round again and then one of these Thatcham residents would be on the blower complaining to the farm of low flying. A hot air balloon bouncing in and out of their gardens they would tolerate. On this day after we had wheeled DJ out of the hangar and made her ready for flight, Fred said, 'I will give you a treat, we will go and do a bit of low flying'. We headed out to that farm on the Will's Estate up on the North Hampshire Downs. This was on the estate where an aunt of mine was the cook in the large house. As we slid low over some hedges, I noticed a row of gentry waving their guns in the air at us. In the wartime, what we were about to do was known as hedge-hopping. A quick word of warning to my captain and we slid out of there as quickly as we could. Until then, neither of us had given any thought about disturbing shooting parties. I knew poor old Fred was worried. Back on the ground he said to me, 'You will tell nobody'. I agreed.

For many years, the group's president was Ramsey. This is the name that we knew him by. His full title was Squadron Leader D. L. Ramsey-Smith. He lived in the village of Grateley. This was just up the railway from the place where I was born. Sadly, like so many others that I am writing about, he has also gone on to that place way up in the sky. Old parachutists may remember him when he flew Rapides for them from out of Thruxton. Thruxton was once a wartime airfield where Whitley bombers had flown from when they had dropped parachutists on a special raid on the French coast. Now all of this is past history, but what happy days they were. Fred was forced to sell his DJ. It was then flown by Peter Henley who was to give me my last ride in her when at the Woburn Rally in the year 2000. She was then painted in her old pre-war colours of the de Havilland School of Flying. It was then sold on and hangared at White Waltham. One day she was flown from out of there by a fellow and a girl passenger. I do not know the full story, but it was said that the aircraft had spun-in. I saw the crash site on the television news the night before going to the 2005 Woburn Rally. Looking at the wreckage, it looked as though she had spun in flat. If she had gone in nose first, then her engine would have finished up in the front seat where I normally sat. When wheeling DJ out of the Thatcham hangar by lifting on her tail struts, for some reason that we never knew, she felt much heavier than what HU did. I had been spun in HU, but never in DJ. Mind you, it had come close at one time if Freddie had not shouted to me, 'I've got her'. Fred had spun his DJ, but I had never seen him do it. This has now made me wonder, was DJ still heavier at the tail. If so, then might this have been a contributing factor. Also, how many flying hours on Tigers had that pilot had. I have never heard the results from the investigation that followed. I do know that all Tiger Moths were not the same. DJ was Hatfield built and HU was Cowley built. There must have been a difference. We found out that a Cowley made rudder would not fit on DJ.

Her remains had been carted off to Farnborough for that investigation. In Freddies hands he could do anything with her. Even land her on a sixpence, that is, if you knew what a sixpence was. Seeing her crashed on the television spoilt for me that years Woburn event. In my den I now have the centre from a damaged prop that had once pulled me across the Solent on two occasions when it had been fitted to HU. This now has a clock fitted in the centre of it. When DJ finally left the farm at Thatcham, she did so in pieces. Her fuselage went to Woodford and her wings went up the road to the Newbury Aeroplane Company at Denford. These to be rebuilt for its new owners. I happened to walk into Ben's workshop just as he was about to remove the fabric from the lower port wing. I then said to him,' Will that registration come off in one piece'. 'I do not know', he said. I was to come away from his workshop with a roll of old fabric tucked under my arm. On this was the registration G-ACDJ. I offered it to Fred, but he said that he was promised a similar piece that was to be framed of the registration taken from off of the fuselage. He told me to keep it, and it is now pinned across the ceiling of my den.

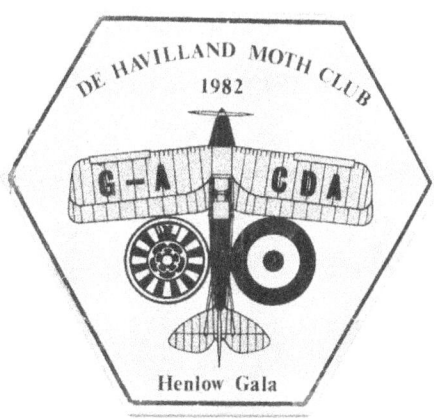

Flying at Cranwell

Peter and Ian Trask on Seven Barrows

HU by the D.H. Memorial stone

Flying with Captain Fred

Tigers were designed to be inverted, but only in the air

Brother William, Mark Peters and DJ

Self standing by HU with her brand new C of A on the 8th of March 1986

I took this photograph of HU where she came to rest on the 5th of June 1986 prior to dismantling her. A Tiger Moth's wings were not designed to be folded. Any stupid fool can fold a Tiger's wings, but it takes a much more clever person to unfold them again

YE'LL TAK' THE HIGH ROAD

This could well have been included in the previous chapter Roman Tigers, but I considered that it was worthy of a chapter on its own. I also could well have called this chapter, 'Barnstorming de Havilland'. One event which I had been looking forward to immensely was the Moth Club's Famous Grouse Air Rally. This rally was being sponsored by Matthew Gloag & Sons Ltd, of Perth. They are highland distillers and I for one can recommend their fine Famous Grouse Whisky. I also always enjoy looking at their advertisements on the television with their grouse strutting about. Both of the Thatcham Tigers, DJ and HU were booked to take part in this rally. This was being flown from Hatfield to Strathallan with staging stops all along the route. This rally was celebrating the fiftieth anniversary of the sealed Gipsy engine that had been fitted into the D.H.60 Moth G-EBTD. It was then flown 51,000 air miles in 600 hours.

My pockets were quite shallow when compared with many other peoples. Because of this, I had to find the cheapest way of getting to Strathallan and joining in the fun. Marcus Barton, one of our group members was going to fly a Piper Cherokee 140, known to many as a Cherry Tree. This he was flying from Booker to Strathallan and then returning on the following day. This was just the one night away. I then agreed to go a share in this aeroplane. For some reason that I have now forgotten, Marcus could not have the aeroplane. Now I had missed out in the chances of flying to Scotland with the Moth Club. I was not to be out done. I decided that I would motor up in my Simca van. I would take B & B's or if I could not get any, then I could sleep in the van. I would then take my time on the return journey when I would call in on some fellow northern cartridge collectors. This way I could then exchange a few old shotgun cartridges. I would also call on some gun shops and try and seek out some of these old cartridges so that I could add them to my growing collection. First though, I would motor to Hatfield as I wanted to see the large gathering of vintage de Havilland aeroplanes.

I drove into Hatfield completing the first leg of my long journey. Here I met up with Stuart McKay who was in constant demand here and everywhere all at the same time. He then told me that he had some flight cancellations and that there were now some seats going spare in a Rapide or a Heron. I made a quick phone call back home and Daphne agreed that if I could, then I should fly. I chose a seat in a Dragon Rapide and then drove back out of the airfield to try and find a safe place where I could leave my van with all the kit inside of it. This I managed to do by finding a friend from my childhood days who now had a business in St. Albans. He was the elder brother to Bruce, my old playmate, who was that A.T.C. corporal who had got me my very first flight in an Airspeed Oxford at Greenham Common. Here I was made most welcome. I could safely leave my van and they even found me a bed for the night.

The next morning, the day of the start of the rally, I took very limited kit from my van and was kindly driven back to the airfield. On the grass was a fine gathering of old deHavilland aeroplanes. These were; D.H.60 Cirrus Moth, D.H.80a Puss Moth, D.H.83 Fox Moth, seven D.H87B Hornet Moths, four and at one time five D.H.89A Dragon Rapides, D.H.114 Heron, D.H.C.1 Chipmunk and forty-one D.H.82A Tiger Moths. What a grand sight that these old aircraft made. There were so many of them that it was impossible to take a photograph of them all with just one shot. I was detailed to ride in the Rapide G-AIYR. This Rapide had landed at Hatfield with a dicky starboard engine. This was then diagnosed as having a cracked cylinder head. It was with thanks to an engineering team who had worked late into the night that I was able to fly up north in this aircraft on the following day.

Two other aeroplanes present with de Havilland connections were the two Thruxton Jackaroos. These were; Maurice Brett with G-AOIR and Tim Williams with his G-APAM "Myth". This time Tim was taking along with him Sheila Scott who had at one time owned the aircraft and had given it its name. Peter Trask was being crewed by now, the late Ron Hamill in our group's Hotel Uniform. Fred Terry was being crewed with his Brother William in his DJ. Peter leCoyte was being crewed with a Calleva member, Paul Herring. Now sitting on the Hatfield turf, Peter's T5424 had developed a fuel problem which required draining the nineteen gallon tank. I have now forgotten what the actual problem was, but I was asked if I would help, which I did. This then took some organising before they would let me into the actual aircraft park. All of these aeroplanes were to fly to Strathallan except for a few. These were; the D.H.60 Moth, the Puss Moth, the Fox Moth and the Chipmunk.

If you had asked me if I believed in gremlins before I went to Scotland, I would have told you that I had an open mind on this subject. These little invisible creatures were to breed on the many aeroplanes which were to fly during the war. They were known to be troublesome and the war being over, some of these were still around. Ask me now and I will tell you that I think that there is still a breed of them in Scotland. I do not know which was worse, the Scottish midges or the Scottish gremlins. Both of them are not very nice. These northern gremlins had decided to pick on the Calleva Group, the nasty little so-and so's.

It was decided by our chairperson, Bill Hardy, that as the Calleva aeroplanes, as they were to fly so far from Berkshire, that they should have a back-up team. Bill and his wife Paddy now also deceased, and along with their daughter Georgina, would motor up by road in Peter Trask's large Triumph estate car. This they would load with the aircraft's tools and spares such as a spare Tiger Moth wheel and other aircraft items that they could fit in. The plan was that Bill and Paddy would then fly HU to Ireland from Strathallan and Peter and Ron would return back home in the Triumph, so much for their planning. One could not do much about any problems arising over the sea, but there could be no more-back up for in Ireland or their return journey. Where their plan went hopelessly wrong was by loading the car with so much aircraft spares and not loading any car spares.

I could not take much of my kit on the aircraft and so I just took some personal kit and a light summer sleeping bag. I had not taken my suit and this was to stop me from attending the main function in Scotland. As I was not booked in anywhere, the chances were that I might have been forced to sleep rough. On that morning the atmosphere on Hatfield was electric. My only grouse was that one was not allowed to walk around the aircraft. It was while fixing T5424's fuel problem that the sad news filtered in that G-ACDA, the oldest Tiger that had just been restored had been completely destroyed. It had been painted in its original colours of the de Havilland School of Flying. These colours were the ones that it had worn when it was with No. 1. E.R.F.T.S (Elementary Reserve Flying Training School). Other aircraft in that batch were the Tiger Club's DC and Captain Fred's DJ. On one of its first flights after restoration the pilot had managed to stop the engine. Instead of making a dead stick landing, he had chosen to dive the Tiger and windmill start the engine. The recondition engine being on the tight side refused to start. He was then committed to a dead stick on a short notice. All may have been well but for some high tension power wires. The Tiger hit these which arrested it in the air. This had then caused a fire to break out and its occupants had to climb down the mainplanes and drop to safety as the Tiger burnt out above them.

Having watched most of the Tigers fly away in waves at a time, it then became our turn to leave.

I sat in the front port seat in the cabin. George Aird and his wife Lorna crewed us. George had been a lucky chap as he had bailed out of a B.A.C . Lightning at nearly zero feet and had got away with it. George having the seat in the nose and Lorna sat behind him and opposite me. I then enjoyed her company all the way to Scotland. As we started to roll out of Hatfield, the last person I was to see was Richard Riding, the then editor of 'Aeroplane Monthly'. Richard had kindly given me a reception voucher which was later to provide me with a most welcome meal. As I have said, I was now flying, but I had no reservations booked. I was what I called barnstorming all over again.

George made two stops for us on our route. These were both at Tiger Moth refuelling stages, Hucknall and Sunderland. Our flight to Strathallan then went as follows; Take-off from Hatfield 10.40, Over-fly Old Warden -, Land at Hucknall -, Length of stay at Hucknall 00.58, Take-off from Hucknall 12.53, Land at Sunderland 14.11, Take-off from Sunderland 14.11, Length of stay at Sunderland, 01.39, Take-off from Sunderland 15.50, Low beat-up and land at Strathallan 17.20. Total flying time 04.30, Length of journey time 06,40.

The Rapide G-AIYR in which I was about to fly in I had last seen a year previous at St. Just on the tip of Cornwall. She had then belonged to Viv Bellamy who used her to fly trips around the rocks of Lands End. She was painted in similar colours as the last aiworthy D.H.86 Express G-ACZP. These colours were silver, black, red and buff. This D.H.86 ended her days when the undercarriage collapsed after a tyre burst when landing at Barajas and the breed then became extinct. It was while we were having a holiday at Trevarren that I took our youngest son Alan to St. Just for him to enjoy his first flight. We had planned to have gone up in YR, but due to a lack of people to fill it, we had to be content with Viv flying us around the rocks in the Cessna 172A G-BAAL. Now on the 30th of June 1979, at last I was going to fly in her. She was now owned by Mr and Mrs Ivan and Heather Rendall who were basing her at Chester. Heather was a school teacher and she came along with us in the rear. Ivan was also flying his way to Scotland, but in the Tiger Moth G-BAFG.

We enjoyed a pleasant trip with good viz all of the way. To help pass the time we did a competition of spotting landmarks and noting down the times. George maintained an altitude of 3,000 feet and we all kept our eyes open for the many other aircraft that were flying the same route. Having gazed down on Old Warden it was not long after, that our Rapide was lined up for the grass runway and our descent into Hucknall.

At Hucknall in the new mown hay, all of the taxi-ways had been cut out of the long grass. This hay had collected in large wads on the tail skids of the many Tigers, much of which then got carted off to Sunderland. Here I was to meet up with Bill, Paddy and Georgina Hardy who had made very good time in the Triumph estate. Peter and Ron were also on the ground with HU. Here I managed to find enough time to take a few photographs. I was enjoying myself, have camera, must travel. All of the Hornet Moths had over-flown Hucknall and had made straight for Sunderland. The rest of our time here was spent busily man-handling the many Tiger Moths along the freshly mown taxi-ways to the refuelling points. Due to this we did not find enough time for a cupa, but it was all good fun.

Back up in the air, we all enjoyed our leg to Sunderland. All along our route we were for- ever overtaking Tiger Moths. George refused to fly in close to any of them unless it had been already arranged. I had to be content with long range shots and as in those days I had no zoom, they did not come out very good. I did try my luck when we overtook HU and T5424. Our route had taken us slap over Newark where I had relatives. On landing at Sunderland, George hit the brakes a little too hard. All was well as we still had plenty of air flowing over the tailplane and the old girl did not stand on her nose. He had corrected in time. This old girl had seen better days and was in need of a restoration. My seat belt would not do up, so what, I had flown with the R.A.F. without them. Her flaps were also giving trouble. This gave Lorna the job of holding down a lever each time that we made a landing. Now at Sunderland, I was to find that Fred and Brother William had also made good progress for they were already on the ground. I then joined them for a bite to eat and a most welcomed cup of tea.

Our last leg was a most beautiful one. The sun was out and the high clouds cast most pleasing shadows on the moors below. The Firth of Forth came up and to our front were the distant highlands. We were too far east for any filming of the Forth Bridges. I did not know it then, but as we approached the Scottish soil, those kilted gremlins were waiting for me. We then caught up with the Rendall's Tiger Moth that Ivan was flying and so George then flew in close. With a beautiful background of the moors, this was a chance for some air to air photography. I went to wind on my film when I then discovered that I had taken my last on that roll. By the time that I had changed the film, the Tiger was way behind us. Though I did not realise it, those gremlins were on to me.

On reaching Strathallan which is located in a very beautiful setting, George first made a fly-past before he came in for his landing. We had cruised at about 130 mph. and had arrived before many of the Tigers. Together we all helped in pushing YR up to the refuelling point where I thanked Heather, Lorna and George for my most enjoyable trip. I then left the Rapide and was not to see her again until I was ready for my return journey back to Hatfield. I then made my way to the Strathallan Air Museum where I took a few pictures, or so I had thought. I was still not aware that I had a gremlin sitting on my shoulder. I then used my meal ticket that Richard had kindly given me. Feeling much better now I had satisfied my stomach, I was then about to try and find a place where I could rest my weary head for the night. It was then that I met up with the Hardy family. They had made very good time in travelling all that long distance by car. Paul Herring had a house in Dunfermline and he offered me the hospitality of sleeping in it if I could get there. Paddy and Bill then made sure that they would fit me into Peter's Triumph estate. The spare Tiger Moth, wheel along with a few other items were placed in a Strathallan's store. This then made room for me in the Triumph.

A perfect day had gone and it was now getting late as I joined Bill and his family in Peter's Triumph. Georgie had been driving hard all day and she was still behind the wheel as we set up through a mountain pass from Auchterarder on route for Dunfermline. Our driver, although still of high spirits was now tired. We then met a car with bright headlights. This was some place between Glen Eagles and Glendevon on the A.823 in the Hochil Hills. It was then that a fallen rock came into contact with the near side of the car. Being well loaded, the impact flattened both of the near side tyres. It also destroyed the front wheel rim so making that wheel u/s (Unserviceable). That fallen rock had stopped us. Whenever you see a sign beware of fallen rocks, it means what it says, one should have kept a good look out for them. There was only one thing that could be done and so Georgie and I did it. We walked all the way back to Auchterarder to get help. Have you ever broken down with a beautiful girl in the early hours of the morning? Well doing it in the circumstances that we were in I cannot recommend it. Back at Auchterarder we phoned up for the services of a breakdown association. The walk to the village had not been too bad as it was a fine night and it was all downhill. The coming back was to prove a little different. There were no mobiles phones then as they had not yet been invented. As I was the only person who was carrying a breakdown card, I was nominated as being the driver.

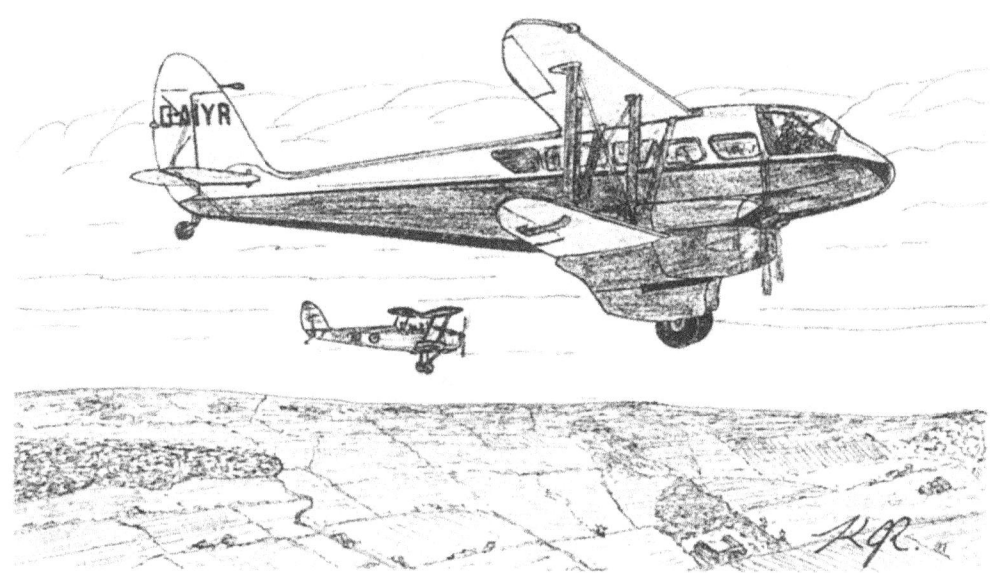
We were for ever overtaking Tiger Moths

Now that we had contacted the breakdown service, Georgina and I then was faced with the long uphill trek back to the stranded car. We had got to where the car was in sight when the breakdown association shot past us in a Land Rover. It had just come from Auchterarder. Had we had been told, we could have had a lift back. At our damaged vehicle, this chap then started splitting hairs. He considered that we had not had a breakdown, what we had was an accident. All of us did not agree with him. All that I can say about him was, that he was not a very very nice man at all. Eventually he made a decision. He took us all back to Auchterarder where he woke up a garage and got our wheel fitted with a second hand tyre. The spare wheel was then fitted to replace the damaged one. The car was once again sitting on air. It was only then that we found that the front wheel would not turn. It was pressing hard on a bent telescopic shock absorber. The breakdown man then radioed his HQ and they told him that the car was to stay where it was and that he had to take all of us in his Land Rover to Dunfirmline. We did manage to force the car off of the road. No way would Bill agree to abandoning the car and leaving all of the aircrafts toolkit with it. There was only one thing that I could do and that was to spend what was left of the night in the car. That sleeping bag then came in handy, but oh, what a most uncomfortable night.

I managed to sleep in bits and bobs. With the daylight I awoke early to a most beautiful morning. Sitting on a fence very close to the car were two ravens preening their feathers as they got ready for their days flying activities. Alas, the light was too poor for a photograph. By the time that the light was strong enough, they had departed. The sun came up red over those high hills and just below me there were several oyster catchers and other waders taking their breakfast. There was to be no breakfast for me. I half expected that Peter might come by air looking for his car. My thoughts went, perhaps if he did, then he might throw me a food parcel. The food voucher that I had used was now long gone and I was hungry and thirsty. I did not know if Bill could have raised Peter, but he did not wish to worry him at this point in time. Back in Dunfermline they had made a plan. This was to purchase a narrower tyre so that they could then move the car. They had borrowed another car and had a mechanic fellow along with it. Our back-up team then arrived back at the Triumph just after mid-day. I was thrust a food parcel through the window and they also dropped Paddy off along with me. The poor dear, she was more tired than what I was, for she just fell into a deep sleep on the grass. The front wheel was removed and away they went with it. Much later they returned with a narrow tyre fitted. The wheel was then fitted back on the car and the wheel revolved, just.

By now thirst was killing me. I had been drinking beer the night before and my tongue was that dry that I kept it still in my mouth. The car now being mobile, we motored slowly back to Strathallan airfield. The first thing that I did was to get a drink. The second thing was to have a wash and brush up. Now that we were feeling refreshed, Paddy and I started to walk down the long rows of de Havilland aeroplanes. It was then that an announcement came over their speakers. A watch had been found. I then told Paddy that it was mine. I had removed it when I had taken that wash. Not liking to keep throwing good watches away, I then left Paddy and started to retrace my steps. While on my way to retrieve my watch there came another announcement over those speakers. 'If there is a doctor present, will he please go down to where the Dragon Rapides are parked'. I thought to myself, 'Oh, I do hope that no one has walked into a revolving propeller'. Little then did I know that this announcement was due to Paddy. She had seen Peter's new Tiger Moth for the first time. Being still very tired, she had stepped back to photograph it and had tripped over some equipment and had done her back in. Hundreds and hundreds of Scots had descended on Strathallan to look at the large gathering of de Havilland aeroplanes. Yet in less than five minutes, we two had both had announcements made for us over those speakers. After we had got Paddy as comfortable as was possible, the rest of that day was spent in looking round some car scrap yards. This to find enough pieces that would make the car serviceable for the journey back south. What we failed to do was to obtain another spare wheel.

That night we motored back to Dunfirmline without any more troubles. I then spent a more comfortable night sleeping on a settee. The next day and it was back to the airfield. Due to poor Paddy's back, Bill flew her back to Thatcham, but not without an incident. They had been forced to give Ireland a miss. Peter Trask and Ron Hamill motored back in the patched up Triumph. Halfway across the Firth of Forth road bridge they were met with a puncture. Peter was not a member of that breakdown association, but Ron was. Ron then became the official driver. Their problem was that they had no spare wheel. We had not given that a thought. I just wonder how many of us had gremlins sitting on our shoulders. It took them several hours getting that car sitting back on air again. Peter leCoyte also had a problem as a gremlin had followed him all the way back to his base. He landed back safely on to the farm from where he had first taken-off only to taxi into a fence that was not there when he had left. This damaged his Tiger Moth and those gremlins had not yet finished with me.

Back on the airfield there was a change round. Heather Randell for one had decided to fly back in the Heron. I stayed with the Rapide. George then flew us back to Hatfield as follows; Take-off from Strathallan 12.25, Land at Tees-side Airport 13.50, Length of stay at Tees-side 01.38, Circuit and low pass at Old warden 17.00, Touchdown at Hatfield 17.15, Total flying time 03.12, Length of journey time 04.50.

On my return trip I sat on the right hand side and level with the wings. The weather was fine, but as we got further into England, so the clouds thickened. We over-flew Sunderland and landed at Tees-side. Here we kept as one party and had a meal. This airport turned out to have been a very expensive place for landing fees. We could just get a glimpse of Newark through the clouds as we flew over the top of it. George then dropped us down through that sea of cotton wool and we enjoyed some fun in trying to identify the many old wartime airfields. We saw the airship sheds at Cardington and made a circuit and low fly-past at Old Warden. This brought two mechanics out to take a look at us. They did not even wave, their expressions were more like, 'Hell, I hope they don't land here'. Perhaps it was just as well that we had not landed.

Back at Hatfield we met up with Stuart McKay again. That troublesome number one cylinder on the starboard Queen had developed a bad oil leak. YR was to have flown out again, but quite a lot of oil had been lost. As the mechanics were not quite sure from where the oil was leaking from, they decided to ground the aircraft. It had given us a good ride and it had got us all back. One chap that I met on the aircraft was Jim Norman. He was living on the same housing estate as where I had left my motor and so I hitched a ride with him. After he had showed me his Tiger Moth that he was rebuilding, I was given a nice cup of tea. It was then back to Victor's house to pick up my van. Here they would insist that I took a hot meal with them before they saw me away. How nice it had been to have made so many friends.

In the air as we were leaving Scottish air space, the film caught up in my camera. For reasons not known to me, this always happened to me while I was in the air. I should have left well alone until I had got back home into a dark room. I tried to fix it in the aircraft and in so doing, I lost every shot that I had taken on it while I was in Scotland. This was the air museum, the place where I had stayed with the broken down car, the lot. All the same, I had enjoyed my barnstorming experience, although it had not turned out like I would have liked it to have done. I had missed out on all of the flying at Strathallan. Yes, I now think that there were a lot of gremlins in Scotland and as far as I am concerned, the Scots are welcome to them. Perhaps they had been responsible for all the trouble that we had with Hotel Uniform's propeller. It had all started from after she had been flown on a trip up to the north.

Rendall's Dragon Rapide at Hatfield

Peter's Tiger Moth at Hatfield

A few of the many Moths at Hatfield

WAY DOWN UNDER

I was made to take an early retirement at the end of 1984 from my job of working for B.T. When I was about to leave, my overseeing officer said to me, 'Don't worry, all of the time is now your own. There is a whole wide world out there just waiting for you to explore'. Maybe there might have been if I had been getting a wage packet as thick as his. All the same, I had never left England's shores and I had often told Daphne that when the right time would come that we would take a holiday of a lifetime. Over the years I had made a pen friend with Geoff Shawcross in Australia through our hobby of collecting and exchanging shotgun cartridge cases. Geoff and his wife Jeane were willing to have us stay with them, and so it was that we decided to take our holiday in Australia.

Since then I have been to Switzerland and twice in the U.S.A, also to the Channel Islands. In doing this we have flown in airliners. But to France and Ireland, we have made several visits and each time we have gone by sea. The first time that I visited the U.S.A. I flew across direct. On my second visit I changed flights in Iceland. I do enjoy doing things a little different whenever I can. On my first visit to the States I went over with a pal from our United Kingdom Cartridge Club. Our hosts were Dale and Lois Hedlund. Dale was also into writing books on old shotgun cartridges, though they always called them shotshells. Sadly Dale is no longer with us. On our visit he kindly took us on a tour across the northern states as far as Yellow Stone National Park. What a beautiful place it is, but it is a ticking time bomb. One day it will very likely blow its top and scatter thick ash all over the prairies. While on this trip I was given the chance to visit several aviation museums and also, Oscar's Dreamland. This housed hundred of old tractors and traction engines. We also enjoyed some Indian and folk museums, but I am now getting carried away from our Australian holiday. I like all flying, but I am not so fond of flying in the heavy metal. I would much rather be flying in an open cockpit with the wind blowing in my face. If I have to spend money being confined to a metal tube then I like to make the best of it. To get to where you want to go we have to be thankful for these large jet liners. I have been very pleased to have flown in some of them, but I do think that they are contributing to the global warming. Hot air rises and these liners are high in the sky. The fumes that they leave behind them continue to rise upwards. Most fumes from off of the ground are washed back down to earth such as acid rain. That is why we once had a midland area that was known as the Black Country. If I have to travel on one of these jets, then I always try hard to get a window seat. I do enjoy looking at the various clouds and if the cabin staff allow, the stars and the night sky. A sun rise above the clouds can be very spectacular and beautiful. To me, this is far more pleasing than watching an-in-flight-movie. Apart from the R.A.F. Comet II's, my flight to and from Australia were my first in large jet aircraft. With several of my first time flights in different forms of aviation, I have experienced problems. Our Australian flights were long and of no exception. I will relate to these in this chapter, but I will not bore you with the others. Just one thing though, and this about Icelandair. Before we took-off they went through all the emergency drill. What a waste of time that was. Had we had gone down in all the white-out that we flew over we would not have lasted for ten seconds.

For many years I had my heart set on experiencing a flight in a flying boat. I had long given up on obtaining one in a four engine Short British made boat, but I still had hopes of flying in a twin engine flying boat. Now by going to Australia, Air Whitsunday's Grumman Mallards were flying trips out to the Great Barrier Reef. This was also one reason why I chose Australia. Later while down under, I was then told that the amount of money I would have needed to have done this would have over stretched my budget. I did not wish to upset my hosts and so I cried off. As I write this, I still have not managed to fly off of the water, I guess that now I am in my mid-eightys that I have now left it far too late.

Back in the previous October, Tim Williams and Henry Labouchere had flown the de Havilland Puss Moth G-AAZP "British Heritage" out from England to Australia. That is the way that I would have preferred to have flown there, but a little bit more on their trip later on. Daphne and I were to travel by airliner. We had bought our passage with the Philippine Airlines. We were to travel from London's Gatwick Airport, to Melbourne's Tullamarine Airport and having a stopover in Manila. This being the airlines base in the Philippines. This was to be a fresh experience for both of us and I do think that it is worth telling. On having that Australian trip, it is now my firm opinion that small aeroplanes are to be enjoyed and that large aeroplanes are to be endured. In other words, light aeroplanes are more appealing and large aeroplanes are more appalling. Having recorded in my log every flying hour that I had made, then I felt that I had to keep on doing so with these expensive flying hours.

When globe-trotting, one finds ones-self flying with or against the clock depending in which direction you are travelling in. The sun is moving from the east to the west and so if you are travelling east, the days and the nights are much shorter, but the flying hours remain just as long. In fact, they seem to be much longer. For this reason I will not state any times of arriving and departing at the various staging stops along our route. Our flight number was PR741 and we were due to depart from Gatwick at 14.15 on Sunday the 21st of April 1985. The stops along our route were as follows; Orly, Paris; Zurich, Switzerland; Dubai, United Arab Emirates; Bangkok also known as Krung Thep, Thailand; We were then to land at Manila in the Philippines at 19.00 their time on the following day. Here we were to have our overnight stay in a hotel with a room with twin beds and a bathroom attached. The following morning we would enjoy a sight-seeing trip that would be given by the airline. We were then to depart on their flight number PR209 at 22.00 their time on the Tuesday. We would then fly through the night and land at Tullamarine at 07.25 on the Wednesday, the 24th of April.

As this was to be our trip of a lifetime, I was determined to be at the airport in good time. I wanted to allow for any road hold-ups, and to be sure to obtain a window seat. This as it turned out was to have been a big mistake on my part. British Airlines then booked us in on behalf of the Philippine Airlines. We were the first to book in and to see our luggage away. I had secured for us a window seat in a non smoking compartment. Having booked in, we then said our farewells to our family that had brought us there as they were not to see us again until another three months. We then had to wait the long period of time before boarding.

At last the time came and we passed through the security and boarded the Boeing 747 Jumbojet N-743PR. Take-off was at 15.10 and our first leg to Paris was the shortest. Here we came down through the clouds having taken just forty-two minutes. Before ever I would fly, I always made it a practice to walk once round the aircraft and to do my own inspection. Here I was not allowed to see the outside of the ship, let alone walk round it. Where ever possible I had liked to have shaken things to make sure that they were firm. Looking out through the cabin window, those podded engines were doing a good job of shaking them-selves. At our next stop in Switzerland we were to sit on the ground for much longer than the time it took us to fly our first leg. We did manage to get one distant glimpse of the Alps as they had been poking through the solid cloud layer beneath us. We had been travelling along at around 33,000 feet.

Having sat in the aircraft for that long period at Zurich, our take-off came and we flew into darkness. Those pretty little dark haired Filipino cabin crew girls would insist that we kept the widow shutter blinds down. We were flying in very troubled times through the middle east and I did not know the route in which they had flown us on. This leg to Dubai in the Persian Gulf took us five hours and fifty-five minutes of flying time. Having landed in the dark, the crew then suggest to us that we walked down the boarding stairs and stretched our legs. I had never before trodden on foreign soil before in my life and so we got out of the aircraft. Having done so, we were then instructed by some airport staff to board a bus to the terminal buildings. Not wishing to get marooned there with the jumbo leaving without us, we refused their offer. This refusal then found us surrounded by guards each holding and pointing guns. Eventually they persuaded the rest of the passengers to leave the aircraft and then we were all driven to the terminal buildings. We were now in the tropics and being night it grew bitterly cold. Having stretched our legs inside their terminal, we then had to be taken back to the airliner. First though, they gave us a search. My camera was snatched from me and wanged through a machine. 'Does not hurt cameras', I was told. I had never ever thrown my camera the way that they did, and what is more, they never said if that machine could damage the film. Next it became Daph's turn. Her handbag was then rooted right out in front of all. It was my belief that the only reason that they got us away from the airliner was so that they could search us. I was not sorry when we left there and I certainly would never make a point of ever returning to that place.

Dubai was all lit up and in pitch darkness it looked very pretty from the air. In the far distance and off to port were two very large fires that looked like oil wells that had got out of control and were in need of capping. It had been a very short night as we had been flying against the direction of the sun. From our cabin window, the desert sands were seen to have blown everywhere. While at Dubai, the airline had given their airliner a complete crew change. We were still in the same aircraft and our new captain spoke with an oriental tongue. Within minutes from take-off and we were once more back above the clouds. We did get just a glimpse of down below where the land gave way to the water as we set out to cross the Arabian Sea and then on to India. Having spent the night in darkness from leaving Zurich I was looking forward to viewing India from above. It was not to be, our new crew were determined to keep us in darkness. All the window blinds were pulled down and they showed a duty free film to show what they were selling. This they then let run for three times and over. Where we were sitting was to the far left of the screen and it was hardly visible. The picture quality was so bad that it was all distorted and as being out of focus. At long last they stopped it. I slid my shutter blind up as did many others only to have them snapped down again. They then set out to show a film. It was not until we were nearly at Bangkok that we were allowed to see daylight again. We could now look down on a tropical cost line and could enjoy the towering cumulus and the ever moving clouds. I had missed seeing India.

At Bangkok we were made to sit in the jumbo in tropical humid heat for over one and a-quarter- hours. The leg that we had just endured in darkness had taken us five and a half hours. Our last leg to Manila was to be a shorter one. Altogether we had spent sixteen hours and forty minutes in the air. By counting the lengths of time while sitting on the ground, we had sat in that jumbo for just under twenty hours and this did not include the time when at Dubai. Though we had both been very tired and travelling in darkness, neither of us had managed to get any sleep.

Our next shock was to come. At Manila, everyone else claimed their luggage, but ours had not been put on the aircraft. We had no idea as to what had happened to it, the lot had all gone astray. All that we had were the cloths that we were standing in and it was very hot and humid. My small hand baggage was already a little overweight and it only contained my camera and photography equipment. For the loss of our luggage, we had to thank British Airways. The airline had booked us in at the Mid Town Hotel. By the time that we had filled out the necessary forms over our missing luggage, the bus for the hotel had left without us. Another complaint to that airline had them lay on a special car to take us to the hotel. This was driven by a young filipina girl who drove at breakneck speed as she chatted away to another girl that was sitting beside her. All of this on the right hand side of the road while other cars dashed across in front of us from out of the many side roads. How they managed to miss each other I do not know. By now it was quite dark and the heat had cooled off. It had been quite a long drive to that hotel.

At long last we reached it. We were both now looking forward to getting our heads down as we were in need of sleep. It had been many hours since we last slept in England. This hotel looked very nice on the ground floor, but oh-dear, upstairs it was a very different story. Down stairs it was all top show. Our toilet would not flush and the electric light gave one flash and stayed permanently out. Daphne managed to find a candle in the bath room. Lots and lots of different little bugs were walking across the beds. In fact, they were everywhere. I was badly in need of a shave and had no razor. I left Daphne locked in her room and went down stairs. Here I managed to borrow a blunt razor from some Germans who were in the bar. I then went back to my room where I took a cold shave. I then left Daphne again and return the razor and in so doing I stopped and had a quick drink with the German lads. On returning back to our bedroom, Daphne had got upset as she had thought that something had happened to me. We did sleep very well , but only because we were both dog tired. Our hotel had been all top show when you entered it and these conditions went for the rest of Manila. In the morning we were both set to make complaints. We tried the light switch and to our surprise the lights came on. What was more, the toilet then flushed. It had been like having a bad dream. Well what was the use, we were to be moving on anyhow.

Having both slept like logs, we had to rush our breakfast in order to catch the motor coach which was leaving from the front of the hotel to take us on our conducted tour. This we had paid for in with the airline tickets and we did not intend on missing out on it. The Filipino girl who was conducting us in the coach was very good at her job. From her we then learnt quite a lot about the Philippine people. We both very much enjoyed our tour and we found their city, if that is the correct word, to be spotlessly clean with no litter anywhere. All of its people were very charming. What really got to us was seeing so much poverty nearly everywhere that we looked. There were scores of young children in the streets begging for money. Most of the housing was just rusty tin shacks forming a shanty town. But in other select parts there were brick built mansions, but no middle class. There seemed to be nothing between the two classes. The cities electricity supply was routed on poles which ran along the fronts of the buildings in each street. Having worked on overhead telephone construction, I marvelled at how all of their plant kept functioning and remained standing during the tropical monsoon storms. It did not then surprise me why we had no working electric lighting throughout the night. During the monsoon season, several of the city streets could flood up to a depth of three feet. Children would then swim in them.

Manila's streets were crowded with jeepneys. These colourful and very decorated vehicles are modelled on the American forces wartime jeep. They have been given longer wheel bases and many do not have glass in their window frames. Along the tops to their flat hoods and not bonnets as these are derived from American vehicles, are often seen many cast metal horses. It was told to us that the more horses the driver had on his hood and not under his hood, then the more girl friends that he had. We were also told that the sex ratio when we were there was one boy to every three girls. When I was on my own talking with a Filipino girl over our missing luggage, she then said to me, 'Have you got your wife with you'. I replied, Yes'. She then said, 'Oh such a pity'. These jeepneys were allowed to run on bald tyres.

Our coach was driven to some public gardens. Everywhere you looked it was spotless and tidy. These people were poorly paid, but they did keep the place tidy and free from any litter. Here we were shown many water lilies and our guide told us that the name 'Manila' stood for, the town of the water lilies. The coach then left the built up area and it took us to the American Forces Cemetery. These grounds were well kept up. They contained thousands of American lads that had failed to make it back home. There was row after row of Italian marble white crosses, each one a serviceman's grave. All had been killed by the Japanese in the interest of world piece. For each grave there must have been many more who were not found or who had died at sea. At this cemetery there is a tall shrine with a portrait of the Virgin Mary on an inner rear wall. She is all worked in a marble mosaic. This tall oblong shrine has on each side of it and to its rear some ventilating blocks. On the hour it plays a tune, being like a large musical box. Also on the inner walls are some large colourful war maps. Two of theses, are the Battle of Midway and the China Burma India theatre. All in coloured marble. Although very beautiful, it was also very sad.

We were very concerned about our missing luggage and this was at the backs of our minds all of the time that we were taking that coach tour. Because of this we got the coach to drop us off at the airport while the rest of the passengers went shopping. Their airline office still had no news that they could give us. As we were walking along in despair, a Filipino lad that we had seen when we filled in those forms called us over. 'Ahh Ms Ruterrrforrrd, I have some news for you, I have traced your luggage. It had been sent to Malta and not to Manila'. Having now got to know these people, I found this news hard to swallow as we had only just come out of their airline offices. Secretly, I hope that he was right. 'It should catch up with you in a few days time', he said. As it turned out, he was right. The only thing that I saw out on the airfield that looked of interest was a Curtiss C-46 now painted in civy colours. It was too far out for my camera to stretch. I was just hoping that it might still be there when we made our return flight and then I might see it at close quarters through the airliner widows. As it turned out, due to many delays, it was to be dark again when we made our return back to Manila. Stuck at the airport we then spent the rest of the day in dodging tropical storms and the endless people who did nothing else but beg for money. This we did while the rest of the passengers were enjoying the shops. In filling in the time, we bought some duty free drinks in their duty free shop that would not except their own Philippine currency. We then had to pay them 200 pesos in order to leave the place. This we were never told about when we purchased our airline tickets. The loss of our luggage had completely spoilt our stop over. Having paid our departure fee, we were more than pleased to be welcomed aboard on our next flight. This was number PR209 and it was flown in the Douglas DC-10, RP-C2114.

I had heard of the poor record that DC-10's had got. One of them crashing by having an engine fall off and another one crashing due to a cargo door failure. This I just kept to myself as I did not wish to upset Daphne. On our flight from England to Manila we had sat next to a Tasmanian chap and he had not smelt too sweet even though he had his luggage with him. We were more than happy to see that they had sat him on the other side of this very wide cabin. Again we were lucky to obtain another window seat in a non smoking compartment. This time we were placed on the port side and a little bit further back being over the main spar. That Tasmanian chap had in his luggage some old iron rivets that had come out of the S.S. Great Britain. He was trying to keep them out of the eyes of the custom people. Also in my hand luggage I had a box of very old empty cartridge cases for my host in Australia. They were non-explosive and were all very collectible. I considered that what the eye did not see, the better it might be. In this airliner the outer seats were in rows of two. In the Boeing 747 they had been in rows of three. We both thought that the DC-10 was much nicer and quieter to fly in than the Boeing.

The take-off from Manila was dead on 22.00 on the Tuesday the 23rd April and in darkness. It was a night flight and we both tried hard to sleep again, but without success. As the sun came up from the east, and we were sitting on the port left hand side, we were able to enjoy a most beautiful sunrise above the clouds at some point over Australia. The morning star shone directly above it as the sun started to come into view. I took several photographs of this but my camera refused to do it justice. If ever you get a chance to view a sunrise above the clouds, do not miss it.

This flight being the last leg of a very long journey gave us seven hours and forty minutes of flying time. As we had built up speed, a large vortex came away from the engine support pod. We were then shown the same film that they had tried to show us in the Boeing, but this time it was not distorted. On both aircraft we had been catered for very well. Our only grouse had been the downed window blinds and the duty free film lasting so long. On this flight we could not see anything below until at the end of our journey. We landed at Melbourne at 07.15 Victoria time. I purposely have not said Australian time because on this continent you can travel through time zones. It was now Wednesday morning and we had to sit in that large Douglas a little longer. Two chaps with an aerosol can in each hand walked down each isle from nose to tail spraying us and the interior. This spraying was to kill any Philippine bugs and we had seen plenty of them. Daphne had been wearing a necklace made from seeds which the Filipino girl had given her as a good luck charm. Luckily it was never noticed. Tim Williams had told me that before they would let Henry and himself climb out of the Puss Moth, that they also had been forced to stay put until they had been sprayed by an aerosol can.

Having cleared customs and this did not take us long as we had no luggage, we were then met by our hosts, Jeane and Geoffrey Shawcross. This was the first time that we had ever met. They had motored through the night the whole length of Victoria in order to pick us up, and we were more than pleased to see them there. They were to do this for a second time within the week as we returned back to that airport and to go back through customs as we collected our belated baggage. This we did wearing borrowed clothing. At Tullamarine Airport we received a payment of seventy five Australian dollars (Approx £36). This was enough for Daphne to purchase a change of undies and myself a pair of socks. I do not know what would have happened if our cases had not be found. I guess that we would have lost out. And so ended our first trip in large aeroplanes, and it had to be endured.

We were both to fall in love with this most beautiful country and its people. Even though the odd person considered us as winging poms, though I am sure that they were just winding us up. The natives did live with a lot of nasties down under, but they had learnt to live with them. For the next three months we had to learn how to tolerate them as well. Where ever we went we were always made most welcome. How I grew to love that country and being so different to England. Eucalyptus gum trees covered the country in hundreds of different varieties from the most graceful ghost gums with their white trunks to the many ragged paper barks. All of these were full of beauty and charm. Being such a large country it then required a large sky to cover it. We found that the sunsets would stretch way into the centre of it. There was a lot of bird life and these were most colourful. I am here referring to the feathered ones, though some of the sheilas were very nice and these came in all shapes and sizes. Having now seen the country, we both now secretly regretted in not emigrating to it when we were much younger. In those days we were both living close to our parents and we had provided them with some small grandchildren. Having not seen it or its people the decision had been too great for us to make. Jet liners were not then flying around the world like they are today. Geoff had been willing to sponsor us. We were now about to find out about all of those things that we had missed out on. It is true that we would have missed old England, but England is no longer the free country that it was in my childhood days. We found Australia to be much more free and easy with its large outdoors. The U.K. is now too overcrowded. I was born in a gamekeepers residence way deep in woodlands and I have grown up to enjoy a certain amount of solitude. Out here in Australia there was plenty of it and just for the taking.

Jeane and Geoff made us welcome. When we first sat down with them to take our first meal, we did not like to over indulge. Geoffrey noticed this and he said,'Look you two, if you don't eat, you will not shit, and if you don't shit, then you will die'. After his speech we both then got stuck in and enjoyed our food. They took us all over Victoria and a sizeable chunk of New South Wales. At one time in our travels we came close to the South Australian border, but we did not cross into it. We made our residence in their home in the small hamlet called Bamawm. This being a few miles to the south of the Port of Echuca which is situated on the southern side of the Murray River. From Bamawm we were to take several trips out in different directions. We were shown the outback with its ever changing salt bushes. The state forests and the mountain rain forests. Phillip Island with its many fairy penguins as they waddled ashore. The Great Ocean Road and the Grampian National Park. We did not do bad, but there was plenty of other things that I have wished that I could have seen. Many years later, our Daughter Linda along with her husband, Barry took a package tour to Australia. Although we were out there far longer than what they were, they did get to cover more ground and to see many things that we had missed out on.

While down under I took the opportunity of looking over some of their old aeroplanes. This Linda and Barry did not do, but they would not have wished to have done so anyhow. One of these was the world's last airworthy Westland Widgeon high wing monoplane. At the time of our visit, it was owned by a grand old gentleman named, Arthur Whittaker. Several years previous I had sat next to Arthur while at a deHavilland Moth Club banquet in Stevenage, Hertfordshire. This being the same evening that vandals had vandalized my Citroen car. Little did I then realize that I would be visiting his country and nearly on his door step, that is, considering the size of his country. One hundred miles distant is not very far when you consider the size of Aus'. I mentioned about Arthur to Geoff. Geoff then said, 'I think that he may be in our phone book, ah yes, here he is'. Geoffrey then phoned him and a visit was arranged to go and see him and to look over his lovely old aeroplane. At that time it was Australia's oldest airworthy aircraft. Since then a de Havilland D.H.60 Moth may now have taken claim over this title. Around the time of our visit, this old Widgeon had been starring in a film called 'A Thousand Skies'. It was also soon to go away for a few more shots to be taken. This delayed us for a week or so, but eventually a visit to Arthur's home in Boort was laid on. Geoffrey's old brown Holden car was loaded up and together we all headed off in a westerly direction travelling along many strait dirt highways to Boort. Many of these straight dirt roads had smoother surfaces than some of England's metal clad roads. The day of our visit was Sunday the 19th of May.

On the day of our visit we were to find poor old Arthur in bed with a dose of flue. We were to visit Arthur in his bed. He then told us that the last time that he had suffered with flue was when he was staying in Stevenage in England. Arthur's brother Len, on who's farm the old Widgeon was kept, stood in for his brother. He took us along with some other people that Arthur had invited on that day to look over his old bird. At their flying field we were to find an open corrugated iron clad hangar with its three outer walls shielded with sugar gum trees. In this small farm building the old Westland was sharing it with an Australian built Turbulent. The Widgeon was a Mark III parasol monoplane that was the same age as myself. It had started its life back in 1928 with the constructors number WA.1695 and it was first registered in England as G-EBUB. It then was sold to Australia where it was allotted the registration G-AUHU and it was given the name "Fleetwing". Later on, along with other Australian civil aircraft it was given a registration change to VH-UHU. This old bird was then sharing the same last two letters as our group's Tiger Moth back home,' Hotel Uniform'. When she had first arrived in Australia she was then owned by Milton Kent. In the December of 1950, after spending twenty-two years in Kent's ownership, the old aeroplane then passed to Ross McCullum and later on to A. J. Murray. Both of these gents had based her in Sydney N.S.W. (New South Wales). In the April of 1953, Reginald St Chad Young purchased it and took it to Yanco in the southern part of N.S.W. He was an oldish man and never quite managed the art of learning to fly. The old Widgeon then languished around under cover until Arthur rescued it in 1957. Since then it has remained in the T.L.C.(tender loving care) by the Whittaker brothers.

With a high wing parasol aircraft it is not that easy to keep the upper wing surface clean. This we found out only too well with the upper surfaces of the top wings of the Tiger Moth. With the abundance of wild birds and having an open hangar, the need to protect the old fabric on the upper surfaces was very important. Bird droppings on fabric are not to be recommended. The Whittakers had found a solution to solving this problem. As they never folded the wings on their Widgeon, they had fixed a protective cloth up near the roof in their hangar and it went the full length of the Westlands wings. Cords were strung along and left this cloth at each corner. By unfastening them and then by pulling on them, it would then raise the cloth off of the top surface of the wings. This in the same manner that one might higher or lower a washing line. This cloth was then suspended in the hangar roof so that the aircraft could be wheeled out. The reverse procedure was then applied when the Widgeon was put back away.

I was to see it and to take photos of it while it was still painted up for its role in the film. It had been playing the part of another Westland Widgeon that was now long gone. This one was registered G-AUKA and was named "Kookaburra". It was in the April of 1929 that the real "Kookaburra" was being flown by Keith Anderson and H. S. Hitchcock who had gone out searching the outback bush for the overdue Fokker F.VII/3m trimotor G-AUSU named, "The Southern Cross". This being the same name which was later to be given to Captain Blair's Short flying boat. The old Fokker had been forced down whilst it was being flown by the two Charlies, Charles Kingsford-Smith and Charles Ulm. Whilst searching for this old Fokker over this inimical terrain the "Kookaburra" suffered a tappet problem. The crew could see the problem unfold on them as the engine of the Widgeon had got open valve gear. Being forced to land in the bush of the Northern Territory's Tanami Dessert they had managed to have got down safely without doing any damage. To get back in to the air again required a much longer run and this they failed to do. They had even tried burning the bush. Due to the extreme heat and a lack of water, they were both to perish. The Fokker "Southern Cross" was later found and made it back safe. The "Kookaburra" was not so lucky. A Thornycroft lorry with a search crew came upon the "Kookaburra" when it was far too late for its occupants. The lorry had got low on fuel and so the tank on the Westland was drained to replenish the Thornycroft. The wings of the Widgeon were then folded and she was left out in the bush. I fail to see why they could not have taken it in tow, but they must have had a reason. Out there it then became lost again when a search failed to find it. A surveyor, Vern O'Brien relocated its remains in 1961. In 1974 or 1975, a party hoped to recover its remains for a museum, but it had gone missing again. As I write this, I am not sure, but I seem to remember reading that it had been found once again.

Whittaker's Widgeon was of all wooden construction and its wings were designed to be folded. With a wing span of nearly thirty-six and a half feet it was powered by a 90 h.p. A.D.C. (Aircraft Disposal Company) Cirrus engine. While we were present, Len Whittaker had tried to start this engine, but without Arthur being there, it point blankly refused to start. We all had a good look at the old bird and I was able to take a few close-up photos of her before we pushed her back into her corrugated hangar. Behind the hangar was what was left of a burnt out Tiger Moth that had not served the Whittakers so well as the old Widgeon.

I had not been able to see the Widgeon fly at Boort, but I was later to see it fly when at Wangaratta when Joe Drage took her aloft. While at Wangaratter, Geoff and I stood talking to Arthur Whittaker who had now got over his flue. He then told me that had he not had been ill in bed on that day of our visit, then I could have had a ride in her. I have since wondered about this as I do not think that he knew how strong the wind was. He then said to us, 'That Widgeon was built with a boxed type spar, just how long can one safely keep flying her'. At his age he was not keen to undertake a rebuild. As I write this I do not know her present history. Let us hope that the Australians might be able to enjoy seeing a Widgeon in the air in the years to come. Twice I had been told that she had starred as the "Kookaburra" in film making. She is now a part of Australia's history.

While we were staying in Bamawm, I was given a local trip from the Echuca Aerodrome. This was in a blue and white Cessna 172 that was registerd VH-WYG. I was picked up from Geoff's house by a local farmer and his son who were friends of Geoff and his family. They were Keith and Peter who motored me to the aerodrome where I was introduced to our pilot, Ted Baker. As the car rolled up to a stop we caught him doing his B.F.I (Between Flight Inspection). My first job was to load a new film into my camera so that I would not need to do so once in the air. Keith and Peter had decided that they wanted to sit in the rear. I was pleased about this as it gave me the chance to sit on the right side of Ted. The part of Victoria where we were staying was all state irrigated. Farms being fed by water from channels and the catchment area was way up in the Great Devidling Range of mountains far off to the east. We were staying in a state bungalow as Geoffrey was a water bailiff by trade. He now owns this property. We took-off from a hard runway, and once we had made some height, Ted latched on to the main irrigation channel that took us in the direction of Rochester that is locally known as Rochie. This part of Victoria is flatter than a pancake and a forced landing out here should not have proved too difficult. The ground below us was divided up by many straight water channels and the dirt roads were just as straight. First, Ted circled around Rochie where he owned a news agents business. He then made for Lockington. After taking a good look at these two towns we then left Lockie and headed for Bamawm. Here I had a chance to take a few pictures of Keith's farm and Jeane and Geoff's home from the air. I very much enjoyed this little trip, and as it turned out, it was the only time that I got to fly in an Australian registered aeroplane. It was very noticeable to see just how dry the land was when one got away from the irrigated area. It was very dry on the northern side of the Murray River, this being in New South Wales. This part of Australia was just coming to the end of a long drought at the time of our visit.

As we left Bamawm, Ted kindly gave me control of the Cessna. He then told me that I would find it much more heavy than a Tiger Moth. My thoughts then went back to that take-off at Blackbushe. This aircraft had a push-pull wheel instead of a joystick and I found it to be more like driving a car. I then headed the Cessna back in the direction of Echuca. On Ted's instructions we crossed the Murray where we circled Moama. Below us was the Rich River Golf Course. In the club room down below we had recently enjoyed a jolly good evening. Daphne and I had then won a dancing prize, though I could not think why. I then handed the control back to Ted so that I could take a few more pictures. These were of the two towns below, one on each side of the Murray with its wharf and many paddle boats. A week or so previous we had taken a river trip on one of these paddle boats and the steam boat "P.S. Pevensey" had got stuck in the mud whilst it was avoiding us. Ted then lined the Cessna up with the runway and brought us in for the landing. This little trip logged me another forty-five minutes in the air. How nice it had been to fly in a light aeroplane again even though it had only been a spam-can.

Back home in England we had a young Australian join our group for a while. His name was Jon Robinson. While staying in England he had been out to my home just the once to look at my collection of shotgun cartridges. Cartridge collecting was a hobby that he had also shared in. When I had decided that I was going to take this holiday I had written to Jon and told him what we were about to do. He kindly wrote back and suggested that we stayed with him for a week. Jon and his family lived at Fitzroy in the suburbs of Melbourne. He owned an Australian built Tiger Moth which he kept some distance from his home. Due to his pressure of work, I was never to see or to fly in his Tiger. This was not his fault as he was determined that I should have done this, even though we did spend a week with him. Jon was still keen that I should fly with him and he was trying to arrange a visit to an air strip at Bamawm along with some other Tiger Moth owners. Our trip back to England came before it could be finally arranged, and so I never did get to fly upside-down, down under.

I had only been in Australia for a few days when I set my eyes on an Australian built Tiger Moth at Essenden Airport. This was an all silver Tiger that was registered VH-CEJ. CEJ being the same letters as those on Jan's Fox Moth. It brought memories of our group's silver Tiger back home. It was sharing a workshop with the fuselage frame of a Hawker Demon and a part rebuilt Spitfire. Both of these projects were being worked on. Also in this hangar workshop was a war worn Bell P-39 Airacobra that was minus its Allison engine. It looked as though it had spent many years in a jungle and it may have been salvaged from out of New Guinea. Out on the airfield were many light aircraft and it was here that I was to see my first Nomad. The Nomad is a high wing twin engine general purpose aeroplane that was designed and built in Australia. This one was yellow overall and registered VH-CRI.

One of my intensions in coming to Australia was to fly in a Grumman flying boat. This did not happen. It was while I was visiting many of the smaller airfields that I spotted a Lake amphibian registered VH-XPS and a Republic Seabee that was registered VH-MJO. My enquiries led to nothing. I was told that the Seabee was not even airworthy. At Essenden there was based a PBY Catalina amphibian. Although it was airworthy, it was not sea worthy. Its long range had made it ideal for land survey work. I did try very hard to find a seaplane, but I was out of luck.

Geoff and Jeane took us on a trip to Swan Hill where we paid a visit to the Pioneer Settlement. This was a purpose constructed village of old buildings containing lots of early equipment that the early settlers had used. Such items like, early wind pumps, tractors and steam ploughing engines, but nothing that was aeronautical. What we did see just before we got to that town were many sections from Catalina flying boats. These had been gathered up together in a large garage yard. Close by was Lake Boga being in the Murray Valley. Lying on the ground in this yard were frames from the turret blisters. At that time, Planesailing who's 'Cat' was based at Duxford were asking in the aviation magazines for any whereabouts of turret blisters. I then wrote them a letter and included some photographs. I do not know if my letter had been of any help to them as I never had a reply. At that time I was told that there might have been some complete Catalinas on the bed of that lake.

Back in 1996, I was sent a newspaper cutting showing a static Catalina flying boat which had been assembled from sections for display by the Lake Boga Lions Club. It had no engines in its cowlings. This cutting also gave some very interesting history about Lake Boga. If Japan had invaded Australia in those dark days of 1942, a secret flying base on the shores of this remote lake in the western corner of Victoria would have then played a vital part in defending the country. This was believed to have been the only inland base of its kind in the world and it was one of Australia's best kept secrets. Lake Boga was the home of Australia's Catalina flying boats. Aircrew training also played a vital role at this base. It had then become a common sight to see a flying boat in the air above Swan Hill. Then service men and women would work tirelessly to overhaul, repair and refit Catalinas, Martin Mariners and some Dornier flying boats. All of these being used by the R.A.A.F. (Royal Australian Air Force) and allied forces for a range of tasks which included, submarine bombing, mine laying, rescue and intelligent work.

Construction of this base was completed in 1942 and the base became No. 1 Flying Boat Repair Depot of the R.A.A.F. It opened as the Japanese carried out their 25th air raid on Darwin. This was just a few months after the off-shore flying boat base at Broome had been attacked by Zero fighters. Fitted with long range fuel tanks, flying boats would return to Lake Boga in stages from remote locations. With concern that this base might be seen from the air, the Department of War went to great lengths to camouflage the new roadways and the buildings so making them look as if they were an extension of the town, but it was not possible to hide the many flying boats. At times there were as many as twenty flying boats anchored on that lake and it became home to one hundred airmen and airwomen. On the ground tall fences concealed most of the base's operations from the public view. The Lions Club uncovered an old R.A.A.F. bunker. This they were to restore as a museum. How I would like to have been able to have gone back to Australia and to visit the place.

Now at the time of our visit, the equivalent to the British Shuttleworth Trust's collection at Old Warden, were Joe Drage's collection of Australia's old aeroplanes. These had been based at Wodonga, but it had just made a short move to Wangaratta. Here the local council had stepped in with some finance. An extremely new large blister type hangar had been erected to house this fine collection of old civil aeroplanes. This new building finally took its shape when all of the many tie-wires had been fully tensioned up. On the outside it had been painted all over in white. In large letters that could be read from the ground and the air was the wording, 'Drage Airworld' in black. On the Sunday the 9th of June 1985, it was the official opening day of this new Airworld and the A.A.A.A. (Antique Aeroplane Association of Australia) had arranged a spectacular fly-in.

From Geoff's, I then got in touch with Jon Robinson. He then promised to fly up to Bamawm in his Tiger Moth and to pick me up. Together we would then fly one hundred miles east and attend the grand opening. On that morning I was all set and waiting with my ears cocked up for the sound of a Gipsy Major when Geoffrey's phone rang. It was Jon from Fitzroy. Down at the coast it was blowing a gale. He was very sorry, but he did not think that it was the weather conditions that he should take his Tiger flying. At Bamawm and also at Wangaratta the weather was perfect. Jon had kept his Tiger about forty miles inland. Had he had gone there, conditions could have been different. Jon apologised for his bad weather and he suggested that I might start looking for a car. This incident emphasized one of the problems in keeping an aircraft too far away from ones home. It was an incident that could quite well have happened here in England.

Whittaker's Widgeon

Catalina sections in a garage yard

Good old Geoff then stepped into the breech and offered to take me in his car. Although he was sorry for me as I would not be flying, I think that deep down he was pleased as he had wished to enjoy that day as well. On the Saturday, the day before, he had taken me to the Echuca Steam, Horse and Vintage Rally. This was a two day event, but on going to Wangaratta we were then not able to enjoy the second day of this event. Both of these two events were being held on the Queen's Birthday weekend.

On the Saturday I had enjoyed seeing many old rare wood burning steam traction engines, a working team of five heavy horses and some oxen pulling a log buggy. There were also many vintage tractors with names such as, Lanz Bulldog, Ronaldson-Tippet and Hart Parr Australian Special. Most of the old steamers were new to me, if that makes sense. They were all wood burners and they made good use of the Murray River Red Gum. There were vast quantities of fallen timber lying in the state's forest. This wood gave out a great heat when used on a fire in doors. Good burning wood that it was, it was not so easy to split. I remember when Geoff was splitting a log, he then came across a red backed spider. These were not the kind of things that you should let nip you. Several of those steamers were quite interesting, to quote just a few of them. An English made Ransome steam wagon with its makers number 35138; Two very old Foden steam wagons; Several English Colonial traction engines; A stationary engine from Barrows of Banbury, England; From the U.S.A, a Case steam roller; From Australia, a Cowley steam roller. I have mentioned some of these just to let you know what we were missing out on in Geoff taking me to the Drage Airworld.

Geoffrey headed his Holden towards Wangaratta and we arrived there in time to see most of that day's events. On that day we both did see that old Westland Widgeon take to the air. All the same, I did feel that I would have loved to have taken to the air in it. This was when Joe Drage decided to fly it. We were to miss a lot of the flying that was taking place while we were walking around this new 123m x 42m x 10m stressed arched hangar building. This new building also housed a 140 seat restaurant, a lounge display and a workshop. Joe and Margaret's historical collection had been purchased by Wangaratta City Council that had hoped that this collection would then place their city on the map and then to have made money while it was being run by Joe himself. Given time and they were all to become very disappointed.

Before Daphne and I had left on our Australian visit, both Ben Cooper and Tony Woollett had asked me that if I got a chance, would I please go to town with my camera on the British Aircraft B.A. Eagle Mk.II, VH-UTI as both needed to get close up details of it. It makes me feel sad as I write this, but both of these grand chaps are no longer with us. I now seem to have out-lived all of my mates. We made our visit long before the Eagle VH-ACN with its constructors number 138 arrived back in this country. Ben and his team at the Newbury Aeroplane Company were then to restore this old three seat aeroplane when it reverted back to its original British registration G-AFAX. This was the only Mk.II Eagle that was given a fixed undercarriage. None of these delightful low wing aeroplanes had survived the war in the UK. I once read somewhere that a C.O. (Commanding Officer) of a Scottish M.U. had made a bonfire of them, but I am not sure if this is true. I approached Joe with my request to photograph their yellow, silver and black Eagle all over. Joe's reply to me was, 'Sure, just go your hardest'. I think that my set of photographs may have helped a little in the restoration of G-AFAX. I was once told that I could enjoy a ride in a B.A. Swallow, but like many promises, it was to come to nowt.

Having photographed that Eagle inside and out, we then set out to look at all the other interesting old aeroplanes that filled up this new hangar building. To help in breaking up the vastness of the place, large triangular cloth sheets were installed. These were in the alternative colours of blue and pink. Why they had chosen these two colours I do not know as aeroplanes do not have different sexes. To my utter amazement, hidden behind one of these pink sheets was Tim William's Puss Moth "British Heritage". I had known that it had been here, but by now I had expected it to have been crated and well on its way back home by sea. My heart felt for it, being left out here all of this time like some forgotten child. When she saw me, I felt that she had tried hard to smile, but just could not bring herself to do so. Tim crewed by Henry Labouchere had flown her out to Australia to commemorate the historical flight that Charles James (Jimmy) Melrose had made in 1934. This the 50th anniversary of the MacRobertson Air Races that were flown from Mildenhall in England to Melbourne in Australia. This 21 year old Australian had flown his Puss Moth VH-UQO "My HIldegarde" all on his own to England. He then made the return trip all of the way back solo in the air races. You may notice that I had called this event in plural as there were two sections, this being the speed and the handicap. He also became the only solo entry to complete the races. Tim and Henry were not a solo flight and they also took very much longer in ZP. This was because they had got plagued with magneto troubles which had been due to a firm who had supposedly overhauled them. But let us not forget that Tim's Puss was now on fifty-four years old. Sad to say, but two years after this race or races, Jimmy was to lose his life when he was flying his own Heston Phoenix through a storm in South Australia. This aircraft registered VH-AJM had carried his initials in its registration. He had named it "Billing" after his uncle, N. Pemberton Billing who had founded the Supermarine Aviation Company in England. It was thought that a wing had failed after it had been struck by lightning. Daphne and I had been at Mildenhall when Tim and Henry had taken-off at the start of their Australian flight. I believe that I was the only person to capture them on film as they taxied out for their take-off on their long journey.

We had gone to Mildenhall where we were to see Tim and Henry leave. This was on Sunday the 21st of October 1984. We watched them take-off with Australia firmly planted in their minds. Tim was to tell his own story in a book which he never got around to having published. He has since told me that he intends to put all of this trip in a book which he hopes to write on the life of his Puss Moth ZP. This would be a book which I would very much treasure to have on my book shelves. I then told him to hurry up and get started as I still want to be around when he publishes it. As together we witnessed the start of their anniversary flight, so they were carrying the race number 16. This was the same number that Jimmy Melrose had carried on the sides of his fin. As I stood gazing at ZP in the Drage Airworld, I then thought of what Ben Cooper had said to Tim Williams while I had stood talking to them back in England. 'Ken is going out to Australia to turn your engine over for you'. I was just about to step over the rope when Geoff said to me, 'You had better not, this place is now filling up with people'. These 1934 air races were those in which the de Havilland Comet G-ACSS was flown into victory. This Comet named "Grosvenor House" had just gone an expensive restoration and so that it was then flown back to Melbourne so that it could participate in the State of Victoria's 150th anniversary celebrations. But this time she did not fly all of that way on her own, this time she flew there in a Qantas Airways Boeing 747. Unlike Tim's Puss Moth, it had long since gone back to Blighty.

So that I will not bore you here, I will give you a few details of those lovely old aeroplanes at Wangaratta with a mentioning of their colours that were in this new building. This' towards the ending of this chapter. There were also many other interesting light aircraft out on the flying field. These ranged from a modern canard to a vintage Klemm L-25 that was registered VH-UUR. Unlike Jan's G-AAUP back in England, this one had been given a longer nose and was fitted with an American flat-four engine. It gave it bags of power as it was flown by a very elderly gentleman. Everything looked all wrong about it. It was painted white overall with black registration letters. These had been applied above on the port wing and below on the starboard wing. What made it look horrid was that these wing registrations had been applied so that they read from the front of the aircraft instead of from the rear. This being the wrong way about. The tops of the fin and rudder were rounded off making it a later model. To make sure that you did not miss seeing its modern engine, the rocker box covers were picked out in a bright red.

The Flying Doctor's Nomad VH-MSF

Commonwealth CA-28 Ceres VH-SSY at Wangaratta

Drage Airworld, Wangaratta

Australian built Tiger Moths were there in full force. Some of these that I had taken pictures of were, VH-AKE, VH-DFJ, VH-KVH, VH-SSI and VH-TIG . There were also many others. There was an Auster Aiglet being VH-WMM and an all red Fokker Tri-plane replica. Also there was a Chipmunk. Geoff and I then enjoyed watching some tied together from their wing tips Tiger Moths and they put on a very good show. To sum up, Wangaratta was a very good day out and I was glad that I never missed it. Not long after I had got back home I attended our deHMC Moth Rally that was held on Woburn Park. I then chanced to hear some Aussies nattering over some photographs. One cannot fail to hear their lingo. They were showing photographs that had been taken on that day at Wangaratta. I then said to them that I had got some similar photos that I had taken and that they were in my car. With this, I then went back to my motor and got them. They then told me who owned each aircraft. They also told me that if I had seen them on that day, then I most certainly would have gone upside-down while being down-under. Yep, sod's law had stepped in again.

Daphne and I both very much enjoyed our stay in Australia. It was a beautiful land of eucalyptus, kangaroos and bird life. Everywhere that our hosts took us, the scenery was always on the change. I did very much enjoy the outback with its ever changing bush and red soil, it was all so beautiful. I enjoyed the abundance of the colourful bird life. Also those large dark coloured wedge tailed eagles. While out here I treated myself to a zoom lens for my camera and this then allowed me to get a few shots of some of their feathered bird life. There were birds of all sizes and I will name just a few. Pretty little silver eyes; the Superb Blue Wren; Honey Eaters and the Flame Robin. A little larger in size were Zebra Finches; various Green Grass Parrots; Crimson Corellas and various coloured Cockatoos. Grey and pink Galahs flew around in flocks in a similar way in which our wood pigeons do. Although many of these birds were most beautiful, I cannot say that their screeching noises that some of these parrots made was quite as pleasant. There were two kinds of

Australian Magpies. These were nothing like our magpies and they made a carolling sound. These calls can often be heard while you are watching Australian soaps on the telly. Their magpies are not always nice as they have been known at times to attack people.

Then there were the larger birds. To name just a few of them. Herons of several different kinds; Spoonbills; White Egrets and several kinds of Hawks; Flocks of Ibis would invade a field. They then came down to land like Horsa gliders on a L.Z . (Landing Zone). There were large Crows, but no rooks. Similar to back home there were large flocks of Starlings; Sparrows and a few Swallows. I could quite well go on, but I must mention the colourful laughing Kookaburras. The most common of the sea birds were the Silver Gulls. Pelicans could often be seen either at the coast or on inland waters. We had expected to see more Kangaroos; Wallabies and Emus in the wild, but these animals seem to like to stay away from humans. Kangaroos like to go walk-about when it gets dark and they often become road casualties. Like our badgers, it is not good for your motor if you run over them when they are left dead in the road. Many Australians fit roo-bars to the front of their vehicles so as to help protect them. Due to these hazards, Geoffrey was not keen in motoring long distances after the sun had gone down.

At Broken Hill, there is a Royal Flying Doctor's base and we all went there for a visit. Here, visitors were catered for. We were shown a film on how their organization worked. One could view through a glass patrician as to what was happening in their radio room. This room took on the duties of a doctor's surgery. On display they had various items of equipment from the past until the present. While we were at their centre, they gave a lot of praise to their fleet of Nomad aircraft. Over on their airfield we were shown over their Nomad VH-MSF. The fellow that showed us over this high wing and fixed undercarriage aeroplane did not give it the same amount of praise as what their control centre did. This Nomad was the very same aircraft that had been used in making the Flying Doctor program that has been shown on the television. It had an all white colour scheme with dark green letters and dark green and buff trimmings. The badge that is illustrated in this book was applied to each side of the fuselage in black. It was while we were on this airfield that an active R.A.A.F. Dakota made a visit. This one was A65-95 and it was in an all metal scheme with a white top to its fuselage. It had a black and yellow rudder and it carried the wording, Royal Australian Air Force in red.

Before we were to return back home, we then spent a week staying with Jon Robinson and his family. Jon took us to a house he had in Lorne which was down on the Bass Straight. Here the surf beaches were a paradise. In that area they had had some very nasty bush fires. The blackened eucalypts trees were now starting to burst into fresh green growth. It must have been terrible living around there when that fire was raging. The new greenery looked for all the world like bunches of mistletoe. During our weeks stay, Jon took me to see some of the local airfield and air museums. I am now not able to remember at which particular airfield that it was that I saw the various aircraft. Amongst the many modern aircraft there were a sprinkling of old timers. To name just a few. Winjeels; Wirraways; Wackett Trainers; a Curtiss Hawk; a Bristol Beaufighter and a Dakota. In one hangar there was a Sopwith and the deHavilland D.H.60 Gipsy Moth VH-UKV. The first of the airfields that Jon took me to was , Point Cook. Here the R.A.A.F. had a museum for visitors like me to enjoy. Several of their aircraft had been put out to grass and so I took some photographs of them. These were; English Electric Canberra A-84-208; Douglas Dakota A-65-108; Gloster Meteor Mk.7 A77-702 and the North American Sabre A94-910. The first part of the R.A.A.F. number is the type number in service. The second part of the number is the individual number in that type of aircraft.

On the opposite side of the airfield and facing us was the non-flying replica of the Fokker F.VII/3m tri-motor "Southern Cross". I was not able to go and view it at close quarters, but from where we were standing it looked like the real thing. The real thing was at Eagle Farm, Brisbane. Rather a long long way away. This ground replica had been made for the film, 'A Thousand Skies'. This was the same film in which Whittaker's Widgeon had been filming in. During our weeks stay with Jon he took me to Berwick Airfield. In a hangar there was a blue North American Hard IV with the registration VH-USB and named "Lady Southern Cross". Its cowlings had been removed and its blue and silver paint scheme was then about to follow suit. I said to the urk who was working on it, 'This should have been an all wooden aeroplane. He then made a reply, 'No way would we ever have a wooden aeroplane in this hangar'. To the rear of this Harvard was a Miles M.3 falcon that was part covered by dust sheets. Its true registration I do not know. It very likely also starred in that same film. If that was not a wooden airframe, then what was.

It was while we were motoring from one place to the other that I obtained a copy of a very old document. For the life of me I have forgotten just how I came by it, but I guess that its original could quite well be at some place in Australia. As I found it most interesting, I will include a copy from my copy here. It had obviously been copied very many times.

DRAGE AIRWORLD AND DISTANT DOCUMENTS

Listed below are some of the most interesting aircraft with a few colour details that were present in the Drage Airworld Museum when I was at Wangaratta. Following on from this list are some copies of documents of early American aviation. While out in Australia I was on the constant look out for old bric-a-brac. I now do not remember where I got these. Looking at them I would say that they have been copied many times over. Where are the originals, don't ask me. I would like to think that they are in the United States, but they might be at some location in Australia. I am including them here as I consider them to be very interesting.
First though is that list of Wangaratta aircraft.

Auster Autocar VH-BYD
Cowslip yellow overall with red trim outlined with a thin black line. The undercarriage legs were red and the wheels were yellow.

Avro 643 Cadet. VH-PRT.
Built in England in 1938. White overall with red letters. These were above on the starboard top wing and below on the port bottom wing. The side registration was across to top of the rudder. Brown wing struts. White wheel leg struts. Black wheels. A tail wheel was fitted.

B.A. Eagle 11. VH-UTI
Seating was provided for two passengers to the rear of the pilot on a bench type seat. Retractable undercarriage. Deep yellow fuselage trimmed in a gloss Brunswick green outlined with black. The wing letters being across both wings above and below. All flying surfaces silver. Leading edges to wings and tail plane were yellow. Interior upholstered in brown leather.

Beech 17 Staggerwing. VH-ACU
Retractable undercarriage. White overall with red trim. Red registration letters on rudder.

Beech 17 Staggerwing. VH-BBL.
Retractable undercarriage. White overall with red trim. Black registration outlined with red across rudder, above on top starboard wing and below on lower port wing.

Cessna Airmaster VH-AVZ
Deep metallic blue with white and red trimmings.

Chrislea Super Ace. VH-BAE
British built and spent its first ten years in New Zealand. It was white and a deep cream. Black trimmings. Registration letters were in black and were on the upper starboard wing.

De Havilland D.H.60 Gipsy Moth. VH-ULM.
Fitted with low-pressure tyres. Deep blue fuselage. All flying surfaces in a deep yellow except for the rudder, which was chequered in black and white squares. Varnished outer wing struts. Wheels and fuselage letters were white.

De Havilland D.H.82 Tiger Moth. VH-BSD.
Coupe top fitted. Silver overall with red cowlings, undercarriage legs, and wing registration and fuselage flash. Wheels silver. Black registration on rudder.

De Havilland D.H.84 Dragon. VH-AON 'Puff the Magic Dragon'
Australian built. Silver overall including spinners, struts and wheels. Middle blue registrations in small on starboard top wing and below on bottom port wing. Also across the sides of the rudder. 'Puff the Magic Dragon' painted in light blue and red etc, on each side of the nose. Built in 1942.

De Havilland. D.H.85 Leopard Moth. VH-UHE.
White with middle blue trim in a kind of modern style. It did not look right on a pre-war aeroplane and I though that it looked ghastly.

De Havilland. D.H.89 Dragon Rapide. VH-BGP.
Having spent most of its working life in New Zealand, it came to Australia in 1957. silver overall and trimmed in red in the following places: The nose joining the fuselage trim line, engine cowlings and nacelles, top half of fin and rudder, registration letters across lower half of fin and rudder, registration on top of starboard upper wing and below on lower port wing. Silver undercarriage trousers and spinners with flashes.

De Havillan D.H.94. Moth Minor. VH-ACS.
Open cockpits. Silver overall with small black registration on fin.

De Havilland D.H.A.3 Drover. VH-AZS and being ex VH-DRF.
White overall with dark blue trim and wording along tops of fuselage. Drage's historical Aircraft Museum.

Genairco Biplane. VH-UOG.
Tow open cockpits and an inverted engine. Silver overall with blue engine cowlings. Red registration letters and outer struts.

Lockheed 12A. VH-ABH 'Silver City'.
Was used during the war to carry VIP's (Very Important Persons) around in Australia. Polished metal overall. Red nose and engine cowlings with red flashes. This then outlined in white. 'Silver City' in capitals on each side of the nose in black. The registration letters were across both wings in the pre-war style in red.

Stinson Reliant. VH-CWV.
White overall with black fuselage letters on fuselage sides and on the wings in the post war style.

Taylor J.2.Cub. VH-UYT.
Deep yellow overall. Black cowlings, wing struts, complete undercarriage and registration letters. These across the fin and in the post-war style.

Commonwealth CA-28 Ceres. VH-SSY. May not have belonged to the museum. Might have been a visitor?
Silver overall. Black nose apron and registration letters across the fin and rudder.

The badge on the Nomad VH-MSF

SIGNAL CORPS SPECIFICATION, NO. 486.

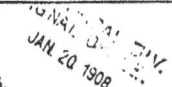

ADVERTISEMENT AND SPECIFICATION FOR A HEAVIER-THAN-AIR FLYING MACHINE.

TO THE PUBLIC:

Sealed proposals, in duplicate, will be received at this office until 12 o'clock noon on February 1, 1908, on behalf of the Board of Ordnance and Fortification for furnishing the Signal Corps with a heavier-than-air flying machine. All proposals received will be turned over to the Board of Ordnance and Fortification at its first meeting after February 1 for its official action.

Persons wishing to submit proposals under this specification can obtain the necessary forms and envelopes by application to the Chief Signal Officer, United States Army, War Department, Washington, D. C. The United States reserves the right to reject any and all proposals.

Unless the bidders are also the manufacturers of the flying machine they must state the name and place of the maker.

Preliminary.—This specification covers the construction of a flying machine supported entirely by the dynamic reaction of the atmosphere and having no gas bag.

Acceptance.—The flying machine will be accepted only after a successful trial flight, during which it will comply with all requirements of this specification. No payments on account will be made until after the trial flight and acceptance.

Inspection.—The Government reserves the right to inspect any and all processes of manufacture.

GENERAL REQUIREMENTS.

The general dimensions of the flying machine will be determined by the manufacturer, subject to the following conditions:

1. Bidders must submit with their proposals the following:
    (a) Drawings to scale showing the general dimensions and shape of the flying machine which they propose to build under this specification.
    (b) Statement of the speed for which it is designed.
    (c) Statement of the total surface area of the supporting planes.
    (d) Statement of the total weight.
    (e) Description of the engine which will be used for motive power.
    (f) The material of which the frame, planes, and propellers will be constructed. Plans received will not be shown to other bidders.
2. It is desirable that the flying machine should be designed so that it may be quickly and easily assembled and taken apart and packed for transportation in army wagons. It should be capable of being assembled and put in operating condition in about one hour.
3. The flying machine must be designed to carry two persons having a combined weight of about 350 pounds, also sufficient fuel for a flight of 125 miles.
4. The flying machine should be designed to have a speed of at least forty miles per hour in still air, but bidders must submit quotations in their proposals for cost depending upon the speed attained during the trial flight, according to the following scale:

    40 miles per hour, 100 per cent.
    39 miles per hour, 90 per cent.
    38 miles per hour, 80 per cent.
    37 miles per hour, 70 per cent.
    36 miles per hour, 60 per cent.
    Less than 36 miles per hour rejected.
    41 miles per hour, 110 per cent.
    42 miles per hour, 120 per cent.
    43 miles per hour, 130 per cent.
    44 miles per hour, 140 per cent.

5. The speed accomplished during the trial flight will be determined by taking an average of the time over a measured course of more than five miles, against and with the wind. The time will be taken by a flying start, passing the starting point at full speed at both ends of the course. This test subject to such additional details as the Chief Signal Officer of the Army may prescribe at the time.
6. Before acceptance a trial endurance flight will be required of at least one hour during which time the flying machine must remain continuously in the air without landing. It shall return to the starting point and land without any damage that would prevent it immediately starting upon another flight. During this trial flight of one hour it must be steered in all directions without difficulty and at all times under perfect control and equilibrium.
7. Three trials will be allowed for speed as provided for in paragraphs 4 and 5. Three trials for endurance as provided for in paragraph 6, and both tests must be completed within a period of thirty days from the date of delivery. The expense of the tests to be borne by the manufacturer. The place of delivery to the Government and trial flights will be at Fort Myer, Virginia.
8. It should be so designed as to ascend in any country which may be encountered in field service. The starting device must be simple and transportable. It should also land in a field without requiring a specially prepared spot and without damaging its structure.
9. It should be provided with some device to permit of a safe descent in case of an accident to the propelling machinery.
10. It should be sufficiently simple in its construction and operation to permit an intelligent man to become proficient in its use within a reasonable length of time.
11. Bidders must furnish evidence that the Government of the United States has the lawful right to use all patented devices or appurtenances which may be a part of the flying machine, and that the manufacturers of the flying machine are authorized to convey the same to the Government. This refers to the unrestricted right to use the flying machine sold to the Government, but does not contemplate the exclusive purchase of patent rights for duplicating the flying machine.
12. Bidders will be required to furnish with their proposal a certified check amounting to ten per cent of the price stated for the 40-mile speed. Upon making the award for this flying machine these certified checks will be returned to the bidders, and the successful bidder will be required to furnish a bond, according to Army Regulations, of the amount equal to the price stated for the 40-mile speed.
13. The price quoted in proposals must be understood to include the instruction of two men in the handling and operation of this flying machine. No extra charge for this service will be allowed.
14. Bidders must state the time which will be required for delivery after receipt of order.

JAMES ALLEN,
Brigadier General, Chief Signal Officer of the Army.

SIGNAL OFFICE,
WASHINGTON, D. C., *December 23, 1907.*

Form No. 13.

Signal Corps, United States Army.

These Articles of Agreement entered into this ——————tenth—————— day of February———, nineteen hundred and eight——, between ————Chas. S. Wallace————, Captain————————————, Signal Corps, United States Army, of the first part, and Wilbur and Orville Wright, trading as Wright Brothers, of 1127 West Third Street, Dayton, in the county of————————Montgomery————————, State of——————Ohio——————————of the second part, WITNESSETH, that in conformity with copy of the advertisement, specifications, and proposal hereunto attached, and which, in so far as they relate to this contract, form a part of it, the said————————————————Chas. S. Wallace, Captain,—————————————— Signal Corps, United States Army, for and in behalf of the United States of America, and the said ——————————————————Wright Brothers—————————————————— (hereinafter designated as the contractor) do covenant and agree, to and with each other, as follows, viz:

ARTICLE I. That the said contractor shall **manufacture for and deliver to the United States of America,**

One (1) heavier-than-air flying machine, in accordance with Signal Corps Specification No. 486, dated December 23, 1907.

ART. II. That the deliveries of the supplies and materials herein contracted for shall be made in the manner, numbers, or quantities, and for each number or quantity, on or before the date specified therefor, as follows, viz:

That complete delivery shall be made on or before August 28, 1908.

ART. III. All supplies and materials furnished and work done under this contract shall, before being accepted, be subject to a rigid inspection by an inspector appointed on the part of the Government,

Art. VI. That in case of the [failure] of the said contractor to perf[orm the] stipulations of this contract within the time and in the manner specified above, Articles I to III, inclusive, the said party of the first part may, instead of waiting further for deliveries under the provisions of the preceding article, supply the deficiency by purchase in open market or otherwise, at such place as may be selected (the articles so procured to be the kind herein specified, as near as practicable); and the said contractor shall be charged with the increased cost of the supplies and materials so purchased over what they would have cost if delivered by the contractor on the date they were received under such open-market purchase.

Art. VII. It is further agreed by and between the parties hereto that until final inspection and acceptance of, and payment for, all of the supplies and materials and work herein provided for, no prior inspection, payment, or act is to be construed as a waiver of the right of the party of the first part to reject any defective articles or supplies or to require the fulfillment of any of the terms of the contract.

Art. VIII. The contractor further agrees to hold and save the United States harmless from and against all and every demand, or demands, of any nature or kind for, or on account of, the use of any patented invention, article, or process included in the materials hereby agreed to be furnished and work to be done under this contract.

Art. IX. Neither this contract nor any interest herein shall be transferred to any other party or parties, and in case of such transfer the United States may refuse to carry out this contract either with the transferor or the transferee, but all rights of action for any breach of this contract by said contractor are reserved to the United States.

Art. X. No Member of or Delegate to Congress, nor any person belonging to, or employed in, the military service of the United States, is or shall be admitted to any share or part of this contract, or to any benefit which may arise therefrom.*

Art. XI. That it is expressly agreed and understood that this contract shall be noneffective until an appropriation adequate to its fulfillment is made by Congress and is available.

Art. XII. That this contract shall be subject to approval of the Chief Signal Officer, United States Army.

IN WITNESS WHEREOF the parties aforesaid have hereunto placed their hands the date first hereinbefore written.

WITNESSES:

John J. Mullaney as to] *[signature]*
Albert Larurere as to] C[apt.], Signal Corps, U. S. Army.
C. E. Taylor as to]
H. H. Hoffman as to] *Wright Brothers*
by Orville Wright

APPROVED: FEB 28 1908 , 190

[signature]
Brigadier General,
Chief Signal Officer of the Army.

*Here add to any contract made with an incorporated company for its general benefit the following words, viz: "But this stipulation, so far as it relates to Members or Delegates to Congress, is not to be construed to extend to this contract." See section 3740, Revised Statutes.

(EXECUTED IN QUINTUPLICATE.)

RETURN TO UP OVER

Together both Daphne and I had fallen in love with Australia. Where ever we had been, we had been treated with kindness and it made us proud to have been called poms. We had been taken nearly all over the State of Victoria and had spent a week or so in its capital, Melbourne. Here we had stayed with our friends, the Robinsons. While here we had visited the shrine and had seen in their book the names of my father's two elder brothers, Richard and William. Together they had emigrated to Australia. They then became Australians, but they were not to be in Australia for as long as what we were. The Great War had started and together they joined up with the Diggers and returned back to Europe, but they were not to see their home again. Having gone through the Gallipoli campaign, they were then both killed in France. One of them never to have been found. We had been shown a little bit of New South Wales with its salt bush and opal mines. We had been taken to where the tall trees grew in the rain forest and where Fairy Penguins came ashore on Philip Island. Visits had been made to lakes, rivers, national parks, bird sanctuaries and nature reserves. Our hosts had taken us from the flat country to the mountainous country and we had enjoyed all that we had been shown. We were both now getting a little home sick and those many new friends that we had made we were now about to leave all of them where we had found them, on that beautiful continent. To me it was like closing a lovely book, and then passing it on, never to see it again.

That country loved its old aeroplanes and so did I. In that short time, I had grown to love Australia with its most interesting old aircraft. We were now about to travel back home on some new aeroplanes. Our flight was booked for the 5th of July from Tullamarine Airport. Take-off should have been at 10.30 in the morning and we had been requested to arrive at the airport by 08.30. Our flight back home was again with the Philippine Airlines and our change in flights being back in Manila but this time without a stopover.

During the dark hours we were up long before 05.00. Jeane and Geoff, bless them, were also up with us. Once more they did a trip for us in those early dark hours. As we motored south, all eyes were kept wide open for those menacing kangaroos that had no road sense. This time they were taking us to the airport and they were not to bringing us back. We had stayed with them for a long time and we had been strangers before we had met. It was now the time to leave, and to let them live their own lives along with their own family. For us, it was time to return back to ours. We said our fair well in darkness to Bamawm. That little place so far away from our home that will always stay treasured in our memories. Together we did that long trip south through Victoria. As the sun came up, we saw no more kangaroos. Geoff and Jeane had got us there in plenty of time. Our hosts had planned their day by spending some time along with their friends in Melbourne. We then thanked them and said our goodbyes. As it happened we were leaving Australia in some of their troubled times.

There was a strike taking place at Sydney Airport of fire fighter and crash crews. That airport had ceased operating. Due to Sydney's problems, double the amount of air movements were being made at Melbourne. Congestion was everywhere and with this there were long delays. Having settled our departure fee, we were made to stand in long queues along with our baggage for the rest of the morning. Eventually it was announced that our flight would be fed in an upstairs restraint and not in the air. Due to this strike, no hot food could be taken on to the airliner. We then sat down and rested our very tired legs while we ate our lunches. This then made us feel a little better. Our luggage was then checked in again and we crossed our fingers that we might see it when we got back to England. Having found our departure gate we passed through the security only to find just as much chaos on the other side of customs. We had to walk out to our aircraft crossing over concrete aprons and carrying our hand baggage as we went. Not all of the passengers were as pleased about this as what I was. It gave me the chance to look at all of this large aircraft and to be able to take a photograph of it. This airliner was the Douglas DC-10, RP-C2003. Having spent the whole of that morning herded around like a pack of animals, it was now 12.30 as we were lifted off of the Australian soil. At long last we were on our way home, but our flight back to Blighty was to be far from a good one. We had departed tired, four hours late. Well never mind, we had been told that we would have had to have waited for four hours in Manila for our second flight on the Jumbo. Perhaps we should go straight from one airliner and on to the other. We had not grown that fond of the place and no way did we wish to go the other side of customs and pay them another 400 pesos to leave again. As it happened all of that had just been a bit of wishful thinking.

One thing that I had been looking forward too, was seeing Sydney and its harbour bridge. While being down-under, we had not travelled that far north. I had consoled my-self that I would see this from the air on my return flight as we were scheduled to land at Sydney. Now thanks to those Sydney strikers, we were not to fly that way. I felt a little cheated having decided to fly with the Philippines. I had missed seeing the Alps, except for a fleeting glimpse. I had missed out in seeing India and now I was being robbed of seeing Sydney. All of this should have been a good excuse to have gone back again. Instead, our flight took us straight across the east side of central Australia. It was only then that the vastness of this great continent came home to me. Most Aussies live around its outer edges and not so far from its coasts. In the centre it was barren desert. We were flying at well over 30,000 feet and the air was crystal clear. Below us it looked like large dried up salt lakes that stretched for hundreds of miles. It was not the place that I would have liked to have made a forced landing in. This part of our flight was uneventful and we were served with some cold snacks and some china beer. Our landing in Manila was in darkness instead of daylight and it still had that tropical smell about it.

The thought of getting off of the Douglas and on to the Boeing made me wonder if they would get our luggage moved over in time. Still, if it went astray for the second time, at least we should have some more clothing back home. I need not have worried, their departure board gave our flight as being another four hours late. Their only excuse was that this Boeing had been held up in Europe, but they gave no explanation as to why. We all sat around and none of us slept. Having been shoved about we were all tired. Our four hour wait had turned into nearly five by the time that we entered that Boeing 747. This one was registered in America like the previous one, and it was N-742PR. All the way back to England we both tried hard to sleep, but again neither of us could manage to do so.

We were towed out backwards from the terminal building. The large Boeing then taxied out to the main runway where we took-off into a dark rain filled sky. Soon we were well above the wet weather and were flown at 35,000 to 39,000 feet. Our first leg was to Bangkok and this gave us two hours and forty-five minutes of flying time. Here we sat, or dozed, in the airliner for one hour and twenty-five minutes. Our next leg was to Pakistan. This leg took us four hours and eleven minutes. Once there, we then sat and dozed for three quarters of an hour. Our next leg was the longest one, and oh boy, did we get tired. This was to Frankfurt in Western Germany. This leg had taken us seven hours and twenty-two minutes of flying time, talk about get some in. It had been a long dark flight as we had been flying in the same direction as the sun. We did catch up with it because on this leg it started to get daylight. Before leaving on our holiday, dear old Captain Fred Terry had given me one of his cards requesting that I might be given a visit to the flight deck. On my outward journey I had tried to use it but without success. On this long leg I decided to try my luck again. I handed it in to the young cabin girl who said she was not that hopeful, but she did say that she would take it to the captain. She then returned and told me that I could go and pay him a visit. That visit to the flight deck was really worthwhile. Although no one spoke to me as they both seemed to be busy. I stayed there for a short while. There was not the slightest sound of any engine noise, I felt sure that I could have slept there. Sitting up in the nose it was not possible to see any of the rest of the aircraft that was trailing along behind us. The only noise was the swish of the airflow passing over the front of the airframe. It was like being in a gigantic glider. While I was here I took a picture of the two captains at work and I think what I might have been looking at could have been the coast of the Black Sea.

They, that mysterious they, would not allow us to leave the Boeing while at Frankfurt, but eventually conditions proved otherwise. We had sat in that airliner for about the time of our usual stay when the captain's voice came over the speakers. My thoughts were, at last we shall be making our final hop back to Britain. Not so, 'We apologize for a short delay, our ground crew have found a fault with the starboard stabilizer. There will be a short delay while they mend it'. Just after this, one of the passengers came up front and said, 'They will not mend this in a hurry. There is a great big hole the size of a cartwheel and a crack all across the top of the wing'. I then went back and took a look at the damage through the window from where he had been sitting. There was an enormous hole that was elongated and it was in the starboard inner flap. Directly above this there was a long crack or a line going up across the upper skin of the wing. We had to continue sitting around in that cabin and then the cabin air conditioning packed up. Outside it was dull humid and thundery. Inside it got very hot and all of us passengers were complaining about the lack of ventilation. These conditions then forced the German authorities to allow us off of the aircraft. They then transported all of us to the terminal buildings in bendybusses. Many of us passengers were dry and thirsty and in need of a drink. We were all most astonished when we found out that a one pound coin was not enough to buy a cup of tea. Several of us then got together and pooled our monies. By doing this, we each had a can of soft drink. I then had a feeling that we may have had more cans than what we had paid for.

After another five hours delay we were driven back to the Jumbo. The apologetic captain's voice came back over the speaker system. It was a pity, but I do not think that he heard all of the remarks that were said back to him. He did get a kind of a hand clap. The ground crews had patched it up. I decided not to go and have another look at it. What you did not see, then you would not worry about. It would have been interesting to have known what had caused all of that damage. The object must have been about three feet long and three feet wide. Yes, I was brought up all of my life to work in the old measurements. Whatever it was, it had done damage to the upper skinning of the wing. We were sat towards the front and this could only be seen from the rear. By this time, I was now far too tired and past caring. This, our last leg was another hour and ten minutes in the air and the aeroplane then held together.

Daphne's legs and feet had swollen and she could no longer put her shoes back on. Luck had it that she had changed her shoes for slippers which she had kept in her flight bag. All of us passengers were well and truly over-tired and the customs people were very good as they did not detain any of us. Our eldest son, Clifford and his wife, Kate along with our little granddaughter Beth, had left Berkshire in the early hours of that morning. It had now gone 19.00 and we should have landed at 09.30. This time our luggage was still with us. Cliff, Kate and little Beth had hung around that airport all day. They did not know where we had got to. After several announcements, they then removed our flight from the arrival boards. The only information that they were given was that this flight had been held up in Germany. This then convinced them that we had been hijacked. This then made them all the more determined not to have gone back home until they knew what had happened to us. As we were that relieved to see them still there, so they were just as much relieved to see us stumbling around those barriers.

Walking out to the DC-10

Our captain had been very apologetic and our passengers had also realised that the troubles were not of his making. The airline had fed us as well as it could. With bomb blasts, blow-ups and hijacks, all airline security was on very tender hooks. Our flights to Australia and back had been far from the best. Are there such things as, international gremlins? I just don't know. We may have been just the unlucky ones. I had taken thirty films in Australia and had brought them all home in a special lead-filmed covered bag for processing. Due to that cabin temperature rising to such high levels in Frankfurt, many of the photos on the outer side of the rolls were ruined. I started to navigate Clifford around the south of London. As I attempted to do so, I then fell into a very deep sleep. What a way to get in some more flying hours. Since then I think that the Philippine Airlines have ceased their international flights. When we had got over our jetlags, our family then gave us a grand and unexpected welcome home party. They surely must have missed us.

MAINLY ON THE LIGHTER SIDE

Mike Janaway, the son of the farmer at our Calleva's base and myself made several aviation enthusiast trips together. We flew with Peter 'Tiny' Ward from Biggin Hill where we enjoyed a flight over our capital city in the Dragon Rapide G-AIDL. We did this in the April of 1983. This was the same Rapide that I had flown in over the Humber Estuary in 1980. Together we took a trip from Bristol in Air Atalantique's Dakota G-AMSV that had '50th Dakota' painted on its nose. Our pilot on that occasion was Captain Scheerboom who had at one time flown with our Captain Fred Terry. The Dakota had been the air transport work-horse of the allies during the Second World War. We were very keen to fly in the axis aerial work-horse, the Junkers Ju.52/3m. To gain this experience we needed to go abroad. To do this, we booked up on an enthusiasts tour with George Pick Airtours. This was to Dubendorf in Switzerland.

First I had to motor Daphne up to Newark where she would spend a week with some relatives while Mike and I were away. I stayed the night with Mike and his wife, Linda. We left Thatcham very early in the morning on the 24th of August 1989. Our departure from Heathrow that was due out by 09.50. We arrived in plenty of time so that we missed all of the early morning rush hour traffic. By doing this, we each secured a window seat as we were flyers and wished to see out. At the airport we met up with George Pick and his nice lady assistant, Valerie Kilby. We were then introduced to the rest of the lads that had booked to go on this tour. Together we saw our luggage away and then we made for the departure gate. Our flight was Swissair No. 803 class Y. It was in an Airbus Industries A.310 that was registered HB-IPC.

The Airbus was very quiet to ride in and I soon got carried away with my camera taking pictures of the strange wing complex. It was a very pleasant flight to Zurich as we were flown across France. Those who were sitting on the starboard side were treated to a view of Paris. Being sat on the port side we missed out on this. For most of the way we were flown above fine scattered small clouds at a height of 33,000 feet. Our flying time was one hour and ten minutes between take-off and touch-down.

At Zurich we had to put our watches forward by one hour so that we were right with Swiss time. Having gone through the customs, we then placed our luggage in some lock-up lockers. An airport coach then gave us a round tour of the flying field and the airport. While on this tour I was able to purchase a fine diecast model of the early Swissair's Lockheed Orion CH-167. This I purchased from the Swissair's Employees Discount shop. The prise that I paid for it was equivalent to £2. 50p, in english currency. To complete our first day with George, we were then given a most interested guided tour of the Swissair's maintenance base. Here we then met up again with the airliner that had not long brought us. The most interesting old aeroplane to me that was in those buildings was the red painted Komte AC-4 Gentleman HB-IKO. This aeroplane being a single engine high wing monoplane. From Zurich Airport we were driven in a coach to Uster. Here we then bought ourselves a meal in a restaurant close by our hotel the Illustrious where we then spent three nights.

On the Thursday morning, we all took a train ride from Uster to Dubendorf. This town had its own airfield which was used by the Swiss Air Force. It also housed their air museum and it was the operating base for JU-Air's three Junkers Ju.52/3m vintage trimotor transports. It had become a beautiful sunny day as we watched the first flight of George Pick Airtours passengers take-off in one of the three Ju.52/3m's. The /3m standing for three motors. When we arrived, all of the three Junkers were lined up on the grass. Two of them were a silver colour overall and the other was a muffin-grey or sandstone colour. On this Friday, the two silver Ju.52's flew while the sandstone coloured one stayed on the ground. Our flight was to have been the next day. As it happened, the two silver corrugated transports were not on the field. That Friday we had to content ourselves with the museum and the rows of parked aircraft.

On the Saturday we awoke to find that we had wet weather. The Swiss Air Force could not have been too pleased either as they were holding a mass fly-past. With their Swiss Alps all around the area, this had not been the kind of weather that they had been wanting. Not to worry, play it by ear was the theme of the day. By the time that our train arrived in Dubendorf, the cloud base had started lifting. We were due off on our flight as soon as we got there. Our section was then booked in with JU-Air and we walked out to the vintage airliner via their museum. Only one Ju.52 was on the grass and we made for that. Mike, myself and another fifteen passengers. Our captain and a female hostess climbed up a short yellow ladder as we all boarded HB-HOS / A-701. Once we were all on board, they started up the three B.M.W. (Bayerische Moteren Werke) radial engines. Good weather or bad weather, we were at last on our way. They did tell us that they had plenty of spares that would enable them to keep these old birds flying for years to come. Also they had a stockpile of unused B.M.W. engines.

Having reached the active runway, we then took to the air like an over sized Klemm. She was not as sprightly as a DC-3, although she was fitted with an extra engine on the nose. It was very quiet to ride in considering that it did not have much in the way of interior upholstery. It was built like a girder bridge having a very strong airframe and it was most delightful. Once up in the air we were given the freedom of the cabin and we were welcomed up front. I was the first one up there. Camera shutters were now clicking all over the aircraft including my own. We slowly made height through the damp haze and headed off into the mountains. As we continued to make height, so the viz cleared and the mountains seemed to grow in size. The largest of them were still capped in snow. We were flown over various lakes with side-wheel paddle-steamers on them as we followed through the valleys. Our trip took us over several small towns, but I did not know what they were. It was far from perfect weather, but it had been better than what we had been expecting.

Being here in Switzerland and flying in a 1930's aeroplane was like putting the clock back in time. We were ambling along at about 6,000 feet and flying past some very rugged mountains with masts and little buildings on the tops of them. How the devil did they manage to get up to them? This was when the film in my camera ran out. As I reloaded with a new film, a Swiss Air Force Super Puma, known to them as a Supa Pooma, caught up with us and formated. He then flipped from our left side to our right side by flying over our top. I was only just in time to take three very quick snaps of him. By now we had been flying for some time and our forty minute flight time was fast running out. This time we were in luck as due to some jet fighters activities over the airfield our captain was forced to do a lot of tight turns over a pine wooded area. This then gave us fifty-three minutes in the air from take-off to touch-down. We had been in the old Junkers for over a good solid hour.

Later on and during that same morning, we were to watch all three of these Junkers formate on each other and fly over their base prior to the start of the 50th Anniversary Flypast. Flying in HB-HOS on that Saturday was on the aircrafts exact 50th anniversary of when the Swiss Air Force had first taken delivery of it. All three of these Ju's were once Swiss Air Force machines. They were now civil aeroplanes but they still retained their old service numbers as well as their civil registrations. The Swiss were very proud of their old Junkers airliners. It had been very nostalgic. The last time that I had seen a Ju.52/3m in the air was when I was at Cosford in 1947. One of which was registered G-AHOG, to me it was then a flying pig. No way now could I associate these old Swiss airliners as swines or flying pigs. All three of them had red fins and rudders carrying the Swiss white cross. This was far nicer than a swastika.

Mike and I had both enjoyed our visit. Most of George's party were to return back on the Monday. We along with another couple had been booked to return on the Sunday. We were due to fly out from Zurich at 17.15. Come the Sunday and it was one torrential down pour. Due to this wicked weather, we were given a coach tour of the town before they dropped us off at the airport. I think that we were very lucky to have got that Ju flight in. We had enjoyed our tour, our flying, the air-display and the museum, but not the weather. It was now back home on the A.310 Airbus HB-IPB.

We saw our luggage safely away and again we were lucky to obtain window seats. Our return flight was over Germany, Belgium and the North Sea. My mind went back to all of our wartime bomber aircrews that had flown back this way often with difficulties. We climbed up through a layer of cloud into the late sunshine. The cloud tops were most beautiful as they reminded me of the vastness of the Australian bush. Always there, and always on the change. We saw several distant aircraft as this cloud layer began to break up as we reached the North Sea. On the let down over the Thames Estuary we lost a lot of height very quickly. I then received a severe pain in my right eye and across the right side of my forehead. It then turned into pins and needles. This I have never experienced before. By the time that we had landed it had gone. We had flown into an airway congestion. Due to this we were kept flying very low over the centre of London. This sightseeing tour we did not expect. With late sunshine shining on all of the buildings and the many neon lights beginning to shine out, our capital city took on a splendour all of its own. By this time I had used up all of my 400 speed film, hard luck. Our captain made a nice landing and it took us some time to taxi to the terminal gate.

And now for the lighter side of aviation. Mike and I had decided that we would like to take a trip in an airship. I wrote a letter to Airship Industries (UK) Ltd, in Baker Street, London. Their reply came back. Yes we could charter an airship. Their letter was short and so I will print it here. Dear Mr Rutterford. We are always pleased to hear from aviation enthusiasts but unfortunately we do not charter an airship by an hour. Our minimum charter period is in fact one day and the charge is approximately £7,000. I hope that this will answer your query. Yours sincerely, Algy Williams. Public relations manager. At half the price of a Tiger Moth, this then ended any thoughts of our Calleva Group having an outing in their very expensive airship. I had written to them on the 6th of December 1984. Their short reply was dated the 3rd of January 1985. They must have had second thoughts about chartering out their airships. I will again quote from their literature. Following the overwhelming success of our introductory trial in the early Summer of 1986, Airship Industries is pleased to announce SKYCRUISE – an airship sightseeing service over London scheduled to commence on the 30th March 1978. It then went on. SKYCRUISE will be operating the thirteen seat Skyship 600 airship for this service, offering flight departures approximately every one and a half hours from Radlett Aerodrome in the village of Park Street, 2 miles south of St. Albans, Hertfordshire. At last, a chance to fly in an airship. Mike and I added our names to their list of would be passengers, but we did not hear any more about it. Apparently they had been inundated with requests for flights from the public. Then during the early months of 1987, Airship Industries advertised their SKYCRUISE over London. We then could fly with them on the 6th of April at 13.30. At long last we had a booking. The price of each seat being £125 per seat during the summer months.

We were both set ready to go when the news came that their two airships, the 500 and the 600 ships had been moored to their masts when a gale had sprung up. This gale then increased into a hurricane velocity. Both of their ships were forced to ride out these storms. Fortunately both ships held at their masts, but they both suffered damage. This incident forced them to cancel all of their bookings. Later on we were offered a new date. This was on the first day in June 1987 and during their peak flying season, but our prices would remain the same as for the off-peak. I wrote back to them and excepted their offer.

I drove over to Mike's home at Thatcham and arrived there by 10.00. A quick phone call to their base at Radlett, and yes, our flight was still on. We were to be third time lucky. First though, Mike had to pull a trailer load of cattle up to Reading Market. It was the old Calleva rule number one, all farming had priority over any flying. I then followed Mike up in my old VW camper van. Mike's father, Joe Janaway then drove the Land Rover back to Thatcham and Mike then climbed in to my old VW and we then proceeded on to Radlett. We motored up the M.4 and then the M.25 and we eventually arrived at the old Handley Page's historical airfield with plenty of time to spare before our flight was due. Together we watched the flight which was scheduled before ours fly away to the capital city. We were to find that there is a lot of work in getting an airship loaded and away. This gave me an excellent chance to take a few photos.

After a wait which seemed hours, the ship returned and we were driven out to her on the airfield. She had been moored to a mast which was fitted to a heavy vehicle. Once the airship had settled, it was held steady by two gangs of four young people. Four more young people were then grasping the sides of the cabin or gondola. By having to employ such a large number of ground staff, one could then see the reasoning of the very high costs of flying in their airships. Before we left their head quarters which was constructed from portakabins, they had weighed us with our cameras or any other baggage which we would be taking with us on that flight. At the main gate and at their HQ they had to employ more staff. All of that weighing in made me wonder what they would do about the weight of the loss of fuel when used up on a journey. A young lady name Jackie was on her first day with the firm. She was also told to take her first ride in an airship along with us. What a lucky girl she was. For all of my life I have never been paid to fly although I have enjoyed quite a lot of free flying. Though she did not say much, she was obviously very nervous as she gazed out at the sights of London by never leaving the centre of the gondola.

As two passengers got on, so two passengers disembarked. By using this method, it stopped the ship from floating up and taking the ground handlers along with it. It was not possible for it to have got away, but its tail could have risen up vertically. As soon as we had stepped into that ship we were airborne as that ship was at a tethered flight and had actually never landed. Think about it, but this period I would not accept as flying time. It was one minute before 17.00 when we were released from the mast with an upward slope and headed off out in the direction of our capital city.

Having been given our seats, we then had to belt ourselves in with lap straps. When 1,000 feet was reached we were then allowed the freedom of the cabin. As we had not been fully loaded , we could all enjoy looking out of the ample window area. These windows were large and three of them could be slid open. Over London I slid one back and poked my camera out and took a photo of one of the ducted propeller units. These were designed to tilt up and down. Having done this, I was then asked to keep my camera inside. They were afraid that I might have bombed London with it. I had no wish to throw my expensive camera at the city, but I could see their concern. We were told that by lifting up these opening windows that they could then be lifted out and used as emergency exits. Only they did not tell us where the parachutes were stored. Obviously, we were not allowed to try these windows out. Had we had jumped out of them it would have given them some weight problems.

Our trip to the capital and back took us close to the busy Elstree Aerodrome. On the ground were many modern light aircraft and in the centre of these was a Spitfire wearing the P.R.U. (Photo Reconnaissance Unit) blue paintwork. Over the city we found it to be encased with haze and the sun did not shine. We were flown at a speed in which a Tiger Moth would have stalled at. It gave me plenty of time in which to change my camera lenses. Mike and I had already over flown some of this area when we had taken that flight from Biggin in the Dragon Rapide G-AIDL. Up in this Skyship 600 registered G-SKSC, the pace was leisurely. We were flown over the central area to the north of Old Farter Thames as we travelled eastward. We then crossed the river to the east side of the Tower Bridge. I was surprised by the amount of greenery that there was all around that Bloody Tower of London. There was none of those grounded ravens to be seen. Our trip took us back past Westminster and Buckingham Palace and I managed to take a nice selection of photographs . As we made our return, through the distant haze, the Hendon Air Museums with the large Beverley transport in its grounds could be seen. What a wicked shame it was that after flying it in there, they then decided to break it up.

When flying in an airship one is conscious at all times of a sideways swaying motion. Not at all unpleasant, but it was there. She was truly a ship of the air. If one became sick, would it be airsickness or sea sickness? It would have to be air sickness, but the conditions might have been similar. So far as I write this, I have never been air sick or sea sick, but there is always the first time for everything. Both of the pilots up front were not positioned away from the cabin like captains are in an airliner. As they flew this ship they had no rudder pedals. Each pilot had one foot placed across the top of the other. This did surprise me as the medical thinking is that the crossing of legs and feet is very bad for the blood circulation.

Just before we had taken-off from Radlett, a man was rushed out from their terminal to join our party. He had been notified of the flight within the last hour. As he was a publican in the village of Park Street he had just been offered this free flight. This was because objections had been made in the granting of a drinks licence to the airship terminal. He paled on with Mike and myself and before we left for Berkshire, we joined him for a drink in his pub. Ours was the last flight of the day. In order to disembark from their ship, so bags of ballast had to be loaded on board so that the ship would not rise at its tail end. Should there had been an emergency and we all had had to have jumped out of those windows, perhaps the last one out might have broken his neck. Flying in that Skyship had been a very pleasant experience that had been well worth waiting for and taking. They had given us good value for the money spent.

My only hot air balloon flight so far, came like a bolt out of the blue. It was a Thursday evening at 17.30 of May 1974 that my phone rang. On the other end was Phillip Prout. Who also worked for the same firm as what I did. He was telling me to get my skates on if I would like a balloon flight. Previously I had got him a ride in a Tiger Moth and in return, I was to obtain a balloon flight along with the Tiger Moth pilot. I did get my balloon flight, but I do not know about the Tiger Moth pilot. I had to present myself down at the balloon field at Marsh Benham by 17.00. The trip was to be in the Twilley's Balloon Team's Thunder Balloon G-BERD named "Twilley's Goldfinger".

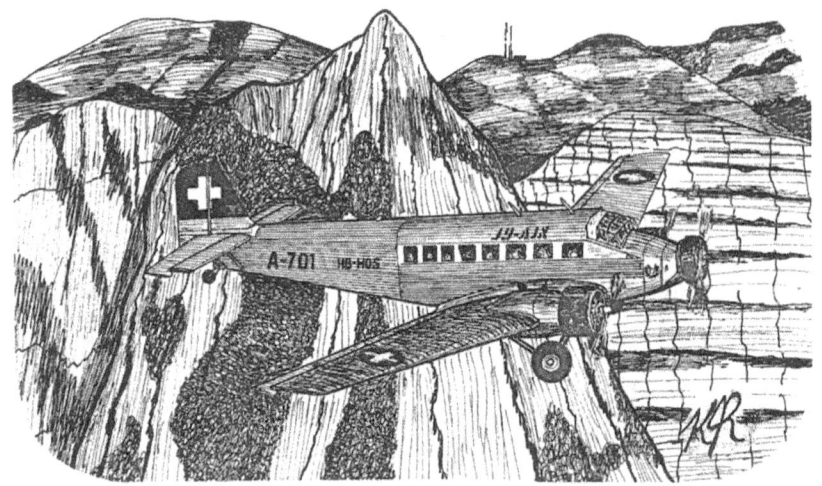

Flying between the Swiss mountains

Bobbing between the trees

I arrived at the field where I then met up with Phil and several other people. The Dante Balloon Group was also about to fly their Cameron V-65 balloon G-BIGY named "Gemma" at the same time as our flight. Phil had brought his parents along with him and he intended that he would get all three of us on our first balloon rides on that evening. No time was lost as the balloon was unpacked from its large boxed trailer. First out was the basket and the burners, ect. Then it was a large bag that contained the envelope. Assembly was well under way when our pilot, John Green arrived on the field accompanied with his wife, Sheila. The envelope was opened out and the basket attached. A motorised fan was started up and this very quickly inflated the envelope. The gas burners were ignited and I was instructed to give Phil's dad a hand to pull on a rope which was attached to a parachute in the crown of the envelope. This may well be the last time that I flew with a parachute. This then allowed the balloon to stand up vertically with the bottom of the basket sitting on the ground. I took one or two photos and was then past a hard hat and a pair of gloves. I was then ordered into the basket along with my pilot, John Green.

Orders were then given to those not in the basket. 'Hands on basket'. After a few burns it was, 'Hands off basket'. We then slowly lifted off into the air. Drifting off towards the south we waved back at those standing on the ground and they waved back at us. While all of this had been going on, the Dante Group had been busy rigging their balloon by the side of "Goldfinger". We cleared the wood by the side of the field and headed towards the railway as "Gemma" lifted off behind us. It was a good job that mine had been the first flight and that I had got a 400 speed film in my camera as the light was deteriorating fast. Flying across the water meadows and the copses at just over tree top height was a sheer delight. I had waited a long time for this flight and it could not have come at a more lovely time of the year. The new spring greenery was now at its best. We saw deer scampering away and the wood pigeons circling in the trees below us. Our height of travel was from 200 feet to tree top height and at times, below. All of my flight was taken in climbing out of the Kennet Valley. I watched with interest as a big willow tree came towards us. I should have said, we came to it. Just when I expected that we would crash into it, the air that was flowing around both sides of the tree neatly carried us to the right of it. We cleared the railway lines with ease but our basket was nearly placed in the water of the Kennet & Avon Canal. John then asked me if I could swim as two young girls waved and giggled at us from the tow path. It was just after this that the Dante balloon crossed the railway lines at less than five feet. Lucky for them that an express train was not coming. After this they quickly made height and headed off in another direction. They were to terminate their flight long before "Goldfinger".

My pilot then made several burns as we started to rise up the wooded slope and out of the valley. Then the top of a tall fir tree stopped the basket dead. I kind of expected us to sink down between the trees as we stopped in mid air, but the balloon could not stall. John just pushed the top of the tree to one side and we continued on our way. How pretty the countryside looked from tree top height, the woods the river and the reeds. The sun was going down in one hazy big red blob. We must have been on the dividing line between trespassing and low flying. We crossed the road at the top end of Hampstead Marshall and with this came the end to my flight. Here John told me to prepare for a landing. Balloonists seem to get away with landing on any persons ground without having the owner's consent. Myself, I can see no difference between camping the night on persons land without that persons consent than making a landing in a hot air balloon. Not that I wish to be a spoil sport, but land owners do get aeroplane pilots booked for low flying when they are at several hundred feet while these balloonists seem to get away with bobbing in and out of fields and just missing chimney pots.

I put the gloves back on and held on to the rope handles that were on the inside of the basket. Don't ask me how, but John just settled us down close to the road with the balloon resting on the bottom of its basket. I was instructed to stay put and not to jump out. I had spent twenty minutes up in the air, well just, and I had flown less than two miles. I could not have flown lower. It was not my favourite way to fly, but it had been enjoyable and relaxing even though I could not have sat down. A car soon came along the road and pulled up and Sheila stepped out. John then gave her a cone that he had picked off of that spruce tree that we had ran into. 'He always brings me a pressie', she said. Phil's parents then drove up in the recovery vehicle. Phil's father then stepped in and I was then told to step out. This landing was known to them as the first intermediate. 'Hands on basket' and a burn or so to be followed by 'Hands off basket' and "Goldfinger" rose up into the air taking Phillip's dad on his first balloon flight. I will not go into the rest of that flight, but Phillip's mother also managed to make her first balloon flight on that evening. By the time that this three in one flight ended it was dark and the balloon was in need of having navigation lights. The balloon then had to be packed up in the dark and carried for some considerable distance before it could be finally be loaded into its boxed trailer. I then had to be driven back to that balloon field at Marsh Benham where my camper was parked up all on its own. That balloon registration was, G-BERD.

For the technically minded, I will finish this chapter with a few details of the Skyship 600. It was a conventional non-rigid airship. The envelope had no internal structure. The rigidity of the gas container or hull being entirely maintained through the positive pressure of the helium gas in which it was filled. Now I will list some dimensions and performance figures: Gross volume, 6,666 cu.m; Length, 59.0 m; Diameter, 15.2 m; Overall height, 20.3 m; Tail span, 19.2 m; Gondola length, 11.7 m; Cabin length, 6.9m; Cabin width at the maximum, 2.6 m; Cabin height, 1.9 m; Disposable load, 2,340 kg; Maximum speed, 60 knots; Endurance, 24 hours. This information I have taken from a brochure.

Boarding the Ju. 52/3m

The Junkers Ju. 52/3m HB-HOS / A-701

I might have made a Zeppelin raid over London

The Bloody Tower

SEEING IS BELIEVING

To believe in something, then one has to be absolutely sure about it. To me, when I see something with my own eyes and if some other person sees it as well as myself, then I can believe in what I have seen. That phrase, 'There are many more things in heaven and earth than meets the eye'. How true it is. In church we say these words when reciting the Creed, 'I believe in all things visible and invisible'. Believe you me, there are quite a lot of them. Just because you cannot see them is no reason to think that they do not exist. Some of those things that you cannot physically see may be nice and on the other hand, some could be down rite evil. All I am saying here is that there are strange things that can be seen, also there are other strange things that cannot be seen, but they might be experienced. Our great grandparents would not have believed that today, you can talk to people all over the world on a mobile phone and also use it to take coloured pictures. What I am trying to get at is this, just because you do not understand them, it is no reason to say that they do not exist. I now firmly believe in such things as ghosts, demons, phantoms, unseen forces which may be good or evil, in a life after death, visiting UFO's and that a few large wild cats prowl our countryside. I also believe in a gypsy's curse, but this I class as an evil force.

Most of the things that I am writing about here happened when I lived in the countryside. I have since had to give up the life of living in the sticks for that of living in the bricks. Although I am now a townie, I am still very much a country man at heart. From my bedroom window, I gazed out across the distant fields to a wood. My eyes rested on a distant black object that I had not seen there before. It was in a field about twenty yards from the woodland fence. This object then sprang sideways. That was no deer and so I rushed down stairs to get my video camera. By the time that I got back up to the window I was just in time to see this large animal enter the wood. Although I was not in time to have caught it on camera. It had obviously caught for its-self a meal, most likely a rabbit. This large black animal was also seen by a lady in the village that was walking her dog.

A fortnight later I was driving Daphne down to the next village. As we passed under a bridge that carries the M.4 Motorway, Daphne remarked, 'What is that strange animal'. I had not seen it as I had been busy looking ahead. I pulled my faithful old camper up and then slowly reversed her back close to the bridge where I could safely park. I left my vehicle to investigate. What I saw above the bramble cover was a thick round black tail with a white or a silver tip to it. This cat like tail was vertically place and was slowly making towards the motorway fence and embankment. As it got close to the fence it then lowered its tail out of sight. The rest of the animal was hidden from me by the vast amount of bramble cover. No way would I risk trapping such an animal up against a fence and I was never to see it again. It had only been a stones throw from me. I reported my sighting to the local gamekeeper. He thought it to have been a dog that had been abandoned from the side of the motorway. I know what I saw and I can tell you that it was no dog. This sighting happened over twenty years ago. I would now think that the large cat that we saw would now be dead. These cats roam large distances and it is quite possible that they are breeding in this country now that they are out there in the wild.

On many weekends I have enjoyed going back into the country where I could walk the woodlands. Sadly, this I can no longer do. On this weekend I had quietly made my way along a woodland path and I had got to a place where two paths crossed each other. I stood in the centre of this woodland cross-roads to see if I could see any deer grazing. From behind me and in thick cover there came such a rumpus which stopped as quickly as it began. I turned around but I could not see what had made it. Then I heard a loud panting from an animal. Not being a very brave fellow, but I hope, a sensible one, I quietly retraced my footsteps back the way that I had come.

The very first time that I tried out my video camera was on a fine but blustery day. I took it along to some woodland which in those early wartime days had served as our playground. At the time of my childhood, it had been a large area of a very fine grass which had been surrounded by scrub and gorse bushes. One evening several of us children had been playing there and the light was fading fast. It was then that we all experienced what we took to be a heavy horse galloping at close quarters. The sound and the vibrations could have been counted in seconds. All of this had started very suddenly and it had stopped just as abruptly as it had started. Together we all stopped playing our game and retreated back home. We were never to play there again once it showed signs of becoming dusk. On the day that I tried out my new camera, this ground had changed from that of my childhood. This area of ground had been cleared of the scrub and had been planted with pine trees. My Father helped in the planting. Then in 1987 we had a hurricane. This then flattened all of these pine trees. The estate had employed contractors to clear this ground of storm damage so that it could be replanted. Now it was just one wide open clearing.

As I was busy using my camera on the movements of the foliage, I was then at the far end of this clearing. It was then that I noticed a lorry that was some distance away from where I was. It was a short wheelbase light grey in colour and it was fitted with a tilt to the rear of its truck. I immediately stopped my photography and started to make my way towards it as quickly as I could. My thoughts were that contractors must still have been working down in the lower end of this woodland. I had parked my vehicle tight to the other side of the gate and I would be stopping workmen from going home. This truck then swung on to the hard track after it had picked its way across the tree stumps. As I made my way, I remember seeing a dinner plate size diff' cover to the centre of its rear axle. No sooner had it entered the track, it then made a sharp turn to the left in the direction of the houses where I once lived. Relieved that my vehicle would no longer be in the way, I commenced operating my camera. A thought then crossed my mind, where did that lorry go. On the left hand side of that track a ditch had been re-dug and beyond this it was one mass of self seeded saplings. I went and took a look. There were no wheel markings and no grass had been flattened. There were no ways that it could have crossed that ditch. I did not hear the sound from that lorry, but then there was a very strong blustery wind blowing. Back at my vehicle I then noticed that the grass and a briar had grown up through the bottom rung of the gate. I then drove down the road and looked at the other gates. It was obvious that none of these gates had been opened for weeks. It was then that it sunk in that I had just seen a phantom lorry. It had come from the same direction as where we had once heard that galloping horse. If only I had kept my camera rolling. If only I could have had some other person with me who could have witnessed it as well, if only! On looking at the route across the clearing that this lorry had taken, it had followed a sewer track that had been trenched in to feed the houses where I had once lived. This sewer was provide some forty years previous and after my parents had moved from there. On thinking about it, that lorry which I had taken to have been a real one looked as though it had been of the type that was common to the 1950'.

It is a pleasant change to get away from aviation for a while as I write this chapter. My brother Dick and I lost our Mother in 1964 due to a terminal illness. On that very night that we lost her, her spirit paid a visit to a life-long friend of hers that she had made during her single days when she had been in service in a large house. This old lady lived eight miles distant in Hungerford. That night our mother appeared to her in her bedroom. The next day she came to our parent's home in

Stockcross enquiring, 'What is wrong with Elsie'. None of us had given it a thought to have got in touch with her and to tell her that she had been very ill. Prior to our Mother's death, my wife Daphne had a similar experience. Her younger sister Margaret was killed when riding pillion on a motorcycle. That same night after the accident she paid a visit to our bedroom. My wife did not wake me until afterwards. It was a moonlight night and Margaret got out of her coffin and went across to my wife. She spoke to Daph and she said, 'Don't worry Daph, I am only sleeping'. With this she turned and went back to her coffin. As she turned, Daph described her as being split open down her back and padded with cotton wool. When we went over to her home in Lambourn, this was exactly as we were to find her. Each one of us has a spirit. As I see it, 'You must believe in God and try and lead a good life and you then you will stand a chance of living another better life when you enter into the next world'.

In this chapter you will find that I am deviating away from things aeronautical, but I have a feeling that I should do this. To write this, it is not so easy without mentioning other people's names. I feel that they have a right to privacy, and so I will do my best to speak of people and places without placing names to them.

At the close of 1984 I was forced to retire early from my job of climbing telephone poles. Daphne and I then took that three month vacation to Australia. It was a holiday of a lifetime in which I fell in love with that beautiful country with its colourful fauna and its people. All the same, there were many things that did not work out as I had planned. Speaking for myself, I had missed out on several aeronautical things that I wanted to see. The trip in a Grumman flying boat to the Great Barrier Reef, just to name one of them. A friend with more wealth than I will ever have, offered to give me so much money if I took a trip with him to Australia. He shared the same interests as those of myself. At first, Daphne had agreed to me going. Later, she had second thoughts about it and did not wish me to go. One thing led to another and we had a row. I slammed the door and walked off down the road blaspheming. It was then that I really was knocked off of my feet. An invisible force with the power of a tornado picked me up and dropped me to the ground. Bruised, I then picked myself up. That force had brought me back to my right senses. It was not the nicest way to receive an almighty power, but it put me firmly in my proper place and from then on it changed me, and for the better I hope. There was a time before I joined the Calleva Group that I would spend many Sundays shooting pigeons. One day I got into conversation with my local vicar, the Reverent Nigel Sands. In my conversation I said to him, 'There is no need to visit a church on Sundays, every religion is just another road that leads to our maker', or words to this effect. Since then I have listened to many of his sermons. His reply to the statement that I made, I shall never forget. It was, 'Yes my boy, but make sure that you are on a right road when the time comes'. How right he was.

ET is with us and has been for at least the last seventy years. During Hitler's war, many aircrews had what they called foo-fighters flying along by the sides of them. It was in 1972 that my village of Wickham, Berkshire was visited by a UFO which was seen in the village by at least two people. It was a pulsating orange object. On that night it worried the children's home at Hoe Benham which is another village in the same parish. It also got a mention in the Newbury Weekly News. The South West UFO Aerial Phenomena Society (S.W.A.P.S.) came along asking questions about it.

I was told by some of my workmates of how they had seen a cigar shaped object that they said was larger than a World War One airship. I could not see any reason why they should make up such a story. They were in a telephone lorry on their way to Wallingford. This UFO was stationary over the top of the Didcot Power Station. Their thoughts were that somehow it was pinching electricity from that station. They then lost sight of it due to some bends in the road and some trees. To their surprise, when the power station came back into their view again this large object was nowhere to be seen. I do not know if it was around the same time or not, but a cousin of mine and her husband living in Newbury had looked up into the night sky and they had described to me a similar object motionless over the town. They stood looking at it for some considerable time and they told me it was lit up with various colours. Eventually it moved off, but when it did so, it did it at a very fast speed from being stationary. Another workmate was driving his van across Bucklebury Common when he saw a disc shaped object that he described as the size of a dustbin lid take to the air from close by him. As it rose into the air he described it as being a very fast zig-zag flight.

Now I have only seen two UFO's that I can be sure of and these were seen by hundreds of other people. Of all places, it was while we were watching a SBAC (Society of British Aircraft Constructors) air show in the 1950's. Unfortunately I have now forgotten which show that it was, or if it had been on a Saturday or a Sunday. I had taken a mate with me on the pillion of my motorcycle and we were both stood on what then was known as the hill watching the flying. There then became a lull in the flying display which was most unusual. As one aircraft finished displaying then another one then followed on in. During this lull, we noticed that the crowds close to us were pointing up to the sky above us. We looked up to see what they were pointing at. High up in a patch of blue sky were two shining round objects. All of a sudden one shot off at such a high speed that no known aircraft of today could possibly have managed to have done so. Pilots would not have stood that G force. We then looked at the other one' this then left at speed like the other one only in the opposite direction. Whatever they were they had been watching that air show. A monthly aviation magazine that I will not mention here by name had started printing articles on early Farnborough air shows. I wrote a letter to its editor telling him of the fastest things that had ever flown at a Farnborough show. He wrote back to me telling me that he would print my letter in the next issue. He did not do so and he stopped these articles on the early Farnborough shows. Much later on I had a chance to meet up with him in person. He just refused to talk about it and more or less shut up like a clam. I guess that some person or persons had warned him not to print it. I suspected this, and so I did not push him. I feel sure that our government and the U.S.A. are hiding many things from their citizens. Judging by what I have read. I think that some of these UFO's could be highly dangerous and if so, then the public should be told about them. They should have the right to know.

Why is it that so many governments will not come clean and tell their citizens what is going on? I have enjoyed a lifelong hobby of collecting old shotgun cartridges both live and empty used cases. I have written several books on this hobby. Aeroplanes and shotgun cartridges have been my two main hobbies. When I was a much younger chap I was exchanging used shotgun cartridge cases by post with a chap named Bruce Kemp in New Zealand. In a letter to him I happened to mention that our landscape was being changed and reshaped due to a small beetle. This was the Dutch Elm Disease. Though what the Dutch had to do with it I do not know. He then wrote me back and he told me that he had just returned from the U.S.A. He said in his letter that this same beetle was killing off their trees as well. Those elm trees had stood through all weathers for hundreds of years and all of a sudden along comes a little beetle and destroys them right across the world. Why then should these fine old trees and also the younger elm saplings be dying at the same time in two different parts of the world? I remember that I kept his letter for ages and then shown it to many people who would not believe me until they had read it for themselves. When the U.S.A. landed on the moon they were very fussy about not bringing home any moon bugs, or was it that they may have seen something on the moon that they did not want disclosed. Is it not possible that UFO's might have brought these beetles to our planet Earth. If so, then might aliens also have brought Aids here as well? Here is some more food for thought. A hole was found that was getting larger in the southern ionosphere. All the nuclear testing was done in the southern hemisphere. Is it not possible that this is what damaged the ozone layer. If it was, then I bet that they will never admit to it.

Now back in the 1930's, I had a nightmare of waking up as being bound up in a spiders web. In later years I spoke about this to my brother Dick. To my surprise, he then told me that he had experienced the same thing as what I had. He had thought that he had been the only one that had been troubled with it. If only our parents were still alive and we could confer with them. It was like waking up with thick black lines moving around the room. At that time, Dick and I were sleeping in separate bedrooms with a dividing wall separating us. This same rear window with its dividing thick woodwork came against this dividing wall. This window then let daylight into both bedrooms. Now might there have been a spider outside of that window that was working on a caught insect in that web? Could that doomed insect have sent out waves that telegraphically had transmitted that we had both violently had picked up? One night I was watching a television programme about a chap who had devised a way to record minute sounds. A sound like the interior of a tree trunk as it swayed in the wind. He also produced a sound of a spider wrapping up an insect in its web. It was then that this same sound that I had endured all those years ago came flooding back to me.

During the war years when I was a teenager, I was cycling to work one morning when I happened to glance up at a window as I cycled past. I was to see a young girl of my own age that I knew. She was completely naked and was bending over close to that window with her breasts hanging down as she was pulling on a lower garment. Now in far later years there was a time when I had been very disturbed in my sleep. I was that fidgety and restless that it upset my wife so much that I grabbed a sleeping bag and made for the down stairs sofa. Being so tired and restless and finding it hard to drop off back to sleep, I was in a very drowsy state of mind. My mind then shot back a few years to the time when I had seen that girl at her bedroom window. It then started to examine her as only a doctor would as to what the rest of her body might have looked like. I was in such a restless state and perhaps I could better describe myself as being half asleep and half awake. It was then that I was completely woken up by a voice that came out of my head. It said, 'Jesus Wept'. Not only that, but it repeated, 'Jesus Wept'. From that moment onwards I was no longer restless. I am positive that some form of presence was latching on to me. My horrid thoughts had driven it right out of my mind.

Daphne and I were touring the Lake District in our Volkswagen Transporter camper. While there we made a visit to another cartridge collector. It was then that the news hit us of the Hungerford shootings. Now we had some family connections with Hungerford. Just around the corner from where Michael Ryan had shot his mother and burnt down the houses we had a young granddaughter. Mrs Ryan was well known to Daphne as she had been working alongside of her in the country Elcot Park Hotel. Although I did not know of any of the Ryans, this upset us so much that we had to terminate our holiday and make for home. All through my life I have been brought up with shooting, guns and cartridges. Even Daph's Father and brothers had owned shotguns. Although I did not know of Michael and had never met his mother, it became hard to believe that he who had used guns along with the police could suddenly act the way that he did. So what may have gone wrong? As I have already said, I do believe that there are forces that are invisible that exist. They can be good or they can be downright evil. I think that it is possible that Michael may have been a little highly strung. According to what Daphne had told me, his mother had given him everything that he had wanted and that he had been a spoilt child. It is my belief that an evil force had singled him out and had latched on to him. It had been that strong that it had completely taken him over. As a person, the last thing that he would have done would have been to kill his mother and burn down his home. How can any government make any laws that can stop an evil force? This evil force may still be operating all around the world.

I have already told you just how primitive our living was when I lived with my parents at Wickham Heath. This I did in the chapter, 'My Village School Days'. For toiletry through the night we relied on a jerry. No, not a German, but a chamber pot known as a gozunder. This because our bucket lavvy was out of doors. In order to cut down the amount of fluid in the gozunder, it became a common practice for us lads on dark nights to empty our bladders in the woodland to the rear of our home. After all, these bedroom slops were thrown out in the same area on the following morning. It was while I was attending to my needs of nature that I experienced something most strange. The ground was covered with snow and the moon shone brightly on this snow and cast shadows on the ground between the fir trees. My eyes were gazing along a path that ran into the wood leading to our chicken pen. I saw what looked like a giant of a man standing motionless on the path about eighty yards away. I thought that I must be seeing things due to the shadows. I rushed back in doors and told my Father and my brother Dick to come out and have a look. Dad declined as his ears were tuned in to a radio programme. Dick followed me back out. The moon was shining just as bright, but there was nothing on that path to be seen in the place that I had seen that very tall man. Many years ago according to some old maps, a road which would probably had been nothing more than a track, had crossed through that pathway. I was never happy after that in closing up our hen-house after dark. Did I see a ghost, I shall never know.

Now I will tell you of a more recent happening. My son and his family live in an isolated dwelling in woodland. This had been built on the site of an ancient fortification. It was on a fine sunny weekend afternoon that my wife and I decided to call on them. We did not know if they would have been at home or not, but it was on our way home anyhow. We noticed their car parked by the house and so we thought that someone might be in doors. We knocked on the door, but all that we did was to start their dogs barking inside the house. Their dogs do know us, but only when they can see us. As we got no reply we sat on an outdoor seat that was close to the door. We rested and took in the magnificent woodland views. The dogs continued barking and then we both heard our daughter-in-laws voice calling out to the dogs to be quiet. Together we then both called out her name as her voice faded into the distance. The dogs did ease up on their barking for a short while. I said to Daphne, perhaps she is taking a bath, go round to the other side of the house and find out if she is, then she should hear you. We then went back to our motor where we discussed the mystified circumstances. We had both heard her voice and we had both called out together. It was then that our granddaughter arrived home. She unlocked the house and we went in and had a cup of tea. While we were drinking the tea, the telephone rang. It was our son and his wife, they had both gone out on the motorbike and were over fifty miles away in Northamptonshire. Their dwelling was reputed to have been haunted, but by what, we did not know. Our family have now lived there for several decades but have never experienced anything of the paranormal. I have since asked several men of the church if they can explain what we both witnessed together. They could not come up with an answer. .

To wind up this chapter, I will mention crop circles. When I was a youngster I presumed that all circles are round. All though some crop circles are circular, many of them are as round as some of the many Swindon roundabouts. I do except that some of these are made by people in the dark using planks of wood, etc. This though I cannot except for all of them as they are far too complicated for people to make in the dark on a short summers night. Who or whatever it is that is making them has got a high rate of intelligence. To start with, they only appear when the crops are nearly ripe. Also, they choose the right kind of field in which to be formed and I have yet to hear of one that has been divided by a hedgerow.

In order to see the beauty of these large circles, one needs to fly over them in an aircraft. I had the good fortune to be taken on a flight in a Cessna 172. The pilot owner of the aircraft was going to take some photos of a newly formed crop circle. We located this and it reminded both of us as being like a large ball of wool. With thanks to my past tuition that I had been given in a Tiger Moth, I was able to take over control while the owner took several photographs of it. I then managed to take a snap shot of it for myself which I will include here though it is not a very good one. Now on the 29th of December 2000, my home was targeted by snow circles. That night we had a fall of snow. In the morning there were snow circles on our front concrete apron to the front of my car. To prove that it happened I took the enclosed photograph that is copyright to me. It shows the postman's footsteps passing through the middle of them. Now what caused these snow circles and why? I could not see any more of them anywhere else. I do know that one can have dust devils, or swirls in very hot weather, but this happened at my home in very cold weather. These snow circles have made me think that the weather may have a part to play in some circles, but I cannot except this for all of the crop circles. Here I must stop. Just one nice thought to end with. It is God that holds the hand with all the trump cards in it.

Snow circles on my driveway

Our son's home is in the centre of the photo

My home is between the struts. Note the proximity of the motorway

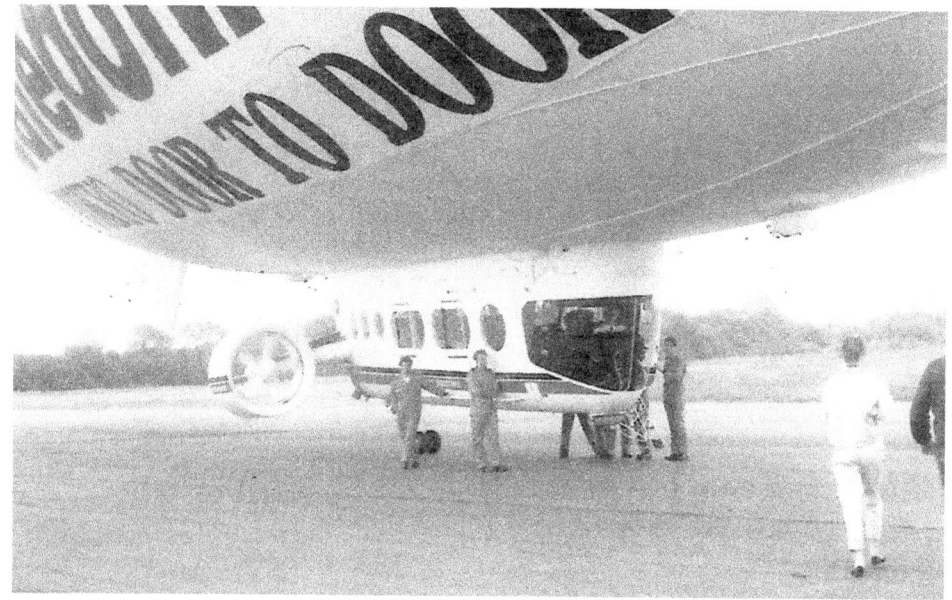

About to board the Skyship at Radlett

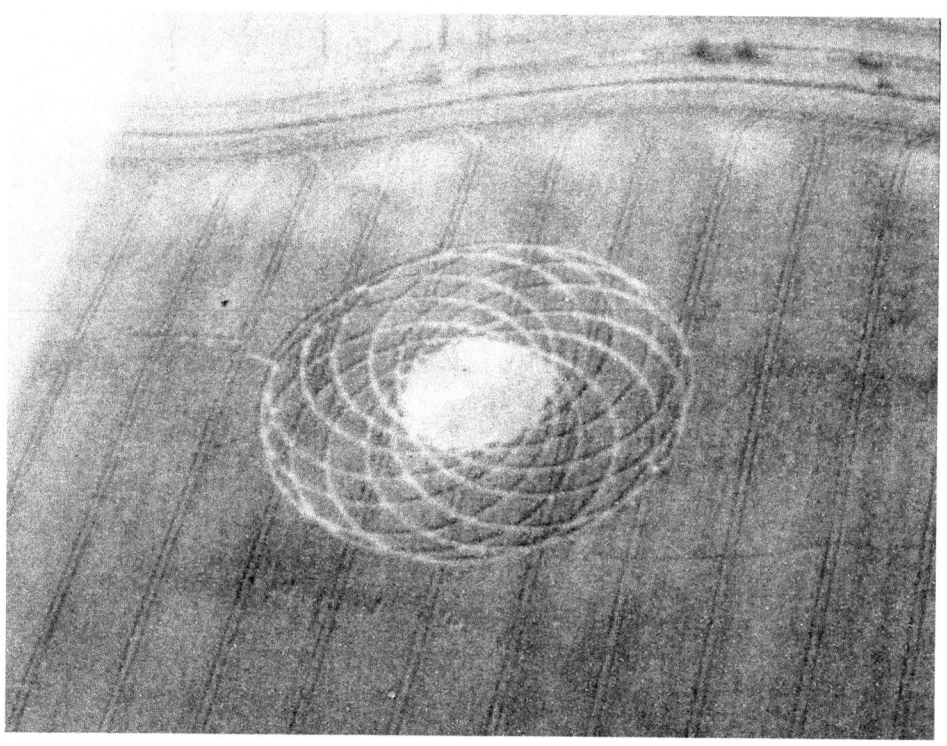

The ball of wool crop circle photographed from Cessna 172N G-OVFR

WITH THE AIRCRAFT RESTORERS

I first got to know Arthur Christian at Walkeridge Farm through my job with G.P.O. (General Post Office) Telephones. Later on, Cliff Lovell was to move into his farm premises. From Cliff's workshops, many old civil aeroplanes have been restored and thanks to him, many interesting light imports have come on to the British Register. Arthur introduced me to Clifford and his team of workers. Ever since then, I have always been made most welcome whenever I had stepped into his workshops. With my interest in aircraft photography I have nearly always carried a camera with me. I like to keep one on my motor. Due to this, Cliff then dubbed me as,' Ken the Camera'. I have had several little trips aloft with Cliff over the years and one of which I have mentioned in the chapter, 'Up in Yours'. This was in the Fox Moth G-ACEJ. I believe that the first aeroplane that Cliff restored was the old 1931 de Havilland Puss Moth G-ABLS. From that he went on to more complicated and larger aircraft. One of these was the de Havilland Dragonfly G-AEDU which came back to England from South Africa in the early 1980's. Together with Mike Freeman, Cliff's firm restored it for Tony Haig-Thomas. The Dragonfly was not the easiest airframe to restore. In 1954, B.E.A. (British European Airways) obtained F-OAMS but it proved too difficult for them to restore. Five years later it got restored at Eastleigh and became G-ANYK when it then flew in a pretty blue colour scheme.

To be successful in this business you have to provide good workmanship for the amount of money that is spent on the project. Each old aircraft that has been restored or given a new paint job then becomes a travelling advertisement for the firm that did the job on it. A good advertisement and more orders could then be coming. It was in Cliff's workshops that I first got to know Ron Souch and the late Ben Cooper. Both of these chaps then became very successful in running their own businesses and becoming known for their standards of workmanship. I well remember Clifford saying to me when I had to take that early retirement, 'Go and find yourself an old aeroplane'. It was a bit too late in life for me to have done that.

One day Tim Williams walked me round his outbuildings and shown me some freshly decorated brick sheds. These I would think may have once been used for milking cows. 'In here', he said, 'we have Ben Cooper moving in to restore old aeroplanes and he is going to build a replica of an Avro 504N. He was extremely pleased that an aircraft business was starting up on his premises. Ben and his wife Jan moved in assisted by Martin Honeychurch. They did not build the Avro, but they did restore the de Havilland Fox Moth G-ACEJ. This had been a wooden aeroplane and every stick in it had to be replaced. The rest of it had burnt to ashes when a modern aircraft crashed on top of it at Old Warden. I would think that this task as the Newbury Aeroplane Company in which they had become, was to be far more complicated than building an Avro 504N. After the sad death of Ben, his wife Jan has continued to keep the business up and running. Many an award winning aircraft has come from out of their workshops. The B.A. Eagle Mark II, G-AFAX being just one of them.

In 1985 on my retirement, Daphne and I took that trip to Australia. (See, 'Way Down Under'). Having returned back home, one evening we invited Jan and Ben to come over to Wickham to look at our Australian photographs. While looking through these, my phone rang. It was for Ben. A lorry had pulled up at his workshops in the late evening and in pitch black darkness. On its high flat bed was the B.A, Swallow Mark II, G-ADPS. 'I am most sorry', said Ben, 'but we have to go'. He then asked me if I would mind going along with him as he would need all of the help that he could get. Together we managed to get it unloaded from off of that lorry. 'You will get a flight in this one day', said Ben for all of your efforts. Although sincerely intended, my Swallow flight never came. I did at one time do an odd job or so for Ben and one of which I remember was removing the Pobjoy engine from out of PS.

My first flight back in England after returning from down-under was with Ben in his vintage Klemm L-25 1a, G-AAUP named "Clementine". I had called in at Jan and Ben's workshops only to be offered a surprise ride in their delightful old Klemm. Ben suggested that I slipped back home and changed into my old clothes as the old Salmson air cooled radial delighted in throwing a fair amount of oil back over its aviators. Being forewarned, I went back home and changed. I did not waste any time, and I was soon back at the Anvill's flying field where I was about to experience my delight. As I arrived, so a cream-yellow Luscome Model 8A landed and taxied in for Ben to adjust its slow running. Then three cars came rolling down the lane, first Martin, then Ben and then Tim.

Ben then set me to work with an oilcan. I had to squirt oil all over the open rocker gear. Only to find that most of this then got slung back at me. Well I had been pre-warned and should have known that an engine of this vintage likes to splatter one's goggles and face. There had been no change in the design since World War One. Only since then, face masks had gone out of fashion. Both wings were then carried out of the small hangar and held in position while eight retaining pins were pushed home. These pins were also secured by four very long spring pins with one application. To make sure that these could still not fall out, there was a wing joining band on each side. These bands filled the gaps between the outer wings and the centre section. These were slid into position from underneath and then locked home with case-type fasteners. Also to be connected up were the aileron controls and the A.S.I (Airspeed Indicator) tubes.

The engine started on the first swing and it revolved clockwise when viewed from the front. It then barked out little puffs of blue smoke from each exhaust stub. It sounded great and the rockers of the valve gear took on a steady blur as the throttle was eased forward. Ben then ordered me into the front cockpit with several cautions on how not to tread any holes through his wing. This done I then made an effort to sort out the straps of the seat belt. By the time that I had accomplished this, "Clementine" was moving down the grass runway that had lighting to each side of it. As we gathered motion, I was amazed that we had lifted off of the grass and stayed floating in the air. This truly was great stuff. Ben then set of aviating around the local fields and through the gaps in the hedges. Ben was a flyweight, but I well and truly made up for his small size. As we slowly made height, "Clementine" then took on a game of chasing her own shadow. After flying several of these figures of eight, Ben gradually coaxed his Klemm away to the west and we flew a large clockwise circle of Hungerford and Kintbury. While over Kintbury, Jan had recognised the sound of their "Clementine" and had stepped out of the house to give us a wave of encouragement. How I enjoyed that old aeroplane that was of my own vintage. It was just how I had expected vintage aviation to have been. Low on power, the smell and the sound of the engine, the wind through your hair and the taste of the oil. On top of all of this, it felt so good to be flying above old England in an open cockpit and enjoying the summer air with all of the pleasant greenery below. It was not possible to hold a conversation between the two cockpits and so I just sat back and took it all in.

That grass runway then came back into view and with a few short bursts from the Salmson which sounded delightful we passed over the hedge and came to a stop half way down the runway. Ben then told me that he thought that one cylinder had oiled up and that it did not help the rest of them. Ben then jumped out and lifted her up by the tail and pointed her in the opposite direction. I thought to myself, 'be careful Bennyboy as if that prop should touch the ground it could damage the turf'. Ben then climbed back in and with a few more delightful bursts from that old radial he returned us back to the hangar.

We then tied "Clementine" down for the night in the lee of the hedge. She then settled down for a rest like all good old ladies should. I then thanked Ben for giving me that chance to sample some aviation that I might never get the opportunity to ever do again. It was also thanks to Tim and Martin for their help in the fixing on her wings. It had been twenty minutes of sheer enjoyable delight and fun. The kind of flying that would have taken place when I was no more than a babe in some person's arms. Ben and I were then the last to leave the field. Nine years later on, Ben was to give me another surprise flight in their rebuilt Fox Moth G-ACEJ. I have already mentioned one flight in this aeroplane and so I will not do so for a second time, delightful that it was. Not that long after being given my flight, UP was to be restored and she must have been under restoration for a couple of decades. Her engine was sent away to be rebuilt and the late John Greenland did a lot of the work on her airframe. She has now been returned to the air again and she now wears a greyish-green and silver colour scheme. It is a joy to see her back in the air where she is once again back in her element.

With the breaking up of the Calleva Group, I was then retired and in need of a small job. This now being well over twenty or so years ago. Ralph Jones of Southern Sailplanes purchased what was left of what had been the group's Tiger, HU. Being in need of a job, I asked Ralph if he had any work going. He invited me to go along and so I spent the best part of a year there. I more or less went along with Hotel Uniform. While I was here I was given the job of putting her back on wheels. Ralph taught me a new trade in how to work with fibreglass, to profile glass sailplane wings and to work on renewing the C of A's on Robin and Super Cub aircraft. I worked here until I was forced to go into hospital. When I came out, I then cried knife and pulled up the stumps.

Ralph was a nice chap but he did have a light triggered temper. Once you got to know him, this you never then did worry about. I found him to be far more relaxed when he was up in the air flying. But then, this could go for many of us. I can once remember in conversation telling him how I had thought about learning to fly but I had not done so because I thought that I would never have managed to have kept it up. His reply to me was, 'You should have done it'. How easy it is to be wise after an event. Ralph is another one of those chaps that has passed on. I attended his funeral in Hungerford and as we came out of the church, a Robin and a Super Cub was flown over in formation. It was very fitting. Ralph will be greatly missed by all of those that were into gliding.

You may ask the question, which of those restorers do I think would do the best job. This I could not answer. To start with I do not know the prices that they charged for their work. In this day and age, you usually get what you pay for, but not always. All of those that I have known have turned out excellent work. Since leaving Southern Sailplanes, all that I have done is to sit down and discuss aviation by joining some local groups. I did enjoy a flight in a R.A.F. VC-10 from Brize Norton where Jaguar fighters were refuelled in the air over the North Sea and this was my last flight in a Royal Air Force aircraft. My last flight but one was in Tim's Puss Moth when he kindly flew me out of the so called deHavilland field at Crux Easton. This the same field in which Captain deHavilland had given aeroplane rides to my Father and most of his family. As I write this my very last trip into the air was in wartime Australian built deHavilland Dragon on the 4th of September 2011. It made its way to England and then into Cliff Lovell's workshop where he restored it as a Dragon Mk.I. It then became G-ECAN on the British civil register. This was to be my second flight in this aeroplane. Over the past years I have flown in many old deHavilland aeroplanes but so far I have never managed to hitch a ride in a D.H.90. Dragonfly. Now at nearly eighty-five years young I now find it more difficult in getting in and out of many of the light aircraft as my arthritis is seeing to that.

I had joined clubs in which to fly radio controlled model aircraft, but I never quite managed to land the things properly. I think that I could have made a better job of flying a Tiger Moth than flying those models. Now having arthritis in most of my joints my aviation interest was sitting down in a chair for a couple of hours once in a while with the Swindon branch of the U.3.A. (University of the Third Age). On mentioning the U.3.A, just one little story that I believe came from out of one of one of their newsletters. It is on the lighter side and it was titled, 'Engineer versus management'. Telling you this story will be a good way for me to wind up this book.

A man in a hot air balloon realised he was lost. He reduced altitude and spotted a man below. He descended a bit more and shouted out, 'Excuse me, can you help me? I promised a friend that I would meet him an hour ago, but I don't know where I am'. The man below replied, 'You are in a hot air balloon hovering approximately 30 feet above the ground. You are between 40 and 41 north latitude and between 59 and 60 west longitude. 'You must be an engineer', said the balloonist, 'Everything that you have told me can be technically correct, but I still have no idea as to what I can make of your information and the fact is, I am still lost. Frankly, you've not been much help so far'. The man below responded, 'You must be in management'. 'I am', relied the balloonist, 'but how did you know'? 'Well', said the man on the ground. ' You do not know where you are going. You have risen to where you are due to a quantity of hot air. You have made a promise that you have no idea as to how you can keep it and you expect people below you to solve all of your problems for you. The fact is, you are in exactly the same position that you were in before we met, but now, somehow it has now got to be all of my fault'.

Southern Sailplanes, Membury

Removing the 90h.p. Pobjoy Cataract from B.A. Swallow

'CLEMENTINE' - centre photograph, fixing on her wing

'GLADYS' - Second from bottom, L to R, Martin Honeychurch, Ben and Jan Cooper

TWO PAGES FROM MY LOG BOOK

RECORD OF FLIGHTS

Date	Aircraft Type	Markings	Pilot	Journey	Hrs.	Mins.	Remarks
				Brought forward..	57	34	
18/4/82	Puss Moth	G-AAZP	Tim Williams	Folly Farm Hungerford Wiltshire	00	15	Local (Dusk)
30/4/82	Tiger Moth	G-AJHU	Bill Hardy	SX. - SX	00	50	Local
31/5/82	Puss Moth	G-AAZP	Tim Williams	Folly Farm-Henlow-F.Fm	01	45	Very very nice.
9/6/82	Leopard Moth	G-ACMN	Henry Labouchere	LANGHAM	00	33	With Aunty Annie.
11/9/82	Tiger Moth	G-ACDJ	Fred Terry	S.X.	00	07	Local
18/9/82	Tiger Moth	G-AJHU	John Colour	Wisley Warren KC	00	15	Local.
18/9/82	DH.60G Moth	G-ABEV	Ron Souch	" "	00	05	Surprise flight.
9/10/82	Tiger Moth	G-ACDJ	Fred Terry	Siege Cross	00	10	Rear cockpit.
				Carried forward..	61	39	

RECORD OF FLIGHTS

Date	Aircraft Type	Markings	Pilot	Journey	Hrs.	Mins.	Remarks
				Brought forward..	163	59	
4/7/94	Dakota IV	G-AMPZ	—	HURN-IoW-HURN	00	30	COMPLIMENTARY RIDE
21/8/94	Tiger Moth	T5424/JoA	Pete leCoyte	Woburn Park	00	13	FIRST VIDEO SHOTS FROM LIGHT A/C
21/8/94	Hornet Moth	G-AELO	Mark Miller	Woburn (local)	00	20	DELIGHTFUL
27/8/94	Tiger Moth	T5424/JoA	Pete leCoyte	Lotmead Fm - Uffington WH - Lotmead, Swindon	00	20	FIRST CUBAN EIGHT
27/10/94	Fox Moth	G-ACEJ	Den Cooper	Folly Farm Alvediston/FF	00	25	A/C JUST REBUILT
8/5/96	VC.10 K	XV102 1st FissonVC	d'Adrian Smith	Brize Norton North Sea Brize	02	50	REFUEL TORNADO FIGHTERS AIR TO AIR PHOTOGRAPHY SEAT TO REAR OF PILOT
15/7/96	B.N. Islander	G-BNXA	Ned Coackley	Caernarfon Airport - Snowdon back to Airport	00	25	HOT AND SUNNY.
2/9/96	Tiger Moth	T5424/JoA	Pete leCoyte	Lotmead Farm	00	10	LOCAL Geoff Shawcross also flew
8/7/97	Cessna 72H	G-AXBH	Dennis Milner	Popham/Sandown low	01	40	Via the Needles
				Carried forward..	170	52	

A PICTURE GALLERY

Having been known by some people as 'Ken the Camera' and by many other names by some other people which I will not disclose, I think that out of the many thousands of photographs that I have taken over my many years that I should show a small selection of them. Photography of aircraft and other subjects has been an important pastime in my life. This being so I have decided to end this book with a small selection from my many photographs. It has been a hard decision as which photos to have chosen out of the many. A few of them are relevant to what I have written in this book, but not all of them. I just cannot help in being a little bias to de Havilland, so please forgive me for this.

I purchased my first camera, a 127 Vest Pocket Kodak folder while I was in the R.A.F. and this would then fit into my tunic pocket. Just after the war, film for it was very hard to come by. I then found a photographic shop in Bath that would develop and then reload my spools with ex-air force pan (panchromatic) film. Mostly due to that film, sometimes I got good results and at others, very poor results or nothing at all. While I was at Colerne I joined their photo hobby section. Along with a chap named Shepherd, I have now forgotten his first name, we would share a darkroom together. I tended to remember the surnames as these were what were called out at the start of every working day in the hangar on roll-call. One rigger was named Spong. His name was always called out as Spongggg' with a ring to the end of it. On leaving the R.A.F. my brother Dick and I would develop and print our own photographs. Living at Wickham Heath we had no electricity. All of this was done by using paraffin lamps. We did our developing in a small cubby-hole under the stairs with the use of a specially made lantern that you could change a coloured glass depending on the type of film in which you were developing. This was done by the dish method. All of our printing was done on the kitchen table by exposing the sensitive paper for so many seconds to the paraffin lamp. From the 127, I then went on to the 120 and 620 size films. In those days, all films were in black and white and many of the old negatives are still as good as when we first developed them. Then I always recorded where and when I had taken my photographs, but with the coming of 35 m strips of negative film, these with aeroplanes and other subjects all mixed in together, my recording system then collapsed.

With the introduction of the 35 m film, it first started off in black and white and then colour was to become standardized. This then stopped me from developing my own films. Now with the coming of the computer, I am now able to print some of my thousands of coloured 35 m negatives and slides, but these slides seem to have lost a lot of their colours.

The few photographs that I have picked out for this gallery are in no special order. They are just as they have been picked. My first photograph shown is of our first car named "Odette" with my wife Daphne and our daughter Linda standing by. Our first son Clifford is just visible inside the car. This was my first vehicle that I started carrying a camera in. The next photo is of the Calleva Group's second Tiger Moth. It was taken while I was working at Arthur Christian's farm. This was long before I joined that group. Please note that my telephone vehicle is in the background. You can now see that I often carried a camera while at work. Following on is the pranged remains of Elliotts 'Newbury EoN. This I took when I worked for that firm in their Albert Works in Newbury. It was a hand held time exposure and here I must stop. Below each photo will just be shown the type, the registration when not clearly visible, the place where taken and the date. This is only when I have had this information to hand. All that it remains for me to say now is, please enjoy.

1934 Austin Seven, Thatcham

DH82A Tiger Moth, Hannington, 18/08/66

Newbury EoN G-AKBC, Newbury, Circa 1953-54

DH94 Moth Minor Coupe, Panshanger, 14/06/52

Spitfire IX ML181 (with erks), Colerne, Circa 1946-47

Miles M25 Martinet T Mk1 JN435 QK-6, Colerne, 1947

Spitfire XIVE PR RM802, Colerne, 1947

Spitfire XIVE MV378, Colerne, Circa 1947

Meteor IV RA441, (before) Colerne, Circa 1947-48

Meteor IV RA441, (after) Colerne, Circa 1947-48

M19 Master TT MKII, Colerne, 1948

DH82A Tiger Moth T6126, Colerne, 1947

Kronfield Drone, Southend, 20/06/53

BAC Super Drone, White Waltham, 03/05/52

BA Swallow 2 (cirrus) G-AEWI, Benbridge IoW, 05/06/49

Kronfield Drone, Duxford, 30/10/83

Sparton Arrow G-ABWP, Southend, 20/06/53

Blackburn B2 Trainer G-AEBJ, Denham, 02/08/54

Avro 638 Club Cadet G-ACHP, White Waltham, 03/05/52

Avro 594 Avian 4M G-ABEE, Hatfield, 23/06/51

Taylor Watkinson Dingbat G-AFJA, Hannington

Piper PA-17 Vagabond F-BFBL, Hannington, 06/06/76

Slingsby T.61A Falke G-AYYK, Popham, 24/07/77

Fairchild F24 Argus G-AJSN, White Waltham, 29/05/50

Bristol 170 Freighter MK32 G-AMWC, Blackbushe

DHC1 Chipmunk 22, Little Staughton, 13/05/78

Comper CLA Swift, Denham, 24/07/55

Comber CLA7 Swift 'Black Magic', White Waltham, 21/08/49

DH98 Mosquito PR16 G-AOCL (my daughter), Thruxton, 05/07/58

DH98 Mosquito Mk36 Convert, Blackbushe, 12/02/55

DH98 Mosquito NF38 VX365, Hullavington, 29/07/54

S25 Sunderland MkV, Hamble, 25/07/53

Avro 688 Tudor 4 'Star Panther', Hurn, 31/07/52

Avro 694 Lincoln RF530 (research Naiad), Farnborough, 11/09/48

HP Halifax BVI RG726, Aldermaston, Circa 1948-49

Beaufighter TT MkX RD854, Andover, 14/09/57

Bleriot XI (unregistered, later G-AVXV), Old Warden, 20/05/51

Hawker Cygnet, White Watham, 03/05/52

Hawker Hart, Hatfield, 23/06/51

Gloster Gladiator G-AMRK, White Waltham, 30/08/52

Messerschmitt Me 110G-4 (unregistered), Andover, 15/09/56

Canberra T4 WT480, St Mawgan, Sept. 1979

Ken J. Rutterford

Tipsy B Trainer, White Waltham, 30/05/55

Chilton DW1 G-AFGH, Denham, 01/08/54

Convair B36 21355, Greenham Common, 21/10/56

Boeing B47B-46-BW Stratojet 12271, Fairford, 09/07/53

Boeing KC-97G Stratotanker 22692, Greenham Common, 19/05/56

Republic F84F Thunderstreak 26667/FS-667, Greeham Common, 19/05/56

Miles M7A Nighthawk, Southend, 20/06/53

Miles M28 Mercury Mk6 G-AHAA, Southend, 13/06/56

Miles M57 Aerovan 4, Southend, 20/06/53

Miles M65 Gemini 1A, Woodley

M2F Hawk Major G-ACYO, Southend, 20/06/53

Miles M14B Hawk Trainer 3, Denham, 02/08/54

Miles M14 Hawk Trainer 3, Denham 14/02/54

Miles M14A Magister, Somerton Isle of Wight, 17/07/49

DH85 Leopard Moth, Somerton Isle of Wight, 28/08/48

DH85 Leopard Moth, Southend, 20/06/53

DH94 Moth Minor, White Waltham, 30/08/52

DH94 Moth Minor G-AFNJ, White Waltham, 29/05/50

DH80A Puss Moth, Thruxton, 21/08/49

DH87B Hornet Moth, White Waltham, 30/08/52

DH83 Fox Moth G-ACCB, Thruxton, 27/08/53

DH83 Fox Moth G-ACEJ, Thruxton, 23/06/76

DH60 Cirrus Moth, White Waltham, 03/05/52

DH60 Cirrus Moth G-EBLV, White Waltham, 03/05/52

DH60G Gipsy Moth G-ABJJ, Hatfield, 23/06/51

DH60G3 Moth Major, Denham

DH84 Dragon 2, Gatwick, 23/07/49

DH86B Express G-ADVJ, White Waltham, 29/05/50

DH90 Dragonfly, Thruxton, 21/08/49

DH95 Flamingo, Redhill, 04/04/53

Auster J/2 Arrow, Somerton Isle of Wight, 17/07/49

Auster J/1 Autocrat G-AIBS, Somerton Isle of Wight

Hintenberg HS9A, White Waltham, 30/05/58

Hilson Praga G-AEUT, 14/06/52

Avro 652A 19 Srs1, Croydon, 29/07/53

Anson MI G-AIXV (spun nose), Croydon, 29/07/53

AS10 Oxford P1089 XP, Eastleigh, 25/07/53

Avro 652A Anson TXX VS505, Colerne, May 1948

DH82A Tiger Moth, Denham, 25/07/53

DH82 Tiger Moth Coupe G-AIZF, Denham, 07/10/54

DH82A Tiger Moth, Bembridge, 05/06/49

DH82A Tiger Moth G-AMBK, Thruxton, 08/07/50

DH89A Dragon Rapide NF875/G-AGTM, 30/10/83

DH89A Dragon Rapide, Hatfield, 30/10/83

DH89A Dragon Rapide NF875/G-AGTM, Duxford, 30/10/83

DH89A Dragon Rapide G-ALAX, Eastleigh

DH89A Dragon Rapide, Biggin Hill, 23/04/83

DH98 Moth Minor, Blackbushe, 29/03/70

Westland Widgeon III VH-UHU (self), Boort Victoria Australia, 09/06/85

Republic Seabee VH-MJO, Melbourne Australia, June 1985

Short S25 Sandringham VP-LVE 'Sothern Cross', Poole, 28/08/76

DHC1 Chipmunk 10, Hatfield, 29/06/79

Ken J. Rutterford

DHC1 Chipmunk 22 (Jackaroo G-APAM to rear), Abbotsley, 11/09/77

Schleicher K13 378 (self), Hullavingtin, 16/03/80

DH85 Leopard Moth, Old Warden, 24/06/79

DH60G Gipsy Moth G-ATBL, Crux Easton, 24/05/81

DH85 Leopard Moth, Hannington, 12/06/77

DH80A Puss Moth, Hannington

Morane-Saulnier MS500, Old Warden, 24/06/79

Percival P6 Mew Gull G-AEXF, Old Warden, 25/06/78

Piper Vagabond, Hannington, 14/02/81

Cessna 120, Popham, 18/05/80

www.ingramcontent.com/pod-product-compliance
Lightning Source LLC
Chambersburg PA
CBHW080358170426
43193CB00016B/2751